# Homicide Hank

The Life of Boxing Legend Henry Armstrong

## Kenneth Bridgham

**Win By KO Publications**
IOWA CITY

# Homicide Hank
## The Life of Boxing Legend Henry Armstrong

**Kenneth Bridgham**

**(ISBN-13): 978-1-949783-09-4**
(softcover: 50# acid-free alkaline paper)
Includes footnotes, index, and bibliography
© 2023 by Kenneth Bridgham. All Rights Reserved.
*No part of this book may be reproduced, or transmitted in any form or by any means, graphic, electronic or mechanical, including photocopying, recording, taping, or by any information storage retrieval system without the written permission of Kenneth Bridgham or Win By KO Publications LLC.*
Cover design by Christian Baldo
Manufactured in the United States of America.
Win By KO Publications
Iowa City, Iowa
winbykopublications.com

To Kenny.
Chase down your dreams.

# Contents

| | |
|---|---|
| Acknowledgments | 5 |
| Boxing's Weight Classes in 1938 | 6 |
| Foreword | 7 |
| Prologue: Tuesday – May 31, 1938 | 11 |
| | |
| 1. A Sea of Cotton | 13 |
| 2. "You Ain't No Jack Johnson" | 20 |
| 3. Melody | 31 |
| 4. Becoming Henry Armstrong | 41 |
| 5. Ups and Downs | 53 |
| 6. The Big Time | 64 |
| 7. "You Can't Jim Crow a Left Hook" | 80 |
| 8. Armstrong & Jacobs: Undisputed | 86 |
| 9. Breakdown of a Champion | 93 |
| 10. "To Live, Men Must Fight" | 102 |
| 11. When Hurricanes Collide | 123 |
| 12. Triple Crown | 135 |
| 13. Keep Punching | 158 |
| 14. A Fourth Title? | 172 |
| 15. The Sweetwater Swatter | 182 |
| 16. Zivic | 193 |
| 17. "To Justify Being Alive" | 211 |
| 18. The Comeback Trail | 217 |
| 19. Sugar Ray | 237 |
| 20. "Tired of Fighting" | 250 |
| 21. God's Ball of Fire | 263 |
| 22. Tolling Ten | 274 |
| | |
| Afterword | 285 |
| Henry Armstrong's Verifiable Boxing Record | 288 |
| Bibliography & Sources | 294 |
| Index | 298 |
| Endnotes | 320 |

# Acknowledgements

I would like to give a special thanks to the following people who have contributed in one way or another to this book.

Thanks to boxing historians Adam Pollack, Clay Moyle, Bob Yalen, Douglas Cavanagh, Bob Mee, and Mike Silver for sharing their knowledge, research, advice, and encouragement.

Thanks to Mandolin Restivo for her support and her editing expertise; my parents for their listening and support; Dena Ley for her enthusiasm for the project and assistance with research; Christian Baldo for his outstanding cover design.

Others who have contributed materially or morally to this book include the members of the International Boxing Research Organization, Lee DeVito of the *Detroit Metro Times*, and Amy Stapleton at *Missouri Life*.

# Boxing's Weight Classes in 1938

Heavyweight – weight limit: unlimited
Champion: Joe Louis

Light Heavyweight – weight limit: 175 pounds
Champion: John Henry Lewis

Middleweight – weight limit: 160 pounds
Champion: Freddie Steele

Welterweight – weight limit: 147 pounds
Champion: Henry Armstrong

Lightweight – weight limit: 135 pounds
Champion: Henry Armstrong

Featherweight – weight limit: 126 pounds
Champion: Henry Armstrong

Bantamweight – weight limit: 118 pounds
Champion: Sixto Escobar

Flyweight – weight limit: 112 pounds
Champion: Benny Lynch

# Foreword

*The Ring*, **November 1937**
author's collection

Henry Armstrong deserves a better writer. Springs Toledo, Thomas Hauser, Jeremy Schaap, Clay Moyle, or Carlos Acevedo would have been my top five choices among living writers to pen the tale of boxing's legendary three-division champion. Come to think of it, Jerry Izenberg's take on Armstrong would be great to read. There is no false modesty in admitting that any of them might have done a better job telling Henry's story.

Back in 1938, the preeminent boxing historian Nat Fleischer dedicated the back portion of a book primarily about Joe Louis to an extended sketch of Henry's life up to that point. Armstrong published his autobiography, *Gloves, Glory and God*, in 1956. Both came out decades before Henry passed away and are long out of print. Since then, no book-length biography of arguably the best fighter ever to lace on a pair of gloves has been published. Since I first became interested in the sport's storied history, this has frustrated me, leaving me to try and do Henry justice. In my opinion, Henry's story should be told often. I wrote this book to enhance his legacy, bringing his story to life for those with perhaps only an inkling of who he was and what he achieved.

One of the challenges of writing about a professional boxer from the 1930s and 1940s is conveying the sport's importance in American culture then. The landscape has changed so that ring exploits of YouTube influencers might be better known to the public than even Muhammad Ali's.

Born in the last months of the 1970s and raised in the 1980s and 1990s without access to premium cable, I grew up when boxing's relevance as a sport in America was in decline. At that time, I might have only been vaguely aware of the current heavyweight champion of the world's name, particularly if it was not Mike Tyson. In my defense, boxing's politics were such a mess that there could be as many as four heavyweight champions at any moment.

Children – particularly boys – in the 1930s could have told you the reigning heavyweight champion's name before they could identify the President of the United States – and maybe the names of the champs from some of the lighter divisions, too, especially if the champ was exceptional, like Henry Armstrong.

In the 1930s, boxing went blow-for-blow with baseball as one of the most popular sports in the nation. But even that does not fully convey its standing with the public to today's reader. Not only were the National Football League, National Basketball Association, and National Hockey League on the outermost fringes of public awareness; this was a time without television, computers, video games, the internet, or streaming. If you and your friends wanted worthwhile, immediate mass entertainment, you had precisely six choices: a radio show, a motion picture, a stage act, the racetrack, a baseball game, or a boxing match. During the Great Depression, you were lucky if you could afford to spend your money on even one of those. When you did, it mattered.

The fierce, powerful, and ruggedly handsome heavyweight champion Jack Dempsey had been the figure whose talents broke both the bank and the barriers for boxing in the 1920s and ushered in a golden age for the sport. Aided by promotional wizard Tex Rickard, Dempsey and his opponent Gene Tunney drew a record 135,000 people to a single fight in 1926, for which Dempsey received a $717,000 paycheck. To put that number into perspective, Babe Ruth, by far the highest-paid baseball player, made $52,000 in the same year. The entire roster of Ruth's New York Yankees earned roughly $241,400 combined for the season. The next year, Tunney, Dempsey's conqueror, received the first million-dollar paycheck ever paid to a fighter. The world's premier boxers were suddenly among America's A-list celebrities.

Even after the retirements of Dempsey and Tunney and the economic devastation of the Crash of 1929, boxers remained idols to the working (and unemployed) classes. Yes, the business of boxing faltered like virtually every other industry, and the multi-million-dollar gates disappeared. But boxing's stars still drew in astonishing figures for the time. In 1935, former heavyweight champion Max Baer made $215,000 for facing future champion Joe Louis. That same year, Lou Gehrig, who had replaced Ruth as baseball's highest earner, was paid $40,000 for his entire season.[1]

Though the heavyweights routinely earned boxing's largest purses, interest and big numbers did not apply solely to the big men. Outstanding men in the lighter division made far more money than their counterparts in other professional sports and far more than the common man. In 1938, when the *New York Times* reported the average household annual income to be $515, Henry Armstrong earned $27,203 in just one of the fourteen fights he had that year.

With such amounts on offer, it is no wonder that participation in boxing was at its peak during the 1930s. The number of licensed boxers rose throughout the 1920s thanks to the sport's popularization by men like Dempsey, Tunney, Benny Leonard, and Harry Greb, and the Depression brought even more activity. Poverty and the threat of poverty meant more men were willing to put their bodies (and lives) on the line for a meal and a shot at financial security. During the 1930s, the number of boxers licensed by the New York State Athletic Commission fluctuated between eight thousand and ten thousand, just in that state. To give some perspective, as of this writing in 2023, there are roughly thirty-three hundred active professional male boxers throughout the United States.[2]

New York City was the center of the industry in the 1930s, but capable boxers came from throughout the country. Men who had day jobs as farmhands, shoeshines, construction workers, bouncers, railroad workers, circus performers, dishwashers, and plain old street thugs fought for their meals in every town and city. Those who endured and succeeded amid this influx of participation were, by definition, exceptional, and as such, they were heroes of their geographic and ethnic communities.

Boxing promotion thrived on interracial, interethnic, and international conflicts in the ring. People of African, Jewish, Italian, Irish, Latin, Asian, and Native descent, along with other ethnicities, faced candid prejudice and social subjugation in the 1930s, some more than others. But they could watch their champions prove their worth under (relatively) fair circumstances in the ring, and they were willing to pay to witness such contests.

"You can't Jim Crow a left hook," Henry Armstrong once observed. And he had a hell of a left hook. His most iconic and memorable matches came against white opponents of Jewish, Italian, and Eastern European descent. Black boxing fans from Central Avenue in Los Angeles, Harlem in New York City, and other enclaves of Black culture throughout America flocked to arenas to cheer him on. The millions who could not afford to do so tuned into radio broadcasts of his fights or eagerly read his exploits in newspapers.

As the reader will discover in the story that follows, Black fighters and white fighters might have officially been equals inside the ropes, but that did not mean that Black fighters of Henry's generation – even the best among them – could expect parity with white boxers when it came to treatment.

"Boxing gave the black man a better break than he received in any other sport," columnist W.C. Heinz once commented, "because it needed him." There was nothing altruistic or even fair about boxing's integration. Racial slurs echoed down anonymously at Black fighters from the stands. White promoters and officials blatantly favored white fighters. They expected Black fighters to take dives against popular white opponents. The handlers of Black heavyweight champion Joe Louis went to great pains to portray him as conforming to non-threatening stereotypes to avoid offending fragile white sensibilities. Managers and promoters took advantage of their systematically uneducated and impoverished Black boxers with abusive contracts and practices. White sportswriters never thought twice before describing Black champions as bestial, savage, or cowardly — not just as individuals but by nature. Once the bell rang, a Black boxer fought more than just the white fellow in the other corner. He was fighting a system dependent upon his degradation.[3]

Despite these obstacles – in fact, *because* they triumphed over them – Black boxing champions of the 1930s like Henry Armstrong, Kid Chocolate, Joe Louis, and John Henry Lewis meant a great deal to Black Americans of the period as symbols of growing confidence and hopes for a better future, even in the face of a Great Depression. For all its popularity, baseball was not integrated. It offered no example of Black men succeeding against white opposition. In mainstream Hollywood films, talented Black performers were relegated to roles as savages killed by whites, enslaved people working for whites, servants to whites, and simpletons inferior to whites, if they appeared at all. The participation of Black people in mainstream American politics was virtually non-existent.

In the 1940s, Nobel Prize-winning sociologist Gunnar Myrdal visited an Atlanta public school for Black children and found that not one student was familiar with Booker T. Washington, W.E.B. Du Bois, the NAACP, or even the Constitution of the United States. Nor did they know who President Franklin Roosevelt was or even what a president did. But several knew who Joe Louis and Henry Armstrong were. This pointed to white society's suppression of ideas and education for Blacks. But it also left Myrdal to conclude that, for Black children in need of hope in a society that subdued it, Louis and Armstrong had "symbolically fought the Negro struggle and won." Or, as boxing historian Bert Sugar once put it, they "became twin lighthouses, illuminating the path." What Black boxers like Louis and Armstrong did with their fists was revolutionary in the 1930s and 1940s.[4]

That would not have been possible if Henry Armstrong – one of fifteen children born in the deepest poverty in Jim Crow Mississippi – had not been a brilliant boxer; some say the very best. His accomplishments inside the "squared circle" of the boxing ring were enough to inspire people throughout the nation to keep fighting their own fights. Here's hoping they will continue to do so.

# Prologue
## Tuesday – May 31, 1938

The night sky was starless over Long Island. An obscuring layer of clouds threatened rain all day, but it never came. Even if the sky had been clear and constellations of mythic heroes lit up the heavens, the tens of thousands of people shivering inside the sprawling Madison Square Garden Bowl in Queens could not have noticed. An illuminated square at the center of the outdoor stadium, roughly twenty square feet of canvas walled by rope, transfixed them. Despite the chilly air and the late hour on a weeknight, despite the event's repeated postponement due to rain, despite the lingering money worries of a Great Depression, they had paid for their tickets and waited through five preliminary bouts to watch welterweight boxing champion Barney Ross of Chicago defend his title against featherweight champion Henry Armstrong of Los Angeles.

In a dressing room inside that vast wooden arena, challenger Armstrong shivered too, not with cold but with nervous energy. His deceptively skinny legs skipped ceaselessly. Sometimes they glided in circles. Then they darted side to side, forward and backward in step with a beat only he could hear. His compact, heavily muscled torso twitched, bent, rolled, and wove in a similarly unpredictable fashion, flinging sweat in every direction as it did so. From out of two massive shoulders, his arms tossed gloved fists in rapid punch combinations at a ghost only he could see.

The ghost could change forms, second to second. Jabs slashed the faces of the Klansmen who once terrorized his family while they hid in a Mississippi swamp. A blazing uppercut felled one of the thugs who murdered Henry's older brother in the streets of St. Louis. A looping right hook caved in the face of the Texas sheriff, who hid behind a gun as he forced Henry out of town in the old days of hopping freight trains. A body shot ripped out the guts of one of the innumerable boxing managers, promoters, and officials who swindled him out of victories and money even as he bled for them.

Soon enough, the ghost was not a person but a phantom of the formless evils that had plagued him and the people he loved – The slavery into which his beloved grandmother was born. The disgusting Jim Crow laws that tried to humiliate his people. The tuberculosis that stole away his mother when he was just nine years old. The poverty and starvation of the Great Depression that once tormented his family and was still wearing away at the soul of America.

He punched faster, harder, with both precision and rage, as though he were trying to rip open the air.

Minutes later, he was in the boxing ring, his body still pulsating with fury and anticipation under a pile of blankets meant to keep him warm. The sting of the frigid air needled at his pores and shocked his already wired nerves.

In the opposite corner waited the man some experts called the best fist fighter on the planet, Barney Ross. Barney was a multi-division champion; he was skilled, quick, and tough. Henry had hurtled two divisions above the featherweight division where he was king for the shot at Ross, who outweighed Henry by at least eight pounds. Victory would be unprecedented. No featherweight champ had ever taken the welterweight title before. But deep down, Henry also knew it was inevitable. Nothing – certainly no man – could turn him back tonight.

He was on his toes now, dancing to the rhythm of his furious heart. He filled his lungs to the breaking point and snorted the air out quickly. The time was close, just seconds away. Henry's cornermen stepped out of the ring; Ross's did the same. The crowd unconsciously hushed, overcome by anticipation. Henry bit down on his mouthpiece with a grimace. Across the ring, Ross looked relaxed, almost bored, as though he were perusing a newspaper while unsuspectingly stepping off a street corner in front of an oncoming bus.

The bell rang, and all those ghosts immediately appeared to Henry Armstrong in the opposite corner. He plunged headlong into combat, pushing incessantly forward as he had done and would do all his life. Forward. No matter what was thrown at him, always forward. From the very beginning.

# 1.
# A Sea of Cotton

As an adult, Henry Jackson, Jr., known to the world as Henry Armstrong, believed he was born on December 12, 1912, auspiciously the twelfth day of the twelfth month of the twelfth year of the twentieth century. Though historians have always regarded this date as the man's date of birth, census records indicate a four-month-old baby named Henry in the Jackson household as of May 2, 1910.

Like so many families, the Jacksons had suffered through the loss of multiple children to illness, poverty, and lack of access to healthcare. They reported to the census taker that just seven of their thirteen children lived. The Henry born in 1910 might have died before his more famous younger brother's birth, and his parents may have passed on his name; such practices were not unheard of. However, this is unlikely, and Henry never mentioned inheriting his name in such a way.[5]

"A colored fighter never knows how old he is, and nobody cares," Joe Gans, the first Black American to win a world championship, once commented. Government record keeping for births of Black children in Jim Crow Mississippi was disgracefully scant, and no known birth certificate for Henry Jackson, Jr. exists. The 1930 census shows that Henry was eighteen years old, supporting the 1912 date, but it is also possible that Henry's parents forgot their son's date of birth and made up the convenient December 12, 1912 date later. After all, he was just one of their fifteen children. He was always small in stature and would have passed as younger as a child and teen. The December 12 date may be correct, but the year of his birth might have been 1909, which would be close enough to the four-month age given in the May 2, 1910 census document. For this book, then, the date of December 12, 1909, will be used for Henry's birthdate.[6]

Like his thirteen brothers and sisters (two of them came after him), Henry was born in the family's three-room log cabin held together by sod and tar paper on a cotton plantation once owned by Henry's paternal grandfather, a white man. The grandfather impregnated a fourteen-year-old Black girl named Henrietta, after whom their son and grandson would be named. Born in Alabama in 1851, Henrietta had likely been enslaved at the plantation, though she would have been legally free by the time she became pregnant in 1866. The story goes that the grandfather freed and married Henrietta, to the scandal of the community. She gave birth to her son Henry Jackson (Senior) in Alabama. After her husband's death, Henrietta married a Black farmer named Henry Chatman in 1870, three years after her son's birth.[7]

Henry Senior grew up the focus of shame and animosity from those around him, both white and Black. The whites disapproved of his existence because the Jim Crow South abhorred sin and "miscegenation." The Black sharecroppers were no more ready to accept him due to his very light skin and Caucasian features. White people refused him legal and social parity based on his heritage, and Black people did not trust his look or his landowning parentage. Henry Senior was nonetheless a proud man, and when innuendos, insults, whispers, or any other disrespect reached his ears, he did not hesitate to settle the matter with his fists.

Almost as soon as he was old enough to do so, Henry Senior left the plantation. "He had to move out because he'd fight anybody," his famous son told author Peter Heller. Settling on another plantation for a while, he met America Hall, who was either full-blooded Iroquois or half Cherokee and half Black, depending on which version of the story her son told. She was the child of Freeman Hall and Clarice Frierson. Henry and America married, and Henry returned with his bride to the plantation in Lowndes County.[8]

According to the 1910 census, his father was about forty-eight years old, and his mother was forty-one when Henry was born. A 1900 census ages them at thirty-three and thirty, respectively. This suggests that the parents may not have known their own birthdates. Six older siblings still lived in the home when Henry was born, four brothers and two sisters.[9]

A southern sharecropper's shack.

As Henry Senior looked over his newborn namesake, he could not assume that the child would survive long. The father had already had to endure the deaths of six children, and this son seemed particularly small and frail. The eldest son, eighteen-year-old Ollus, thought his little brother looked like a tiny rat and said so. Much to their mother's chagrin, the Jackson children took to calling their baby brother Rat. Tiny Henry would need a strong heart if he were going to survive the winter, let alone a childhood of poverty, labor, and social degradation.[10]

Luckily for him and his family, what Henry lacked in size, he more than made up for in vitality. He was a curious and adventurous baby and toddler, a bundle of energy incessantly exploring the cabin and the surrounding land.

In his earliest years, he conceived of the world as one giant cotton field speckled with unpainted shacks. Work and church defined his ideas about life. The lives of his family, adults and children alike, revolved around toiling in that unending field. [11]

Mississippi cotton sharecroppers

Henry would remember his father as stern and sturdy little fellow with an unassailable character. His mother was also small but strong in both body and spirit and a strict disciplinarian of her children and herself. "She'd have a kid today and start working almost tomorrow," Henry later remembered of her. Unlike her husband, America could be generous and tender when the moment was right. She treated friends and guests as family at the dinner table. Little Henry spent his evenings enveloped by the sound of family and friends laughing, singing, and eating around him in the Jackson home. The older children slept in bunk beds at night, but the three youngest, including Henry, slept side-by-side on the floor.[12]

The only power to compete with King Cotton in the life of a sharecropper was that of Jesus Christ. On Sundays, work in the fields and the home stopped, and the entire community would gather at Frierson's Chapel, the small church built and maintained by the Black laborers. It is unclear if the chapel was named after America's mother's family. Henry enjoyed watching his parents cast off the woes of hard labor and meager survival for joyful, communal singing. As he got a little bigger, the experience of Frierson's instilled in him a strong faith in the Christian God as a god of "charity without question, love without end."[13]

America Jackson was unrelenting in her insistence that her son Henry would grow to be a minister. The boy certainly was unwavering in his faith, for he believed the Lord had spoken to him at just four years of age. Henry had been daydreaming on the front porch of the Jackson home when he heard a voice from "beyond the sky" say to him, "You must go over yonder and do great things. But always remember Me as the giver of all life. I don't want you ever to forget that I am your God and maker."[14]

Another divine encounter came in the woods beyond the family home while collecting kindling wood at night with a brother and a sister.

> ...there was a little pig. It sounded like a pig. You know, you have those kind that was running around the street all the time out there in the country. So it sounded as if this pig was running in the swamps, coming towards the bridge. And my sister always liked to play with the pigs, because she catches them, and she likes them. The pig said, "Squeak," and he ran.... So I'm looking, listening for the pig, too, but I'm hearing another noise of a horse coming down the road in front of us. After you get across the bridge was the road like that curved, and the high stalks and everything was up. There were trees like, you couldn't see them at all, and it was dark, but I heard the horse, and I'm waiting for the horse. I'm looking for the horse, my sister looking for the pig.... I just heard the horse coming..... [When the pig] jumped on the bridge, looked liked to me the horses hooves hit the same time. Plat! Plat! Plat! Plat! Four times. And we could just see the pig, the little black pig, then all of a sudden it began to turn white, and my sister said it was time for her to go. She didn't have any nerve. And then all of a sudden, the pig it seemed turned into a beautiful white dog, and then all of a sudden when it turned into this dog, it just said, "Blip," and went up over me, and over me was a horse, just the head, the beautiful mane and no feet at all, and his eyes like glass, just shining like diamonds. They was just glowing like that, looked like something was breathing. His veins was just like the river flowing, and I looked up at this horse, and I heard my sister crying and hallowing [sic], and I just wanted to ride him, that's all.... When I opened my arms like that, then he disappeared.[15]

Henry would tell versions of this tale throughout his life and continue to believe that this was a sign from God.

By working hard, living off the land, and attending church dutifully, the Jackson family was accepted into the community of Black sharecroppers working the plantation, overcoming the isolation once imposed upon Henry Senior. Despite his mixed Irish, African, and Native American ancestry, Henry Junior saw the Black people of the fields as his people and the whites living in Columbus as "the others." Even still, it was not the concept of skin color or ethnic background that he initially perceived as the dividing factor.

Skin tone did not necessarily define who was white and who was Black in the Jim Crow South, and Henry, whose father could pass for white, picked up on that early.

> See, my grandfather's a white man, and my father was by the grandmother who was an African.... I lived on this plantation, and after my grandfather died, my grandmother gave it up, cut it up and she gave some to my father... and she had the most beautiful place on the Waverly Road. I was a kid running around there, and we got people... you know how those white people did, the colored girls, they had intercourse with them, and they had kids by them. On that plantation, I had cousins out there looked as white as you. I didn't know the difference in people.[16]

There was something other than skin color that separated Henry's people and "others." It was that "others" behaved differently toward Henry's people than they did toward each other. Young children being strongly sensitive to tone of voice, Henry was barely out of toddlerhood when he already perceived that when the others addressed his people, "it was more talking *at* than talking *with*. Mostly it was hard and cold underneath, and even when their words were polite and friendly, their voices were unfriendly."[17]

Jim Crow was more than just legal statutes and signs on water fountains reading "whites" and "coloreds." It was more than just segregation of neighborhoods and schools under the false pretext of "separate but equal." For the people who lived it, it was a code of daily behavior meant to reinforce Black people's subjugation as second-class citizens in perpetuity.

As he grew up in an American Apartheid, his parents taught young Henry to step off sidewalks to let white people pass uninterrupted. They taught him to address any white person by "boss," "sir," or "ma'am" while watching the adults of his family accept "boy," "nigger," "auntie," and other demeaning pronouns from whites without complaint. They taught his teenage brothers never to look too long at a white woman because of the white man's fear of "miscegenation." Yet if his mother or sisters were ever harassed or assaulted by a white man, there could be no legal recourse or personal vengeance.

When Henry was five, people across the nation flocked to their local cinemas to see an epic silent film called *The Birth of a Nation*. Directed by D.W. Griffith, the Kentucky-reared son of a Confederate officer, the film was the most inflammatory of its age and maybe of all time. The story portrayed Black people (played by whites in blackface) as lazy, idiotic, and rapists. It construed post-war Reconstruction as a corruption of good government and the abolition of slavery as an unnatural invitation for crime and depravity. The film depicts the birth of the Ku Klux Klan as a means of saving the South from these sins. At its conclusion, the heroic Klan rescues the virginal white actress Lillian Gish from a mixed-race pursuer.

Griffith made extravagant use of the then enormous budget of $110,000 to fund massive battle scenes, a three-hour story, and production values never seen in American film. Those qualities drew the largest American audience in motion picture history to that point, grossing tens of millions of dollars domestically.[18]

Celebrated Black Americans like W.E.B. Du Bois voiced their concerns over the portrayal of their race in the film and the dangers it represented. The National Association for the Advancement of Colored People tried to get the movie banned. Just as they feared, *The Birth of a Nation* brought a resurgence in white supremacist activity throughout the South.

On Thanksgiving Day, 1915, twenty-five hundred former Klansmen paraded through the streets of Atlanta, Georgia, to bask in the pride the film had brought them. Officially disbanded in 1877, the KKK reconvened that night beneath a burning cross. Membership exploded almost overnight. Far from seeking to curb the damage done by the film, President Woodrow Wilson told the press that Griffith was "writing history with lightning." The President was proud to see that the film at one point quoted him praising the old KKK as "a veritable empire of the South, to protect the Southern country." He happily screened the film in the White House accompanied by Chief Justice Edward White, a former Klansman.[19]

*The Birth of a Nation* brought about a regression in the already unbalanced relationship between Blacks and whites in the Deep South back to an even more oppressive and violent time, making Mississippi a dangerous place for a young Black boy like Henry Armstrong to grow up. In an interview for an oral history entitled *Remembering Jim Crow*, Willie Harrell, a Black man also raised on a Mississippi farm but seventeen years younger than Henry, remembered trying to navigate the life-and-death dangers of segregation on a plantation. Slavery might have been legally over, but in a society still dominated by white supremacy, no one enforced a Black person's rights, even to leave. The bosses on Harrell's plantation knew that, and they were brutal.

> If they'd catch you trying to leave, they'd take you back there and whip you, fasten you up in the barn and whip you. It's just like old slavery time. They hemmed me up in the barn like [where] they feed mules, and they whipped me.... Wasn't nothing I could do. They had a whip.... Wasn't nothing you could do, but take it. You try to resist [and] they would kill you.

Henry was lucky to live on land owned by his grandmother. He had no racist white landowner with a whip, but he still had plenty to fear. Growing up in the years of the KKK's resurrection, he saw Black people tarred and feathered in the town square regularly. Henry watched a white landowner whip his neighbors, and he twice hid with his family in a nearby swamp while lynch mobs prowled the area. On both occasions, whites lynched a Black man. After witnessing such events, Henry had recurring dreams that he was white.

Most of the white people Henry encountered lived in the growing nearby town of Columbus, Mississippi, the county seat of Lowndes County (which bordered the state of Alabama). Columbus had a population of approximately 8,988 people in 1910. It and the surrounding plantations lay not far northeast of the Tombigbee River, a tributary of the Mobile River. When the Tombigbee would overflow, it caused havoc for the Jacksons and the other sharecropping families, drowning livestock and crops. One such flood decimated farms throughout the area in 1912, when Henry would have been about two years old. It lasted from February to May, "exceeding in duration any previous flood of record." As a result, the Jackson family home was raised on stilts. [20]

Boll weevils, the cotton-devouring beetles which migrated to the area in the late nineteenth century, were also a terror of the Mississippi sharecropper. While the rest of the country reacted to *The Birth of a Nation*, the Jacksons reacted to a boll weevil infestation that devastated their crops, leaving the family little income. Henry Senior struggled to bring in money, and America was pregnant again. Word arrived from friends and family that he could find work to the north in Missouri, where there were cities and where the Jim Crow laws were not quite so oppressive. Henry Senior was a talented butcher, a skill that came in handy no matter where one lived. Thus, he found himself a butcher's position at the Independent Packing Company in St. Louis, Missouri. Taking his eldest sons, Ollus and Oscar, with him, he left the rest of the brood behind with America on the plantation until he could raise enough money to buy a home for the family.

Times were lean and stressful for America Jackson and her small children while the men were away, and the boll weevils devoured their income. Doubtless, Henry Senior sent some money home to help, but little Henry would retain a memory of his mother's grief and worry into his adulthood. The family rejoiced with relief and excitement after the father sent word to pack their bags for St. Louis. However, Henry Senior reported that there was not enough money and shelter to house all their children. America chose only the youngest few, Henry among them, and left the rest to stay with neighbors or fend for themselves. That choice left America Jackson "a broken woman," Henry later remembered. [21]

The sights, sounds, act, and emotions of leaving Mississippi and the only home he had known gave five-year-old Henry some of the most vivid memories of his lifetime. The clanging, roaring, and smoking of an "iron monster," the first steam engine Henry had ever seen, terrified him into shrinking behind his mother, who assured him everything was alright. Holding her hand tightly, he followed her into one of its cars and sat down next to a window facing the station, out of which he could see friends and family, some of them in tears, waving farewell below. They sang hopeful gospel songs which comforted and calmed him for a time, but as the train first convulsed and then surged forward, and as the people he had known all his life faded into the distance behind, Henry's little heart began to surge once more with excitement, fear, and sadness. [22]

# 2.
# "You Ain't No Jack Johnson"

The first thing Henry noticed upon disembarking from the iron monster in St. Louis was the size of everything. The size of the train station, more significant than any building he had seen in or around Columbus. The size of the other buildings and houses, and the size of the sidewalks encircling them. Even the height of his father and brothers, who seemed taller than he remembered as they stood erect in their fine suits and pride as employed, urban men freed from the degradation of the Deep South's plantations. Then came the sounds: first, the hissing train engines; outside of the station were the clanging streetcars and the noisy automobiles everywhere. He noticed a louder tone in the voices of his father and brothers, too, confidence and pride he had never detected in Black men before.

That pride must have been especially great as the father showed his family around the square, three-room brick house he had obtained for his family at 914 Josephine Street on the corner of Josephine and Papin Streets in the city's South Side. That night, Henry and his brothers and sisters slept in new bunk beds their father had set up around the house.

The other shock of St. Louis was the amount of people. On the plantation, cotton was everywhere when he stepped out of his front door. In the city, it was people that were everywhere; many of them were children, children of different colors. Outside of his house, Henry met and played with boys and girls who were Black and white, Christian and Jewish. Amongst these children, he picked up the nickname Red, thanks to the reddish tinge of his hair. The Jacksons' neighborhood was a tough one. When not sitting through classes in the Toussaint L'Ouverture Grammar School, the neighborhood kids were "outside of class fighting each other – or getting ready to fight – or talking about fights – or nursing the aftereffects of fights."[23]

Another future boxing great, Archie Moore, who was between three and six years younger than Henry (Archie never could be pinned down about his actual age), grew up in the same neighborhood of St. Louis. "Back when I was a kid in St. Louis, a gang fight meant only fists, and it was usually an ethnic thing," Moore wrote of those years. "The Irish against the Italians or blacks took on the Latinos. It was the type of fight that an adult could break up with a few stern words. No killings, that's for sure, maybe a black eye or fat lip. I could hold my own, so I never had to worry." Little Henry Jackson would eventually learn to hold his own, too.[24]

Henry lost his first street fight and came home crying to his mother. She showed little sympathy. "If you have to fight, learn how to fight," she told him. Then she slapped him across the face.

Henry would have to learn to fight, then, because staying out of fights was an impossibility. While St. Louis was not as discriminatory as Columbus, its schools were just as segregated, and the school for Blacks was on the East Side of town. To make it to class and back home each day, Henry, his big sister Henrietta, and the other Black children had to fight their way through the East Side kids who always waited for them. Because Henry was only five, most of the older East Side kids let him off easy at first, and if they did not, Henrietta stepped in to slug the boy who picked on him.

After her second husband died, Henry's grandmother Henrietta Chatman moved from Columbus to live with her son's family in St. Louis. That both Henrys and little Henrietta were all named after the woman speaks to the extraordinary reverence with which the Jacksons regarded her. She would play a central role in the family and in the life of little Henry, who would forever remember her stories of life in slavery and of once seeing the "Great Emancipator," Abraham Lincoln, with her own eyes as an enslaved girl in Alabama. She was a strong woman with an iron will and steadfast beliefs.[25]

Grandma Henrietta's arrival proved sorely needed for the Jacksons, for it practically coincided with the illness of her daughter-in-law. America Jackson had contracted tuberculosis, known as consumption at the time, the leading killer of people in the United States. Her health deteriorated slowly for two years, "a long haul," as Henry remembered it later. He and his siblings tried to help make her comfortable and tend to some of her chores in her last days. She died on Tuesday, October 21, 1919, of interstitial nephritis, a rare kidney ailment that can arise when a patient suffers from tuberculosis. Her death certificate listed her as only forty, but she was likely at least a decade older. Her son Henry was just short of his tenth birthday. Grandma Henrietta immediately stepped in as a surrogate mother.[26]

Well into her sixties, Henrietta was a heavy-set lady with graying hair and weak eyesight. Though not as openly loving as her daughter-in-law, Henrietta kept her grandchildren fed, washed, clothed, and disciplined. As a formerly enslaved person, she greatly valued the education her grandchildren received, and she saw no good reason for avoiding hard work, so she accepted no excuses from Henry when he tried to get out of studying or chores or if she found out he had been skipping school. Though she did not hit or spank, Henry remembered, "she could make a boy feel even worse than if she had." Like America, Henrietta was sure of bright little Henry's destiny to be a man of God; she included it in her nightly prayers.

Outside of the home, Henry found little use for schoolbooks. After the family returned from his mother's funeral in Columbus, Henry found the streets of St. Louis an excellent place to let out his anguish over the loss of his mother. Some bigger kids started bullying him after he refused to play football. They changed his nickname from Red to Sissy. Once Henry confessed this to his older brother John, John taught him the rudiments of wrestling. He proved quick, both in learning and in reflexes.

Soon enough, the confident little scrapper had thrown or pinned every boy his size on Papin Street. Then, in the street fighting kid's version of jumping weight classes, he beat all the bigger boys too. After that, he began taking on two at a time.

Once a kid got a taste of his specialty, the headlock, he never messed with little Henry Jackson again. Even so, the victories came with a cost. He may have remained undefeated in the streets and the schoolyard, but each victory ultimately meant defeat at the hands of his father's spankings for coming home in ruined clothes.

Eventually, Henry came upon a bully who, after being thrown to the ground by various wrestling moves, put up his fists and insisted that Henry box him. No one had taught him any boxing technique, but as far as Henry was concerned, a punch was a punch. He landed a hard right on the other boy's chin and sent him crashing into a coal bin. Henry ran home to brag to John, who laughed and dubbed him "Little Jack Johnson," after the famous former heavyweight champion, the first Black man to hold the title.

Henry realized that knocking a guy down with a punch was much quicker than wrestling him down. That meant less damaged clothing and fewer spankings from his father. Culling together twelve dollars from the money he had saved cleaning apartment building steps, Henry bought himself a pair of boxing gloves he would produce each afternoon after school. Soon enough, he was repeating the same feat he had as a wrestler: beating every other boy on Papin Street. Then he began venturing into other neighborhoods looking for challengers.

To the youngsters of St. Louis, beating a foe from a rival neighborhood gang was a badge of honor. Archie Moore remembered, "Our gangs usually fought over fancied slights or invasions of enemy territory. But most often the two gangs would meet and a representative of one fought a fair fight with a representative 'champion' of the enemy. When it was over the two fighters shook hands and peace was temporarily restored between the warring tribes."[27]

To the Papin Street gang, Henry Armstrong was their champion, the boy they sent to defend their honor in neighborhoods abroad. He found that the best technique was to catch an opponent in the gut first. Then, when they doubled over in surprise, he would clobber their heads. The basic but effective approach followed a boxing axiom he likely had not learned yet. "Kill the body, and the head will follow." In time, he wore the gloves out against the bodies of other boys and had to give the hobby up.

His talents at wrestling and boxing convinced Henry that he wanted to be an athlete, an inspiration that ended his occasional bouts of truancy from school. He entered Vashon High School in 1925 and reclaimed his status as an excellent student. He was a talented writer with a particular affection for composing poetry, an art he would practice for the rest of his life.

In the summers, he kept in shape by running approximately fifteen miles to a job as a pin boy at a bowling alley in Maplewood, Missouri. At Midtown Alley, he made friends with other pin boys who happened to be fans of boxing as well, and he convinced some of them to chip in for some new gloves. Along with these boys, Henry formed an unofficial boxing club that would gather after the Alley closed at one in the morning and spar in friendly matches with one another. As well as acting as organizer and pugilist, he also refereed bouts. By age sixteen, now the victor over every other kid in the club, Henry fantasized that maybe he had what it took to be a real boxing champion.

His more practical side told him to look toward the medical field. The thought of earning good money and helping his family appealed to him, and his grandmother and father were more likely to approve of his being a doctor than a boxer. He admired the wealth of the physicians and lawyers he saw riding in fine cars. Grandma Henrietta still had her heart set on his becoming a preacher, but she agreed that being a doctor was a respectable profession. He resolved to enter college after high school.

Because he completed an extra school semester over one summer, Henry graduated with honors from Vashon High in 1929, a few months ahead of his classmates. Still, he was proud to walk in the graduation ceremony alongside those others later in the year, partly because he had been named Vashon High's valedictorian and poet laureate. He was nineteen, but no one knew it; even Henry probably thought he was sixteen. Draped in a new blue serge suit bought with ten dollars borrowed from a friend, he recited a self-penned valedictory poem from the dais, his family proudly looking on.

The coming decades would prove Vashon High a breeding ground for boxing talent. After Henry, other Vashon alums would include Virgil Akins, Leon Spinks, Michael Spinks, and Devon Alexander, all world titleholders.

A proud honors graduate with plans for a medical career and prosperity for his long-suffering family, Henry fully intended to take his diploma as far as a Black man was allowed in the segregated South. He had no idea that events in his home and the world would make survival tougher than ever for him and the people he loved.

On October 29, Americans opened their newspapers to find headlines declaring the most significant stock market crash in the history of Wall Street, a staggering fall of fifteen thousand points. This event, afterward known as Black Tuesday, had causes reaching as far back as the international politics attending the Treaty of Versailles following the First World War a decade earlier. Despite the widespread optimism over a booming American economy throughout the 1920s, economists had been pointing toward signs of a pending and very severe economic downturn since the early years of the decade: a virtual halt in agriculture exports as European nations focused on repairing their post-war economies; the automobile causing a decline in railway ridership and production leading to downturns in the vital coal and steel industries; corporations refusing to trickle down their profits into increased wages for employees.

President Calvin Coolidge ignored warnings of the coming economic crisis from advisors and political foes alike. His successor Herbert Hoover, left holding the proverbial bag, tried but failed to reverse the subsequent chain reaction of fiscal disasters. For his part, Hoover pointed to Europe as "the great center of the storm."[28]

As many middle-class Americans had invested in the stock market using bank loans, millions found themselves out of their life savings and badly in debt to banks that were desperate to collect on payment or collateral as quickly as possible. Credit faltered. Paranoia about banks folding became a self-fulfilling prophecy as millions closed their accounts, causing five thousand banks to close their doors by 1932.[29]

Farmers in the Midwest, already having had to endure a downturn in foreign demand, found their land ruined by sun-blotting clouds of soil that stripped their region until it became one giant "Dust Bowl."

Realizing that people would have less spending money, manufacturers burdened with huge surpluses began laying off large sections of their workforce, which only meant that even fewer people could afford to buy their products. Soon enough, the factories shut down, and more people were unemployed. Industrial production in the United States fell by fifty percent. By 1932, unemployment in America would approach thirty percent, fifty percent for Black Americans. The national suicide rate had increased by thirty percent.[30]

Wealthy businessmen and supporters of a free-market economy considered the Great Depression just what America needed. Secretary of Treasury Andrew Mellon told President Hoover that the Depression was "not altogether a bad thing," because "People will work harder... Enterprising people will pick up the wrecks from less competent people."[31]

Albert Wiggin, chairman of Chase National Bank, told a Senate committee that the crisis was just a typical side effect of the cycle of healthy "business activity." He tried to convey that there was nothing really to worry about. He believed that the American people had an "infinite capacity for suffering," insinuating that the nation needed to settle down and accept its circumstances in the name of a free market. Wiggins, of course, was doing fine. Not one to test his own capacity for suffering, he had secretly used millions in Chase funds to short-sell more than forty-two thousand shares of the company's stocks to a personal profit of more than four million dollars.[32]

Despite Wiggins' self-delusion, the American people's suffering was indeed beyond their capacity. At first, desperate people turned to the institutions which had always helped through hard times before: their places of worship, their unions, charitable societies, and government agencies. However, those institutions were soon overwhelmed and depleted of resources.

Unable to afford their mortgages and rents, hundreds of thousands of people in major cities throughout the country began to assemble in shanty towns composed of tents, lean-tos, and whatever other kinds of make-shift shelters they could construct. The public dubbed these impoverished villages Hoovervilles to mock the bitter, helpless, and increasingly reclusive President.

The *New York Times* was printing the word "Hooverville" for only the second time when they referred to the shanty town that had assembled on the banks of the Mississippi River in St. Louis, Missouri. That Hooverville was the country's largest, comprising between three thousand and five thousand Americans living in predominantly garbage and driftwood homes. Dollar for dollar and job for job, St. Louis was probably hit harder by the Great Depression than any other city in the nation. By 1931, unemployment there would surpass thirty percent, higher than the highest national average for the entire duration of the crisis.[33]

For Black Americans, the Depression worsened already widespread poverty, unemployment, and prejudice. The National Recovery Act (NRA) to be instituted by Hoover's successor as President, Democrat Franklin Roosevelt, was still years away. Roosevelt benefited from the first widespread voting wave of Black Americans in U.S. history, a reaction to the prior Republican administration's ignorance. When it did arrive, the NRA was hardly a relief for Black Americans, who came to refer to it as the Negro Removal Act. Labor unions and the American Federation of Labor paid little more than lip service to combat racial discrimination in hiring practices.[34]

Left to their own severely limited devices, some Black people in St. Louis formed the St. Louis Urban League in 1929 and began to boycott businesses that catered to Black clientele but employed only whites. Their example sparked a national "Jobs for Negros" campaign of boycotts by similar grassroots organizations throughout America.[35]

The Jacksons kept their home through the lean early years of the Great Depression, but staying out of the squalid Hooverville meant significant struggle compounded by illness, age, and the violent death of one of Henry's older brothers.

"He was a very good-looking boy," Henry told Peter Heller decades later. "He was working out with my dad at this packing company. Because all the girls was falling for this guy he got killed. Some fellows beat him to death because the girls was just falling for him."[36]

The St. Louis newspapers of 1929 and 1930 carried no stories about the killing, and Henry never specified which brother died, nor do any death records from St. Louis and the areas nearby that the author could find.

Henry never described the emotional toll this murder took on him or his family, but one can imagine it must have been shocking and sad. It left just Henry and Henrietta as the only Jackson children still living in the home. The rest had grown up and moved out. It also removed income from the household at the start of the Great Depression.

The Jacksons had no choice but to move on from the tragedy. Though it certainly was not enough to put a dent in the family bills, Henry had his own small income from the bowling alley, and he dreamed of college. Meanwhile, his father and grandmother struggled to hold on to their paychecks. The onset of rheumatism meant chronic pain for Henry Senior at the meat factory job, which had once given him so much pride.

Keeping a job was already hard for a man over forty after the Crash of 1929, but Henry Senior knew that looking for one would be more problematic. "A man over forty might as well go out and shoot himself," was one desperate Depression-era American's view of the situation. A similar hopeless anxiety began to take over Henry Senior as his condition worsened. Perhaps more concerning was the incessant cough he could not seem to shake, an early sign of the tuberculosis that had killed his wife and would one day claim him too. His growing fondness for alcohol did not help matters.[37]

Now approaching her eighties, Henrietta Chatman was going blind, a crisis for any manual laborer. Henrietta worked at a nut factory, cutting pecans out of their shells with a small knife for a few cents an hour. Her grandson first knew of her condition when she came home from work one evening, hiding a hand behind a handkerchief. She went to the kitchen sink and began washing blood from her hand. Unable to see the pecans, she had been repeatedly stabbing herself all day with her knife. Disturbed by the realization that his grandmother was blind and injuring herself, Henry Junior immediately decided to find better paying work so that his father and grandmother need not work themselves into the grave.

Finding work, let alone decent paying work, in possibly the hardest hit urban center in the country was a difficult prospect. "Every morning up before dawn, washed, shaved, and dressed as neatly as possible. To the factory gates, only to find a hundred others already there, staring blankly at the sign: NO HELP WANTED," is how one historian describes the morning routine of a typical urban male during the Great Depression. Being Black would put Henry at a disadvantage to the white men on the job hunt, but he was young and athletic, and he knew those traits would help him if he could only find an opportunity.[38]

One morning, Henry read an ad in a newspaper saying that the Missouri-Pacific Railroad was looking for strong men. He excitedly declared to Henrietta he was going to get himself the job. "You ain't nothing but a boy," she scoffed at him. Undeterred, he grabbed his father's hat, shoes, and overalls. He put on a coat, stuffed it with cotton and rags to look more muscular, and headed down to ask for work. Henry told the foreman that he was twenty-one and got the job.[39]

The older men teased the young newcomer, but the work and the pay inspired Henry. He was especially thrilled to drive spikes into the ground with a sledgehammer, remembering that this was how the great heavyweight champion Jack Dempsey claimed to have built up his muscles. The site was in a St. Louis suburb called Carondolet. His co-workers from downtown all rode the ten miles down the tracks to and from work on a motorized hand car, but Henry liked to show up late going both ways so that he could impress them by running behind the car the whole way, with a hard day's labor in between each trip. When he got home each night, he posed and flexed in front of the mirror, admiring his developing body. "That hammer heaving job sure toughened me up," Henry later told a British columnist. "I recommend it as a fine start for any boxer," he told another.[40]

Even when he was not heaving the hammer for the railroad, Henry spent the evenings secretly developing his body. He later told an interviewer:

I was a small little fellow, but I was very strong because I secretly had a desire to become a great athlete and I would do training (while unbeknownst) to everyone, in fact I would do them secretly. What I would do, I bought all kinds of training equipment and I took them to my basement when we were living over on Josephine Street and this is where I religiously went into training and getting myself into condition. And then I would get up in the morning, early morning, before going to work or school and I would run. I would run around Forest Park. I was just a maniac for running, and I guess you know when I started fighting they used to call me "Perpetual Motion," and "Other Side Hank," you know, and all those names. And this stamina that I acquired in my youthful days really helped me.[41]

Before long, Henry was bringing home twenty dollars a week as a railroad hand, making him the primary breadwinner for the Jackson household, just as he intended. Still, the desire to be a great, wealthy professional fighter nagged at him. He became something of a pet to the older men on the job site and made friends by talking about boxing with them. His co-workers waived off his claims that he would be a great fighter someday.

"A Negro fighter has to be mighty good," someone reminded him, "so good that he simply can't be overlooked – and even then the going is hard." The fellow knew what he was talking about.[42]

Since the dawn of gloved championship boxing in 1892, there had been just seven Black world champions before 1929, and just four of them from the United States. One of those was Jack Johnson, who had held the world's heavyweight championship between 1908 and 1915, during which time he became the most hated man in the country. The heavyweight championship, a title which conferred upon its wearer unofficial recognition as "Emperor of Masculinity" throughout the sporting world, had been exclusively the property of white men before 1908, if only because the white champions drew a "color line" in refusing to face Black challengers, citing various racist excuses.

Only after being tempted by a thirty thousand dollar guaranteed purse did champion Tommy Burns upend precedent and scandalize his white fans by accepting a fight with Johnson. Easily battering Burns about the ring until police stopped the fight to avoid a riot, Johnson quickly did everything that could offend white America, which amounted to nothing more than living the life he wanted without deference to the sensitivities of the white public. He quarreled with, disobeyed, and fired his white managers. He moved into a white neighborhood. He bought the finest clothes and automobiles and loved to flaunt them before news cameras. He romanced and married white women with equally unabashed pride. He relished humiliating every "Great White Hope" promoters put before him. His July 4, 1910, victory over revered ex-champion James Jeffries sparked deadly race riots throughout the country.

**Jack Johnson**

Harassed by the government, collecting death threats as quickly as he spent his dollars, and facing trumped-up charges of "white slavery," this son of two actual enslaved people went into exile in Europe, where he drank, engorged himself, and lost his motivation, eventually losing his title in a dull fight with the gigantic challenger Jess Willard in Cuba in 1915, the year *Birth of a Nation* was released.

Jack Johnson's victories in the ring, extravagant lifestyle, and refusal to bow to the expectations of white society made him an idol to Black American men and boys throughout America for generations, Henry Jackson included. Most whites and even some Black people felt quite differently, seeing Johnson as a poor influence or representative for Black people. Two days after his victory over Jeffries, the *Los Angeles Times* warned Black readers against taking pride in the win. "Do not point your nose too high. Do not swell your chest too much. Do not boast too loudly. Do not be puffed up," the white writer instructed them, lest Johnson's example influence them to take their ambitions in "a wrong direction."[43]

Even after he lost the title, white America remained traumatized by Johnson's insistence on being an indomitable Black man. Between 1915 and 1929, only two Black men (light heavyweight Battling Siki of Senegal and middleweight Tiger Flowers of Georgia) were given a shot at a world boxing championship; none received a shot at the heavyweight belt until 1937. Both Siki and Flowers won their overdue chances at glory. Still, talented Black men like Sam Langford, Harry Wills, Jeff Clark, Eladio "Black Bill" Valdes, Larry Gains, George Godfrey, Robert "Jamaica Kid" Buckley, and William "Kid Norfolk" Ward were all denied championship fights and big money purses primarily because of their skin color.

**Kid Chocolate**

Then came Eligio Sardinas-Montalbo, a skinny, dazzlingly quick, two-fisted ex-newsboy out of Cerro, Cuba. At some point, while compiling an undefeated amateur record and then going undefeated in his first twenty-one pro fights in Havana, winning all of them by knockout, Sardinas-Montalbo acquired the stage name of Kid Chocolate. Just eighteen years old and roughly 126 pounds, he arrived in New York in 1928 to become a star almost overnight, thanks to his graceful style and high-volume punching. He fought in Madison Square Garden, the most famous boxing venue in the world, and began tearing through the featherweight division.

In a highly anticipated matchup at the Polo Grounds in New York on August 29, 1929, Chocolate faced another rising star in the division named Al Singer, a white puncher out of the Bronx. Experts figured the fight to determine the coming champion. It garnered a gate of roughly $225,000, a record for a non-title fight in the lighter divisions. Fans were disappointed by a lackluster affair in which the Kid emerged the victor by controversial decision. As it would turn out, Kid Chocolate and Al Singer both became world champions in the coming years.[44]

Henry would later repeatedly tell the story that not long after the Kid Chocolate and Al Singer fight, on lunch break at the railroad, a gust of wind blew a copy of the *St. Louis Post-Dispatch* to his feet. He picked it up and read of the fight. He read a headline stating that the Kid was paid $75,000 for the match. The payday stunned Henry. Some quick calculations told him he would have to work about seventy-five years on the railroad to see that kind of money. Turning to a co-worker, he insisted he would be a professional boxer and earn $75,000 for a single fight someday. He left work that day to the sound of grown men laughing behind him.[45]

The headline for the *Post-Dispatch* on August 30, the day after the bout, read, "KID CHOCOLATE AWARDED DECISION OVER SINGER IN 12-ROUND BOUT." There was no mention anywhere in the article of the fighter's payday. However, Henry's memory might have confused the paper's name with that of the *St. Louis Star and Times*. Underneath their August 30 headline were the words, "Cuban Negro, $40 Preliminary Fighter Two Years Ago Draws Down $50,000." Regardless of the paper's name or the amount of the payday, young Henry Jackson was amazed and inspired.

That evening, Grandma Henrietta was just as skeptical as Henry's co-workers but was not amused. She still believed that her grandson should enter medical school and become a doctor. "You ain't no Jack Johnson," she insisted. He tried to tell her he could make enough money as a boxer in a year to pay for medical school, but she remained opposed to the idea. Nonetheless, Henry went about installing a punching bag in the basement.[46]

# 3.
# Melody

Pine Street YMCA, St. Louis, MO

Henry had promised a wedding ring to his high school sweetheart, sixteen-year-old Velma Tart. But supporting his family on his railroad salary left him no money to save for a ring, and he seemed directionless. Frustrated at Henry's lack of prospects, Velma broke up with him and married another man. The railroad job ended in a layoff, and after a brief stint as a dishwasher, Henry Jackson spent the next year working in a hat shop until five in the afternoon.

After work, he always headed down to the local YMCA on Pine Street, where he worked on his physique and boxing technique. Four stories of red brick, the Pine Street Y was a community center for Black people in St. Louis. Founded in 1887 by John Boyer Vashon, the local educator after whom Henry's high school had been named, it provided Black residents with access to a gym and a swimming pool, facilities from which whites banned them. There was a boxing ring, too.

It was during one of his workouts there that Henry ran into Harry Armstrong. Though they would later tell the press that they were halfbrothers, Henry and Harry were of no relation. Harry had fought at various locales around the South, though this author could find no prior record for him. A 5'5" light heavyweight, he had been no great shakes as a fighter, "just another palooka," as he put it. But he had experience. Henry had known him for years, but they were not yet close friends.[47]

Harry was there to give pointers to a protégé of his, a lightweight named Eddie Foster. He spotted Henry walking in and asked him why he was carrying a pair of boxing gloves.

"I'm a boxer," Henry told him. When Harry scoffed, Henry said, "I boxed bigger guys than you."

"OK," responded Harry, pulling gloves over his hands, "put 'em on."

After lacing up the mittens, Henry charged forward, launching wild swings at the other man. Punch after punch missed the astonishingly elusive Harry, who returned fire with left jabs that only infuriated and disoriented Henry further.

Harry called time and explained that being a good boxer meant more than throwing random punches and being able to take a good shot to the chin; it also required skill and defense.

Harry next instructed Henry to dodge his next left jab by stepping to the right and crossing over Harry's jab with a right hand.

"Can you do it now?" challenged Harry, and he shot out that straight left. By the time it fully extended, Henry was out of the way, letting loose with a right hand as instructed. Harry did not expect the speed; the next thing he knew, he was on the floor.

"Boy, you can punch," Harry said, rubbing his sore jaw as he stood up. The two headed to the showers, and while there, Harry began to think about managing this quick-handed, aggressive puncher. Listening to Henry sing in the shower, Harry devised the boxing moniker Melody Jackson for his newest charge.[48]

For decades, the best way for a young Black aspiring boxer to make his name locally had been in the racist spectacles known as the battle royal. Poor Black men and boys were put on stage, blindfolded, and made to fight it out for the amusement of primarily white men (though Black audiences also enjoyed battle royals) who tossed coins at them. The last man standing was allowed to walk home with his prize, the coins he picked up off the ground. This was how legendary future champions like Jack Johnson and Joe Gans first won notice in their communities. However, Henry Jackson wanted no part of the battle royals. Offered an opportunity to make his debut in such an event, he passed. "I wouldn't go for that," he later remembered. "I was really too proud."[49]

The typical route to notoriety out of the question thanks to his charge's self-respect, Harry Armstrong was able to work out the chance for Henry to instead participate in the Amateur Athletic Union's upcoming boxing tournament. Meanwhile, he kept Henry in the ring sparring with Eddie Foster and instructed him in the rudiments of boxing technique. Henry was easily dominating Foster in no time.

When Harry and Henry turned up at the St. Louis Coliseum for the tournament on Thursday, March 20, 1930, they found there was only one other "colored" kid in Henry's featherweight (126-pound) weight class, one Jimmy Burch. Since Missouri law segregated all boxing matches, he would be Henry's only opponent, and the winner of the match would be the amateur colored featherweight champion of the West.

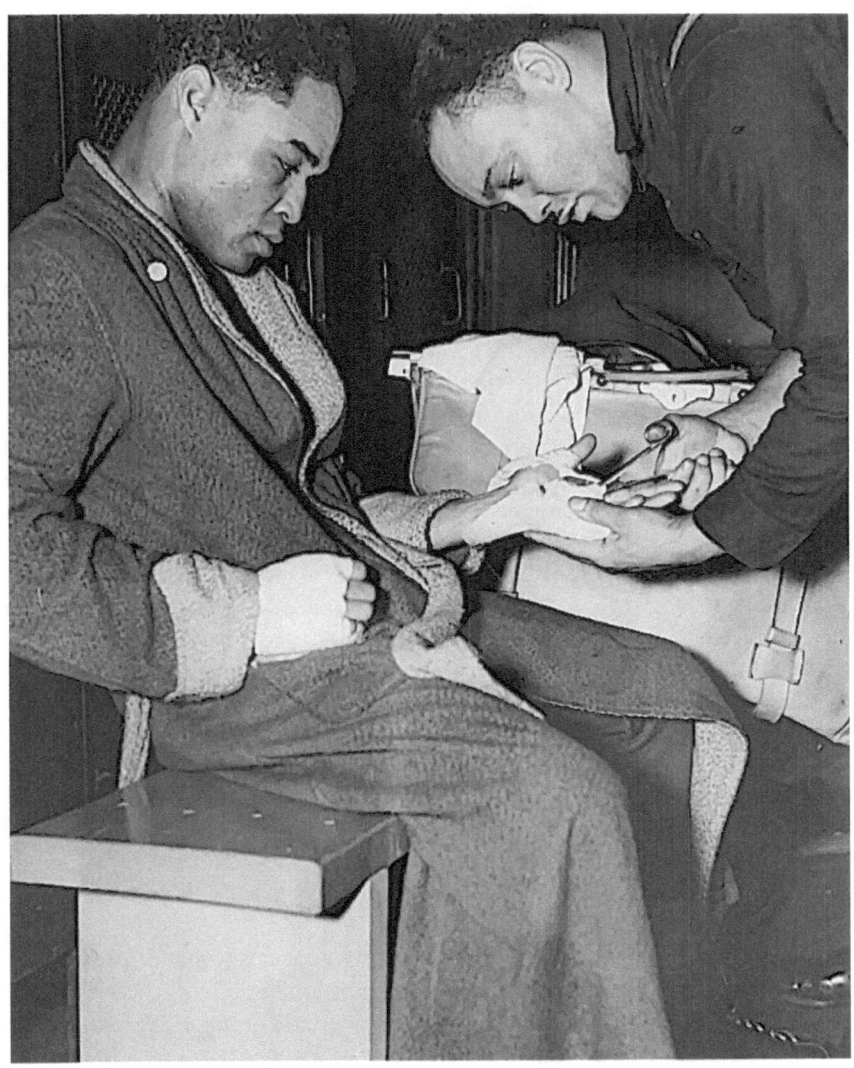

**A beautiful friendship. Harry Armstrong cuts the wrap off Henry's hand after a fight**

Henry was already familiar with Burch's reputation as a hard-hitting local kid. According to Henry's autobiography, Burch also proved quick. He outpunched Henry in the opening round. At the start of round two, Burch appeared to be already chasing a knockout. He sent home a terrific right hand to Henry's head. Though briefly stunned, Henry later said the blow angered him and helped him get into the fight. He went wild with rage and charged at Burch, who was quickly overwhelmed by the aggression. Burch successfully dodged several of the blows, but at least one made it through, and it was enough. Burch was out cold in round two, and Henry "Melody" Jackson was a regional amateur boxing champion after his first organized boxing match. Handed a trophy in his first organized boxing match, Henry was impressed to find out that it was worth ten dollars.

"Other boy smacked Henry and broke his nose the first punch," Harry Armstrong later remembered of that fight. "Next round, Henry bobs out, throw his right. Bongo, down goes the other boy for the count."[50]

The results of the fight reported in the *St. Louis Post-Dispatch* and *St. Louis Argus* on March 28 both list "Henry Jackson defeated James Burch, one round, technical knockout," suggesting Henry finished the fight earlier than he or Harry remembered. These were likely the first times his name appeared in print outside a school yearbook.

The publicity stemming from the fight prompted a self-styled local promoter, George Boyd, to organize a four-round rematch between Jackson and Burch for the opening of the Swartz Athletic Club at 2602A Pine Street. To populate the preliminary bouts, Boyd went into the streets and told the Black kids there that the winner of each bout would win a five-dollar certificate redeemable for boxing gear at a local Spaulding store. He brought those who volunteered to the club on October 28, 1930. Despite Jackson and Burch being the only experienced amateurs, locals packed the house. Henry later remembered that Burch broke his nose for the first and only time in his career as an amateur or professional boxer. (Harry remembered things slightly differently, saying that the broken nose came in the first fight with Burke.) Henry again reacted with rage, suddenly attacking Burch and knocking him out of the ring to score a third-round knockout victory.

Henry presented his winner's five-dollar certificate the next day at the Spaulding store. "Well, buddy," he was told by the man behind the counter, "this guy sent about three or four of you guys down here. You go back and catch that guy. He's nothing but a thief. He ain't left no money down here for nobody." Incensed, Henry headed for the Swartz Club. There, he found Boyd's partner working on disassembling the ring. The partner was just as upset. He told Henry that Boyd had skipped town with the almost three-hundred-dollar gate.[51]

Upset by his first encounter with the many con artists that populated the sport of boxing but still proud of his championship, Henry resisted the pleading of his family to leave boxing behind and pursue preaching. On March 19, 1931, just one day short of a year since winning the AAU title, a 130-pound Henry Jackson scored a first-round technical knockout over Roy Johnson at the North Side YMCA

By that summer, Harry Armstrong thought it was time for him and Henry to make some money in the fight game, and the pickings were slim for finding quality Black featherweights in St. Louis. Harry decided they should head for Pittsburgh, Pennsylvania, then one of the hottest boxing towns in America.

Henry and Harry regularly read the *Pittsburgh Courier* and the *Chicago Defender*, two of the leading Black newspapers of the day. They read in their pages stories of fighters like Jackie Rodgers and Jimmy Thomas drawing big gates by winning fights in Pittsburgh. Henry felt confident he could do the same.

With dreams of the big money he would make, Henry bragged to friends that he would be in a long black limousine fit for Kid Chocolate the next time they saw him.

Harry, Henry, and Eddie Foster packed into a 1927 Nash automobile with a German shepherd and a bunch of sandwiches made by Grandma Henrietta, and they hit the road in June 1931. After a few days of traveling, they arrived in Pittsburgh around three o'clock in the morning and pulled over on Wiley Street to sleep until daylight. They then found accommodations in a boarding house on the same street, and Harry Armstrong set out to book some fights for his fighters.

Call it the Smoky City or the Steel City. *The Atlantic Monthly* later called it "Hell with the lid taken off." Pittsburgh was all those things back in the first part of the twentieth century. A labyrinth of molten steel, smoke-belching furnaces, and mountains of black coal, the city was populated by grim-faced, multicultural laborers proud of the stone and metal metropolis they had built.

Even by 1931, Pittsburghers could already boast a long tradition of world-class fighters. Men like Dominick McCaffery and Frank Moran had fought for the heavyweight championship in 1885 and 1914, respectively, though neither had managed to win the title. There had been a top-tier lightweight in Jack McClelland during the turn of the century. However, Pittsburgh boxing was best known for producing middleweight champions during the 1910s and 1920s, specifically Harry Greb (regarded by many as the best fighter the division had ever seen), Frank Klaus, and George Chip. Even as the 1930s dawned, the city had many young fighting talents on the way up, including Jackie Wilson, four brothers named Yarosz, and five brothers named Zivic. If Henry and Eddie wanted to make names for themselves against quality opponents, Pittsburgh was a hotbed of such talent, even if most of it came from the same two families.

Harry placed an announcement in the *Pittsburgh Courier* sports page announcing their arrival. The trio haunted the Center Avenue YMCA, but no promoters took notice. They then moved to a gym owned by businessman and racketeer William "Woogy" Harris. Again, nothing happened except the dwindling of their meager savings. Soon enough, there was no money for rent, and the friends subsisted on a diet of just cabbage, pork, and bread.[52]

In desperate need of food and the cash to buy it, Henry ran into promoter Jules Beck at another gym and begged him for a chance to fight on one of his professional cards. Beck agreed to put him in an event at his Myers Bowl venue in North Braddock scheduled for a week later.

Beck likely saw little potential in the starving youngster from out of town. He was nothing more than a body for Beck to feed to a local star to make the hometown boy look good. "If a billy goat could talk, sign a contract and otherwise meet the boxing commission's requirement, Beck would try and get him matched," noted a Baltimore newspaper.[53]

Beck planned to toss the starving little no-name from the South in with rising local prospect Jackie Wilson, a future featherweight titlist. Henry cared little for who he fought so long as he could eat afterward. He later estimated that he had lost five pounds in the previous few days from starvation.

The well-connected promoter ensured that *The Pittsburgh Courier* ran an article praising Melody Jackson as "particularly promising." The write-up, easily the longest of Henry's life thus far, embellished Henry's record, unless the claimed wins over Les Darcy, Red Grover, and Jimmy Du Valle ("an outstanding featherweight in the South") were not covered in the St. Louis papers. Henry's fabricated "pro" record stood at twelve victories (eight by knockout) and one defeat. A shorter second paragraph described Eddie "Mississippi" Foster as "a very clever and elusive fighter."[54]

While preparing at the Fresh Air Gym, Henry initially sparred with Eddie to prepare until Eddie injured his back in a fall. Then Henry himself hurt his side badly. In some stories, he said he was injured while sparring with local welterweight Jackie Murray; in others, it was in a fall while doing his roadwork. He worried about a cracked rib but could not afford a doctor any more than he could afford to pass on the fight.

The night of Monday, July 27, 1931, was a hot one. Henry, using his stage name Melody Jackson, arrived at the open-air Myers Bowl in Braddock, Pennsylvania, for his first professional bout only to find out Jackie Wilson was a no-show due to an injury of his own. His opponent was instead Al Iovino, an Italian American southpaw from Swissvale, Pennsylvania. Henry had never faced a southpaw in the ring before but did not object to the substitution. "I'd have piled right into a cageful of lions and tigers on the promise of a good meal," Henry later reminisced.[55]

"A killing puncher," was Pittsburgh fight manager Bunny Buntag's assessment of Iovino. "He was not just a fellow who knocked you out. If he hit you, he killed you." The compliment was tragically true. Iovino had once killed a man in an amateur bout.[56]

The Swissvale southpaw had been an accomplished amateur, but since turning pro, he had won just seven of sixteen outings in the talent-rich Pittsburgh scene.[57]

The fight, scheduled for four rounds, was the opening bout of a four-fight event headlined by a match between veteran New York welterweight Thomas "Bucky" Lawless and Pittsburgh's rising star Teddy Yarosz.

Jackson weighed 120 pounds to Iovino's 122. As would become his trademark for the rest of his career, Henry rushed out of his corner at the opening bell and tore into his opponent with abandon. Iovino met him toe-to-toe, resulting in a thrilling battle while it lasted. By the third round, his quick pace, malnourishment, injured ribs, and Iovino's blows to his empty belly began to sap Jackson's energy. After Iovino capitalized with "a long overhand left that found its target," Henry crashed face-down on the canvas with less than thirty seconds left in the round. He did not beat the count, losing his first professional bout. In the main event, Yarosz remained undefeated in forty-six fights and looked good in winning a unanimous decision over the New Yorker.[58]

Al Iovino

"I always could hit," Iovino bragged years later. His win over the man who would become Henry Armstrong earned him a footnote's place in boxing history, but it would be his last win. After two back-to-back losses (one to Jackie Wilson), he retired from the ring later in the year. He served in the U.S. Army during World War II and passed away in 1968 at age 59.[59]

Henry received thirty dollars from Beck for his losing effort. He, Harry, and Eddie immediately rushed out for food. "With thirty dollars you can get milk, steak, chops, and everything," Henry later mused.[60]

Just four days after the loss to Iovino, Henry was back in a boxing ring, this time at Hickey Park in Millvale, Pennsylvania. The promotion by Bill Dumer was conspicuous as a rare "all negro" boxing event. Henry's opponent was Sammy Burns, "the coming star among the lightweights," from Pittsburgh's Hill District, who had won five of his seven bouts.[61]

Well-fed on his earnings from the Iovino bout, Jackson weighed in at 124 ¾ pounds, more than four pounds heavier than he had just a few days earlier. Burns was heavier at 128 ¼, but the weight advantage did him little good. "I beat this kid terrible," Henry would later remember. No longer weakened by hunger or distracted by his sore rib, he dropped Burns twice in the opening round. Rising from three knockdowns in all, Burns nonetheless made it to the closing bell of the six-round match. Melody Jackson gained his first professional victory. The *Pittsburgh Courier* described him as "the best-looking fighter in the lot."[62]

Eddie, fighting on the same card under the name Mississippi Foster, lost his match by knockout. Still, he and Henry both received thirty-five dollars each for their efforts.

Discouraged by his loss, Eddie made it known that he wanted to go home. Harry and Henry conferred with each other on what to do. Henry had found work as a sparring partner for the slick young bantamweight Jimmy Thomas at a dollar a day, but that was not enough to pay the expenses for all three men (Thomas would go on to become a ranked contender but never got his title shot). Jules Beck wanted to match Henry with Chico Cisneros, an experienced Mexican fighter with many losses but also big names on his record. Should Henry win against Cisneros, promised Beck, he would get a shot at Chicago star Eddie Shea. Still, neither Harry nor Henry was sure he was ready to step up his opposition yet with just two pro bouts behind him.

Wary of his fighter being fed to the lions, Harry tried to find a better-connected Pittsburgh manager to navigate Henry's career on the local scene. He offered Henry's contract to Gus Greenlee, a bootlegging and gambling figure from the Hill District, a predominantly Black community. Greenlee's interest in sports would later lead him to found the city's legendary Negro League Baseball Team, the Crawfords, but Melody Jackson did not strike him as a promising investment. "The bait didn't interest me," he remembered several years later. Greenlee would later sign on to manage future light heavyweight champion John Henry Lewis.[63]

The three fighters' hopes for promising boxing careers in the Smoky City looked more dismal each day. Meanwhile, money was tight again, and autumn was fast approaching; Henry was wary of the Pittsburgh winter cold he was hearing so much about. He told Harry they should leave.

The trio decided to detour to Chicago to visit one of Eddie's brothers, and they stayed there for a week. The largest city Henry had ever been to, Chicago had a thriving boxing network not unlike Pittsburgh's, and Henry decided to explore. He visited the local gyms and watched featherweight contender Eddie Shea, heavyweight contender Kingfish Levinsky, light heavyweight Larry Johnson, and a good-looking lightweight prospect named Barney Ross work out.

On the return trip, they encountered a vicious storm, and the wind tore up the canvas roof of the Nash. They arrived in St. Louis sodden with rainwater, Henry sitting in the back seat with the German Shepherd. As friends watched the old car squeak and rattle through the city streets, Henry was all too aware that he was not in the limousine he had promised them would accommodate his return. They arrived at Henry's home first, and as he got out of the car, the three friends agreed that they would try again once they raised more money.

Henrietta welcomed her grandson back with a filling pot of stew. In the following days, friends came by to greet Henry and hear his tales of success, forcing Henry to admit the opposite. Embarrassment and depression kept him awake at night, frustrated at the backward step. Only a visit from his sweetheart Yvonne convinced him to venture out with her to a friend's home.

The people there teased Henry, and he furiously stormed out with Yvonne at his side, swearing to show them he could make it as a boxer. He told Yvonne he would head to California and that he would have the money to marry her when he got back. With that, he thanked her for her support and loyalty and headed home to lie awake in bed and think up his plans for heading West. He had to move forward.

Henry spent the following evening in the train yards, observing the men who hopped trains and their methods. After all, he had no money and decided "hoboing" would be the method to get to California and his dreams of success in the ring.

The term "hobo" was a shortening of "hoe boys," a name applied to the itinerant people who illegally stowed away on trains as a means of travel. Most travelers were farm laborers before economic circumstances left them without jobs, hence "hoe boys." The desperate search for work forced them to sometimes travel across the country, often following the changing seasons.

It could be a hazardous way to live. Private security workers, called "bulls" by the hobos, were hired by railroad companies to keep stowaways off their trains. Police were traditionally not friends of the hobo either. Though most hobos were cooperative with one another, violence between individuals was not unheard of. Then there were the falls, crashes, and other ways of getting injured or killed. At least sixty-five hundred people perished because of accidents or violent altercations related to hoboing in a single year.[64]

This lifestyle had existed in one way or another long before the Crash of 1929. The great heavyweight champion Jack Dempsey, a sports superstar of the 1920s, proudly regaled the press with stories of his days as a hobo before finding fame. However, hoboing became so prevalent during the Depression that it was a fact of life not just for those who hopped trains but for virtually every community in America. Towns and cities were perplexed by and sometimes frightened of the hobos drifting in and out. More than two million men and thousands of women resorted to hoboing at one point or another during the Depression.

To a dreamer like Henry Armstrong, the promise of a reward made the risk irresistible. When he woke the next morning, he set out for the house Harry and Eddie shared. Eddie was out, but Henry told Harry his plan. Harry, an experienced hobo, came around to the idea. When Eddie came home, he opted to stay put. Henry and Harry would be on their own for this trip.

Harry returned home to say goodbye to his family and pack his bags. Then Eddie drove him and Harry to the station at Carondolet, said farewell, and drove home. The duo leaped aboard a train heading west on the same track Henry had helped build two years earlier, waving goodbye to Eddie.

The duo spent the night shivering in the rain and bouncing between various trains. The next day, they mistakenly hopped aboard a train going south instead of west from Kansas City. It took them to Shreveport, Louisiana.

At Shreveport, Henry found himself in the same Deep South prejudice he had escaped in Mississippi. He discovered that the bulls there most enjoyed beating the Black hobos.

Finding a hobo camp on the outskirts of town, Henry and Harry gathered wood to bring to a fire surrounded by a group of resting and sleeping men. Henry dropped a log in the fire as a sort of payment for admission. The duo began to settle down and warm themselves when a burly, bearded white man nearby awoke and sat up.

"What are you niggers doing laying down here with these white people?" the big man shouted.

Henry was shocked, and his temper flared. Unaccustomed to this kind of overt racism from his years in St. Louis, Henry was preparing to stand his ground and settle the matter physically with the bigot when Harry counseled him to keep his cool.

"You don't know where you are," Harry whispered. "You're not in St. Louis. You're not at home. You're in a foreign country down here." He pointed out the sound of a westbound train coming in the distance and convinced Henry to swallow his pride and head for the tracks.[65]

"If you want to stay healthy and out of jail down here, you've got to play Uncle Tom," Harry warned his friend after an encounter with a racist Texas sheriff the next morning.[66]

They spent that day hopping trains to continue their westward travel and were finally on a train headed into California that night.

After sunrise, bulls kicked all the hobos off the train near San Bernardino. From there, they proceeded on foot down Highway 110 and delightedly feasted on oranges from the groves before hitchhiking into Los Angeles. Arriving at night in the rain, they wandered to a Christian shelter where they were allowed to sleep in the attic on the floor.

In the late 1930s, when Henry was a world-famous boxing champion, Nat Fleischer, editor of *The Ring* magazine, talked to him about his arduous trek and noticed that the eleven-day journey crisscrossing the country had left its mark on the young man.

> That trip to California is still one of the nightmares of Henry Armstrong's life. His face becomes serious and slightly sinister when he speaks of the jungle camps from which they were chased by other hoboes, the railroad police, the days without food and the many privations of life on the road to which they were subjected.[67]

"I know what it is to be broke and hungry," Henry said of those days to another journalist while at the peak of his career, "and I don't aim to ever be that way again."[68]

# 4.
# Becoming Henry Armstrong

In Pittsburgh and Chicago, Henry had seen cities where boxing thrived. Still, Los Angeles had been a boomtown of boxing activity stretching back into the nineteenth century. The Los Angeles Athletic Club opened its doors in 1880, with boxing as one of its options. Boxing matches and exhibitions were happening at Turnverein Hall as early as 1885. James Jeffries, the legendary heavyweight champion, had grown up in the area around that period.

As California cities go, San Francisco had an even longer boxing history dating back to the Gold Rush. However, as the Hollywood studios established themselves in the 1920s, the glamor of their stars made the City of Angels a metropolis of newcomers, and ambitious boxers were among those arrivals. The Great Depression also boosted boxing talent, as more young men were willing to put their bodies on the line for a payday, even if the wallets of fans (and consequently promoters) had begun to empty. Every neighborhood had at least one local boy to be proud of as he laced up the gloves to represent them against neighboring communities.

Los Angeles eventually eclipsed San Francisco as the center of boxing activity in California, and by the time of Henry's arrival, had been home to stars such as Fidel LaBarba, Jackie Fields, Ace Hudkins, Dynamite Jackson, Les Kennedy, Speedy Dado, Young Peter Jackson, and Alberto "Baby" Arizmendi. Big fights happened in venues like the monolithic Olympic Auditorium and the vast Wrigley Field. Despite all this activity, the city had yet to produce another fistic celebrity of Jeffries's caliber in the twentieth century. Henry Jackson fantasized incessantly about being that star as he crossed the country by train and automobile.

He and Harry spent their first several days in L.A. bouncing between shelters and scrounging up food. They would shoplift their meals using the pockets of Harry's long coat.

They also introduced themselves to the Los Angeles boxing gyms: the Manhattan, Ringside, and Main Street gyms. However, they failed to garner any fights or even find Henry a willing manager.

Harry decided the best course of action was to forgo the pursuit of paid bouts and establish Henry's reputation through the amateur ranks. They agreed that the *nom de guerre* Melody Jackson would have to go to hide the fact that he had already turned pro back in Pittsburgh.

"People are calling us brothers anyway," explained Harry, "so let's make it official. Long live Henry Armstrong!" The pair advised the State Athletic Commission that they were brothers, a lie both would cling to through much of the rest of Henry's career.[69]

At the suggestion of another fighter, they presented themselves at the doorstep of Tom Cox, an inspector for the state boxing commission and promoter of "bootleg" boxing matches. With Harry praising Henry heavily, they convinced Cox to sign Henry Armstrong to a five-year management contract.

In 1955, Henry told Al Stump of *Sport* magazine that his California amateur debut had been two fights in a single night in South Gate: the first bout a win and the second a draw. In 1957, he told the *Santa Maria Times* sports editor that he was so battered and exhausted after the trip from Missouri that he embarrassed himself in his Los Angeles debut. In his autobiography published a year later, he recalled that his first amateur opponent in California was Archie Grant, whom he defeated easily in a match near Pasadena, followed by a second-round knockout victory over a forgotten opponent a couple of days later. A dislocated shoulder brought a brief pause in ring action, but he was back at it a month later.[70]

In later life, Henry claimed to have gone undefeated in between 85 and 125 amateur fights in 1931, but most of these are not verifiable in contemporary newspaper reports available to this author. Manager Cox was heavily ensconced in L.A.'s "bootleg" boxing scene. These were unregulated battles put on by and fought by men who did not have licenses or sanctioning from the state to do so for multiple reasons. Organizers put them on in back rooms, basements, and other secretive venues without newspaper advertising — only those in the know could attend.

Also called "smokers" or "buckets of blood," bootleg boxing shows were common before, during, and after the Great Depression, but the need for extra money made them especially popular in this period. Henry received three dollars per fight for his initial smokers. The organizers and audiences expected him to fight any man in front of him, regardless of weight class. "I'd fight welterweights, middleweights, almost heavyweights, and I only weighed about 126," he claimed. Many great fighters developed this way, and many more never amounted to anything in the boxing world. Henry claimed to have sometimes engaged in three to four a night, bouncing from one secret club to another to collect multiple purses.[71]

"I'd have to knock my man out early so I could get over to some other stadium for another fight I had billed the same night," he remembered decades later. The first fight was to have money to pay his manager. He would pocket the funds for his second fight to feed himself and Harry.[72]

Smokers are likely the reason for his claims of having fought in more than eighty amateur battles, though fighters were paid small amounts for bootleg victories and could thus be considered semi-pro.

The earliest newspaper report this author could find was in the *Los Angeles Evening Express* of November 11, 1931, indicating "Joe Lugon, Lincoln Heights Athletic Club, vs. Henry Armstrong, Pasadena, 133 pounds" to occur in Pasadena the following evening. The author could not locate an article with the results of this fight, but the claim of being undefeated is untrue. On November 19, Jimmie Garcia knocked out Henry Armstrong in the first round of a fight in Burbank's Jeffries Arena (named after the great heavyweight).

Harry Armstrong would lace on the gloves when Henry was injured and needed rest. Harry was less successful in the ring than his "brother," but they estimated they averaged about $1.50 per bout, factoring in the unpaid amateur contests. They had to pay a dollar per bout to Tom Cox, but winners were also routinely rewarded with watches and other prizes, which they could then pawn for cash. In this way, as their reputations rose in the amateur ranks, Harry and Henry wound up taking home about twenty dollars a week between them for a time.

With money loaned to them from Cox, Henry and Harry bought a shoeshine stand on the corner of Seventh and Wall Streets in 1932 and went to work there seven days a week (unless it rained), charging five cents to shine a pair of shoes and fifty cents for a pair of cowboy boots. With tips included, they often doubled their money. Supplementing their income from their fights, they would continue to operate the stand into 1934.

Olympic Auditorium, Los Angeles, CA

1932 proved an eventful year for Henry in the ring. On January 28, he took part in the AAU Southern California boxing championships at the Olympic Auditorium in Los Angeles. He was one of eleven fighters entered in the featherweight division. Henry won the tourney by beating San Diego's Ace Bergerren in a semi-final bout the *Los Angeles Times* reported as "one of the best in the tournament" and then winning a close decision over San Pedro's Perry Thompson in the finals. This earned him notice in most of the state's major newspapers, a place in a tournament against San Francisco's champions, and a place in the Olympic trials in Los Angeles that Summer.[73]

Through trial and error, Henry developed his signature style, learning what worked and what did not the hard way. As writer Al Stump, who saw

Henry in action, later described it, "In a light crouch, Henry weaved his whole upper body like a cobra on the attack, never still, always poised to strike. Meanwhile, his high-held elbows and the top of his hunched-down head absorbed the [opponent's] best hooks and uppercuts." His punches came in fast and devastatingly hard. Though later reporters seemed most impressed by Henry's short left hook, his personal favorite was his wild overhand right. "When that looping right really connected," Henry boasted, "the opponent usually didn't know anything more, until revived after the count of ten."[74]

Henry displayed a remarkable ability throughout his career to take excessive punishment and keep plugging forward. There were subtle tricks he developed in these early years which aided him in absorbing the punches. Crouching forward, he rolled his upper body and shoulders left to right, up and down. This posture made him a smaller, moving target and allowed him to roll with the impact of incoming fire, lessening the damage. He kept his head down and his eyes watching his opponent's feet. This left his opponents with only the hard top of his skull as a target. His elbows were tucked close against his short ribs to protect them. He crossed his forearms underneath his chin to shield his face at other times. In either case, he purposely kept his arms close and punches short when he could, making it difficult for his opponent to hook their arms around him and pull him into a clinch.

Henry earned a reputation for relentless aggression and forward momentum. The weaving of his heavily muscled upper body was a means to an end: to get inside his opponent's jabs, bury his head in their chest, and unleash his left hooks and overhand rights.

Sportswriters, opponents, and trainers would later routinely compare Henry's constant work rate in the ring to that of a machine. There was nothing mechanical about Henry's approach nor his endurance, however. He fought with passion and fury. He possessed a deep well of stamina that came not from fossil fuels but from his humanity, determination to achieve, self-belief, and discipline.

Henry learned his trade on the job. He fought often and, in the early years, improved from match to match. In February of 1932, he fought five times. The wins started piling up in May and June, with at least six coming in that period.

The Olympic trials came to L.A.'s Olympic Auditorium on July 1, 1932. The winners would advance to the national finals in San Francisco later in the month, and the victors there would comprise the U.S. Olympic boxing team.

Making the U.S. Olympic team and winning a medal was not yet the sure ticket to national and international stardom it would become in the second half of the twentieth century. Still, victory in the Olympics carried a certain prestige as a standout among the world's amateur boxing ranks and would at least win Henry a strong hometown following to take with him into a decent start as a professional. That was all in the future, of course. For now, Henry had a crop of talented California featherweights to fight.

Henry recognized some of the names on the list of featherweight entrants; he had battled Augie Soliz and Joe Grajade multiple times that year. He had lost an unpopular judges' decision to Grajade in May. Nonetheless, Henry made it to the semi-finals, where he claims in his autobiography to have won a hard-fought decision over white southpaw Brassie Mitchell. Unlike in Missouri, boxing matches were not legally segregated in California (though some promoters avoided them). The papers make no mention of a match between Armstrong and Mitchell and indicate that Mitchell was overweight for the tournament.[75]

In the tournament finals, Henry took on Johnny Hines, the betting favorite to win in the featherweight class from the tournament's start. Henry had been itching for a fight with Hines for some time, but the white fighter's manager had not allowed a fight until a chance at the Olympics forced their hand. Approximately ten thousand people were in the stands, by far the largest crowd Henry had yet boxed before.[76]

Henry later remembered that he was robbed of the second round when the referee declared that Henry fouled Hines with a low blow; Henry insisted it was a legal punch just below the heart that "lifted him off the floor." In Henry's view, he dominated the rest of the fight. When the announcer gave the verdict in Johnny Hines's favor, Henry said, "they almost had a riot there that night." Yet, according to the next day's *San Pedro News-Pilot*, "Johnny outboxed and outslugged the negro and looked good."[77]

Henry and Harry met Cox the next day at the Main Street Gym. They had been talking about turning Henry professional for some time, and after the loss in the trials, Henry figured that would be the next step. Instead, Cox and Harry decided that Henry would take another shot at the Olympics, this time as a bantamweight (118 pounds). They had learned that the Los Angeles branch of the AAU had decided that the winner in that class stood less of a chance than Henry, who had given a good enough show against Hines that they offered him the spot as the Los Angeles bantamweight representative in the national finals. Henry cringed at the thought of the work and starvation required to drop roughly eight pounds, but he agreed.

Henry later told author Peter Heller that, while starving himself and wondering how he would get the money together for a trip to San Francisco, Cox matched him with "one of the toughest Mexicans I've ever fought in my life," Perfecto Lopez. This author could find no newspaper article to confirm this matchup between the pair. Earlier in the year, on March 12, he lost a decision to Lopez. Even if he got the timing wrong in his tale, Henry's memories of the bout were vivid because of some support he got from one of Hollywood's elite that night. As he told Heller:

> He was a lightweight. I was only a featherweight trying to get down to 118 pounds. We fought at the old Main Street Gymnasium. I will never forget this. Mae West heard of my dilemma in 1932. She herself and her manager come down to the Main Street Gymnasium and she said she was going to help draw the crowd if possible. She came, and

this guy got a decision over me. She was there with her manager all in that beautiful white like she used to wear, stunning as ever. She was sitting right in my corner. She always loved fights. She saw the fight, and I was told that she gave my manager close to a hundred dollars to make the trip to help me.[78]

With West's help, Cox gathered the funds for the trip to San Francisco while Harry focused on an intensive program to cut Henry's weight. On Saturday, July 16, the trio traveled to Frisco in Cox's 1930 Ford and found a place to stay on Turk Street. A boxing gym was on the same street, as was a park, allowing Henry to train, do roadwork… and starve himself. Since July 3, Harry had kept him on a diet of no breakfast, half an orange for lunch, and a small lamb chop with one piece of toast for dinner. Harry strictly rationed water, leaving Henry feeling drained and irritated come fight time.[79]

On July 20, the day of the trials, he weighed in at 117 ½ pounds and immediately gorged himself on a big meal. Scrawny and weak, he survived a knockdown and a broken tooth to stop Frank Gallucci of Portland, Oregon, with a hard right hand in the third round. [80]

In the next day's second round of the tourney, he faced Oakland, California's Jess La Barba. He lost another decision he felt he had won, and the crowd agreed. "The gallery boys hooted the verdict," reported the *San Francisco Examiner*, "apparently figuring that Armstrong who landed the harder punches was entitled to the decision." That ended Henry Armstrong's dreams of Olympic glory. He blamed the loss on being severely weight drained. Irritable because of hunger and frustrated by the loss, Henry was even more out of sorts after Cox pocketed the leftover money from the trip and the fight and rewarded Henry for his efforts with a single chocolate bar on the drive home.[81]

One week after the Olympic trials opened, the Dow Jones Industrial Average tumbled to its lowest point during the Great Depression, 41.22 at closing. In 1932, the economic crisis overflowed into social and political turmoil in America and abroad. A group of Iowa farmers hanged a judge about to foreclose on their land. A deadly standoff between three thousand demonstrators and police in Dearborn, Michigan, lasted five days. Tens of thousands of veterans from the Great War marched on Washington, hoping to have their 1945 pensions released early. The result was a violent confrontation between this "Bonus Army" and the active U.S. Army, not a good look for the incumbent Hoover administration.[82]

It was an election year, and most expected the Democrats to trounce Hoover's Republicans. But few held real hope of change. Many discouraged Americans were moving to more radical political voices, socialist and Communist firebrands previously on the fringes who were becoming powerfully mainstream. Calls for and fear of revolution were widespread. In Europe, ultra-nationalist political groups were using the crisis to threaten minorities and enemies and secure frightening levels of power.

That summer, the United States won more Olympic gold medals (forty-one) than the second, third, fourth, and fifth-place nations combined. Success in the Games was a rare bright spot among incessantly gloomy newspaper headlines.

Despite his disappointment in the trials, Henry decided to turn pro. Times were brutal, and he needed cash like everyone else. A week later, Cox, who only managed amateurs, sold Henry's contract to pro manager Wirt "One Shot" Ross for $250.

Ross was one of the most successful and sought-after managers in Southern California. He managed Albert "Chalky" Wright, a rising featherweight contender then at the start of a 35-fight undefeated streak. His most prominent star of the moment was Young Peter Jackson, the reigning lightweight champion of California. Ross's stable of fighters and knowledge of the fight game impressed Henry. He signed a five-year contract with Ross, and Ross loaned him five dollars to keep himself fed.

Wirt Ross professed to have an expert's eye for untapped fighting talent. He was known to walk up to a well-muscled stranger on the street and ask him if he wanted to be a "pro-fessional pugilist." If the fellow agreed, before he knew it, Ross would have him in a set of boxing trunks and posing before flashing cameras while the manager introduced his new protégé to the press with a name fit for a carny. Ross liked naming his "discoveries" with show biz monikers like Haystack Sloan, King Solomon, or the Dalton brothers and dressing them up in accompanying costumes.[83]

Associated Press sportswriter Bob Myers described Ross as "a handsome giant of a man with snow white hair, bright blue eyes, and two sets of diamonds, one of which was real."[84]

"Ross was a stout, portly Kentuckian who sported a thick Southern accent and a wide sombrero hat," Henry later recalled. "A large diamond stickpin glittered in his necktie. He resembled the comedian, W.C. Fields, not so much in the way he looked as in his manner."[85]

He liked to pass himself off as an ignorant country bumpkin, the better to outhustle unsuspecting opponents across the negotiating table. An old Army man and an inveterate storyteller, he claimed to have traveled the world from Panama to Alaska and the Philippines to New York. In his strong Southern accent, Wirt Ross told tall tales of his "grandpappy" killing Yankees during the Civil War. Some people called Ross the "Old Rebel."

Loving a good laugh, he was a walking joke encyclopedia, albeit one with a short temper. He was also a gambling addict, prone to pulling a pistol and saying he only needed "one shot" if he felt cheated. Gamblers and boxing people took to calling him "One Shot" Ross. His insistence on fair play was not reciprocal, however. He was not above making under-the-table agreements about his fighters. When the deal was right, he would not so subtly let his fighter know it was a good idea to take it easy on a particular night.

Before he bought Henry's contract, the wary manager wanted to see his potential investment in action. He had seen Henry in the amateurs, but the pro ranks were another matter. The fights lasted longer and were generally against better opposition. Ross put Henry in the ring with Chalky Wright for some light sparring. According to *The Ring* magazine's West Coast correspondent, "Armstrong 'murdered' Wright, putting him on the deck twice and cutting him to ribbons in one round." Rescuing Chalky from further destruction, Ross called an end to the session and headed out to put one of his diamond stick pins in hock so he could afford to buy out the contract.[86]

Henry was relieved to make the switch. "[Cox] never gave me a cent of money," he remembered years later. "He didn't even want to feed me."[87]

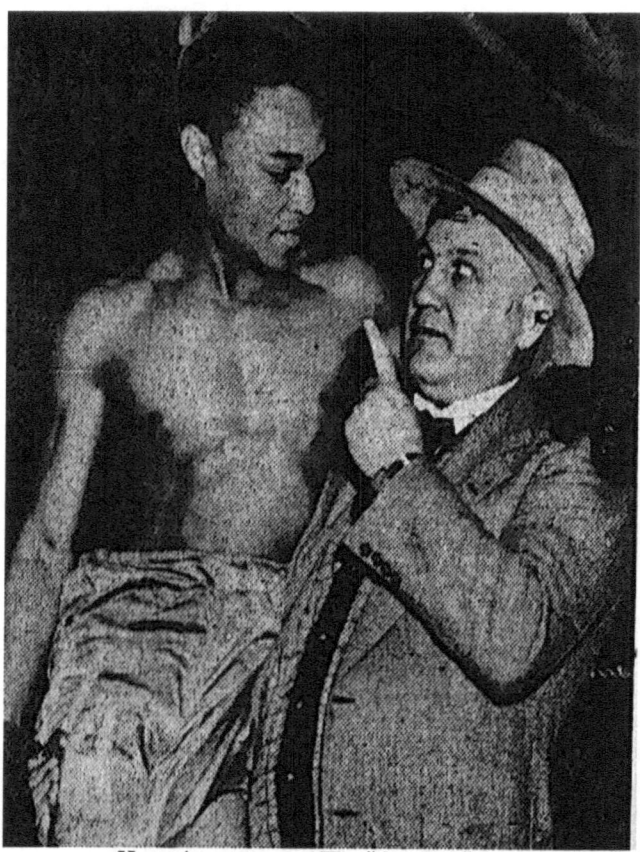

Henry Armstrong and Wirt "One Shot" Ross
*Oakland Tribune*, November 27, 1935

On August 26, 1932, the *California Eagle* reported that Ross, "hustling manager of the west's largest fight stable with the finest suite of training and dressing rooms," had picked up Henry Armstrong, "who left a string of K.O.'s all through this winter's trials only to get a bum decision in the finals up north." A day later, the *Los Angeles Times* ran a giant photo of Henry, maybe his first time getting his picture in the paper. It was a picture of Henry biting into a large slice of watermelon.

Held on Tuesday, August 30, at the Olympic Auditorium, Henry's California pro debut was one of several undercard fights, hardly the main event winning gold in the Olympics might have gotten him, but it paid him fifty dollars, more than Henry had yet garnered for a fight. His opponent would be Eddie Trujillo, whom the *Daily News* reported as having won thirty-nine consecutive fights as an amateur. Trujillo was making his professional debut.

As the *Daily News* reported the next day:

> Armstrong hit the Mexican lad with a right to the jaw in the first round and knocked him down for a two-count. Trujillo got up and pasted the negro all over the place, almost to get himself an even round. In the second, Trujillo picked up where he left off in the first and gave Armstrong a nice pasting. Armstrong weathered the round and came on to take the third from the Mexican battler with a hard right on the jaw just before the bell rang. Trujillo speeded up in the fourth and took it by a slight margin and earned the decision from referee Frank Harlborrow.

Henry recognized that he had deservedly lost the fight, the second time he had lost a professional debut. He was thankful for a respectful ovation from the crowd for his efforts but could not help feeling guilty for letting down the hopes of his fans, Harry, and Ross. Losing his next fight on September 27 against Al Greenfield certainly did not help, especially since it was on the undercard of a fight featuring the featherweight star Freddie Miller, which would have been a chance for Henry to make good before a larger crowd. Greenfield already had twenty-seven pro victories behind him when they fought, and Henry later felt that Ross had over-matched him.

In his autobiography, Henry claimed that his long-awaited first pro win came in a six-rounder against one Johnny "Mickey" Ryan, but California newspapers have no evidence of this bout. The case is the same with Henry's claims of victories over Young Bud Taylor, George Dundee, and Perfecto Lopez before the year's end. Boxing historian Nat Fleischer and his *The Ring* magazine included these and several other victories from the same period in accounts of his boxing record. However, the only wins verifiable by newspaper evidence between the loss to Greenfield and the dawn of 1933 were victories over Henry Hernandez, Gene Espinosa, and Clarence "Young Corpus" Corpuz, all in December. Newspaper evidence shows that most of the bouts Armstrong and Fleischer described as happening in 1932 occurred in the next year.

Ross matched his fighter tough; some say too tough. Greenfield, Espinosa, and Corpuz had 108 pro bouts on their cumulative records. Henry beat two out of three, but Ross kept him busy against more experienced fighters through the following year, too.[88]

With the opening of 1933, Henry graduated from four-round fights to six-rounders and fluctuated between the featherweight (126 pounds) and lightweight (135 pounds) divisions. On March 21, as the opening fight on the undercard to the featherweight championship event between Freddie Miller and Speedy Dado at the Olympic Auditorium, he picked up a stoppage win over the vastly more experienced Paul Wangley of Minnesota.

Henry was making between fifty and seventy-five dollars per fight and expanded his shoeshine business to include two more stands. He and Harry went in together on a furnished five-room apartment and bought a radio.

Henry's first fight with Severo "Kid Moro" Bascon, one of many talented Filipino fighters in the Southern California area, was memorable for several reasons. Held on November 3, 1933, at the Pismo Beach Arena, it was Henry's first ten-round matchup and his first main event pro fight. It was also the first in a savagely contested three-fight rivalry.

**Kid Moro**
*Los Angeles Times*, **December 12, 1933**

Moro could be called Henry's first world-class opponent. Having won just eleven of his twenty-three pro fights, he sported a spotty record. However, like Henry, his handlers had matched him tough from the start of his career. His 1919 pro debut was in Manila against Filipino superstar Pancho Villa, a future Hall of Famer. Moro had a win over power-punching future middleweight champ Ceferino Garcia and was just coming off a hard-fought loss to Henry's friend Young Peter Jackson, the lightweight champion of California. The papers recognized him as the "lightweight champion of the Orient."

But the most memorable thing about the first Armstrong-Moro fight was its mayhem. No one who saw it would forget one of the most chaotic nights in California boxing history.

From the start, Henry knew he was in his most brutal battle yet. The cleverer boxer, Moro accumulated a lead in the early rounds, but Henry persisted and won the latter rounds "by sheer fighting heart," reported the *San Luis Obispo Tribune*, calling the fight one of the most thrilling in the venue's history. At the end of ten rounds, referee Fred Gilmore, the only judge for the fight, raised Henry's hand to signal his victory.[89]

Moro threw a fit, screaming at the referee, waving his fists about, and yanking at the ring ropes. The large Filipino contingent in the crowd was even more incensed. Egged on by Moro's manager, a mob invaded the ring, at least one brandishing a knife. They assaulted Gilmore until police officers rescued him and got him to safety.

Meanwhile, Henry and his cornermen tried to make their way quietly to the dressing room. One man from the crowd kicked Henry, and Harry had to hold his fighter back from retaliating. Returning to their dressing room, they noticed Wirt Ross was nowhere to be found; he had fled the arena when the riot broke out.

Henry and Harry hid in a bathroom stall and exited the building through a window. Henry was still in his boxing trunks and robe, so Harry gave him parts of his own clothing to cover up. Fighter and trainer hitchhiked their way back to Los Angeles, where they entered Jack Dempsey's Barbara Hotel to get some sleep. In the lobby, they discovered Wirt Ross, who greeted them as though nothing had happened and immediately set about making plans for Henry's upcoming fights.

Though the referee had declared the fight a victory for Henry and subsequent historians have marked it as such in the record books, the California State Athletic Commission overruled Gilmore's verdict, and it was officially declared a draw. The controversy gained Henry more press than ever, teaching him that any publicity was good publicity.

The well-matched duo fought two more times between 1933 and 1934 in front of large crowds attracted by the reports of their initial encounter. Each was a hotly contested battle and ended in a draw verdict.

Though Henry's work in the ring in 1933 had not been without its blemishes, it had been a year of progress. He had moved from four-round undercard fights to ten-round main events, gained much broader press coverage, and racked up twelve wins (six by knockout) against one loss and five draws. He avenged the only loss (to Baby Manuel) with a ten-round decision victory in his first outing of 1934.

Most importantly, he was learning his trade. The amateurs and smokers had certainly provided an education, but the professionals brought on better competition and more challenging fights for higher stakes. "Every one was a war," Henry later remembered of his early bouts as a pro.[90]

In July 1934, it looked as though Henry would pick up a three-month suspension from the California State Athletic Commission for failing to show up for a fight with Perfecto Lopez, a man he had beaten in a thrilling contest just a week earlier. Organizers had scheduled their subsequent encounter for July 24 on the undercard of a fight between heavyweights Tom Patrick and Hank Hankinson. Neither fight sparked much of the public's interest and sold only about two thousand tickets. The fighters involved knew that would leave little left over to pay them, and whatever they received would have to be split with their management and cornermen. Henry claimed a broken hand the day before the fight but refused to let the Commission inspect the injury. Patrick did not show for the main event, for which he received a full year's suspension. Henry got his suspension overturned by fighting and stopping Lopez on August 28.

By the end of September, Henry had lost just once in two years and thirty-two fights. He had beaten many of the best featherweights and lightweights in California. The local press was now declaring him "Wirt Ross's latest black menace" and "the uncrowned featherweight champion of the world." The *California Eagle* saw in Henry "more of the real 'killer' instinct than any other colored fighter on the coast." That month, the California Athletic Commission recognized him as the state featherweight champion. His purses were going up, and with his shoeshine stands losing money due to dishonest employees, Henry and Harry closed the business.[91]

Even with all the praise from California sportswriters and the good money coming in, Henry had yet to test himself against a legitimate contender for the world featherweight or world lightweight titles. Wirt Ross and the reporters could proclaim him the uncrowned champion all they wanted. Nobody outside California would listen until he could get another contender in the ring and beat him.

# 5.
# Ups and Downs

**Alberto "Baby" Arizmendi**

Experiencing success as a professional prizefighter gave Henry the confidence to move forward in his personal life, too. In 1934, he proposed to his girlfriend, Willa Mae Shandy. Born February 5, 1912, in Texas, Willa Mae moved to Los Angeles with her family as a child. She was the twenty-two-year-old stepdaughter of a Baptist pastor, Reverend Walter L. Strauther. She and twenty-four-year-old Henry married at Strauther's church on August 7, 1934. Before the year was out, she would be pregnant with their first child.[92]

While Henry enjoyed his first weeks of matrimony, Ross negotiated a fight in Mexico with Alberto "Baby" Arizmendi, a longtime contender for the world's featherweight championship recently won by Freddie Miller. Neither fighter knew it then, but Armstrong would wind up facing Arizmendi more times than any other topflight boxer in his career, a total of five bouts (Perfecto Lopez, a lesser opponent, also battled Henry five times).

Arizmendi was born in either 1913 or 1914 in Torreon, Mexico. When infantile paralysis left him hospitalized at age six, doctors recommended shadow boxing as part of his therapy to recover. Before he turned eight, the determined youngster was already participating in his first organized boxing matches, and by thirteen, he was fighting professionally. Hence the nickname "Baby." In 1932, he mounted a one-man fistic invasion of Los Angeles while still a teenager. He whipped some of America's best little men, including Fidel LaBarba, Speedy Dado, and Newsboy Brown, all of whom were stars in the California area. Hollywood elites like Clark Gable and the Marx Brothers were ringside at his fights. Mae West's "ample bosom rested on the bottom rope at the Hollywood Legion Stadium every Friday night" that Arizmendi fought.[93]

The Baby traded wins in two bouts with Miller in 1933 and lost a one-sided ten-round decision to former multi-division champion Tony Canzoneri in March 1934. He rebounded by winning the New York State Athletic Commission's recognition as world champion with a dominant beatdown of Mike Belloise in New York City. He returned home to a massive celebration in Los Angeles's Latin Quarter, including a parade and a dance at the Shrine Auditorium. He was only the second (after Battling Shaw) Mexican-born boxer to win a world title in boxing.

In November, the Mexican Boxing Commission announced that it recognized Arizmendi as the featherweight champion of the world. Still, all other sanctioning bodies outside of Mexico and New York recognized Miller. Rumor had it that Miller would sign to defend his title against the winner between Arizmendi and Armstrong.

Ross got Henry a guaranteed purse of fifteen hundred dollars, plus a percentage of profits from the gate, by far the most the young fighter had ever seen. The manager and fighter drove to Nogales, Arizona, and caught a train to Mexico City. It was Henry's first time outside the United States. It was Arizmendi's homecoming fight in his native country after becoming a star abroad.

Mexico's fight fans were thrilled to see the matchup, and Henry was surprised to see a band serenading his arrival when he stepped off the train. On the way to the Cosmos Hotel, he spotted low-flying airplanes above pulling banners welcoming Henry Armstrong to Mexico.[94]

Because Harry had to stay behind in California to keep his day job (He had quit his prizefighting career by this point), Ross found Henry a Mexican trainer named Tony Rocha, who made a point of taking the American to run in the hills around Mexico City to acclimate him the higher altitude.

Knowing this fight was the most important of his boxing career so far, Henry trained hard but became troubled by a conversation with Ross.

"Don't get too anxious, son. You're not supposed to win this fight," the manager told him.

Henry questioned Ross's meaning. Ross then asked him to "take it easy in this fight."

When Henry told Ross to speak plainly, Ross replied, "Just fight to go the full ten rounds." Despite this, Henry claimed he went into the fight without suspicion that Ross had agreed to a fixed decision.[95]

Twenty thousand fans filed into the open-air National Stadium in Mexico City on the evening of Sunday, November 4, a national record for a boxing match in Mexico to that point. Under a clear sky and in the surprisingly chilly air, the two highly regarded featherweights put on a ferocious fight from bell to bell, slugging it out without let-up.

Decades later, Henry continued to insist that he carried Arizmendi through the fight at Ross's insistence. He was astonished at Arizmendi's determination and ability to take his best punch but noted that "they had to practically show him to his corner at the last round." However, the referee did not see it that way and awarded the decision to Arizmendi.[96]

The American United Press correspondent agreed it was an easy win for the Mexican champion. "Arizmendi gave a courageous exhibition in last night's battle, fighting aggressively despite a broken left wrist. Superior boxing ability carried him through," read a story in sports pages throughout the United States. The correspondent accused Armstrong of repeatedly fouling with low blows, drawing boos from the crowd. He needed a police escort to protect him on his way to the dressing room.[97]

Arizmendi now also claimed Armstrong's recognition from California as champion. Miller initially agreed to unify the championship in a third battle with Arizmendi, but the fight never came to fruition.

The loss mattered little to Henry, not when he had fifteen hundred dollars coming to him. He celebrated that night, hitting the local bars and nightclubs. It was not until later that somebody told him that bandits had stolen the entire gate, including his share of the purse.

Henry needed that money, not only because he had already spent his savings and had no money to get back to the United States, but because Willa Mae was pregnant with their first child. Henry meant the purse from his first big fight to help his new family get off on the right foot. Making matters worse, Henry fell ill, which he blamed on exerting himself so hard in the cool air on the night of the fight. That meant he could not get another fight right away in Mexico to fund his return.

While Henry recovered, Harry Armstrong arrived in Mexico, and Wirt Ross set about arranging a fight to help offset some of their losses. Henry had recovered enough by December 1 to stop Joe Conde in a Mexico City bull ring. Two weeks later, he knocked out welterweight Ventura Arana. Henry's record for 1934 consisted of 13 wins, 6 of them by knockout, the lone defeat to Arizmendi, and a draw with Kid Moro.

In its year-end rankings for 1934, *The Ring* magazine, the self-proclaimed "Bible of Boxing," rated Baby Arizmendi the number one contender for Freddie Miller's legitimate featherweight championship of the world. Still, Arizmendi's manager could not get Miller's people to commit to a fight.

The Mexican champion's handlers sought another respected opponent for the New Year's holiday. Boxing tickets sold well on holidays in Mexico, and no one wanted to miss out on the cash windfall. Since the first fight with Henry Armstrong (listed as the number eight contender in *The Ring*'s January 1935 rankings) had brought a national record gate, and since Armstrong was still marooned in Mexico, they approached Ross about a second match. Even though Arizmendi's title would not be on the line (the fight would take place over the featherweight limit), Ross and Armstrong were ecstatic at the chance to make big money again and signed the contract without hesitation.

Again, Arizmendi's manager approached Wirt Ross about a fix.

"Tell that nigger of yours he's got to lose a lot surer this time," said Arizmendi's man. Ross agreed, but Baby's manager was not satisfied. He also wanted Harry's assurance, and he got it.

His concerns mollified, Arizmendi's man told them he knew where they could bet two thousand dollars on the Mexican fighter. Harry told him he did not have that sum but accepted a cash loan from the manager. "I had to make it look good," Harry later told writer Jim Tully.[98]

The second bout between Henry Armstrong and Baby Arizmendi occurred at El Toreo de Cuatro Caminos, a Mexico City bull ring. Henry was again awed by another crowd of twenty thousand on hand to watch him fight their hometown hero on New Year's Day. An assurance from Ross that there was no need to take it easy this time further energized Henry. Wirt and Harry had no intention of keeping their agreement with Arizmendi's manager. Ross told Henry to get revenge.[99]

Henry would remember the rematch with Arizmendi as "a two-man preview of blitzkrieg and total war." Both men incurred severe cuts, Henry worse than he had ever been. The men bled all over each other through twelve rounds, the longest distance Henry had yet gone in a fight. The thin air of the high altitude bothered him. Nonetheless, when he returned to his corner at the final bell, he sat on his stool, confident he had won.[100]

"I beat him so bad till he couldn't see," he later told author Peter Heller.[101]

But the victory was not to be. Harry later said, "they picked Arizmendi up from the floor and raised his hand."[102]

Henry and Harry may have felt robbed, but the United Press agreed with the decision. "Arizmendi won eight rounds as he counter-punched and boxed his way to the victory," reported their correspondent. Of course, sportswriters were not immune to bribery from managers and promoters.[103]

At least Henry got paid this time. Not the purse. The promoters disappeared before paying that. But Harry was able to collect on his bet and shared it with Henry.

Henry stayed in Mexico long enough to get into the ring with another Mexican featherweight star, Rodolfo "Baby" Casanova. He lost by fourth-round disqualification for a low blow in a fight he was winning. Government officials held up his purse as they investigated the foul, but they eventually paid him.

That made for three losses in his five fights across the border. Henry, who insisted the blow was legal, began to feel as though he never would get a fair shake from referees in Mexico City, especially considering the notes he had been receiving by mail before the Casanova fight, threatening in Spanish, "If you knock out Casanova, you will be shot!"[104]

When word came that Willa Mae had given birth to their first child, Lanetta Armstrong, on February 24, Henry finally got out of Mexico and headed home, taking the first plane flight of his life to do so. Meeting his daughter instilled in Henry a sudden sense of responsibility and redoubled his seriousness about making advances in his boxing career. Lanetta's arrival also inspired a renewed need for family in him, and he paid to have his ailing father and grandmother relocate into his new house in Los Angeles at 715 E 55th Street.[105]

After almost six months away and two of his fight purses unpaid, combined with travel expenses, medical expenses, and more mouths to feed, it was imperative Henry get more fights. He returned to the California rings by stopping Sal Hernandez in two rounds at the Olympic Auditorium on March 19. Then it was back to Mexico City to drop yet another referee's decision in a matchup with Davey Abad on the undercard of a Baby Arizmendi title defense. Henry then went undefeated in his next nine matchups in the States (including a revenge victory over Abad) before facing Philadelphia's Joseph Loscalzo, better known as Midget Wolgast, who had just lost the flyweight (112 pounds) championship of the world earlier in the year.

Loscalzo had been a troublesome youth in Philly. Like Henry, he enjoyed a good scrap in the streets and was known for beating up much bigger boys – and one schoolteacher, an act which landed him in reform school.

Turning professional at just fifteen years old in 1925, he took the name Midget Wolgast after a famous local fighter, Bobby Wolgast. Less than five years later, the New York State Athletic Commission recognized him as the flyweight champion of the world. Nicknamed "Greased Lightning" because of his striking hand and foot speed, Wolgast was an unpredictable fighter known for befuddling his opponents by switching from the conventional (right-handed) to southpaw (left-handed) stances. In his prime, which is to say between 1930 and 1934, he was virtually untouchable.

After winning the title, Wolgast virtually cleaned out his division and those nearby with wins over Willie La Morte, Speedy Dado, and Small Montana. He successfully defended the championship just once with a decision over Ruby Bradley. A world traveler, he fought in New York, Indianapolis, Honolulu, Montreal, London, Paris, New Orleans, and Los Angeles before losing his championship to Montana in Oakland, California, on September 16, 1935.[106]

Wolgast was a noted ladies' man, with movie star Mae West among his many lovers. One jilted woman attacked him while he walked to the ring and drew first blood before Wolgast's opponent had a chance.

**Midget Wolgast**

Though still just twenty-five years old, Wolgast was already a veteran of nearly two hundred professional fights and was considered shopworn. He was moving permanently up into the featherweight division and sought to prove himself with a win over Henry Armstrong.

Wirt Ross recognized the importance of Henry's fight against such a well-known ex-champ. He was concerned that racism might rob his fighter of victory should the match be close. He cautioned the State Athletic Commission to be careful in picking the referee. Alan Ward of the *Oakland Tribune* saw the logic in Ross's worry.

"It is sad but true that some arbiters are inclined to discriminate against Negro boxers," commented Ward. "There is an unwritten rule with many of them that if a Negro fights on an even basis, he loses. If he has a slight edge, he is given a draw. Of course, if he delivers a lopsided licking to his opponent, there's little else to be done save raise his hand."[107]

The event, held on Wednesday, November 27, 1935, at the Oakland Auditorium with Armstrong and Wolgast headlining, garnered a dismal

$1,300 gate, which puzzled the promoters and sportswriters. "Those staying at home missed a splendid fight," reported the *Oakland Tribune*. Henry, the bigger, younger, and considerably fresher man, took the ten-round decision. Wolgast showed several flashes of his old skill and showmanship; some felt he deserved the nod. As for the writer for the *Tribune*, he believed the decision was correct. "If you doubt that the 'Midget' received a beating, you should have glanced at his face after hostilities had ended," read the paper. "He was a mass of bruises, swellings, and lacerations."[108]

Already known as a man who loved the nightlife, Wolgast's personal and professional life fell apart after the loss to Armstrong. His first wife had left him, likely fed up with his womanizing and drinking. He fought on for another five years but spent more time at the bottom of a bottle than he did in the gym, losing more fights than he won. The former champion retired in 1940 after losing a six-round decision to unknown Bill Morris in Lancaster, Pennsylvania. Afterward, he worked as a trainer until he died in a Philadelphia bar in 1955 at just forty-five years of age. Joseph "Midget Wolgast" Loscalzo was posthumously inducted into the International Boxing Hall of Fame in 2001.[109]

Henry closed out 1935 by stopping Alton Black on cuts in Reno, Nevada on December 6. The year had gotten off to a rough start with three losses in Mexico. Excluding a draw with Perfecto Lopez, Henry had won his eleven other fights, six of them via the short route, and had bested a former world champion in Wolgast. California once again recognized him as the state featherweight champ.

In his year-end boxer rankings for 1935, *The Ring*'s editor Nat Fleischer praised Henry's forward momentum in the sport. "Henry Armstrong, Pacific Coast Negro featherweight, is one of the most formidable ringmen in the division," he wrote. Fleischer encouraged his readers to "Watch this lad this year. He is expected East in the near future and should make the division hum with activity." Fleischer ranked Henry as the number three contender for Freddie Miller's championship, right behind European champion Maurice Holtzer and Henry's old Mexican rival, Baby Arizmendi.[110]

Henry must have been proud to finally win the notice of Fleischer, who was considered the journalistic sage of all things fistic in America. But perhaps nothing about 1935 elated him more than becoming a father and buying his first home for his new family. It had been a successful year, indeed.

Henry did not have much to celebrate on New Year's Day when Mexico City judges handed a gift decision to lightweight Joe Conde over Henry Armstrong after ten rounds. Feeling that he was robbed yet again by Mexican boxing officials (*The Ring*'s correspondent concurred with Henry's belief), Henry went to Wirt Ross and insisted that the manager get him a fight back in California.[111]

As it turned out, coming home was not the solution. Montana's Ritchie Fontaine "proved a revelation" when he scored a clear decision over Henry after ten hard-fought rounds on February 26, 1936, in the Oakland Auditorium.[112]

"Nothing but gameness and smart generalship kept [Armstrong] from losing by kayo. The rough tactics, typical of Fontaine, did not affect Armstrong, who badly mussed up the face of his tough foe," reported Louie X. Campbell of the *California Voice*, the Oakland-based Black newspaper. In the days following, Henry revealed that he had broken a knuckle on his right hand in the sixth round of the furious fight.[113]

After a month off to heal, Henry "punched Ritchie full of holes" in a March 31 fight at the Olympic Auditorium in L.A., despite Fontaine's six-pound weight advantage.[114]

After two more victories that Spring, Wirt Ross brought Henry the news he had desperately wanted to hear for over a year. Henry would get another shot at Arizmendi on August 4, at Wrigley's Field in Los Angeles.

Henry was ecstatic. Bitter about what he saw as two hometown decisions over the border, he had been waiting to prove his dominance over Arizmendi in the States. The fact that he would be making his debut at the massive Wrigley Field sweetened his satisfaction.

**Wrigley Field, Los Angeles, CA**

Big boxing matches had been happening at Wrigley Field for about a decade, at first under the auspices of promoter Dick Donald. After Donald's retirement, his rival Jack Doyle, already the promoter at the Olympic Auditorium, took over. The Olympic featured shows more often and was considered the center of boxing in Southern California. Only the rarest, most anticipated, and richest fights happened at Wrigley Field. The first two boxing shows in California to garner one hundred thousand dollars or more happened in the late 1920s under Doyle. The Great Depression had made it impossible for those numbers to happen again anytime soon. Even so, with its twenty thousand seats and two decks, fighting there still held a prestige for California fighters that no other venue could offer. For Henry, fighting there against Arizmendi meant he was guaranteed two thousand dollars, his largest purse yet.

Henry sequestered himself in the Main Street Gym for a five-week training regimen, the longest time he had ever had for a single fight. Harry Armstrong finally quit his day job to focus on training Henry full-time.

The night of August 4 was cool and cloudless in California, perfect weather for a boxing match at an open-air park. As Henry pulled up to the park in his car, he was thrilled to see hundreds of eager fans waiting in line outside, primarily people of color. The sight also made him nervous. For the first time, he felt a responsibility to his Black fans to do them proud. Wirt Ross and Harry Armstrong looked at him strangely and seriously in the dressing room as if instilling their hopes in him. Henry always felt anxious for himself in the minutes before a fight, but now he felt the weight of others' hopes on his shoulders. Even so, he considered himself better prepared for this fight than ever, "in the pink of condition." As was his custom, he began incessantly shadowboxing. His brain hummed with thoughts of how much his future, Harry's, Ross's, and his family's depended on the next hour. He wanted his fans to go home proud as well. "It's up to me," he told himself.[115]

Almost eleven thousand people attended that night, and Henry felt all twenty-two thousand eyes looking him over intently as he stepped outside and approached the ring. He climbed in. The announcer introduced the fighters. The referee gave his instructions. It all passed like a blur as Henry felt his heartbeat quickening with anxiety.[116]

The bell rang, and suddenly Henry felt like someone else had taken control of his body, a being of pure rage. Rage at the injustice he felt at those decisions in Mexico City over a year earlier. Rage for the titles and big purses that could have been his. Rage over all the fighting he had had to do to get himself another chance at Arizmendi. It all suddenly seemed to explode within Henry and fueled his arms into a buzz saw of punches. He was faintly aware that Arizmendi was punching and landing too, and Henry wondered why he did not seem to feel any of them. His own punches just kept coming, with no thought of bobbing, weaving, or protecting himself. He barely noticed the rounds passing by, and at no point did fatigue enter his mind or body.

Henry was thrilled when the last bell sounded and someone told him the fight was over, but not because he was tired. He was still full of a previously untapped thirst for violence. He was thrilled because he knew he had reached a new level as a fighter, one he had not known was possible. Somehow, the pressure had brought out a stronger, more aggressive Henry Armstrong. Returning to his stool, he thought, "This is the greatest fight so far."[117]

Others thought so too. Fighter-turned-writer Jim Tully was there and more than impressed. "He was no longer the meek boy," wrote Tully, who had met Henry a few days earlier and found him disarmingly humble and quiet. Tully was almost disturbed that the personable youngster had become "a ripping, slashing, tearing fighter." The shock gave way to fascination. "The Negro's blows, hard and accurate as five-pound sledges, were everywhere," Tully continued. "So was Arizmendi."[118]

"Double barreled destruction vomited in the Baby's face 60 seconds of every minute and every minute of every round," wrote Bill Potts in the *Los Angeles Examiner*.[119]

Petey Sarron, now the generally recognized featherweight champ after beating Freddie Miller, sat ringside. As the fight progressed, a ringside reporter watched Sarron's face turn white. The champion constantly shifted around in his seat.

Paling perceptibly as he blinked with frightened eyes that saw Armstrong, the infernal machine, smoke the idol of Mexico out of the ring with burning, searing leather to take every one of the 10 rounds... Sarron aptly expressed the sentiments of 16,000 hysterical, stunned spectators when he said:

"I'm glad I'm not the one in there with Armstrong tonight."[120]

From the moment he stepped out of the ring until he went to bed in his home that night, Henry found himself lost in a whirlwind of handshakes, back slaps, and congratulations from friends, family, and dozens, if not hundreds of members of Los Angeles's Black community. In between it all, he found time to down a quart of ice cream and inform his wife and daughter of the good news.

"Henry Armstrong, Central avenue's perpetual motion contribution to fistiana, was recognized as the new featherweight champion of the world last night after he'd handed Baby Arizmendi, Mexican 126-pounder, a decisive licking in their ten-round battle for the title at Wrigley Field," Henry read in the *Los Angeles Times* the next day. "Armstrong, the negro buzz-saw, kept up a continuous attack throughout the full ten rounds and Arizmendi never won a single round." The writer noted that Arizmendi's back barely left the ropes to which Armstrong pinned him the entire night.

On the same page, Henry saw the first photos of a Black man named Jesse Owens setting a new world record for the long jump at the Berlin Olympics, one of several Owens victories which would infuriate the Nazis overseeing the Games.

Potts noted that Owens, Armstrong, and Joe Louis collectively represented a new era in Black athletics, which he dubbed "the charge of the black brigade."[121]

After four years of battling as a professional in the California boxing rings and elsewhere, the Mexico and California commissions now recognized Henry Armstrong as the featherweight champion of the world. He had just beaten a great rival recognized by many as the best featherweight on the planet in dominating fashion, avenging two prior losses. Just hours later, Sportswriters throughout the country were singing his praises.

Henry Armstrong had entered his prime.

# 6.
# The Big Time

Henry Armstrong had conquered the west coast boxing scene. He was the most exciting boxer Californians had ever seen and was streaking through the biggest names the state could produce. After beating Baby Arizmendi, he quickly racked up three more wins in three weeks, including a fourth-round knockout of the tough Juan Zurita at the Olympic Auditorium. Still, Henry was not satisfied. He longed to prove himself against the nation's best, and that meant fighting in New York City.

New York scribes like Nat Fleischer of *The Ring* had been anticipating his arrival amidst the streak of victories Henry had assembled in California. Most of the action in boxing happened in New York City, including in the featherweight division of late. The featherweight championship picture had been a mess at least since 1932. Two sanctioning bodies were recognized by the American public when determining the world championship. The New York State Athletic Commission (NYSAC) had influence because the money was there – and consequently, most of the big fights. In 1921, thirteen other state commissions formed the National Boxing Association (NBA) to offset the NYSAC's outsized influence.

Initially, both organizations recognized the same man as champion until the undisputed titleholder Christopher Battaglia, alias Battling Battalino, failed to make weight for a sanctioned championship match with Ohio's Freddie Miller in 1932. After that, both organizations bestowed their championship belts on different men. By the start of 1936, the NYSAC recognized Baby Arizmendi as the world's featherweight champion, while the NBA picked Miller. *The Ring* magazine, recognized by its large readership as the trustworthy source on all things boxing, also managed its unofficial rankings and recognized its own champions. They liked Miller for the championship and gave him their belt.

On May 11, 1936, Miller lost an upset decision and his portion of the championship to Petey Sarron of Alabama in Washington, DC. That same month, the NYSAC stripped Arizmendi of their title, feeling that he could no longer make the division limit, even though he did so in his August bout with Armstrong, which he lost. California and Mexico recognized Armstrong as champion because of that fight, though their decisions carried much less clout than those of the other sanctioning bodies.

Meanwhile, New York handed over their belt to local boy Mike Belloise without his having to win it in the ring. Then there was the European Boxing Union, which recognized France's Maurice Holtzer as champion. By early September, *The Ring* ranked the top fighters in the division as follows:

World's Champion: Petey Sarron
Contenders:
1 – Henry Armstrong
2 – Mike Belloise
3 – Freddie Miller
4 – Baby Arizmendi
5 – Ned Tarleton
6 – Dick Corbett
7 – Willie Smith
8 – Tony Chavez
9 – Fillo Echeverria
10 – Maurice Holtzer[122]

If Henry wanted undisputed recognition as the world's champion, he would have to defeat both Petey Sarron and Mike Belloise, and his best shot at doing that was in making the pilgrimage to New York City, where the big crowds and big money might lure both men into the ring with him. The only problem was that, for all of Wirt Ross's influence on the West Coast, he had few connections in the Big Apple. Henry also suspected that Ross was in trouble with organized crime figures in New York.

Henry and Harry had been dissatisfied with Ross and had secretly begun searching for a new manager. They distrusted his wheeling-and-dealing with other managers, as in the Arizmendi fights. They saw he was not the man to help Henry take the next step in his career.

Their friend Langston Hughes, the poet, introduced them to writer Jim Tully, a former hobo and boxer. The purpose of the meeting was to discuss writing, but the conversation quickly turned to Henry's boxing career, "the stuff that makes writing," as Hughes put it.[123]

In his own words, Tully had been nothing more than "a bruiser with a whalebone body and a granite jaw," but he felt he understood boxers and boxing. He was an early composer of celebrity profiles, with Charlie Chaplin, Clark Gable, Diego Rivera, Jack Dempsey, and Walter Winchell among his subjects. Both Armstrongs impressed him, and he considered buying Henry's contract from Ross. He told them he would get back to them after the Arizmendi fight.[124]

After witnessing Henry's thrilling performance that night, Tully was even more convinced that Henry was a future world champion. But he was also convinced he couldn't manage the fighter. The fight roused him so greatly that he knew boxing would take over his life should he sign on with Henry and Harry. He told Henry, "I can't make it," explaining that he did not want to sacrifice his writing career. Henry understood.[125]

Little did Henry know that events were taking place to remove his attachment to Ross and set him on the road to success in New York without Tully's help. On the night Henry beat Baby Arizmendi, two famous film stars sat ringside at Wrigley Field. Al Jolson was the popular song and dance man (and blackface performer) who had almost single-handedly introduced

Hollywood and the world to "talkies" in the Warner Bros. film *The Jazz Singer* in 1927. The soundtrack consisted of one song ("Swanee," ever after Jolson's signature tune) and a few lines of dialogue ("You ain't seen nothin' yet!"), but that was enough. The film was a box office sensation. "There had been previous attempts at sound cinema before," notes film historian Mark Cousins in his book *The Story of Film*, "but this film was well-funded and widely released." Seemingly overnight, motion picture palaces wired for sound, and sound movies, especially musicals, were being produced at a frantic pace.[126]

One of the biggest stars to rise out of these early musicals was Ruby Keeler, the acting, singing, and dancing star of Ziegfeld's Follies and the hugely successful and influential musical films *42nd Street*, *Gold Diggers of 1933*, and *Footlight Parade*. Jolson and Keeler had married almost immediately after meeting in 1927. The couple had a big home in Hollywood and had shown up that night at nearby Wrigley Field to watch the hometown fighter Henry Armstrong in action.

**Al Jolson and Ruby Keeler**

Keeler noticed a familiar face sitting in the row behind her and Jolson. It was Eddie Mead, the New York fight manager. Known as "Fat Eddie" in the fight game and "Beef Stew" (after his favorite meal, which he allegedly ate for breakfast every morning) to those on more friendly terms, Mead was a heavyset veteran manager firmly ensconced in middle age, with a widow's peak hairline and a chubby face. The look implied sluggishness to the unimaginative, but Mead was a boisterous, animated fellow with an everyman charisma.

"The fight mob called Mead a 'colorful character,'" sportswriter Eddie Muller later remembered of him. "He came from the old school of managers. He spent money as fast as he made it.... Mead was one of those stay up late guys.... He never quit trying even when he was broke, which was on more than one occasion." So far, the entirety of the 1930s had been one of those "occasions" for Fat Eddie Mead.[127]

Keeler and Mead had known each other years earlier as young residents of the Lower East Side, a predominantly Jewish section of New York City. The son of an iron founder, he ran a barber shop on Forty-Sixth Street before taking up boxing management. Mead had briefly found his way to the heights of the sport by orchestrating the career of Joe Lynch, a fellow New Yorker who was the bantamweight champion of the world during the 1920s.

He was not without his shady connections and accusations of dirty trickery. A rival manager once accused him of inserting a small iron bar into the gloves of his fighters. Since Lynch's retirement in 1926, Mead's fortunes had waned, and part of his income now came from transporting stolen jewelry for the then little-known Los Angeles bookmaker Mickey Cohen to New York to fence the pilfered goods. Hence Mead's most likely reason for being in Los Angeles at that moment, with the bonus of engaging a couple of his current fighters in L.A. bouts. The movie star hugged the fight manager before action got underway in the ring.[128]

"That's the kind of fighter you should be handling," a thrilled Keeler exclaimed to Mead toward the middle of the fight. By then, Henry had asserted control of the action.

"Yeah, I should have him, but there're five thousand reasons why I won't," retorted the down-on-his-luck Mead. "That's what Ross will want for his contract after tonight – five grand."[129]

Long before this, Ross had once offered to sell the contracts of Henry Armstrong and Young Peter Jackson to Mead for a total of fifteen hundred dollars. At that time, Mead had been in L.A. managing Davey Abad, a decent fighter out of Panama. He had been in Abad's corner in the Olympic Auditorium on May 28, 1935, watching Henry Armstrong trounce poor Davey. But Eddie was not so much focused on his own fighter as on the little dynamo in the opposite corner. He knew Wirt Ross and knew he could do a better job of managing this Armstrong kid than Ross. After the fight, he approached Ross, who offered to sell Henry's contract with Jackson's as a package deal. Eddie agreed and told Wirt to meet him the next day at a racetrack to sign the contracts.

In truth, Eddie didn't have the money; he was a notorious loser at the races, and there was a depression on, after all. He and Abad had not even netted one hundred dollars for the Armstrong loss. Eddie spent the day scrounging the funds together in loans from friends, maybe Mickey Cohen. Ross was late to the meeting the next day, and gambling addict Mead spent that time betting on two races. By the time Ross did arrive, Eddie no longer had the cash to buy Henry's contract. A little over a year later, Eddie Mead was kicking himself.

On the morning after the Armstrong-Arizmendi fight, Mead's phone rang. Al Jolson, Ruby Keeler's rich and famous husband, was on the other end, yawning after a mostly sleepless night of pestering from his wife. Jolson said that if Mead could convince Ross to sell Armstrong's contract for five thousand dollars, he would put up the money. Mead immediately ran down Wirt Ross to make the offer.

Ross ran the idea by Henry. Henry asked Jim Tully what he thought of the deal. "Mead and Jolson are both right people," was the reply. "None better."[130]

Henry told Ross he was good with the change, and Ross told Mead the deal was on. Mead rushed to the movie studio where Jolson was working to tell him the good news and hatch another plan: They would pay Mead the five grand but tell the press the sum was ten.

"That'll make us look a lot bigger," Mead explained, "and get us a lot of good publicity." With Jolson's consent, Mead instructed Henry to go along with the story when interviewed by the press, and the fighter did as instructed.

Ross and Mead met on Friday, August 21, to finalize the deal. After reading of the ten-thousand-dollar purchase price in the papers, Ross refused the check for five thousand.

"The papers say it's ten grand... and ten grand it is!" Ross insisted with Henry present.[131]

His bulbous face turning red and his body quivering with rage, Mead shouted a barrage of curses at Ross, who stood his ground. Eventually, Mead calmed down enough to agree and asked Ross to give him a day to come up with the funds.

Too embarrassed to return to Jolson for more money, Eddie Mead turned to another Hollywood big shot for funds. George Raft was another movie star he knew from back in New York. Eddie had even managed George's brief and unimpressive career as a prizefighter in the early days.

Raft had grown up in the Hell's Kitchen neighborhood of the Big Apple, and like Mead, he had his share of underworld connections dating back to childhood, most notably Bugsy Siegel and Owney Madden. The FBI believed he had connections to other gangsters such as Frank Costello, Joey Adonis, Jack Dragna, and Longy Zwillman. With Madden's financial backing, he relocated to Hollywood in 1927 and, after surgery to correct a cauliflower ear, got into the movies as a bit player. He became a star after appearing in the classic 1932 gangster picture *Scarface*. Though not much of an actor, Raft was very handsome, became a heartthrob leading man, and developed a persona of menacing cool that worked well for the gangster characters he often portrayed on the silver screen.

A George Raft and Frances Drake publicity still for the film *The Trumpet Blows* (1934)

Authorities suspected Raft of fixing a fight on Madden's orders on at least one occasion. Madden owned a controlling interest in the Italian heavyweight Primo Carnera and was orchestrating his rise to the championship of the world through a series of fixed fights. In 1930, Raft allegedly drugged his friend Eddie Peterson on the night Peterson was to face Carnera. Peterson collapsed under a "grazing" left hook in the opening round.[132]

Always harboring a more than passing interest in boxing, Raft jumped at the chance to own a piece of Henry Armstrong's future.

"You don't have to go to Al. I don't want to be mixed with that guy," Raft said. He had just one requirement. "Just keep my name out of it and you just give me the five grand back when you get it." That was the agreement.[133]

Mead brought the ten thousand to Ross, who released Henry from his contract. The press afterward reported that Eddie Mead and Al Jolson were Henry Armstrong's managers, with Mead handling the business and Jolson providing the financing and a bit of star power. Even Henry was unaware of Mead's deal with Raft, though he did regard the actor as a friend.

Wirt "One Shot" Ross continued his career as California's most colorful manager for decades, his most successful later fighter being Freddie Beshore. But by the time Freddie got his shot at heavyweight champion Ezzard Charles in 1950, Ross had long since sold off his contract. The "Old Rebel" passed away in 1960 at age eighty-eight.

Eddie Mead (standing), Al Jolson, and Henry Armstrong

If Henry had doubts about signing with Mead and Jolson as his new management, they disappeared within days of signing the contract. By then, the duo had already arranged his shot at NYSAC featherweight champion Mike Belloise. Even better, Henry would not have to leave home. Belloise was coming to L.A.

A Bronx fighter who had come up in the talent-stocked gyms, clubs, and arenas of New York City, Belloise was crafty and quick. Because of his tricky defense, quick counter-punching, and his ability to fight effectively in both the orthodox and southpaw stance, he was nicknamed "The Bronx Spider." A pro since 1932, he was a veteran of over two hundred amateur bouts. *The Ring* rated him the world's "cleverest" boxer in 1936. As of October of that year, he had a record of 49 wins against four losses and five draws. One of those losses came after fifteen rounds against Baby Arizmendi for the NYSAC title. Since gaining that title, he had defended it once with a ninth-round knockout of the even more experienced Dave Crowley. Many fight fans were picking Belloise to defeat Henry.¹³⁴

Mike Belloise, "The Brooklyn Spider"

Originally scheduled for Tuesday, October 20, the fight was pushed back a week due to Henry recovering from the flu, only providing more time for the public's anticipation to build. Advance ticket sales spiked.

"Henry Armstrong's 'public' was conspicuous in front of the Olympic yesterday afternoon and the day before his fight with Mike Belloise. Chauffeurs of a couple of city garbage trucks parked their chariots on Eighteenth street and rushed to buy their fight tickets at the box office," reported the *Los Angeles Times* the day after the fight.

By fight time, 10,400 fans had taken their seats in the Olympic. Henry later admitted that he got a slow start in the fight, claiming he was still feeling the weakening effects of his bout with the flu.¹³⁵

"Armstrong had no easy time of it with the little Italian, who threw punches with such abandon and direction that for a spell it was believed he would win the fight," reported the *Los Angeles Daily News* the next day. The clever and swift New Yorker was on top of his game, and Belloise's son later said it was "perhaps his greatest bout," considering his performance and the quality of his opponent.[136]

Henry came on stronger as the match progressed and took rounds nine and ten decisively to close the show. When they returned to their corners after the bell, Belloise sported a cut eyelid while Armstrong bled from his nose and mouth.

At the bout's end, referee Abe Roth, the only judge for the fight, raised Henry Armstrong's hand, and Al Jolson "howled with delight." But the decision was hardly unanimous as far as the crowd was concerned. Hoots, boos, and catcalls erupted across the Olympic in protest. Mae West shouted a torrent of vitriol from her ringside seat at Roth. "I couldn't help but get a kick out of that," Belloise later confessed to the *New York Post*.[137]

The press was also divided. Even among the Los Angeles papers, there was some disagreement about how the fight went. The *Daily News* felt the fight was close and that Henry only secured the win in the final two rounds; meanwhile, the *Times* felt that Armstrong dominated every round but the fourth as he "poured rights and lefts to the body and head with almost reckless abandon inside Mike's guard." The *Pasadena Post* called it a "hometown decision," insinuating that Belloise was robbed. Meanwhile, the Associated Press called it "a draw, with an edge, if any, to Belloise for more effective blows."[138]

As sportswriters filed into Mike Belloise's dressing room after the fight, manager Pete Reilly raised hell claiming that Armstrong fouled his fighter with low blows throughout the fight. Eventually, Belloise shushed Reilly and admitted, "Armstrong beat me and he was entitled to the decision."[139]

Most fighters will say that they feel much worse the day after a hard fight than they do on the night of the fight. The bruises, abrasions, cuts, sore joints, sore muscles, and sore head do not hit the nervous system until he wakes up the following day. Even so, October 28 brought a sting deeper than the flesh for Henry.

Word came that the NYSAC had decided they would not recognize Henry Armstrong as champion. For weeks the press had been reporting that the fight would be recognized as such, the fighters signed contracts to that effect, and the NYSAC had not objected. Both fighters came in at 125 pounds, one pound below the required weight limit for a featherweight bout, thinking that the title was on the line, and they fought accordingly.

The Commission reasoned that the fight had been for ten rounds, not the fifteen rounds New York State required for championship bouts. Never mind that fifteen-round fights were illegal in California and that Henry was coming on in the later rounds, and the decision would have likely gone even more his way had it continued. Never mind that the commissioners had known that the fight would go ten rounds. The white New Yorker was still the world's champion, said the NYSAC.

Bill Henry, a sports columnist for the *Los Angeles Times*, told his readers not to get too upset and did so with indisputable logic. "The main thing now is that Henry Armstrong is the champion of Mike Belloise and Henry knows it and Mike knows it and you and I know it. If the N.Y. Boxing Commission doesn't know it – that still makes it unanimous."[140]

Rational though it was, the argument would have been a meager consolation for Henry Armstrong, who could no longer celebrate the title he had thought was his just a few short hours before. Without that title, Henry had little to entice NBA and *Ring* champion Petey Sarron into a fight.

Eddie Mead wisely did not give Henry time to sulk. On November 2, he was already back in the ring, specifically L.A.'s Eastside Arena, where he decimated Gene Espinosa inside 34 seconds. A hard right to the jaw put the Filipino fighter down, his head hitting the mat "with such a terrific thud that it could be heard all over the arena." It took Espinosa's handlers ten minutes to revive him.[141]

Shortly after that, St. Louis promoter Benny Greenburg approached Eddie and Henry about Henry making a conquering hero's return to his hometown for a couple of fights. Henry jumped at the chance, and Harry accompanied him on the train trip home. Willa Mae had gone ahead of them, and Eddie Mead was planning to follow shortly. Lanetta remained in California, presumably watched by a trusted babysitter.

The St. Louis newspapers reported on Henry's anticipated return weeks in advance. When they disembarked at Union Station just before dusk on Friday, November 6, they found the train surrounded by a welcome party numbering approximately three hundred (*The Chicago Defender* reported six hundred) people of both races, including Mayor Bernard Dickmann, other city officials, reporters, and photographers with their popping flashbulbs. Of all the faces present, Henry was happiest to spot that of his older sister Henrietta among the crowd.[142]

Henry's most satisfying part of the day was likely riding from the train station to the St. Louis YMCA in a police-escorted motorcade, with a brief stop at City Hall, where Dickmann presented him with the key to the city. Henry, Willa Mae, Harry, Henrietta, and her husband Abe McConnell rode proudly together in a chauffeur-driven convertible 1930 Packard through the streets. A brand-new black Buick carrying other members of his family followed them, and behind that were about fifty more automobiles, including one transporting a band that provided a celebratory soundtrack as the parade made its way to City Hall and then on through the city's Black neighborhoods.

Henry could not help but remember his promise to one day return to St. Louis in a manner befitting his hero Kid Chocolate, complete with a chauffeured automobile.

Once the parade ended, Henry and Harry took rooms at the Pine Street YMCA, the very same building where the fighter and trainer had worked so hard in the amateur days. They wanted a familiar setting in which to sequester themselves for fight preparations. On the schedule was the relatively inexperienced Joey Alcanter of Kansas City. Despite a limited record, Alcanter had beaten some quality opponents lately and was considered the lightweight champion of Missouri and a contender for the world title. Harry intended Henry to be in good shape for his homecoming fight.

Good intentions aside, the temptations of being a national celebrity were getting the better of Henry. Until the first fight with Arizmendi, he had yet to taste liquor; poverty and a focus on his boxing career had seen to that in the lean years. But being a young and successful prizefighter surrounded by Hollywood celebrities – not to mention a conquering hero returning to his hometown – meant that offers of parties, free drinks, and fast women were always at hand. Once fame hit, Henry began to sample "plenty of the grape, at $40 the vintage bottle," as he later related to a reporter.[143]

The Henry Armstrong and Joey Alcanter fight was supposed to be a co-main event with a matchup between NBA featherweight titleholder Petey Sarron and his challenger Everett Rightmire on November 17 at the Municipal Auditorium in St. Louis. Neither title claimant would come in under the featherweight limit of 126 pounds, so neither man risked his title. However, Alcanter's state lightweight championship was contractually up for grabs.

Fans were excited to see the two best featherweights in the same ring together on the same night, even if they would not face each other. But a few days before the fight, Sarron was dropped from the card without a detailed explanation. Midget Wolgast took his spot.

Henry did show up for his bout, and he won when the referee stopped the fight on the ringside doctor's recommendation before the start of the sixth round. With roughly six thousand fans watching the hometown kid make good, an Armstrong left hook (*The Defender* reported it as a right) not only dropped Alcanter to his knees in the fifth round; it fractured his jaw. "That boy can hit like a Missouri Mule can kick," mused one reporter. Henry Armstrong now added the Missouri State lightweight championship to his collection. Meanwhile, Rightmire became the latest man to defeat the faded Wolgast.[144]

Next up for Henry was veteran California lightweight Tony Chavez, described by a local paper as "one of the hardest hitting ringsters in the game today." Chavez had knocked out Rightmire the prior year. In the lead-up to the Armstrong-Chavez event, Chavez told reporters that he had personally seen Armstrong in action on multiple occasions back in Los Angeles, and he felt that Henry's aggression would make him an easy mark for a counter-punch knockout.[145]

When they met on Wednesday, December 3, at the Municipal Auditorium before an attendance of 6,280, Chavez upset the odds and took home a victory, but it was hardly by knockout. "Chavez took a thorough beating round after round," reported Raymond V. Smith of the *St. Louis Globe-Democrat*, "but he amazed the fans with his durability and courage." As Smith saw it, Armstrong was on the verge of knocking out Chavez in the eighth round when he unloaded "a terrific right uppercut" intended for Chavez's mid-section that strayed low and landed directly to the groin. Chavez collapsed to the floor, rolled across the mat and out of the ring, landing on the pavement below. Someone lifted him back into the ring, and his handlers picked him up to carry him to the dressing room. On the advice of the ringside doctor, the referee declared that Armstrong had fouled Chavez and disqualified him.[146]

As Henry saw it, the punch landed only slightly below the belt line, and Chavez's reaction amounted to nothing more than "a fine piece of acting." It was Henry's first loss after a ten-fight winning streak, the longest of his career so far. That it happened in front of a disappointed hometown crowd in just his second fight home added to Henry's frustration.[147]

**Tony Chavez**
*Los Angeles Daily News*, February 14, 1939

Harry and Henry had chosen an undefeated local middleweight named Archie Moore for a sparring partner in St. Louis. With only six fights behind him as a pro, Moore was a novice in 1936. Archie would go on to one of the longest and most successful boxing careers in history, holding the light heavyweight championship of the world longer than any other man. He would also claim the record for the most knockout victories in a pro career. Henry and Archie became good friends in later life.

A transplant from Mississippi like Henry, Archie grew up in the same part of St. Louis as Henry and trained at the Pine Street YMCA, where Henry had gotten much of his early instruction. Unable to afford transportation, he walked to the gym each day. He was offered three dollars for six rounds of sparring with Armstrong. When Archie arrived at the gym to collect his pay after the Chavez fight, someone told him Henry had left town.

That was not exactly true. Henry was no longer staying at the YMCA, but he was in St. Louis. He and Willa Mae celebrated his twenty-seventh birthday and the Christmas holiday while staying with Henrietta and her husband before returning to Los Angeles.

Rodolfo "Baby" Casanova
*Los Angeles Times*, November 15, 1932

On New Year's Day, 1937, Henry was in a Mexico City bull ring to face featherweight Rodolfo "Baby" Casanova a second time. Since scoring his disqualification win over Henry in 1935, Casanova had picked up victories over some of the division's biggest names, including Baby Arizmendi, Speedy Dado, Joe Conde, Freddie Miller, Juan Zurita, and Kid Azteca. He had lost a few fights, too, but was still a big star in his native land. Suspicious of Mexican judges and referees, Henry sought to end things early. He finished off Casanova in the third round before a huge crowd.

On January 19, Henry avenged another disqualification loss by forcing Tony Chavez's cornermen to throw in the towel in the tenth round of a lightweight match at the Olympic Auditorium in Los Angeles. Knockouts of lesser opponents Winfred "Moon" Mullins, Varias Milling, and Joe Rivers, all lightweight bouts held in California, came between February and March.

Finally, Mead arranged for Henry Armstrong's long-awaited New York City debut. That it would be at Madison Square Garden, the world's single most important boxing venue, speaks to the anticipation with which the East Coast awaited the California phenom's arrival. Henry was thrilled.

Construction on the third building to bear the name of the Garden finished in 1924. Jack Dempsey's promoter Tex Rickard footed the bill for nearly five million dollars. Considered the most spectacular indoor sports arena of its time, the new Garden boasted two tiers of seating and a capacity of nearly 18,500 people.

The Garden was the battleground of the sport's idols, including Dempsey, Gene Tunney, Joe Louis, Kid Chocolate, Benny Leonard, Jim Braddock, Max Schmeling, Jack Sharkey, Max Baer, Primo Carnera, Mickey Walker, Tommy

Loughran, Maxie Rosenbloom, Jimmy McLarnin, Tony Canzoneri, Barney Ross, and Lou Ambers. It was the headquarters of *The Ring* magazine.

Madison Square Garden, New York, NY

It was also the final resting place for the hopes of many fighters whose names neither Henry nor anyone else could remember. A boxer's debut at the Garden was not just his coming-out party for big-time boxing; it was the make-or-break moment where the finicky New York boxing scribes would decide if a fighter had the goods to compete with the sport's true elite. They expected a fighter not just to win but to win spectacularly. If an out-of-state fighter did not pass muster, he was often written off and never allowed a major New York fight again.

Henry expected to fight Aldo Spoldi, the popular lightweight champion of Italy, who had won two fights at the Garden within the prior year. However, on March 11, just one day before fight time, the NYSAC granted Spoldi a week's delay to nurse an injured hand, and organizers selected Mike Belloise as Spoldi's substitute for the March 12 engagement. Because the fight was only for ten rounds, both fighters could come in above the featherweight limit, and Belloise's title would again not be on the line. Henry, Harry, and Eddie Mead were convinced the whole event had been a ploy to get Henry back in the ring with Belloise without the title on the line, just to give the Bronx Spider a revenge hometown decision and vindicate the NYSAC's decision not to recognize Henry as champion.

When the chronically skeptical New York sportswriters got their first glimpse of Henry Armstrong in his hotel room before the fight, they almost felt sorry for him. He sat by the window and distractedly sketched a picture of the city skyline as they asked him questions. He told them about his poetry and talked about learning to paint. He told them he wanted to attend medical school to study hygiene and become a doctor. When he paid attention long enough to answer their queries about the fight, his reply of "I feel I'll do adequately" seemed pathetically humble to the hard-boiled, hard-drinking, hard-smoking, hard-typing scribes of boxing. Surely, they told themselves and their readers, this quiet poet from California was nothing more than an Eddie Mead hype job. They came away convinced Mead was leading his poor lamb to slaughter in New York as a simple cash grab.[148]

In truth, Henry was keenly aware of the importance of the fight and was far from the relaxed daydreamer he presented to the press. He later remembered feeling incredibly nervous, knowing he had to make a great impression on the picky New York fight crowd.

That night was cold, and the Garden was only at about a third of its capacity, with 6,796 people spread around the arena. The vacancy made the place look canyonlike. During his ring walk, Henry shivered with nerves and a chill; his knees were weak. Then, before entering the ring, he spotted George Raft in the ringside seats. He still had no idea about the actor's role as a silent partner in his success, but the actor encouraged him by telling him that he represented all California. Emboldened, Henry assured George he would win and made his way between the ring ropes, ready for a fight.[149]

The next day, the *New York Daily News* had this to say:

> Henry Armstrong, an ebony tempest from out of the West, swirled into Madison Square Garden last nite and swept Mike Belloise off the landscape with a knockout in the fourth round of a scheduled ten-round bout. A left to the stomach followed by a right to the jaw, finished Belloise seven seconds before the bell.[150]

After the fight, holding court in his dressing room while getting a rub down from Harry, Henry came off much more arrogant to the sportswriters than he had in his hotel. Asked to describe the final moments, he told them, "It was really preposterous that he came out for the fourth. His punches were absolutely inconsequential.... He was making futile gestures. Then I slipped over the left hook. That's all."[151]

Decades later, talking with author Peter Heller, Henry admitted it was an illegal right-hand blow to the back of the neck that ended the fight. "I turned him a somersault in the air I hit him so hard," Henry bragged. After the referee counted him out, Belloise stood on wobbly legs intending to keep fighting. Henry had to tell him the fight was over, and Belloise did not regain his full senses until he was in his dressing room.[152]

Later in the year, because Belloise had only defended his version of the championship once since they had handed it to him, the NYSAC stripped him of their recognition as champion. Still, they did not recognize Henry; they declared the title vacant.

With his credentials clearly established in the Garden, ten thousand fans showed up a week later to watch Henry pound out a dominant ten-round decision over Aldo Spoldi. That made Henry the first fighter to box in the Garden in two successive weeks. Immediately after the fight, Henry rushed to celebrations in Harlem's nightclubs.[153]

It was fair to say that Henry had conquered the New York fight scene in just those two fights, a huge step forward for his career. Nat Fleischer of *The Ring* considered Armstrong's furious style "a revelation" and noted that "His determination, his aggressiveness and two-fisted style registered with all the critics." Pat Halsy, an ex-fighter who had once gone eighteen hard rounds with Hall of Famer Terry McGovern, had been a judge for the fight. "I always said nobody hit as fast and often as McGovern," a flabbergasted Halsy muttered after that fight, "but I just seen proof I was wrong." Mission accomplished.[154]

## *Armstrong Knocks Out Belloise; Loser Unable to Come Up for 5th*

### Los Angeles Featherweight Drops Bronx Fighter With Left Hook to Jaw in Fourth Round and Count Reaches Seven at Bell —Donovan Calls Halt at Garden—7,000 Attend

New York Times, March 14, 1937

# 7.
# "You Can't Jim Crow a Left Hook"

Being a Black celebrity during the Great Depression was a tightrope walk. One had to be non-threatening, non-political, and reinforce white peoples' beliefs about their own superiority, especially if one wanted to cross over to the more lucrative white audience. A handful of well-known black intellectuals and political firebrands gained attention by discussing America's issues with race. Still, the Black celebrities who crossed over to white approval and made good money were figures like Bojangles, Ethel Waters, Louis Armstrong, and Hattie McDaniel. All were talented individuals, but their popularity largely rested on their willingness always to appear as though their only purpose for living was to entertain and that they never resented anything about their status as second-class citizens.

For Black boxers, such an act was like forcing a smile while juggling fire. Interracial and inter-ethnic contests had become the norm everywhere but in the Deep South by the 1930s, and defeating white opponents was both a job requirement and a precarious danger. As Henry himself once quipped, "You can't Jim Crow a left hook," as vivid of an image of boxing as the great equalizer as has ever been uttered. Henry and other boxers of color regularly defeated white opponents, an act which made white audiences as uncomfortable as it made Black audiences joyous. Henry and others had to double down on their deference outside the ring to placate white fears or risk a dangerous public backlash.[155]

Joe Louis, a famed heavyweight contender as of the time Henry made his New York debut, is perhaps the best example of this. Like Henry, Joe was the son of Southern Black sharecroppers and the grandson of enslaved people. Like Henry, he left the Deep South (Alabama, in Joe's case) with his family as a boy. The Barrows (Louis's real name was Joseph Barrow) went much further north than St. Louis to Detroit. Like Henry, he had changed his name upon lacing up the boxing gloves.

Though not quite as aggressive as Henry in the ring, Louis was nonetheless a heavy-punching knockout artist, still named by *The Ring* as the single greatest puncher in boxing history over seventy years after he retired. Beginning with Lee Ramage in December 1934, Louis tore through the upper echelons of the heavyweight division in the mid-1930s, knocking out one ranked contender or former champion after another. With each victory, he gathered more fans, particularly among Black people, who saw in him a symbol of upward advancement during the Great Depression and – just maybe – the man to recapture the coveted heavyweight championship of the world for them.

Since the days of the independent and controversial Jack Johnson, Black fighters had been allowed to fight for championships in every division except for heavyweight. Many whites feared that another Black heavyweight champion like Johnson would demonstrate the same unabashed enjoyment he displayed when defeating his Caucasian opponents. Johnson's very public liaisons with white women and the pride with which he always carried himself were also a lingering threat in the minds of whites. They worried that such behavior would prompt other Black people to take pride in themselves or seek social parity with whites. Accommodating this sentiment, the white promoters who controlled boxing drew the unofficial but very real "color line" back across the heavyweight championship after Johnson lost the title in 1915.

If Joe Louis was going to be the man to cross that line, if he was going to be the Black man who beat down a white heavyweight champion of the world, his handlers knew he must follow a specific set of rules and behaviors to appear as non-threatening to the white establishment as possible. Most importantly, he could not smile after beating a white opponent or be photographed with a white woman (although he had multiple white lovers behind closed doors). These rules directly resulted from Johnson's behavior – or rather, white reactions to Johnson's behavior. Joe's handlers viewed his speech impediment and usually deadpan facial expression as blessings, as wary whites could incorrectly dismiss him as mentally slow and willingly submissive and, therefore, non-threatening. He could inspire Black pride inside the ring, but he would reassure white insecurities outside of it.

Just a couple of years into his career, Joe Louis was the most popular Black American athlete in history. Then, overconfident, undertrained, and not yet the heavyweight champion, he was knocked out in a shocking upset to Germany's Max Schmeling, bringing his progress to a stand-still. Black fans who had once mobbed and cheered him suddenly regarded him as an embarrassment, a failure of their hopes.

Louis's loss brought unprecedented devastation to the morale of Black people worldwide. The fight was broadcast throughout much of Europe, Latin America, and South Africa. The immediacy and far-reaching signal of radio had made Louis a new kind of Black international hero, and his defeat brought an equally new kind of widespread sorrow. "An idol… an idol fell last night," read the *New York Post* after Louis's defeat, one of the few mainstream papers to show sympathy to Joe's crestfallen Black fans, "and the crashing was so complete, so dreadful and so totally unexpected that it broke the hearts of the Negroes of the world." Famous Black singer Lena Horne who had broken down and wept along with the rest of her band during the fight, put it more simply. To her and her people, Joe was now "just another Negro getting beaten by a white man."[156]

There was no one to wholly and immediately replace Joe Louis as a symbol of Black pride. Still, other Black Americans from various vocations inherited the splintered pieces of his hero status. In athletics, two men helped fill the void. The first was Jesse Owens, the track star who had proven himself the "fastest man alive" and embarrassed Adolf Hitler at the Berlin Olympics after Louis's loss. Owens returned to the United States as a national hero.

The other, Henry Armstrong, filled Joe's oversized boxing shoes. No other young boxer of any color was as talented and thrilling as Henry, apart from Joe Louis himself. Though he was more verbal and expressive than Louis, Armstrong remained at least palatable to white audiences and clearly tried to be so. Jack Johnson may have been one of his heroes, but Henry was just as willing to be the anti-Johnson as was Louis. He posed for photographers by biting into watermelons. He avoided photographs with white women. If he ever quarreled with or rebelled against his white managers and promoters, it never made the papers.

In those days, reporters did not generally ask athletes their thoughts on social issues, and Henry rarely spoke out about the ill-treatment of Black people in America. Perhaps the vivid memories of seeing fellow Blacks whipped and lynched by whites as a child made him reticent to speak out, and understandably so.

On a rare occasion that he did criticize racist America, he compromised it with understatement and patriotism. "While the so-called American Way hasn't been kind to my people, it's better than any known system," he once told the *New York Amsterdam*. As far as the public was concerned, Henry Armstrong was a quiet, smiling, well-behaved Negro who could fight like hell, and they wanted nothing more from him.[157]

Henry fought like hell on April 6 in the Olympic Auditorium when he knocked out the tough and experienced Pete DeGrasse in the tenth round.

His next opponent was Frankie Klick, a clever San Francisco fighter who claimed to be the junior lightweight champion of the world. Established as a class for fighters competing between 126 and 130 pounds, the junior lightweight division existed in a kind of limbo of legitimacy at the time. Though boxing's sanctioning bodies later recognized it as an official division, many in boxing, including *The Ring* magazine, still refused to do so in 1937.

Still, if there was a junior lightweight class, Frankie Klick was its champ, establishing himself as such back in 1933 with a knockout of Henry's idol Kid Chocolate. Klick was a skilled practitioner of the so-called "sweet science" but lacked a serious punch. By the time he and Henry met in the ring on May 4, 1937, Klick had eighty-five wins on his record.[158]

Henry was the slight betting favorite because Frankie was considered a little long in the tooth (The fight took place the day before his thirtieth birthday). However, the *Los Angeles Times* considered Klick "the best fighter Henry Armstrong, featherweight title-holder, has met to date."[159]

The fight proved less competitive than the bettors anticipated. Before a capacity crowd at the Olympic Auditorium, Henry "turned his Gatling guns loose" on Klick and forced the San Franciscan's corner to throw in the towel in the fourth round.[160]

**Frankie Klick**

Frankie Klick would win just one of his next four bouts before retiring in 1939. He attempted a comeback in 1943 but fared no better and abruptly retired again. He lived to the age of seventy-five, passing away in 1982, but was largely forgotten for the talented champion he was. Upon his death, columnist Bill Soberanes, who had met Klick and many other old-time boxing champions, lamented that Klick never got the recognition he deserved and said that his contemporaries considered him "a prize fighter's prize fighter."[161]

On May 28, Henry returned to Wrigley Field to participate in the undercard of a main event featuring popular local heavyweight Bob Pastor. Henry's opponent was Wally Hally, a fighter out of Hollywood riding a six-fight unbeaten streak, including a ten-round decision over Baby Arizmendi. After a thrilling toe-to-toe battle, Hally's corner threw in the towel in the fourth round just before their man slumped to the canvas under a trademark Henry Armstrong assault. Similar quick knockouts of lesser opponents, Mark Diaz and Jack Carter, followed in June.

Henry traveled back across the country to fight in New York again on July 8. Before a Madison Square Garden crowd of eleven thousand, he dropped cocky Alf Blatch, the lightweight champion of Australia, to the canvas eight times in three rounds before the referee stopped the fight.[162]

"I think he wanted to kill Blatch," the astonished referee later warned Eddie Mead. "You better talk to this boy."

Mead replied that talking to Henry during a fight would be pointless because "he doesn't hear a thing."[163]

Eleven days later, Al Jolson and seven thousand others watched Henry flatten Philadelphia's Lew Massey with similar violence in four rounds in Queens.

The rest of the summer and autumn of 1937 found Henry jumping between cities in the East and Midwest in a chaotic and disorganized crisscross. He fought as often as once every three days, traveling hundreds of miles between fights only to drive the same distance back for another fight elsewhere. It was exhausting but also thrilling, as Henry saw places he had never seen, and the people there saw Henry Armstrong in action for the first time.

Benny Bass, "The Little Fish"
*Atlantic City Press*, **December 20, 1934**

The first stop was Philadelphia's Baker Bowl to face one of Henry's heroes, the Russian-born two-fisted scrapper Benny Bass. Immigrating to Philadelphia with his family as a young boy, Bass fought his first professional bout at just sixteen in 1921 and was a veteran of over two hundred pro bouts by the time he entered the ring with Henry. He had briefly held the NBA's recognition as featherweight champion in 1928, having won it before a massive hometown crowd of forty thousand in a fight with Red Burman, then lost it to the dynamic Tony Canzoneri. He had also claimed the world's junior lightweight championship until he lost that to Henry's other idol, Kid Chocolate, in 1931. Since that time, he had mostly been campaigning as a lightweight. At thirty-two years old, he was riding a twelve-fight winning streak.[164]

Back in 1930, Henry had attended Bass's fight with Davey Abad in St. Louis. It had been the first boxing match he had ever seen. Now, he would be facing Bass himself.

On July 27, twelve thousand fans packed the Bowl near its capacity to watch their hometown hero face the streaking California phenomenon. To their disappointment, the fight was embarrassingly one-sided from the outset. His body worn by hundreds of prizefights, Bass was slow of both hand and foot and mustered little to no resistance to Armstrong's ceaseless aggression. Bass's champion's heart kept him in the ring until the fourth round when five successive right hands rendered him senseless. Though the victory over a name opponent was important to Henry's career, he hated having to humiliate a man he admired.[165]

Finished as a world-class fighter, Benny Bass fought just seven more times before retiring in 1940. He worked as an alcohol salesman and as a court clerk in retirement. Still, he remained a visible figure around the fight game and an advocate for the Veteran Boxers Association until his death at age seventy in Philadelphia. He was posthumously inducted into the International Boxing Hall of Fame in 2002.

Henry was back in New York for a third-round knockout of Irish Eddie Brink in front of 9,032 fans on August 13. Johnny Cabello did not make it through the first round in Washington, D.C., three days later.[166]

"Petey Sarron is wearing the featherweight crown simply because he hasn't bumped into the paralyzing Negro," mused D.C. sportswriter Burton Hawkins.[167]

Before the month was out, Henry made his Detroit debut by stopping Orville Drouillard in five. *The Detroit Free Press* now considered Henry "the best fighting man in the world pound for pound.[168]"

On September 9, at Hickey Park in Pittsburgh, Henry dropped Charley Burns to the canvas five times in four rounds to win by knockout. Jules Beck, the man who had once promoted young Melody Jackson when he was trying to make it in the Smoky City years earlier, promoted the Burns fight. Al Iovino, the local southpaw who had been Henry's first pro opponent in 1931, was in the park that night. Al had long since retired, but Henry left him two tickets for ringside at the box office. "Henry Armstrong is all they say he is," observed the writer for the *Pittsburgh Sun-Telegraph*.[169]

A week later, he was in Madison Square Garden to stop Johnny DeFoe in four rounds on September 16. Then he headed back west to Youngstown, Ohio, where he knocked out Bobby Dean in less than a round on September 22. On October 29, following a drive across Pennsylvania, Henry knocked out Joe Marciente in three rounds in Philadelphia, where his tour of the region had started against Benny Bass.

# 8.
# Armstrong & Jacobs: Undisputed

**Promoter Mike Jacobs and Henry Armstrong**

While Henry was streaking through the East and Midwest piling up knockout victories, Eddie Mead and New York promoter Mike Jacobs were hard at work putting together the much-anticipated championship match with featherweight king Petey Sarron. The winner would be the world's unified, undisputed featherweight champion. Even the NYSAC agreed.

Though not a heavy hitter, Sarron was one of the trickiest fighters in the sport, wily and hard to hit. "Pete is a trim, black-haired little fellow who looks like a prizefighter and talks like a college professor," noted journalist John Kieran. "He has a thick ear, a broken nose, a delightful Southern accent and a happy choice of words."

Born in Birmingham, Alabama, in 1906, he turned pro in 1924 after serving as an alternate at the Paris Olympics. Despite years of success, he did not get his shot at the title until 1936, losing to Freddie Miller. In the rematch later that year, he beat Miller for the NBA and *The Ring* belts. He had defended the championship twice. A noted world traveler, Sarron was in South Africa for a rematch wtih Miller when negotiations began for a battle with Henry Armstrong.[170]

The key figure in arranging the long-awaited matchup was Jacobs, who would be the czar of New York boxing for the next decade. Nat Fleischer, one of the few men in boxing who did not utterly despise Jacobs, considered him "A hard-headed business man, a cool and calm calculator who always had a sound reason for every move."

Journalists John Field and Earl Brown elaborated in a profile on Jacobs's stranglehold over boxing for *Life* magazine in 1946. "In a business not noted for its honesty, he is considered honest, being shrewd enough to see that crookedness does not pay off at the box office," they wrote, correctly recognizing him as "the most feared and the most successful promoter boxing has ever known."[171]

Not everyone found him to be as honest as Field and Brown. Sugar Ray Robinson, one of the sport's biggest stars of the 1940s and 1950s, told them, "Mike will manipulate anybody for a buck.... You don't earn the championship on merit anymore. You buy it."[172]

Jacobs is one of the few figures in boxing who could compete with Henry Armstrong in collecting nicknames. As a young concessionaire and ticket scalper, he was "Steamboat Mike." Later, the fighters in his promotional stable affectionately called him "Uncle Mike," and he often used the moniker himself. "What's in it for Uncle Mike?" was his favorite catchphrase. Those less appreciative of his cold business tactics called him "Uncle Wolf," "Monopoly Mike," "Machiavelli of Eighth Avenue," and other less polite names. "Nothing short of the stingiest man in the world," was columnist Jimmy Cannon's impression.[173]

The great author, screenwriter, and journalist Budd Schulberg once asked a grizzled old fight manager who knew Jacobs, "Isn't there anybody who likes him?"

"His mother used to like him, but she passed on," came the reply.[174]

Fifty-seven years old at the time of the Armstrong-Sarron negotiations, Jacobs had not yet reached the pinnacle of his career. Still, he was ubiquitous in the New York boxing business, recognizable for the ever-present cigar strangled between his poorly done false teeth. Small but dark and penetrating, his beady eyes had stared down many a rival at the negotiating table from beneath the arched eyebrows of a comic book villain.

Just as Henry Armstrong rarely took a backward step in the ring, Jacobs rarely took a misstep in his rise to preeminence in boxing promotion. Raised in a predominantly Irish section of New York, he was the son of Eastern European Jews who emigrated to the States via Dublin. A born hustler, he started as a child hawking newspapers and then pressuring men into buying sweets and sodas for their dates on tourist boats. He invested his profits into buying concession stands on the boats and at Coney Island and hired employees to run them. "After sixteen, I was never broke again," he once bragged.[175]

Soon enough, his booths sold tickets for the boat rides, and then he bought the boats. Ticket selling became his focus, and he became New York's fastest-rising ticket broker, specializing in the arts, entertainment, and sports. Once gaining dominion over that market, he saw the profit in being the man who financed the events, too. Barnum and Bailey's Circus, Buffalo Bill's Wild West Show, Broadway plays, the Metropolitan Opera House, and the Fifth Avenue Fashion Show were all events and venues that benefited from Jacobs's ever-deepening pockets in the first decades of the twentieth century.

Jacobs was not a boxing fan; he was a fan of money. While visiting Nevada in 1904, he finally met a man whose ambitions rivaled his own, boxing promoter George "Tex" Rickard. Rickard was six years away from organizing the historic heavyweight title fight between Jack Johnson and James Jeffries. Years later, Rickard signed Jack Dempsey and was on his way to raking in millions. He promoted Dempsey's fights with significant investments from Jacobs, who naturally got a piece of the action in return.

Jacobs was not attending the fights (Why take up an extra seat you could sell?), but he was attending business meetings about the fights, observing, learning, and making connections. He absorbed Rickard's story-telling abilities and his knack for framing a political or moral struggle around Dempsey's fights, thus rendering his promotions relevant to those who might otherwise ignore boxing. Using this framework, Jacobs helped Rickard assemble boxing's first million-dollar gate between American Dempsey, an accused draft dodger, and Frenchman Georges Carpentier, a decorated hero of the Great War. He may have also helped Rickard put together the financing to build Madison Square Garden.[176]

After Rickard's unexpected demise in early 1929, the Madison Square Garden Corporation surprised many by naming fight manager Jimmy Johnston as its new promoter, leaving Jacobs, until then thought to be the heir apparent, out in the cold. Some said the Garden's board saw Johnston as a less shrewd and consequently more compliant choice.

For a time, Jacobs returned to his ticket brokerage. But by 1934, he was effectively orchestrating a coup within New York boxing's power structure by ingratiating himself to the wife of William Randolph Hearst, the multi-millionaire media mogul. He created a new promotional company called the Twentieth Century Sporting Club and offered a lower rent for events put on by the Free Milk Fund for Babies (Mrs. Hearst's favorite charity) compared to the rates offered by Johnston and the Garden. In a secret meeting, he made prominent Hearst-employed sportswriters silent partners in the Club in exchange for their agreement to give his promotions free and glowing press. Naturally, said writers would be much less enthusiastic in praising Johnston's events.

Initially unable to book shows at the Garden, the Twentieth Century Sporting Club spread out its boxing events between New York's Hippodrome and various ballparks. Johnston had the heavyweight division all tied up thanks to his contract with champion Max Baer, so most stars of the sport's most lucrative division were unavailable. Instead, Jacobs patiently and quietly signed up all the best talents south of heavyweight that he could find. Barney Ross, the slick and handsome multi-division champion out of Chicago, was the first of his big stars.

In the Autumn of 1937, Jacobs put together a "Carnival of Champions" at New York's Polo Grounds. It lasted over four hours and featured eight of his non-heavyweight stars going at each other in title fights. Harry Jeffra took the bantamweight crown from Sixto Escobar. Fred Apostoli stopped Europe's middleweight champion Marcel Thil. Barney Ross defended the welterweight championship against Ceferino Garcia. And Lou Ambers held onto his lightweight honors against Pedro Montanez.

Between his promised percentage to the milk fund and the guarantees for his fighters, the event was a short-term financial loss for the Twentieth Century Sporting Club. However, it had served notice to boxing that Mike Jacobs now had a whole cast of stars in his stable. Jacobs' sportswriter partners spilled Hearst-bought ink all over New York about the Carnival of Champions. Looking at his company's future in the long run, Mike knew the expensive extravaganza had been anything but a flop.

Sitting ringside that night was Jacobs's newest and brightest star, the new heavyweight champion of the world, Joe Louis, who had knocked out Max Baer's conqueror, Jim Braddock, two months prior. Joe did not fight in the Carnival but was brought into the ring to wave to the crowd before the fisticuffs began.

The Twentieth Century Sporting Club's signing of Louis in 1935 was nothing short of a coup in boxing. In truth, Jacobs did not so much steal Louis away from Jimmy Johnston and the Garden as Johnston lost him. Back then, Louis was a knockout-producing sensation in the Midwest. His manager, the dapper Detroit racketeer John Roxborough, thought it time to bring his fighter East. He picked up the phone and put in a call to Johnston. Aware that Louis was a Black man but assuming Roxborough was white, Johnston made the error of referring to Joe as a "nigger" during the conversation. As such, insisted Johnston, Louis must agree to lose to the white men he faced in the Garden. As soon as the call was through – which did not take long – Roxborough phoned Jacobs, and Johnston lost out on the biggest ticket seller in sports since Jack Dempsey.[177]

It was not so much that Jacobs, a Jew raised in an Irish neighborhood, was without racial prejudices; to him, Black people were "schwartzes." It was that Jacobs saw everybody in varying shades of dollar bill green. If Joe Louis could fill arenas to the rafters with Black fans by winning, Mike Jacobs wanted him to win and win often. He saw no need for Louis to throw fights, and that was enough for Roxborough. Louis signed the deal and came East, and two years later, Mike Jacobs had himself a sensationally popular heavyweight champion.

Now there was a smaller Black fighter out of Los Angeles thrilling fans in New York City with his all-out attack and string of knockouts. Jacobs saw snatching up Henry Armstrong as the next step toward his goal of taking Madison Square Garden for his own.

Jacobs approached Eddie Mead about a fight with Sarron. Mead had considered permanently moving Henry up to lightweight and sending him after champion Lou Ambers. However, with Mike Jacobs now presenting a deal, Mead was confident Henry could still make featherweight and take Sarron first.

With Mead on board, Jacobs shot off a cable to Jimmy Erwin, Sarron's manager, who was with his fighter in South Africa. After eight fights abroad, Erwin and Sarron were anxious to return home, and a big payday against

Armstrong would be a welcome homecoming gift. They cabled back, "Request Nat Fleischer, Editor of The Ring, handle all negotiations. Has authority to act as our representative." Meanwhile, they let Fleischer know they wanted a fifteen-thousand-dollar guarantee to put Sarron's championship on the line.[178]

Fleischer had once been an employee of Jacobs's, and he still had some ties to the promoter that stretched the definition of journalistic integrity. He presented Sarron's demands to Jacobs and the rest of the brain trust at the Twentieth Century Sporting Club. The Club was anxious to finally make their move against Johnston with a show in the Garden, and they thought the long-awaited featherweight championship match was the right way to do it. The Club's matchmaker Al Weill offered Henry 12.5% of the gate. Mead refused and held out for a week. Finally, it was agreed that Henry Armstrong would get 14.5% (or 17.5%, depending on the source) of the gate, and Sarron would get a flat fifteen-thousand-dollar guarantee.[179]

Henry had not fought at or under the featherweight limit of 126 pounds since his first fight with Mike Belloise a year earlier. Dropping the necessary weight required a strict diet. The skeptical NYSAC weighed him multiple times in the days leading up to the fight. For the first, he weighed 130 pounds. Two days before the fight, Henry weighed 127 pounds. A day later, he had shot up to 129 pounds. After a day of exhaustive exercise and only beef broth to eat or drink, Henry came in a half pound below 126 on the morning of October 29, the day of the fight. Sarron had no trouble coming in at 124 pounds. Betting had Henry as the three-to-one favorite.[180]

After the weigh-in, to escape the flash bulbs and questions of the press, and the stress that came with his first true championship match, starving Henry made his way to a friend's house for breakfast and then disappeared alone into a bedroom. He could not sleep, but he rested, staring at the ceiling and thinking about his heroes Kid Chocolate, Joe Gans, and George Dixon, little Black fighters who became champions despite the opponents, the pressure, and the prejudices before them. Emerging around seven in the evening, he got into a car with Harry and headed for Madison Square Garden.

They arrived at the arena an hour early. In the dressing room, both Henry and Harry were full of restless energy. Al Jolson stopped in and told them he had bet ten thousand dollars on an Armstrong victory. Henry joked with Jolson to hide his nervousness and give Al some confidence in his wager. He took his typical twenty minutes to warm up before a fight so that he would not be "caught cold" by an opponent; this was an unusually long time compared to most fighters' routines but standard for Henry. He furiously shadow-boxed for seven rounds and then took a rub-down before donning a new dark blue robe with skull-and-crossbones stitched on the back beneath his name, a gift from his wife.

It is customary for the challenger in a title fight to enter first and await the champion. As Henry made the way to the ring with a police escort, a cascade of cheers accompanied him. Nearly twelve thousand fight fans attended, producing a gate of $37,408. The champion entered a short time later and shook hands with his challenger. They had only just met for the first time a couple of days earlier.[181]

Henry's nervousness spiked as ring announcer Harry Balogh reviewed the standard preliminary announcements and introductions. Wanting to get to the fight and burn off this anxiety, he felt angry at Balough for taking so long. Then there were the referee's instructions, also seemingly interminable to Henry.

"He's not fighting a punk now," muttered Sarron as the fighters customarily met at the center of the ring. That only made Henry more impatient to get going. After what seemed an eternity, the opening bell clanged, and Henry could finally let go.[182]

He charged out quickly, expecting to have to chase Sarron down, but was surprised when the champion willingly met him toe-to-toe. Even more shocking, Sarron's quicker hands were getting the better of the slugging. His punches did not hurt much, but they sure came in bunches. In moments, Henry experienced the unfamiliar sensation of having his own back against the ropes as Sarron piled up combinations. Henry did not let up, but he felt himself trailing through the first three rounds.

At one point, Sarron smashed a punch right into Henry's windpipe and followed it up with another hard shot that caved in his belly. For a time, Henry could not catch his breath and felt nauseous. He eventually recovered but had the troubling suspicion that he might have met his match.[183]

"Armstrong was frankly puzzled," reported the *Daily News*. Henry had expected Sarron's speed but not his aggression. It took him time to adjust, but he kept firing back at the champion, and his superior punching power began to show its effects on the slowing Sarron.[184]

In the words of Fleischer, both fighters showed "a brand of courage that only ring gladiators who possess a true fighting heart could show. No finer display had been seen in the Garden ring in many moons."[185]

Gradually, Henry noticed that the champion's knees would momentarily buckle whenever Henry caught him with a good one to the gut. Sarron's aggression was starting to trail off, too. Henry did better in the fourth and fifth rounds, but reporters at ringside still gave those frames to the champion.

Sensing his chance to turn the tables and maybe close the show, Henry came out looking for a kill shot in the sixth. He charged into Sarron, landed fourteen unanswered punches, and "with the suddenness of a cobra striking its prey," he let go of a powerful left uppercut up the center of Sarron's guard. As the champion's head flew up, Henry wrapped around his favorite right cross to the temple, and that was that. Sarron crumpled in a daze to his knees, and referee Arthur Donovan counted him out. It was the first time in a career of over one hundred fights that the skilled Petey Sarron had been off his feet. Donovan knelt to pick up the former champion, and a reporter heard Sarron ask the ref, "What happened?"[186]

Skilled and rugged Petey Sarron received a booming cheer from the crowd as he stepped out of the ring as an ex-champion for the first time. He looked up at them and allowed himself a faint smile in gratitude.

"I just forgot to duck," the former champion told reporters afterward.[187]

"People forget Sarron," Henry pointed out years later, "but he was a good champ. He could punch and take a punch, and he was willing to fight with you."[188]

Sarron fought on, but never again for a world championship. He won eleven consecutive bouts before dropping a decision to future lightweight champion Sammy Angott. After fourteen years in the ring as a pro, he retired in 1939. Later, he moved to Florida and served as secretary of that state's boxing commission. He passed away July 3, 1994, at age eighty-seven and was posthumously inducted into the International Boxing Hall of Fame in 2016.

Donovan counts out Sarron.
*New York Times,* **October 30, 1937**

# 9.
# Breakdown of a Champion

Henry Armstrong was the undisputed featherweight champion of the world, the first in seven years. The NBA, the NYSAC, California, *The Ring*, Mike Jacobs, Madison Square Garden Corporation, and the rest of the world were convinced. As Henry made his way out of the Garden ring and through the arena after knocking out Petey Sarron, his eardrums reverberated with the crowd's roar. They experienced one of the most thrilling championship battles in years, capped with a conclusive knockout. The victor was an exciting young scrapper who could be counted on to provide thrills every time he entered the ring – win, lose, or draw. He had been doing a lot of winning of late. He had been a street fighter, a railroad worker, a dishwasher, a hobo, and a penniless waif. Yet he had triumphed over it all to become a champion. In Henry Armstrong, the people of Depression-era New York, especially the Black fans from Harlem packing the arena, saw their own stories in his past and their hopes in his future.

Harlemites swarmed around him during his walk to the dressing room. Some were familiar faces, but most were elated strangers. He may have been born in Mississippi, raised in Missouri, and a resident of California, but it mattered little to them. Lots of them had escaped the South, too. They patted him on the shoulders and back, asked to shake his hand, begged for autographs, and sang his praises all the way to the dressing room. There, Henry faced a battalion of reporters firing away with questions. At the same time, photographers' flashbulbs exploded in his face. Eddie and Harry eventually forced the newspapermen out and locked the door.

Later, as Henry, Harry, and Eddie Mead escaped the Garden and got in a car, Harry turned to Henry and said the perfect words for the moment. "Those are Kid Chocolate's shoes you're wearing now, so be sure you take good care of them," the smiling trainer quipped. As those words sank in, Henry finally considered the reality of his accomplishment. He thought of that younger version of himself daydreaming about being a boxing champion and having the kind of wealth and fame that the Kid enjoyed, and he felt a sense of satisfaction. That the words came from Harry, the friend who had been with him from the beginning, and a man who used compliments sparingly, made it all even more gratifying.[189]

It was time to celebrate. Eddie Mead dropped Henry and Harry off at the Club Plantation in Harlem, where his wife and friends awaited his arrival for a victory party. He had been here before after making his New York bouts with Mike Belloise and Aldo Spoldi, but that did not prepare him for the reception he received after beating Sarron. A drum roll announced his entrance, and the room otherwise went quiet. Henry felt everyone's eyes settle on him.[190]

Suddenly, cheers went up, and a crowd of people surrounded him. Celebrities he had only seen on stage and screen, on the ball field, or in magazines treated him like a beloved family member and ensured that a free drink was always in his hand. From his entrance to his return to his hotel room, the rest of the night was a blur of champagne toasts, boisterous laughs, hand-shaking strangers, winking women, and swing music.

Henry may have been riding high after the Sarron victory and the adulation that came with it, but Eddie Mead ensured he had no time to rest on his laurels with four non-title fights in two months. By November 19, he was back in the Garden to bloody and then stop undefeated Billy Beauhold in five rounds. Fifteen thousand fans watched, more than had turned out for the Sarron fight. Just four days later, he was on the other side of the state in Buffalo, knocking out Joey Brown in two. A third fight with lightweight contender Tony Chavez in front of a crowd of twelve thousand on December 6 at a Christmas charity event in Cleveland found Chavez unable to survive the first round. Less than a week later, Henry was way down in New Orleans, enjoying the nightlife and knocking out the overmatched Johnny Jones in two rounds.[191]

The easy Jones win capped off a phenomenal 1937 for Henry Armstrong, comprising twenty-seven consecutive victories in twelve months, twenty-six of them by knockout. For the first time, he had not lost a single fight all year. Those who had fallen before him included Mike Belloise, Frankie Klick, Benny Bass, all former champions, and the reigning champ Petey Sarron. He had avenged his disqualification loss the prior year to Chavez with two knockouts. Only Italy's champion Aldo Spoldi had made it the distance. It had undoubtedly been the best year of his professional boxing career to date. Sixty years later, *The Ring* magazine considered Henry Armstrong's 1937 "may be the greatest year of any fighter's career."[192]

Henry finally took a train from New Orleans home to Los Angeles, where his hometown fans feted him with more parties and feasts at cafes and nightclubs. He was home only long enough to celebrate Christmas with Willa Mae and Lanetta before heading back out for New York City, where he collected a special award from Nat Fleischer shortly after the New Year.

The March 1938 issue of *The Ring* magazine, published in January, awarded Henry Armstrong its annual award as "Most Valuable Boxer of 1937." At the time, readers' votes and a panel of experts determined the recipient. In the magazine's scoring system to determine the winner, Henry received 7,235 points, with runner-up Joe Louis receiving 6,005, even though Louis had finally won the heavyweight championship that year, becoming the first Black man to do so in twenty-two years. Henry was the first fighter to receive the vote of every sportswriter polled since the magazine's inception in 1922. He was the second Black man to win the award (Louis had been the first, in 1936). A silver medal personally presented by Fleischer was "the most coveted honor that can come to a fighter apart from the winning of a world championship," at least according to *The Ring* staff member Daniel M. Daniel.

"If there was anybody in boxing last year who made dramatic history, who met all comers, who showed superlative skill not only in his own division but against heavier men, it was Armstrong," wrote Daniel.[193]

"Hurricane Henry," "Homicide Hank," "Hammerin' Hank," "Howizer Hank," "Perpetual Motion," "Hurryin' Henry," "The Tan Terror," "The Black Blitzkrieg," "The Human Inferno," and "The Human Buzz-Saw." A new nickname seemed to be invented for Henry every week. There were plenty more, but those were the ones that seemed to stick. They all captured what amazed the sportswriters and fans so much about the entertaining young fighter: his unique melding of ruthless attack and seemingly limitless endurance.

Henry appreciated the compliments but told a reporter, "They've called me something of a 'miracle fighter.' They've exaggerated on this point, I'm afraid. All I do is to fight my best, keep moving, keep the arms swinging." He admitted that he was mostly out of control during a fight. "I don't know what I'm doing when that bell rings," he told the *New Yorker*.

Whether the sportswriters were resorting to hyperbole or not, such ceaseless fighting ferocity had not been seen in at least a decade, when "The Human Windmill," Harry Greb ruled the middleweight division, but some said Henry outworked even Greb. He came at every opponent as though he were a violent force of nature like a "Hurricane." When he finished with them, they often lay there motionless as though they were the victims of a "Homicide."

The cold, detached persona that took him over in the dressing room beforehand made his bloodthirstiness inside the ropes even more chilling. In Eddie Mead's words, Henry "sweats ice water in the dressing room." Then the bell would ring, and it seemed his blood was on fire with a lust for battle.[194]

His busy schedule and success pleased promoters and fans, but privately he wondered if every fight was on the level. "I'm sure some men I fought against took a dive," he later admitted of this period. He said he knew of one occasion where Mead made at least one attempt to fix a fight, "probably more."[195]

Writing about his career in *Argosy* in 1955, Henry remembered that Eddie's plan for the fix nearly backfired. "The other fellow agreed to take a dive in the fourth round for $2,500; then he tried to double cross me by catching me napping and beating me." Instead of laying down in the fourth like he was supposed to, the opponent attacked, landing several hard blows. In the corner afterward, Mead revealed the plot to Henry, who angrily knocked out the other man in the fifth. "He thought he would catch me asleep and be the big man.... All he was able to collect was an iron-studded KO - without the $2,500." Henry never specified which opponent (or opponents) might have taken payoffs.[196]

On January 12, 1938, *Life* magazine photographer Carl Mydans shadowed Henry for nearly the entire day of his scheduled non-title fight in Madison Square Garden against Italy's Enrico Venturi, beginning with his weigh-in at the NYSAC's office and ending with the fight. *Life* claimed the profile to be "probably the most complete photographic documentation of a boxer's life on the day of a fight." There were photos of Henry reading the newspaper, savoring a steak, walking to the Garden, signing income tax forms, and getting his hands wrapped in gauze in preparation for the fight. Even Eddie Mead made it into a couple of shots. Mydans also captured Venturi's manager Carmine Tarantino losing his temper and getting restrained after an argument over the length of Henry's hand wraps.[197]

The Venturi fight before 12,500 fans on a snowy evening at the Garden caused subsequent headlines due to Venturi's claims of a foul. Henry put Venturi – the former lightweight champion of Europe – down in the sixth round with a right to the jaw. The Italian rose, but Henry let loose another right to the belly, and Venturi dropped to his knees and motioned to referee Arthur Donovan that the blow was low. Donovan issued a warning to Armstrong. Meanwhile, his face red and contorted, Venturi fell backward to lie prostrate on the floor. Suddenly ignoring the alleged foul, Donovan counted Venturi out.

James Dawson, a writer for the *New York Times*, thought "the punch which ended the fight seemed fair." Mydans's photo of the punch, published in the *Life* pictorial, shows that it landed right on the beltline. A doctor who examined Venturi in the dressing room later testified that the blow had likely been below the belt but had not hit the groin.

The NYSAC ordered Mike Jacobs to withhold the loser's purse pending an investigation. They eventually released the purse to Venturi but suspended him for 120 days for his "unsatisfactory" performance and for coming in over the agreed-upon 137-pound weight limit for the fight. The knockout victory for Armstrong stood official.[198]

On January 21 and 22, Henry fought two nights in a row, something he had not done since his amateur days. On the twenty-first, he stopped Hollywood's Frankie Castillo in three rounds. The next night, he finished Tucson's Tommy Brown in two. Both shows were in Arizona.

During the Great Depression, boxing champions fought often, particularly the champions of the smaller divisions. Sometimes they put their title on the line, but they frequently fought in non-title fights, which almost always took place while they were over their division's weight limit.

It was also not unheard of for champions to travel between major cities for these matches. At a time when money was scarce, fighters and their management sought to fill their bank accounts as often as possible, and that meant fighting. This was doubly true of champions of smaller divisions, as they generally drew smaller crowds and smaller gates than their larger counterparts. In the years before television, this meant fighting in cities where people did not often have a chance to see the champ in action, and thus they would be willing to come out. Managers and promoters did not want the New York, Chicago, and Los Angeles crowds to get bored of their stars, so it sometimes did them well to take the show on the road.

Eddie Mead had Henry on a pace of fighting and traveling through 1937 and 1938 that was beyond excessive, even for the Great Depression. The schedule was exhaustingly disorganized. Henry would be fighting in New York City one night, in Los Angeles a few nights later, and then return to New York for another fight a week or so afterward. If the boxing would not wear Henry out, the traveling threatened to. He was not so much moving forward as he was spinning in confusing circles.

In hindsight, boxing insiders and sportswriters criticized Mead for overworking his fighter. Eddie's reasons for doing so may lay in the stories of Fritzie Zivic, the star Pittsburgh fighter who would eventually become one of Henry's great rivals.

In a later interview with Peter Heller, Zivic said that Eddie Mead "was doing a lot of monkey business at the time." When Eddie came up short at the racetrack or did not have the funds to bet on a big race, he borrowed money. According to Zivic, Mead borrowed as much as ten thousand dollars at a time from Mike Jacobs. "He figured he'd get it back," explained Zivic, "he's got Armstrong, and he borrowed some more, borrowed some more." For Jacobs, keeping Mead in debt meant keeping the manager locked in a conflict of interest with his fighter. So long as Armstrong's manager was in his pocket, he could trust that manager to advise Armstrong how Jacobs saw fit.

Of course, Mead was not just borrowing from Jacobs. On the road, where Jacobs was unavailable, Mead went to Henry, who loyally forked over the cash for Mead's next losing bet.

Henry was gambling and losing, too. He would repeatedly lose two hundred dollars on one race and head right back in to bet another two hundred. He had begun to enjoy the life of a celebrity as well. "I was so big, I didn't really know what was happening," he would remember when his days of stardom and wealth were far behind. He now insisted on fifty-dollars-per-night hotel rooms and spent money on ladies who were not his wife, another expensive habit. On one occasion, Henry donated his entire fight purse to the widow of a deceased boxing judge.

To keep the money flowing, fighter and manager needed to keep the fights coming. At first, for a young boxer who had gotten his start battling three or four times a night in bootleg battles, fighting once a week or even every other day may have seemed restful. However, combining that frequency with Henry's all-or-nothing fighting style meant punishing wear and tear on his body and psyche.[199]

The championship, big money, losing bets, loans, parties, alcohol, reporters, fans, managers, promoters, movie stars, women, photographers, and continuous training. Bouncing between Los Angeles, New York, Los Angeles again, New York again, Washington, Detroit, Pittsburgh, New York again, Youngstown, Philadelphia, New York again, Los Angeles again, New York again, Buffalo, Cleveland, New Orleans, Los Angeles again, New York again, Phoenix, Tucson. Fight after fight, sometimes just days apart, yet in different regions of the country.

It all came to a head in late January 1938. Following his knockout of Tommy Brown in Tucson, Henry, Harry, and Eddie were on the road home to L.A. when the stress over it all suddenly overwhelmed Henry. He never revealed what he felt or did during that trip except to say that he suffered a nervous breakdown. The directionless swirling burned him out. Whatever happened, it was concerning enough to convince Eddie and Harry to make a detour to a ranch "rest home" in Fontana, California, and leave Henry there to recuperate.

Albert "Chalky" Wright

Henry barely had time to take a deep breath before Eddie Mead returned less than a week later to pick him up and take him to a fight in Los Angeles. Mead made sure no word of the breakdown made it to the papers.

The L.A. opponent would be no pushover, either. Eddie matched Henry with his friend Albert "Chalky" Wright. Henry had known Chalky for years, from when they were both California featherweight prospects managed by Wirt Ross. In those beginning days of Henry's career, he had served as Wright's sparring partner and had gotten the better of him in plenty of those scraps. But a professional fight was different, and Henry could not afford to take Wright lightly.

Chalky was born in Colorado but moved with his mother to Los Angeles as a child after his father abandoned the family. He turned pro shortly after his sixteenth birthday to help keep food on the family's table. He also spent some time as a chauffeur for Mae West, the glamorous actress and connoisseur of prizefighters.

By the time they met in the ring, Wright was already a veteran of at least 126 pro bouts. Like Henry's early record, Wright's record was peppered with losses (twenty of them, to be exact), most coming early in his career, as he learned his craft on the job. Over time, he developed into a tremendous boxer-puncher with impressive defensive technique as well as precision punching accuracy and efficiency. One of his future opponents, Willie Pep, would later say that Chalky was "the hardest puncher that the featherweight division had had in the past twenty or thirty years." Of late, he had lost a ten-round decision to Baby Arizmendi, but that was his sole defeat in his last nineteen fights. Although the newspaper columns anticipating the fight read like they were advance obituaries for Wright, Henry knew he had a live underdog in front of him.[200]

It was Henry's first fight in L.A.'s Olympic Auditorium in over six months and his first since winning the undisputed featherweight championship. The Los Angeles papers filled their sports pages with ink about the returning hero. "A CONQUERER, returning from the wars of many a canvas battlefield, returns tonight to receive the homage of his hometown crowd at Olympic Auditorium," heralded Ken Frogley's column in the *Los Angeles Daily News* on the day of the fight. "He is Henry Armstrong, possibly the most popular fighter in America today, the lad who has dethroned even Joe Louis as king in the hearts of the colored folk." It was the first time two Black fighters occupied main event status at the Olympic in over a decade.[201]

Ten thousand four hundred fans packed the Olympic to capacity on February 1, 1938. Henry came in at 130 ½ pounds, Chalky at 128 ¼. With both men over the featherweight limit, it was a non-title affair. Chalky used all his guile to survive the first, Armstrong chasing after him. Armstrong scored a knockdown in the second but was impressed that Chalky quickly made it to his feet. A left hook dropped Wright to his knees in the next round. He rose only to have Armstrong on top of him, looking for the finish. Henry landed a big right to the jaw. Wright "seemed to fly through the air several feet to land on the canvas, out cold," Henry later remembered. Once Chalky's cornermen revived him, Henry immediately checked on his friend and was happy to see that he seemed unhurt.

It would take another three years, but Chalky got his shot at the featherweight championship. On September 11, 1941, he scored an impressive knockout of champion Joey Archibald to take the title. After two successful defenses, he lost a fifteen-round decision to the supremely skilled Willie Pep in 1942. Wright and Pep would go on to battle three more times, Pep always the victor. After twenty years and 160 victories in the ring, Chalky finally hung up his gloves in 1948. Gambling losses and alcoholism sapped his savings, and by 1957, he was back living in his mother's home, where he died following a fall at just forty-four years of age.

Though they were friends, Henry did not have much pity for Chalky's fate. By Henry's estimate, Chalky blew about $200,000 in ring earnings. "You see, he'd drink a lot," Henry remembered to Peter Heller years later. "The fellow was just a lucky guy.... He got all kinds of breaks. He bothered around with all the gangsters." Wright was posthumously inducted into the International Boxing Hall of Fame in 1997.[202]

After the triumphant homecoming in L.A., it was back on the road for Henry Armstrong. North to San Francisco to stop Al Citrino in four rounds. Citrino "kept throwing himself in the buzz-saw's teeth. The buzz-saw kept cutting him down," the *San Francisco Examiner* reported.

On to Chicago to stop contender Everett Rightmire inside of three on September 25. Rightmire fainted in his dressing room before the fight. His handlers had to revive him and drag him to the ring, where they propped him up as target practice for the man the *Chicago Tribune* described as a "black rocket."

Then, in a fight in Minneapolis three days later, Charley Burns got blown up by a "Dusky Dynamiter" inside two rounds. That made for four fights in February alone.[203]

A wrist injury suffered in the Burns fight forced the cancelation of scheduled bouts in Los Angeles, New York, and Butte, but Henry still managed to fight two three-round exhibition bouts in a single night for a charity event in Pasadena, California, on March 4 before entering training camp for his most important fight since winning the title, a fourth showdown with his old rival, Alberto "Baby" Arizmendi.

Arizmendi still had two wins in their rivalry over Armstrong's lone victory, and his management did not let the press forget that. Since their last meeting in August 1936, the Baby had not been nearly as busy as the new champion. He had lost a couple of bouts but managed a win over Chalky Wright and was still a ranked contender. Sportswriters considered Arizmendi Henry's first serious threat since beating Sarron.

Again, a capacity crowd of 10,400 paying customers filled the Olympic seats to see this exciting duo go toe-to-toe. Thousands more broke through a back gate and rushed inside after tickets sold out, standing in the aisles to watch the action. All were treated to a classic war that kept them on their feet and cheering almost the entire time. It was a brutal brawl, with both sides accusing the other of repeated fouls.

When the opening bell rang, the fighters went shoulder-to-shoulder at center ring and began using their legs to press each other. Henry was able to move Arizmendi backward. His quicker hands gave him the edge in that opening frame, but Arizmendi came on in a big way in the second round. He landed several clean shots to Henry's chin, and though Henry did not seem hurt, the Mexicans in the crowd cheered wildly for their countryman.

Henry battled back in the third and fourth, and by the fifth, Arizmendi's right eye was nearly shut from the jabs that Armstrong kept in his face. In the eighth, Arizmendi suffered a severe cut. In time, his face became a mask of blood and grotesquely distorted features. Still, the sturdy Mexican hero refused to back off, and remained at ring center, trading blows with a "Human Buzz-Saw."

As the tenth started, Henry intended to do everything he could to keep his twenty-seven-fight knockout streak alive. He abandoned all defense and jabs and tore in with combinations of hooks, uppercuts, and crosses, doing his utmost to put his bloodied rival away. But Arizmendi would not budge; he showed tremendous courage in meeting Henry blow-for-blow and bloodying the champion's nose.

When the final bell rang, both fighters returned visibly exhausted to their corners as the thousands in attendance roared their approval of a sensational slugfest. The referee pointed to Armstrong to indicate his victory, and now their score was even; two wins for Arizmendi and two for Armstrong.

The next day, the newspapers recognized the clear victory for Henry, but they praised Arizmendi's fighting spirit in battling through swelling and blood to make it to the finish and end Armstrong's long knockout streak.[204]

Henry got back to scoring knockouts with wins over Eddie Zivic (of Pittsburgh's famous fighting Zivic brothers) and Brooklyn's Lew Feldman through the rest of March. Zivic went out in four in Detroit on March 25, and Feldman in five in New York five days later.

Henry's team felt he needed more than quick knockouts to keep the public interested, especially now that Joe Louis had regained his stature by winning the heavyweight championship. Fight fans were now saving their money to see Joe's fights, and Mead was concerned that there would be little left over for Henry.

Henry agreed. Now that he had the title, he needed something new to push him forward and keep him from spinning his wheels fighting non-title matches against overmatched opponents until the gas ran out. He needed a sense of direction.

Mead met with George Raft and Al Jolson to discuss a plan for Henry's future. Mead and Jolson then approached Henry together with a novel plan. They informed Henry that he would pull off a stunt that no one had attempted before. He was going to win the featherweight, lightweight, and welterweight crowns, and he was going to wear them all at the same time. That, they predicted, would give him the popularity of a heavyweight and keep the big money rolling in. Big money sounded good to Henry, and he felt to his core that no boxer south of middleweight could beat him.

The proposed stunt was Jolson's brainchild. Henry knew the actor understood little about the fight business, but "Jolie" did know fame. "Him and his Hollywood ideas," Henry thought to himself. Veteran manager Mead seemed enthused by the plan, and that convinced Henry.[205]

"Ok," the fighter said to his brain trust, "get 'em together."[206]

# 10.
# "To Live, Men Must Fight"

**Al Weill**

Surely, Henry would first go for the 135-pound lightweight title before trying for welterweight all the way up at 147 pounds. It made sense to step up one division at a time, and he had primarily been fighting as a lightweight for years, anyway.

At the time, twenty-four-year-old champion Lou Ambers, a skillful yet rugged Italian American battler out of Herkimer, New York, ruled the lightweight division. He had held the title since winning a decision over the hugely popular Tony Canzoneri in 1936. Al Weill was Lou's manager, a wily veteran of the boxing business who also served as matchmaker for Mike Jacobs's Twentieth Century Sporting Club.

When negotiations between Mead, Jacobs, and Weill began for an Armstrong and Ambers matchup in March of 1938, Weill insisted upon an open-air ballpark with a larger capacity. He had no intention of putting the lucrative lightweight championship on the line for the smaller purse of an indoor arena, even Madison Square Garden. Jacobs, meanwhile, wanted to secure his position in the Garden.

Welterweight champion Barney Ross needed to get back in the ring soon, anyway, figured Jacobs. The popular Chicagoan had not fought since

September, when he suffered a hand injury while training for a title defense against Ceferino Garcia. Ross was far more popular than Ambers. A match between him and Armstrong would promise a bigger gate wherever it took place. Should Armstrong lose and the entire triple-champion plan collapse, at least Jacobs would have cashed in with the bigger payday. He stopped returning Weill's calls and informed Mead to prepare Armstrong for Barney Ross.

Weill was beside himself with outrage. He immediately resigned his position at the Twentieth Century Club and would continue to hold a grudge against Jacobs for the perceived slight. He called upon every connection he could to pressure the NYSAC to insist that Armstrong fight for Ambers's lightweight title before he could jump up to welterweight.

While the Commission deliberated this appeal, word came that interested parties in Chicago, Ross's hometown, wanted the bout there. That convinced the NYSAC to allow the Armstrong-Ross matchup before the fight and its proceeds moved to Illinois. Weill and Ambers would have to wait.

At a March 29 meeting, Jacobs and Mead conferred with Ross's manager Sam Pian and members of the NYSAC to work out a schedule for the potential fights for the Spring through Autumn of 1938. The still bitter Weill did not show, sending Ambers's trainer Charley Goldman in his stead. Ultimately, they agreed that Armstrong and Ross would battle for Ross's welterweight laurels on May 26. Should Ross win, he would defend the welterweight strap against Ambers a month later, and then Armstrong would face Ambers for the lightweight title on September 14. Should Armstrong win against Ross, he and Ambers would contest lightweight honors on July 26.

Ultimately, Jacobs warmed up to Al Weill's idea of an outdoor park but scheduled it for the Ross fight, not Ambers. Henry and Barney would fight it out at the open-air Madison Square Garden Bowl, not to be confused with the more famous indoor arena Madison Square Garden.

Another pet project of Tex Rickard, the Bowl was completed in Queens, Long Island, after Rickard's death. With boxing's popularity rising during the 1920s, Rickard wanted a larger outdoor venue to house the growing crowds that would not fit into the regular Garden. Why pay rent amounting to hundreds of thousands of dollars for Yankee Stadium and the Polo Grounds? The wooden stadium sat on asphalt across the East River from the Garden on Northern Boulevard. It had seventy-two thousand available seats and was the site where Jack Sharkey, Primo Carnera, Max Baer, and James Braddock had consecutively won the heavyweight championship between 1932 and 1935. Champion Ross would receive 37.5% of the gate and his challenger 12.5%; Jacobs and company would pocket what remained after expenses.[207]

Taking on and defeating Barney Ross at welterweight would not just be a step forward in the career of Henry Armstrong, it would be an unprecedented leap forward. A little less than two months before fight time, Henry and Harry Armstrong set up a training camp in Pompton Lakes, New Jersey. This was by far the most prolonged period of preparation Henry had ever been granted before a fight, befitting the fight's importance.

The Madison Square Garden Bowl, Long Island City, NY

"Here, during the last fourteen years, probably more fighters have rusticated than anywhere else," A.J. Liebling once wrote of Dr. Joseph Bier's pastoral property just over fifty miles northwest of Manhattan. The accommodations consisted of a seventeenth-century house, a large red barn (converted into a mess hall, rec room and bar), and a group of bungalows, where most of the visiting boxers and their teams resided. The seclusion and outdoors were prized by most New York trainers, but not all the fighters. Liebling overheard at least one boxer reared on the odors and smog of city life complaining about "too much fresh air."[208]

Filipino phenom Pancho Villa was the first significant boxer to train there in the 1920s. Most recently, Joe Louis had made it his training headquarters, beginning with his fight with Primo Carnera in the Summer of 1935.

Henry's team shared the camp with that of Louis, who was preparing to defend his heavyweight championship in a much-anticipated rematch with Max Schmeling, the German who had knocked him out two years earlier. Their camps likely had to schedule their training sessions around each other, but the red barn had a dining area, gaming tables, a radio, and a bar. Louis and Armstrong struck up a friendship over billiards and music in their precious idle hours.

For sparring partners, Eddie and Harry brought in veteran lightweight Charley Gordon, upstart welterweight Jack Murray, and a familiar face from California, Chalky Wright. In their sparring sessions, Wright put Henry to the test so well that Mead's close friend Eddie Walker signed him to a management contract. Walker would eventually guide Wright to the featherweight championship.

As the fight drew closer, Henry found time to sit with John McNulty and Harold Ross of the *New Yorker* and convey his life story. He reflected on his humble beginnings and the struggles in his early days as a starving boxer. He revealed for the first time to the press that his trainer Harry Armstrong was not his brother. But he made sure to credit Harry with being by his side from the beginning of his career, sharing boxcars, money, and food. He admitted to his love of fine linen, which he would buy to have made into custom suits, and bragged of his top bowling score of 268.

But it was Henry's love of reading and writing poetry that most intrigued the writers. The boxer spoke of his admiration for Langston Hughes' writing. Asked to share some of his verse, Henry declined, insisting that it was for Willa Mae's eyes only.[209]

While preparing himself for battle in camp, Henry sat down to scribble a few lines of verse that he would later feel confident enough to share with *Newsweek*:

Even now, journalists are steaming up a bloody combat
Between one Barney Ross, a Jewish boy, and myself,
Negro –
Two fighters of oppressed races fighting each other, just like that.
It doesn't seem exactly sensible or right.
We're not mad at each other; we're just fighting for things
we need.
It comes right back, the same old thing – to live, men must
fight.[210]

Barney Ross would have related to those words, "to live, men must fight." He had lived that truth almost from the beginning and would continue to live it long after his fight with Henry Armstrong.

A sensitive, undersized, asthmatic, and studious child raised in a strictly religious family seems like an unlikely candidate to become one of boxing's greatest champions. Such were the beginnings of Beryl Rosofsky, later to become famous as Barney Ross. In accordance with their orthodox Jewish beliefs, Barney's parents abhorred all violence, even in self-defense. However, after thieves murdered his father in his own Chicago grocery store and his mother suffered a resultant nervous breakdown, the authorities sent Barney's younger siblings to an orphanage. The once obedient and bookish boy went wild in the streets with grief and rage. He became a staple in neighborhood street fights, known for his wild attack and willingness to fight bigger boys; he organized dice games for school friends; police picked him up on multiple occasions, and he was eventually expelled from school.

**Barney Ross, "The Pride of the Ghetto"**

By his own account, Barney became an errand boy for some of Chicago's most successful and vicious gangsters, including Al Capone, Machine Gun Jack McGurn, and Bugs Moran, picking up their laundry, getting their shoes shined, and delivering secret written messages between them. He claimed to have been stunned more than most by the infamous St. Valentine's Day Massacre of the Bugs Moran gang "because I knew every one of the seven men who were killed."[211]

Ironically, Capone, the orchestrator of the shocking gangland slaying, may have saved Ross from a similar fate as those seven victims. Apparently, recognizing that Barney was meant for more than the gangster life, Capone handed the boy a twenty-dollar bill and ordered him to "get off the streets" and "go back to school or get a job." A couple of friends suggested that Barney, known as such a quick and vicious scrapper in the streets, try his hand at boxing. That seemed an excellent way for Barney to make good money, buy a home, and reunite his family.[212]

Rosofsky became Ross to hide the fact that he was boxing from his religious mother. He went on to win the Chicago Golden Gloves tournament as a featherweight in 1929 and then went to New York, where he won the inter-city title. Hooked up with manager Sam Pian, he turned pro the same year and spent the next three years building his record throughout the Midwest, bulking up into the lightweight division in the process. Eventually, he signed with the Twentieth Century Sporting Club as his promoter and became a sensation in New York, too. Once he started bringing in real money and reunited his family, his mother's apprehensions about the fight game faded.

Pian and Mike Jacobs were smart to play up Ross's Jewish ethnicity. Jews had enjoyed a prominent place in boxing's championship history since the bare-knuckle days. They made up a sizable section of the sport's loyal fanbase during the early twentieth century, cheering fistic stars like Abe Attell, Benny Leonard, Jackie Fields, Al Singer, and Max Baer on to victory. With Leonard and Attell retired and Fields, Singer, and Baer moving into the latter halves of their careers, Barney represented a new generation of sporting heroes to Jewish Americans. The press and promoters dubbed him "The Pride of the Ghetto."

"Rooting for him took your mind off worrying about the possibility that there might not be enough money at the end of the month to buy food," boxing writer Bert Randolph Sugar, who was a child in Washington D.C. during the Depression, remembered of Ross. "He filled his fans' hearts with hope when they couldn't fill their stomachs."[213]

By 1933, Ross hooked up with trainer Ray Arcel, the man regarded by many as the best teacher the sport has ever known. A fellow Jew raised in Harlem, Arcel had been a guiding force behind Benny Leonard, Jim Braddock, Teddy Yarosz and other champions when he joined Ross's camp. After Ross, Arcel would work the corners of an all-star cast of boxing legends ranging from Ezzard Charles and Tony Zale to Roberto Duran and Larry Holmes.

Ross fought two thrillers with quick and slick Tony Canzoneri in 1933, winning both the lightweight and junior welterweight (a relatively new division not yet recognized in all corners of the sport) championships in the process.

Then came three wars with slugging welterweight champion Jimmy McLarnin between 1934 and 1935, where they traded that title back and forth. He won both Canzoneri bouts and two out of three with McLarnin. That made him only the third man yet to win championships in three weight divisions if one counts the junior welterweight title; not everyone did.

After winning the welterweight strap from McClarnin a second time, Ross campaigned permanently at welterweight. Big names like Frankie Klick, Ceferino Garcia, and Izzy Janazzo failed to wrest the crown from his elusive head.

Many recognized Ross as the mythical pound-for-pound best fighter in the sport. As heavyweight champion, Joe Louis was the king of the sport, but Barney was the clear standout among the lighter divisions. He was swift of both hand and foot, possessed impeccable technique and balance, and showed a rugged warrior's heart in his rivalries with Canzoneri and McLarnin. He seemed even more unconquerable with a mastermind like Arcel as his motivator, teacher, and strategist.

"Ross, with rare ring intelligence, could adapt to any attack or defense, all the while setting up his opponent," wrote Sugar nearly seventy years later while rating Barney among the top twenty boxers in history. "Stabbing repeatedly with his left jab, Ross could make any boxer look bad, giving him a good beating and embarrassing him for good measure." If Barney had a significant flaw, sportswriters and opponents had yet to find it.[214]

Beyond his fighting prowess and Jewish heritage, Ross's personality and looks added to his popularity. He was polite and charismatic, spent his money on the latest men's fashions, enjoyed the company of movie stars and celebrity gangsters, and looked nothing like the rugged pug he was. His jet-black hair was always immaculately styled. He had dark eyes beneath expressive eyebrows. His full cheeks and beaming smile added to his boyish charm, and there were no scars or cauliflower ears to mar the impression of a pint-sized matinee idol. Ladies who otherwise could not care less about boxing flocked to Barney's fights. Other than Henry Armstrong, no other fighter south of heavyweight could draw the gates that Barney Ross drew. Putting them in the same ring brought the music of ringing cash registers to Mike Jacobs' ears.

"A good big man always beats a good little man." It had been a sports adage at least since the 1860s, its originator long since forgotten. It had been ringing true ever since, with very few exceptions. Sure, some guys had moved up in weight to win titles before. But there inevitably was a massive disparity in talent or age, or sometimes the "little" man possessed a height and frame that allowed him to pack on the pounds and come in virtually the same size or even bigger than the "big" man. At face value, Ross and Armstrong did not have a huge disparity in talent. Both were uncommonly fast, particularly with their hands. Armstrong was an indefatigable slugger, but Barney matched that with supreme boxing skills and had shown a warrior's will to win numerous times. They were both considered the two supreme non-heavyweight talents in boxing.

Ross had every physical advantage but age. They were both twenty-eight, though Henry believed he was three years younger. Ross was the bigger man. He stood about an inch and a half taller than Armstrong. Though Ross had started as a teenage amateur featherweight, he had been fighting as a welterweight for years. Experts expected him to come in around 142 pounds, while Armstrong's frame would require him to stay down around 136 pounds so that excessive bulk would not weigh him down in the ring. Some doubted that Henry was even capable of weighing as heavy as 136. Only Henry's tremendous reputation narrowed the odds to seven to five in favor of Ross.[215]

Henry did not leave Pompton Lakes until the morning of May 26, the scheduled day of the fight. More than anything else, his team's concern was making the minimum 136 pounds required to qualify for the welterweight division and challenge for the title. Anything less, and the commission might call it off for putting Henry at a dangerous size disadvantage.

To put weight on, Mead insisted that Henry constantly drink beer throughout camp, two or three before each meal and three or four after. Mead thought it would stimulate Henry's appetite. "It's the only way in the world we can put enough weight on you to save this Ross fight," he explained. So that the fans and press would not witness Henry's drinking, he and a friend would row out into the middle of a nearby lake to down the brews.[216]

Weighing himself before departure for New York, Henry found he was still not heavy enough, despite eating a massive steak for breakfast that morning. To artificially increase his weight, he began chugging down glasses of water for the rest of the morning. When he showed up for the weigh-in, he could feel the water swaying in his bloated stomach as he stepped on the scale. 138 pounds.[217]

The weigh-in provided Henry and Barney their first chance to speak to one another for any length of time, and they found they enjoyed each other's company. They kidded one another and talked about the possibility of postponement because it looked as though it might rain. Henry thought of the first time he saw Ross, then a young up-and-coming lightweight training in a Chicago gym when the novice Henry passed through the Windy City in 1931, and he was proud of how far they both had come.

Mike Jacobs habitually consulted a farmer's almanac for weather information before scheduling events, particularly at open-air parks. This time, the research failed him. As he feared, bad weather postponed the fight from Thursday, May 26 to Friday, May 27, and then again to Tuesday, May 31. In the interim, many ticket buyers lined up at the Garden box office for refunds. Jacobs was beside himself, but Henry was relieved. The extra water weighed heavily in his stomach on the original fight date, and he was afraid it would debilitate him during the fight. "I was afraid if I was hit I'd burst like a paper bag," he later joked.[218]

As they waited out the rain, Henry and crew returned to Pompton Lakes at Joe Louis's invitation, where Henry continued to train, eat, and drink. Seeing the famous heavyweight puncher sitting ringside at his sparring sessions as if taking notes made him nervous. Later, he learned that Louis's trainer Jack Blackburn wanted his fighter to study Armstrong in action. On the eve of the fight, one thousand fans and sportswriters joined Joe in watching Henry give a public workout.[219]

Not long afterward, Blackburn approached Armstrong and asked, "How'd you like to box Joe today?" Henry was flabbergasted. He fought bigger men all the time, but taking on the world's heavyweight champion seemed a bit much, even if it were just a sparring session. As Henry later recounted the story to interviewer Ted Carroll:

I looked at him like he was crazy, then he called Joe over and asked him if he wanted to box with me. Joe mumbled something, and to this very day I haven't the slightest idea what he said, but I figured the way to treat this was like a gag, so I say, 'Look this big guy is fighting a guy who knocked him out before, and if you want him to stay in the best shape don't let him take any chances with me in there.' Blackburn looked at me and scratched his head, and Joe never changed expression. Then I walked off leaving them standing there.[220]

One good side effect of the postponement was that the NYSAC waived the need for Henry to maintain the 136-pound or more weight requirement. According to Henry, that took some finagling on the part of Eddie. Henry wound up weighing in at just 133 ½ pounds on the morning of the fight. Even at that low weight, rumors spread that Armstrong had attempted to trick the scales by inserting lead weight in his shoes. NYSAC chairman John Phelan personally checked Henry's shoes and feet to make sure and found no signs of tampering. Henry was relieved by the lower weight; he felt trim and energized at 133 ½, as opposed to the bloated and queasy feeling that 138 gave him. The champion came in at 142.[221]

Though clouds threatened rain, none came on the evening of Tuesday, May 31. The temperature was crisp, around fifty degrees, in the outdoor Madison Square Garden Bowl. The threat of more rain and the need to work the next day kept many people at home. The upcoming Joe Louis and Max Schmeling rematch also meant that fans were saving money to see the big men fight. Between thirty and forty thousand fans ("pneumonia addicts," Jack Mahon of the *Daily News* called them) – roughly half the Bowl's capacity – arrived, paying $160,861.[222]

Former heavyweight champion Jim Braddock and his friend Joe DiMaggio of the New York Yankees were in the crowd. Mike Jacobs showed up without a ticket and consequently found his entrance barred by one of the Bowl's guards. His beady eyes glaring hard and cold from beneath the rim of his ubiquitous pork pie hat, the red-faced Jacobs informed the employee that he ran the joint. The guard remained steadfast. "I don't care if you're the King of England," he told Jacobs; "you don't get through without a pass." At this, the fuming promoter found the guard's supervisor and demanded he fire the guard before storming through the gate. A few minutes later, he returned and rescinded the order.

"If he won't let me in, he won't admit the phoneys," the devout capitalist reasoned, and the guard was allowed to keep his job.[223]

The chill in the night air meant Henry walked into the arena wrapped in heavy blankets. Ross had on long pants and wore a cap over his head. Towels covered his shoulders. When they met at ring center for instructions from referee Arthur Donovan, Henry in his blue robe with the skull and crossbones on the back, Barney in a warm, white bathrobe with blue stripes, the champion's height advantage appeared more pronounced than the inch and a half reported.

Ross vs. Armstrong ticket for the original date
Author's collection

After a lengthy conversation between Donovan and Ross's camp about potential fouls, the fighters returned to their corners. Henry's body quivered with nervous energy. He hopped in place, alternating from one leg to the other and pumping his fists in front of him in the seemingly interminable wait for the opening bell.

When it finally came, he bobbed and weaved toward Ross, who met him at ring center and flicked out a series of his famously quick left jabs. Henry ducked them all and began punching away with hooks. The champion returned in kind while circling Henry, hoping to keep the dangerous slugger off balance. Ross tried to backpedal out of the in-fighting and keep Henry away with his jab, but it was useless. Henry simply lunged in with wild lefts and rights that caught the champion on the sides of his head.

Before round one was over, Barney figured out that he would have to duke it out with this "Perpetual Motion" kid. Ross landed several stinging uppercuts that caught his bobbing and weaving adversary square in the face. He had worked on that punch specifically in camp to counteract the shorter fighter's bob-and-weave approach.

The fight quickly became a slugging match, Henry going to the body while Barney concentrated on the head. Both men were quick and aggressive in the early rounds, swinging for the fences, with neither having a clear advantage.

Early in the second frame, Henry caught Barney off guard with a left hook audible to the movie cameras. Putting his head in Ross's chest, he tried bullying him to the ropes, but Barney wisely turned in circles to avoid the trap and planted more sharp uppercuts on the challenger's head. When the round ended, they were shoulder-to-shoulder trading uppercuts.

At its start, the third looked like it would be a highly competitive round. The fighters traded hard, clean shots. But Ross looked uncomfortable with the pace. He was holding more now. By the closing seconds, it was evident his punches were losing steam. Meanwhile, Henry seemed to be only getting started.

Famed newsman Grantland Rice would compare Armstrong's frightening combination of savagery and firepower from the third round on to "wildcats using machine guns as well as claws."[224]

Round four was a thriller. The champion's blows seemed ineffectual to start. He held his left straight out in Henry's face to try and keep him away but to no avail. Armstrong pressed Ross against the ropes for the first time, which seemed to wake up the champion in Ross, who used his legs to push Armstrong back. Barney landed lefts and rights from all angles. For the first time in a while, the re-energized "Pride of the Ghetto" seemed to be getting the better of his challenger.

About halfway through the round, both men rose out of their crouches and flung out wild left hooks. Neither saw the other's shot coming, and both men took a hook square on the side of the head. Henry's entire upper body flung out to the side under the force. Meanwhile, Ross involuntarily skipped twice to his left to maintain his footing. The crowd erupted with a unanimous "Woooaaaah!" To everyone's surprise, neither man went down.

The fighters fell back into a shoulder-to-shoulder crouch, but only Henry threw punches. He pressed the champion backward, forcing Ross to circle away from the ropes again. Barney began letting some uppercuts go again, but there was no power behind them.

In his corner after the fourth, Ross complained to Sam Pian that he thought something was wrong with his arms; he could not put any power behind his punches. "No, kid, it isn't your arms," replied the manager. "I'm afraid your legs are gone. You can't step over to punch like you should."[225]

Blood spilled from the noses of both men as round five opened. Backing away from a shoving match, Ross tried to get his jab working again, but he left it hanging out in the open too long, a tell-tale sign of fatigue. Henry simply sent a smashing left hook around the side to the champion's face, and Ross's left eye immediately began swelling. Ross was missing more now, and Henry frequently trapped him on the ropes. Armstrong was landing four or five punches to one from his opponent.

Trapped in his corner in the final seconds of the round, Barney tried to escape but caught a crisp Armstrong left hook just as the bell rang. His head whipped to the side with the unexpected blow. He was lucky they were near his corner and did not need to go far before flopping onto his stool.

At the start of round six, Ross later remembered, "something happened to my legs. I couldn't seem to move on them, they were like Mack trucks." There was nowhere to go for Barney but the ropes, where he endured a relentless Armstrong assault. He bravely tried to fight back but found no success. When the champion returned to his corner, his team asked him what was happening.[226]

"My legs don't move right...my arms don't move right," Barney told them. "I must have had a temporary shock or something...maybe it'll go away."[227]

It did not go away in the seventh. Ross struggled to breathe and thought he might be suffering an asthma attack. As the fighters neared a corner toward the middle of a round, Barney leaned forward and caught a right hand to the back of his head. Dazed, he did not see a follow-up left hook that caught him clean. He sagged but stayed upright, only to find Henry all over him with hard shots. Ross went into full retreat. "Homicide Hank" sensed his opponent was finished, and he went wild chasing after the champion. Ross escaped execution, but the seventh had been Armstrong's best round so far.[228]

Henry threw all caution to the wind in round eight. Not bothering to defend himself against Ross's flagging jabs, he poured on the punishment. He bled from a cut lip he had sustained in training. A hard right hand sent him into a neutral corner, where Henry unloaded more combinations. It appeared that the end was near for Barney Ross. In the closing moments of the round, Henry planted his feet to prepare a killing blow when Barney suddenly let loose with a dynamite right uppercut that stopped the challenger in his tracks, staggering him just before the bell rang.

"From the ninth round on, gameness alone kept Barney on his feet," wrote Nat Fleischer. "The fans were expecting, moment after moment, for Barney to drop in his tracks." Henry walked right through the champion's punches and immediately pressed him into Ross's corner. All Ross could do was shuffle along the ropes in retreat. Meanwhile, Henry pursued with persistent combinations to the head and body.

Toward the end of the round, a knockout-hungry Armstrong let loose with wild, head-hunting hooks that mostly missed their mark. With Armstrong off-balance from his missed haymakers, Ross surprised him with several sharp uppercuts and hooks. Henry tried to duck but caught most of them in the face. The crowd cheered the champion's best moment of the round, but it proved brief. Henry's arms started pumping again, and Ross appeared too tired to defend himself or keep away.

When Ross went to his corner after the ninth, he asked his cornermen what could be wrong with him. His panicked mind reached for excuses. He asked them if it was a stroke or maybe arthritis. Had he been poisoned?

"It's nothing like that," answered Arcel, who had seen the same thing in Benny Leonard years earlier. He knew what it was. "It's only old age… it just caught up to you tonight…This is your last fight." Barney told him he was crazy and defiantly lunged off his stool to head into round ten.[229]

He walked into a ruthless Armstrong assault to both the head and kidneys. A hard left sent him into a neutral corner, where he tried to fight back, but the round was all Henry Armstrong. Eventually, Ross stopped punching back.

"Stop the fight! Stop the fight!" The horrified shouts echoed down from all sides of the arena. But referee Donovan let the beating go on to the bell.

In Ross's corner, manager Pian was deathly pale, and Arcel threatened to stop the fight. "Don't you dare!" Barney shouted at him before getting up at the sound of the bell.[230]

**Armstrong pummels Ross**

There should not have been a round eleven, but there was. Henry walked through the champion's feeble jabs as though they hadn't been thrown and continued to batter his opponent. He sent in hooks from all directions tirelessly for three minutes straight, hoping to bring an end to the slaughter.

The cries to stop the fight were getting louder, more unanimous. Ross's blood was all over both men. It soaked through Henry's gloves. One reporter described the champion as "little more than a blind and blood-smeared, tottering human punching bag." When the bell finally rang, Henry frustratedly rolled his eyes at the ceiling as he bounced away to his corner, wishing he'd had a few more seconds to end Barney's suffering.[231]

Between rounds, Arthur Donovan came to the champion's corner and told him the fight was over. He was stopping it.

"No, no, let me finish," a distraught Ross begged. He promised Donovan that he would never fight again if he let him finish the fight. Donovan relented after insisting that Ross throw some punches back at Armstrong. [232]

Still, the champion was in full retreat through most of round twelve. Henry showed signs of fatigue, too, but he was still landing the harder punches. Barney, "fighting on courage alone," still got in his shots, particularly a well-timed right uppercut directly to the face, but such moments were rare.[233]

Arcel thought he had seen enough. "Ross was really hurt in the twelfth round, and we were going to stop the fight," he later recalled. But Barney again insisted he be allowed to continue.

"You stop this fight, and I'll never talk to you for the rest of my life," he insisted. Arcel reluctantly agreed.

Overhearing this, Donovan made his way over. "You're on your own from here on in, Ross," he warned, forgetting his responsibility to protect the fighter.[234]

Of course, round thirteen was all Armstrong. He battered Barney with lefts and rights to both the ribs and face, focusing primarily on the swollen right eye. Ross could not hold his arms up. They hung helplessly at his sides. Rolling back and forth with the bombardment of hooks to his head, he took sickening punishment, and by the *New York Daily News's* account, he landed only three punches in return.[235]

The champion could hug and tie Henry up to smother his assault at times in the fourteenth. As his body instinctually entered survival mode, it produced a desperate influx of adrenaline that allowed Barney to land a series of hard lefts to Henry's face. By the end of the round, they were both fiercely trading blows.

Both boxers touched gloves in the center of the ring to start the fifteenth and final round, a traditional sign of mutual respect and sportsmanship. Henry bore in as usual and continued to land lefts and rights, though with noticeably less steam.

For the rest of his life, Henry claimed that he was carrying Ross through the final three rounds out of respect. But the fight film shows he was still a man on a mission, trying to wear down a stubborn, proud champion. He sometimes leaped off his feet to put some extra pop behind the left hooks he tossed into Barney's face. There was no holding back.

As if looking to give his fans one last show before exiting the ring for good, Ross unexpectedly livened things up with combinations of hooks and uppercuts toward the middle of this closing frame. Henry returned in kind, punctuating things with a huge left hook that landed with a loud *whack* and set some in the crowd howling in horror. Mercifully, the bell signaling the end of the fight rang shortly thereafter.

Both fighters embraced.

"You're the greatest," Barney said, and the two fighters walked together to Henry's corner, all smiles. They chatted for a moment before Barney's cornermen showed up to throw a towel over their man. They worked on his bloody, swollen, and bruised face as they walked him back to their corner. To Fleischer, Barney's visage "looked like one who had been crushed by a threshing machine." Similarly, Grantland Rice thought Barney's sides were "as raw and red as if Henry had used a battle-ax."[236]

Referee Arthur Donovan scored twelve rounds for Armstrong, two for Ross, and one even. Judge George LeCron gave Henry eleven rounds, Barney two, and scored two even. Judge Billy Cavanaugh scored ten for Armstrong, four for Ross, and one even. Unofficially, Nat Fleischer felt Henry won eleven rounds, Barney three, and one was even. Henry Armstrong was the new welterweight champion of the world, the first man ever to win both the featherweight and welterweight laurels.[237]

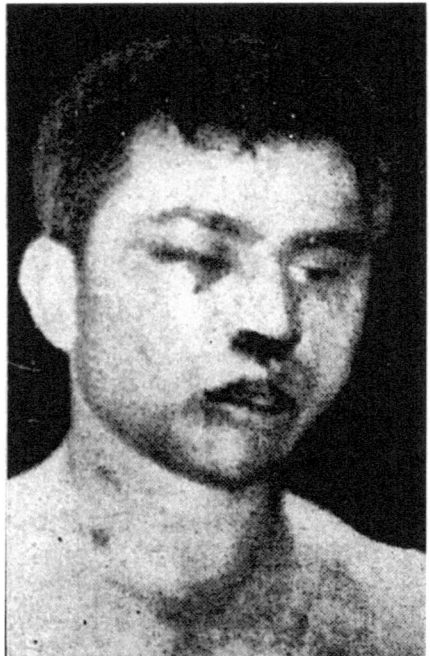

**Barney Ross, after fifteen rounds with Henry Armstrong**
*New York Daily News*, **June 1, 1938**

As Barney Ross left the ring, he was surprised by the eerie silence from the crowd, as though they were mourners at a funeral watching pallbearers transport a casket. It was disconcerting at first, but he later came to value the moment as a touching sign of respect from fight fans, a show of awe not just for the greatness of his wins but his bravery in defeat. Henry Armstrong had made the man many regarded as the best in the sport look old overnight.

"I will never forget truly great champions like Barney Ross in their days of glory," wrote Jesse Abramson in the *New York Tribune*. "He was da Vinci and Rembrandt rolled into one. Tonight, he was old and very tired against this young dynamo, Armstrong."[238]

Rice, awed by Ross's bravery, wrote that the ex-champion was "game to the last drop of blood," adding, "He took a beating that few in the history of the ring could have soaked up and still stood before the charge."[239]

Henry could not have agreed more. "He is mighty game, that Barney," the new champion admitted to the press after the fight. "Even when he could no longer punch he would try rallies and take everything I gave him."[240]

"That was my last fight," Barney told the sportswriters in his dressing room. He said Henry Armstrong was a great fighter, "a punishing, tireless battler who never rests and never gives you a chance to rest." He lamented that he had not gotten the chance to fight Henry when he, Ross, was at his peak. He said he wanted to return to Chicago and sell suits with his father-in-law for a living. "There was something missing in me tonight," he concluded.

After spending the next several days in a hospital recovering from his injuries, Barney Ross kept his promise to never fight professionally again, despite an offer of fifty thousand dollars from Mike Jacobs for a lone comeback fight. He retired with a magnificent record of seventy-two wins against just four defeats and three draws. He was never stopped or knocked out in eighty-one professional outings, not even by a prime Henry Armstrong. In its August 1938 issue, *The Ring* ran a two-page spread of photos of the Armstrong-Ross match and appropriately labeled it "Downfall of a Titan."[241]

Henry always had only good things to say about Barney over the years, referring to him as "a real gentleman" and "the cleverest and finest all-around fighter I ever fought." Many years after retirement, Henry said Barney had the biggest fighting heart he had ever encountered, adding, "Courage was written all over him."[242]

Ross would prove just how much courage he had in the next few years. At the outset of World War II, Barney volunteered for military duty. As a celebrity, he was offered a relatively safe position training military personnel and doing public relations but insisted upon facing the same dangers as any other enlisted man and was assigned to the U.S. Marines in the Pacific Theater.

On November 18, 1942, stationed at Guadalcanal, he volunteered for a small patrol of five Marines to scout out the advance of an Army regiment that would soon follow. They took out a Japanese machine gun nest and were returning when a larger party of Japanese soldiers surprised them and opened fire, killing one of Barney's fellow Marines and badly wounding the three others. That left Private Ross to fend off the enemy alone through an entire night, firing his rifle and those of his comrades and frantically tossing grenades under fire. Shrapnel from a mortar shell ripped up his side, an arm, and a leg, and a bullet shattered his left ankle. Barney fought alone for thirteen hours, trying to keep his friends alive before reinforcements rescued him on November 19. Despite his injuries, he carried one wounded Marine to safety. He had killed twenty-two Japanese soldiers and saved the lives of two Marines, not including himself. The Corps promoted him to corporal and awarded him the Silver Star "for conspicuous gallantry."[243]

Asked for comment on his harrowing experience, Barney quipped, "Those Japs aren't as tough as Henry Armstrong."[244]

After recovering in a military hospital, Ross continued to see action in the Pacific until he permanently returned stateside in February 1943 due to a severe malarial infection that would plague him for years. He became one of the celebrity heroes of the war, meeting public appearance demands of the military to drum up public support. Newspapers throughout the country told of his Guadalcanal heroics.

Meanwhile, Barney secretly fed an addiction first to the morphine hospitals had used and then to heroin. He fell thousands of dollars in debt to support his habit over the next three years, his physical and mental health deteriorated, and his wife left him.

After turning himself in for arrest (the only way to get committed for help with drug addiction at the time), Barney went into recovery at the federal Public Health Service Hospital in Kentucky. Emerging clean, he traveled the country as an expert on narcotic addiction, lecturing at schools, helping other addicts, and speaking before government committees. One of the first celebrities to speak openly about his struggles with drugs, he was an early public proponent of decriminalizing drug use and possession and instead treating addiction as an illness, while supporting heavier punishment for drug "pushers." The movies *Body and Soul* (1947) and *Monkey on My Back* (1957) were loosely based on his struggles with addiction. Ross despised both films but did publish an autobiography, *No Man Stands Alone*, co-written with Martin Abramson, in 1957.

Though he never recovered the financial security destroyed by his lavish lifestyle, gambling habit, and substance abuse as a younger man, Barney remained a well-liked figure in boxing and Hollywood. He sometimes worked as a boxing referee, was a bodyguard for Eddie Fisher and Elizabeth Taylor, and held various corporate public relations positions in his later years.

In 1963 and 1964, his name entered headlines again when he appeared as a character witness at the trial of an old friend from his days as a Chicago street kid named Jacob Rubenstein, alias Jack Ruby, the man who killed Kennedy assassin Lee Harvey Oswald. Ross and Ruby had remained in touch through their adult lives, and Ruby allegedly harbored an almost obsessive hero worship of the champion, even into middle age. Barney testified that Jack was a good friend, albeit one with a frighteningly violent temper.

From the late 1950s until his death, he was a fundraiser (and likely a gun smuggler) for the fight for Israeli independence. Barney Ross, a notorious chain smoker, died of mouth and throat cancer on January 17, 1967, at age fifty-seven. As one of the truly elite boxing champions of all time, he was among the inaugural class of inductees into the International Boxing Hall of Fame in 1990.

While Barney headed for the hospital after their fight, Henry took a shower and headed to a victory celebration in Harlem. As a car carried him to the Small's Paradise nightclub, Henry saw jubilant Black people crowding the streets, cheering his victory with no idea he was riding right by them. When he arrived at the club, it was so packed that he wondered if they had forgotten to leave room for the guest of honor.

Henry later wrote that he was overcome with the feeling of a great, invisible presence around him immediately upon entering the club, and he heard in his head the very same words he had heard as a child on his parent's porch in Mississippi. "You must go yonder and do great things… Don't forget that I am your God and maker. *Remember*?"[245]

Stunned, he stood motionless and silent. His fellow partygoers were perplexed. As they stared, Henry asked to be excused and disappeared into a private room alone. There, he thanked God for his victory and asked why He had spoken to him at this moment, but he received no reply. Eventually, Henry returned to the party and politely partook in the celebration, but he remained distracted all night before making an early exit.[246]

Back in Los Angeles, the residents of Central Avenue, the city's Black community where Henry lived, were just as jubilant over Henry's victory as those in Harlem. The United Press reported that:

> Although Central Avenue hilarity did not produce the usual number of riot calls, enthusiasm was as great as the night Joe Louis defeated Jim Braddock for the heavyweight title. Every radio in the area blared the blow-by-blow description of Armstrong's overwhelming victory over Barney Ross in New York. Newspaper extras were gobbled up by the thousands, and passed from hand to hand with joy.[247]

The June 13, 1938 edition of the mainstream magazine *Newsweek* had a photo of his victory on its cover next to a large-print caption, "Armstrong: pound for pound the world's best fighter?" A brief article inside seemed to answer the question in the affirmative while acknowledging not everything Henry did in the ring was strictly legal. It began:

> Most fighters have two weapons, their fists. Henry Armstrong has seven: his fists, his elbows, his shoulders, and his head. Also he is gifted with astounding endurance and energy, which enables him to fire all seven weapons simultaneously from the word go to the final bell.

After describing the fight, the writer reported that Henry had one hundred and fifty thousand dollars in the bank, a wife, a daughter, and a chauffeur. The Ross victory had brought him a $27,203 payday. "Eventually Armstrong wants to become a clergyman – like his father-in-law," it went on. The article closed with Henry's poem written in training camp about the fight.[248]

The jinx of the Madison Square Garden Bowl remained true. No boxing champion had successfully defended his championship inside its sprawling wooden frame. The Madison Square Garden Corporation also lost thousands of dollars promoting fights there. Sportswriters referred to it as "the Madison Square Garden *Hole*." By 1942, the expansive rows of bleachers were no more, the walls of a post office building standing in their place.[249]

Henry and Willa Mae spent the weekend after the fight in Atlantic City before returning to Los Angeles in early June. Henry took a few days to relax and enjoy the sunshine there before embarking on a new adventure. He met promoter Fred Sommers through Eddie Mead, and Sommers helped organize a softball team with Henry serving as a pitcher. The Champion

Dynamiters spent the next couple of weeks barnstorming Southern California, including a ballyhooed showdown with welterweight contender Ceferino Garcia's team, the Bolo Sluggers. However, the venture quickly ran out of money, and the team was dissolved.

After what felt like too little time back home, he took off for Pompton Lakes to check on his friend Joe Louis and his preparations for the most anticipated sporting event in at least a generation, the rematch with Germany's Max Schmeling, who had knocked Joe out two years earlier.

Now that Louis had the heavyweight championship, many regarded the coming battle with Schmeling as a battle not of men but of ideals. Schmeling was the favorite fighter of German dictator Adolf Hitler and his Nazi government. Joseph Goebbels's propagandists had made much of his win over Louis as a sign of the white man's supremacy over the black man and of German supremacy over the world. With Hitler's heavy re-armament of the German military, anti-Semitic speeches and laws, and the political upheaval he was causing in Europe, many saw war on the European horizon. They saw a metaphor in the fight between Louis and Schmeling, representing the conflict between democracy and fascism. Richard Wright referred to both fighters as "puppets" in "a conflagration of social images whose intensity and clarity had been heightened through weeks of skillful and constant agitation; social images whose appeal could evoke attitudes tantamount to two distinct ways of life in the world today."[250]

Roosevelt and Hitler knowingly participated in their nations' recruitments of Louis and Schmeling as symbols of American freedom and German strength, respectively. They made it easy for promoter Mike Jacobs to utilize Tex Rickard's old good versus evil narrative to sell tickets to the rematch. So did some pro-Nazi protestors who arrived at Pompton Lakes one day to picket Joe's training. Asked by a reporter if he was scared, Joe replied, "Yeah, I'm scared. I'm scared I might kill Schmeling."[251]

At Eddie Mead's suggestion, Louis's trainer Jack Blackburn had Henry give Joe pointers on fighting in his aggressive all-or-nothing style. While Henry and Joe worked together to devise the strategy for overwhelming Schmeling to his satisfaction, the heavyweight champion – a man of few words – turned to his friend and declared with his characteristic concision, "It won't go like it did before."[252]

Newspapers noted that Blackburn was developing a new strategy to nullify the German's dangerous counter right cross. This time, Gayle Talbot of the Associated Press observed, "Blackburn has him wading in and trying to throw punches like Henry Armstrong does." Such a strategy would be a gamble against a skilled counterpuncher, but Blackburn was confident. After all, Louis was a devastating puncher, maybe the best ever. That was why the papers called him "The Brown Bomber," wasn't it? Why not put those hard punches on Schmeling as quickly and often as possible?[253]

Henry Armstrong was part of a cavalcade of American celebrities and politicians on hand in Yankee Stadium for the historic Joe Louis and Max Schmeling championship match on Wednesday, June 22, 1938. Looking around him, he might have spotted politicians and government officials J. Edgar Hoover, Thomas E. Dewey, and Fiorello LaGuardia. There were movie stars like Gary Cooper, Clark Gable, and Douglas Fairbanks; fellow elite athletes past and present like Jack Johnson, Jack Dempsey, Gene Tunney, and Joe DiMaggio; Black musicians Louis Armstrong, Duke Ellington, Count Basie, Cab Calloway, and Ethel Waters. Evalyn Walsh McLean took her seat wearing the Hope diamond. Others of her class with last names like Astor and Roosevelt (including the President's son) sat nearby.

Famed journalists Damon Runyon, Grantland Rice, Jimmy Cannon, and others were on hand to cover the fight, of course., as were reporters representing every major paper in the country and several from abroad. Authors Ernest Hemingway and Richard Wright were present and later wrote their own remembrances of the most important cultural event in a generation.

Champion Louis got in the ring first, and Schmeling followed shortly thereafter. Eddie Mead in Joe's crowded corner alongside Jack Blackburn, two more trainers, and two managers. It was Eddie who had recommended the trademark Armstrong brawling strategy to Blackburn, and Blackburn wanted his expertise during the fight itself.

As it turned out, Joe did not give Eddie much time to offer advice. It was all over just two minutes and four seconds after the opening bell. In true Henry Armstrong fashion, Joe Louis charged out of his corner without giving the opponent a moment to think or breathe. He pounded Schmeling across the ring, hammering hooks to the head before switching to the body. As his challenger retreated along the ropes, Louis followed and crashed home a terrific right hand to Schmeling's kidney that made the German scream so loud that onlookers in the rafters later swore they heard it over their roars of approval. Because Schmeling had turned his back to him, Louis thought the wail came from a woman in the crowd. Max desperately clutched the ropes as though he had forgotten everything he knew about boxing. On came Louis's ramming right hands to the side of the head, three in succession, before Max's knees buckled, and Arthur Donovan jumped in to signal Joe to a neutral corner.

Max righted himself before the ref started counting. Germany's hero took a solitary, hesitant step forward, like a child peeking out of his bedroom door after being punished, asking, "Is it safe to come out now?" Louis was on him immediately, and a single right hand sent Schmeling tumbling forward onto the mat.

As the challenger got up for more, his knees quivered. Joe then went into full "Hurricane Henry" mode and produced an onslaught of left and right hooks around Schmeling's feeble guard, folding him in half. The German's legs were still upright. They were as straight as two steel bars – a tell-tale sign of a hurt fighter. But Max's upper body went flailing to the floor. He caught himself with his hands on the mat and stood up quickly, but only long enough to catch a right to the body and a left hook to the jaw. Max did a belly flop, and his cornermen jumped into the ring before Donovan could reach the count of seven. The fight was over.

Henry had seen celebrations in Harlem after his own title fights. They amounted to a little girl's imaginary tea parties compared to the joyful bedlam and hysteria following Joe Louis's annihilation of Max Schmeling in less than one round. Black people already regarded Louis as, in the words of Wright, "the living refutation of the hatred spewed forth daily over radios, in newspapers, in movies, and in books about their lives." With this new victory, Louis had sent their refutation worldwide.[254]

An estimated five hundred thousand people erupted into Harlem's streets in ecstasy, and many stayed there till sunrise. Tens of thousands more packed the nightclubs. New York's police chief told his men to back off, saying, "This is their night. Let them be happy." It was, reported Porter Roberts in the *Pittsburgh Courier*, "the greatest show of Negro UNITY American has ever seen!"[255]

Similar displays were happening throughout American cities and much of the world. Men and women jumped for joy in the streets of France, South Africa, Panama, Jamaica, and places as remote as the gold mines of British Guiana. In Henry's hometown neighborhoods of St. Louis and Los Angeles, the celebrations were nearly as wild as in Harlem. The Jews of Poland and Germany also celebrated but in a much more private manner.

Henry willingly joined in with the celebrants in Harlem. Joe Louis was now the most beloved Black American alive, a living, walking folk hero the likes of which his people had not known for generations, if ever. Henry certainly would have recognized this that night among his fellow celebrants in Harlem and would have known that there was nothing he would ever do as a prizefighter to eclipse Joe's popularity now. He was OK with that; he was as happy to have Joe Louis to look up to as the rest of them.

# 11.
# When Hurricanes Collide

Henry Armstrong and Joe Louis - Armstrong is wearing his *Ring* magazine welterweight belt around his waist and another personalized "special" belt from the magazine across his chest

Joe Louis and Henry Armstrong, now close friends, had risen almost simultaneously to the peak of the sporting world. Armstrong might not have symbolically vindicated democracy by smashing a Nazi idol as Louis had. Still, after winning the welterweight crown with his thrashing of the revered champion Barney Ross, he too was basking in the glow of unanimous praise.

Black columnist Billy Rowe declared Henry the greatest fighter of all. "Pound for pound, I never have seen his equal," wrote Grantland Rice, a man who had been covering the sport since the first decade of the twentieth century. "One of the greatest fighters ever," said Jack Dempsey. Jack Johnson called him the greatest fighter in thirty years. Not coincidently, Johnson won his championship precisely thirty years earlier.[256]

"Boxing writers have devised a great many nicknames to describe Armstrong," pointed out Damon Runyon. "Hurricane Henry, Homicide Henry, The Human Buzz Saw, etc. They are all understatements." The author of *Guys and Dolls* could not contain his excitement at witnessing Henry's dominance of a bigger, supremely skilled opponent. "A man would have to have an axe in there with Henry to make it even up," he theorized, "and then he would have to be an expert with it."[257]

Almost a week later, Runyon was still raving about Henry in his syndicated column. "We saw a fellow the other night who for single-mindedness of purpose beats anything we have seen in a long time.... Henry Armstrong fills our idea of a prize-fighter to a T-T-T-."[258]

With men like Dempsey and Runyon crowing their astonishment, the Ross win brought Henry to a new plateau of fame. No longer just a rising sports figure, he was a household name, and the intensity of that fame shocked him at first. When he tried to visit the Saks Fifth Avenue store to buy a horse-riding outfit, admirers mobbed him. The situation grew dangerous enough for a police officer to have to rescue him and rush him back to his car so that his chauffeur could drive him to safety.[259]

"Hurricane Henry" Armstrong was scheduled to challenge "The Herkimer Hurricane," Lou Ambers, for the lightweight title on July 26, 1938, in a much-anticipated battle. Hearing of the results of the Armstrong-Ross fight while in training for a bout with Baby Arizmendi, Ambers told the press he was ready to meet Henry anytime. He admitted that Henry was a dangerous fighter, but "I've fought several good men, and some of the best ones I've fought have been my easiest opponents. That's about all there is to say except that I'll be ready as soon as Henry is." On June 7, Arizmendi held Ambers to a ten-round draw.

Despite Ambers's professed confidence, the consensus of the sportswriters was that Ambers would fare no better than Ross. "If you see a little blond man running today like his coat-tails were on fire and glancing back fearfully over his left shoulder every now and then, the odds are you are looking at Lou Ambers," wrote Gayle Talbot.[260]

Should Armstrong win over Ambers, it would complete his intended trifecta: to hold three division championships simultaneously. When Mike Jacobs agreed to host the fight outdoors at New York's Polo Grounds, Al Weill seemed to get his wish. Ambers, as champion, would receive 37.5% of the gate to put his title on the line, while challenger Armstrong would receive 22.5%, a significant improvement over the 12.5% he got for facing Ross. Armstrong's end of the contract included his signing over exclusive promotional rights in New York to Jacobs for three years, the same provision Joe Louis had once signed.[261]

Like Barney Ross, Lou Ambers was the son of immigrants; in Lou's case, Italian immigrants who had settled in Herkimer, New York, a village between Utica and Schenectady along the Mohawk River. Antonio D'Ambrosio, Lou's father, was a saloon keeper. Just as had Henry and Barney, he had changed his name upon becoming a boxer, having been born Luigi D'Ambrosio on November 8, 1913. This made him twenty-four years old and a little less than four years younger than Henry at the time of their scheduled matchup, a sizable youth advantage by boxing standards.

Lou Ambers, "The Herkimer Hurricane"

Luigi had been a hot-tempered bully as a child, with little patience for school or church. In his teens when the Great Depression hit, he started working at a furniture company to help his family make ends meet. His real passion was the boxing lessons he was getting in the basement of St. Anthony's Church from Father Gustave Purificato.

Lou entered the illicit world of "bootleg" boxing around the same time Henry did on the other side of the country in Los Angeles. His career record is possibly missing dozens of early smokers from in and around Herkimer. Young D'Ambrosio could relate to Barney Ross's fear that his mother might one day find out about his being a prizefighter, so he signed up for boxing matches under two different names, Otis Paradise and Lou Ambers. Once word inevitably got out, he went ahead and settled on Ambers.

By 1933, he was an undefeated prospect still in his teens working as a sparring partner for his idol Tony Canzoneri when he met Weill, the French-born businessman who sometimes worked as a matchmaker, sometimes as a promoter. Weill liked what he saw in Lou and became his manager.

Weill was part of a three-man team that included trainers Charley Goldman and Whitey Bimstein, a trio some call the best corner in the history of boxing. Goldman, a former star of the bantamweight division, bore the gnarled hands, mangled nose, and cauliflower ears of a mean fighter, but his students knew him as a patient teacher with a heart of gold. "The part I like best is starting from the beginning with a green kid and watching him develop," he once told *The Ring*. Goldman was revered as "the dean" of boxing by other legendary trainers like Ray Arcel and Al Braverman.

"Name the top fighters of any class, and it's a dollar to a punch in the kisser that I've worked over them sometime or another," Bimstein bragged to one writer, and he wasn't wrong. Whitey worked the corners of more world champions than any other boxing trainer. In the 1950s, Weill, Goldman, and Bimstein would again team up to guide the career of undefeated heavyweight champion Rocky Marciano. In the 1930s, Lou Ambers benefited from their dedication, experience, and craft. Wins over talents like Tony Scarpati, Cocoa Kid, Johnny Jadick, Jimmy Leto, and Sammy Fuller came under their guidance between 1933 and 1935.[262]

Weill maneuvered Ambers into a fight with Canzoneri for the lightweight championship in 1935. He lost the bout, only the second loss of his pro career, but he whipped Fritzie Zivic, Frankie Klick, Baby Arizmendi, Scarpati, and others to earn a rematch. Scarpati died on March 20, 1936, from wounds suffered in his second fight with Lou, a tragedy that would leave its psychological mark on the victor. Lou told Al Weill he was quitting, but the manager convinced him to go on, as did a hug from Scarpati's mother at the funeral service. "But every once in awhile," Lou later remembered, "I'd look in that corner and I'd see like a picture of Tony Scarpati, God rest his soul."[263]

In his second fight with Canzoneri, Ambers outboxed and sliced up the aging legend to win the lightweight championship in Madison Square Garden on September 3, 1936. He had since made two defenses of the title, one of them a second victory over Canzoneri, the other a decision over contender Pedro Montanez as part of Mike Jacobs's "Carnival of Champions" in 1937.

With his unmarked, youthful face, feathery blond hair, and a head two sizes too big for his 5'5" frame, Lou Ambers still looked like the teenager he had been when he got started; but he possessed all the ruggedness and craft of the ring veteran that he was by 1938. Three years earlier, he had fought through the pain of a broken jaw to win a ten-round decision over Fritzie Zivic. Though no knockout artist, "The Herkimer Hurricane" was known to relish a good scrap and wear down opponents with his work rate, not unlike Armstrong. He was also very clever and could box rings around a guy if the fight called for it, as it had against the great Canzoneri. Sportswriters marveled over his hair-trigger reflexes, praising his ability to dash in, land combinations on an opponent, and then escape untouched.

Joe Louis warned Henry about another aspect of the Ambers fighting style. "Ambers has a habit of jumping in to meet a punch," the Brown Bomber told his friend. "He does it on purpose to make punches around the belt land a little low. You keep 'em high, Henry, or it can cost you."[264]

Critical respect from those who knew boxing and a world championship belt around his waist notwithstanding, Ambers was not as beloved by the public at large as were Joe Louis, Barney Ross, or Henry Armstrong; he did not have Joe's size and punch, nor Ross's leading man looks, nor did his record boast Armstrong's streak of knockout victories. But Ambers was an elite talent, and he could fight like hell.

With a long time to prepare for the matchup, Eddie Mead and Harry Armstrong set up a camp at Pompton Lakes. Henry had been fighting primarily as a lightweight for years, and there was no need to pack on the pounds by scarfing down heavy steaks and a half dozen beers daily. He could instead focus on sparring. Eddie and Harry brought in Chalky Wright as a sparring partner once more. Lew Feldman, another well-respected former opponent, also joined his team. In late July, Chalky opened some nasty cuts on Henry's lip in sparring, and Henry had to wear special headgear through the rest of training to allow them time to heal.

Lou trained in Summit, New Jersey. Observers were surprised to find the lightweight champion in slugging matches with his sparring partners, as though he planned to do the same with Armstrong. Most thought Ambers's best chance to win came with relying upon his boxing ability and movement.

"Personally, I don't think Lou is working right for the fight," Canzoneri told the Associated Press after visiting the champ in camp a few days before fight night. "He should move around more, step from side to side, instead of taking all those punches he absorbed this afternoon."

Canzoneri refused to pick a winner of the fight but revered former lightweight champ Benny Leonard seemed to lean toward Ambers in saying his boxing ability was "what it takes to beat Armstrong." Baby Arizmendi, who had faced both men in the ring, predicted an Armstrong victory by knockout.[265]

Ambers expressed his usual confidence in victory. "I'll cut up Henry Armstrong so badly, the referee will have to stop the fight," he predicted. "Don't worry about me."[266]

After Ambers injured his hand in training, Weill requested a postponement from the NYSAC. They rescheduled the bout for August 10.

With their weights expected to be close and with Ambers only three-quarters of an inch taller, Henry would not be at as much of a size disadvantage as he was against Ross. As of the morning of the tenth, betting had Armstrong the favorite to gain his third championship at one to three-and-a-half odds. The *New York Times* felt that the challenger deserved to be the favorite, but only narrowly.

"In his unorthodox way, Ambers is faster than Armstrong and unquestionably more agile than the Californian," assessed the *Times*. "His speed and agility have carried him to the heights. But in punching, resistance to punishment and the ability to administer it Armstrong clearly excels his foe and these qualifications are expected to decide the issue."[267]

Mike Jacobs probably considered throwing his farmer's almanac out of his office window when he looked up at the rainy skies on August 10 and had to postpone the fight again. The attention spans of boxing fans began to wane, and Jacobs could see his ticket sales spiraling down the drain with the rainwater. He moved the fight out a week and took it out of the Polo Grounds, moving it indoors to the Garden.

The fighters returned to their training camps to keep in shape and get in more rounds of sparring. Henry dropped Lew Feldman with a left hook on the chin in the final minute of his final day of sparring. He felt ready. Jacobs, on hand to see the challenger in action, said he was also happy with Henry's preparations.

At the weigh-in on the morning of August 17, champion Ambers came in at 134 ½ pounds and challenger Armstrong at 134, both under the required lightweight limit. The fighters were probably relieved the fight would occur inside, as the day had been sweltering and humid, and the evening was not much better. Twenty thousand fans joined them in the Garden, paying $102,000 for the privilege. The largest crowd that had ever had jammed into the arena left some folks with standing room only.[268]

While preparing in his dressing room, Henry received a visit from a familiar face, Pittsburgh's Al Iovino, the big puncher who had knocked him out in his pro debut. Henry had invited Al to make the trip from his home in Swissvale, Pennsylvania, to see the fight, all expenses paid. The old foes shook hands, and Iovino expressed his thanks and support before leaving to find his seat.

Iovino witnessed one of the most vicious and historic title fights ever. When the first round opened, Ambers got off first with two lefts to Henry's face. The crowd roared its approval, clearly rooting for the champion despite the betting odds. Henry got going with a right-left combination to the head, but only the first punch landed. From there on out, the fighters were tearing away at one another.

After heated exchanges to open the second round, Henry worked his way inside Ambers's two-and-a-half-inch reach advantage and began working over the body. When Armstrong tried going for the head, he found the champion's defensive reflexes were on point. Plenty of punches landed, but Henry was missing more than usual. After the fighters emerged from a clinch, ringsiders noticed a gash above Lou's eye. Whether a punch or a head butt caused it was not clear. The round was another slugfest. Henry closed it with another grazing shot at Lou's chin as if wanting to leave the champion with a little something to remember him by while he rested on his stool.

Taking full advantage of his greater reach, Ambers caught Armstrong coming in with a few sharp lefts to the face at the start of round three, but the rest of the round was Henry's. Lou tied his challenger up, but as soon as the referee separated them, Henry was right on top of him again.

The champion showed a greater effort in round four, and the round was a brawl that saw both men endure punishing blows. In rounds four and five, Ambers began using the right uppercut, the same punch that had been so bothersome to Armstrong against Ross. Henry retaliated with an onslaught of body blows in round five. The pro-Ambers crowd cried "foul" with virtually every body punch Henry threw, but he refused to relent. "He was a perfect little demon, a human cyclone," was how James Dawson of *The New York Times* described Henry at that moment.

**Armstrong and Ambers at war.**

With one second to go in the fifth, Henry surprised Ambers by switching from the body to the head and landing a fast right to the jaw. Lou dropped to his knees. As fighters could be saved by the bell according to the rules in force, the referee did not need to count. Al Weill leaped into the ring and dragged Lou to the corner.[269]

In the sixth, a left-right combination put Ambers back on the floor with plenty of time on the clock. He was up at the count of eight. Sensing his third championship within reach, "Homicide Hank" came in with no thought of defense and threw haymakers from every angle imaginable. Ambers stood up under the assault but could only manage ineffectual jabs in return. He found himself on the ropes trying to protect his body from the constant blows. Both men returned to their stools bleeding, Ambers from the gash above his left eye, Henry from the cuts he had suffered in training on his lip, now re-opened by the champion's blows.

The challenger continued to show an almost obsessive focus on mauling the champion's body throughout round seven. Ambers did land another sharp, well-timed uppercut and tried to dance out of danger, but it seemed to do him no good; Armstrong was always there in his chest, his hands continuously moving, his shoulders rolling, his legs pressing Lou backward. Henry trapped his man on the ropes and only picked up his work rate from there. Referee Billy Cavanaugh had to step in and take the round away from the challenger for a legitimate low blow, but Henry immediately went back to work without a let-up. As the round drew near its close, he shifted his approach to start pounding away at Lou's face.

Henry got careless at the start of the eighth and received three short rights square on the jaw. It was maybe Lou Ambers's best moment of the fight so far. Henry briefly froze in his tracks, but soon enough, those "Perpetual Motion" arms were pumping away again, and the champion's back was on the ropes again. Cavanaugh stopped the action to take yet another round away from Armstrong for punching low.

Henry was bleeding badly from a cut near his left eye, the first facial cut he had ever received in a prizefight. The bleeding lip was bothering him, too; he struggled to keep his mouthpiece in as he spat out blood to be able to breathe.

The champion took advantage of Henry's difficulty in round nine, landing lefts and rights to the head. Henry kept coming in as the round progressed, but he was also walking into accurate, well-timed punches from Lou Ambers, who punctuated the round with three successive left hooks to Henry's jaw.

The tenth saw "Hurricane Henry" and the "Herkimer Hurricane" colliding at center ring in a whirlwind of punches, with Henry getting the better of the action, though his punches were again straying low.

In the eleventh, a jolting Armstrong right rattled the champion and sent him careening across the ring. Henry afterward focused on the body. He lost another round to a low-blow call. Still, he strafed the champion with a series of unreturned punches, including another devastating right to the jaw before the bell rang to end the round.

Ambers got off to a good start in round twelve. He followed a left jab with a one-two combination to Henry's jaw. But by the end, Henry had Lou on the ropes covering up again. The referee took the round away from Henry on a foul call.

Henry's lip continued to bleed profusely. The cut near his eye and his bloody nose did not help matters. Cavanaugh came to his corner after the twelfth round to tell them he was stopping the fight based on the cuts. Appalled, Henry asked why.

"Look at the ring. It's full of blood," the ref replied.

"So what?"

"It's your blood."

"Well, I'm not going to bleed no more."

Cavanaugh was flabbergasted. "If you got that much damn nerve, I'll let you continue," he relented. But he warned Henry, "If you spit any more blood on that floor, I'm going to stop this fight."

Henry agreed. After Cavanaugh left the corner, Harry was about to apply some coagulants to Henry's cuts when Henry told him, "It's all right. I'm not going to bleed no more."

"What are you talking about?" Harry was as perplexed as the referee.

"I'm not going to spit it on the floor," Henry explained. "I'm going to swallow it."

"Oh, you're going to get sick, man, with all this tincture of iodine and collodion in your stomach," his trainer warned him.

"I'm going to win this title," Henry insisted. "Take the mouthpiece out. Don't give me no mouthpiece. Just let me go." Harry followed orders.[270]

A few seconds into the thirteenth, the crowd was on its feet, watching both fighters land heavy blows to the head. Ambers "came forth such as he had never before exhibited, and fought Armstrong to a standstill," reported Fleischer. Henry could feel himself weakening as the round progressed, and he could both feel and hear the blood and chemicals swirling around in his gut. For the first time, he was taking a backward step and then another under Ambers's resurgence. Ringsiders noticed that the challenger's punches were getting wilder; looser. Looking to end the fight, Ambers was tearing him up toward the end of the round.

The crowd was in a literal riot. Fans were not just throwing their hats in the air with delight; they were throwing their chairs, and they shouted Lou's name as they never had before.[271]

They had no idea that the thirteenth round had been a desperate final rally by the champion to retain his title. When the bell rang for round fourteen, the exhausted Ambers got up slowly from his seat and appeared to Fleischer to be out on his feet purely from fatigue. The fighting was mostly the same trading of blows upstairs, but now Henry was doing the much better work. An Armstrong right nearly put Ambers down for a third time just as the round ended, but the brave champion stayed upright.

Lou may have looked worse off to onlookers, but Henry's body had long ago entered survival mode. He would retain only vague memories of the latter part of the fight.

At the start of the fifteenth and final round, the badly battered combatants respectfully shook hands. Both men then did their best to separate the other from his consciousness with stiff blows to the head. For Henry's part, he was fighting on pure instinct. "I got up at the bell and started to swing, and that's all I remember," he wrote later. "I just kept fighting and fighting and fighting and I don't know what happened."[272]

Henry returned to punishing the body after missing a left to Lou's head. Ambers continued throwing desperately at his challenger's bloodied face. Almost as if to symbolize their evenly matched fighting prowess, they landed simultaneous hard right hands as the final bell tolled. Henry returned to his corner, looking to Jimmy Cannon of the *New York American* "like a broken egg-beater on two ramshackle clothespins."[273]

Cavanaugh scored the fight seven rounds for Armstrong, six for Ambers, and two even. Judge George LeCron scored the fight eight rounds for Armstrong, six for Ambers, with one even. Judge Marty Monroe differed, scoring eight rounds for Ambers and seven for Armstrong. Henry Armstrong received a split decision victory.

The decidedly pro-Ambers crowd hooted, hollered, and booed the verdict. Some accused the judges of robbery (as did Al Weill).

Henry was in tears as he walked back to his dressing room. He was now boxing's first simultaneous three-division champion and the only man to win three division championships in a year. It was the goal he and his team had longed for, meant to make him as famous as Joe Louis. Yet he was leaving the scene of his crowning achievement to a chorus of boos.

Despite the crowd's disgust at the decision, the correspondents from *The Ring*, *The New York Times*, *The Journal-American*, and *The New York Post* all thought Henry deserved the win. Fleischer later called the crowd's reaction "one of the most inexplicable and unjustified demonstrations seen in New York boxing in many years."[274]

Henry's mind was a mess. Whether the loss of blood, the sickness of having the blood and chemicals in his stomach, or the blows to his head caused it, there were times during the fight and afterward when he did not know where he was or what was happening. He had hallucinated through the fifteenth that he was fighting members of the Garden crowd and not Lou Ambers. Though he acknowledged his win in the ring, by the time his team made it to the dressing room, he thought he was waking up after Ambers had knocked him out. His team had to tell him that he won the fight. Years later, he had to confess, "I've seen pictures of that moment [the referee raised my hand], but I've got to admit it's a total blank to me."[275]

Once a doctor checked Henry out and confirmed he was alright, Eddie let in the press to ask their questions. The Armstrong team's eerie silence surprised those expecting the customary celebrations. Their subject lay prostrate, face up on a rubdown table, struggling to catch his breath and sucking on a large chunk of ice. "Scars, like crimson, crescent moons, curved above and under each eye," noticed Jimmy Cannon. Armstrong's bloody, gaping mouth reminded him of a hooked fish.

When he could speak, Henry said it was the toughest fight of his career. He welcomed a rematch but said he needed a vacation from boxing. He praised his opponent as "a pretty tough boy [with] a peculiar style. He's hard to hit and can take a punch very well." Eddie Mead then held court over the rest of the makeshift press conference, assuring the sportswriters that Henry was ready to defend any of his three belts against whomever promoter Mike Jacobs chose for him.[276]

The crowd cheered Lou Ambers as he stepped out of the ring ropes. They had come in rooting for the underdog from their home state, and he had held his own against the man many considered the best fighter in the world. He certainly did not look like the beaten man; his face was unmarred outside of a cut above his left eye.

Even so, his antics in the dressing room gave reporters the impression that Armstrong had beaten him silly. Ambers stripped naked, burst into song ("I Want a Girl Just Like the Girl That Married Dear Old Dad"), and then started pacing the room, bobbing and weaving as though Hammerin' Hank were still tossing leather at him. "Whoop-a-doopy," he shouted each time he ducked.

The fact was, Lou was simply in good spirits. And why not? He was $32,000 richer. Once he calmed down, he was gracious and candid in defeat. He praised Henry's relentlessness and said the low blows had not done any damage.

"I don't know whether I won or lost," he admitted, "All I can say is that it was a hard fight and, I hope, a good one."²⁷⁷

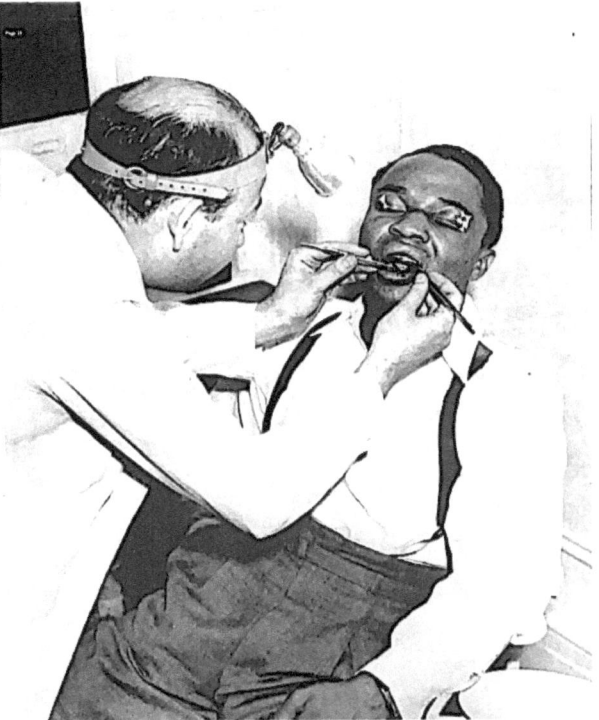

Dr. Schiff stitches up the new lightweight champ
*Life,* August 29, 1938

It was better than 'good.' Armstrong's title-winning effort against Lou Ambers was not just one of the most brutal fights of Henry's entire career; it remains one of the bloodiest, most grueling, and historic lightweight championship bouts in the division's storied history. A week later, revered sportswriter Grantland Rice dubbed it "one of the greatest lightweight shows the ring has ever known, because for 15 rounds there wasn't a minute – or scarcely a second – that they weren't whirling at each other, fighting from rope to rope, in and out of corners and across the ring." Rice went on to say that Henry's victory, "tacked to the other things he has done stamped him as one of the greatest fighters [to come along] in many years." *The Ring* later recognized it as the Fight of the Year for 1938.²⁷⁸

Henry received a payday of $25,000 and eight to fifteen stitches (depending on the source) on the inside of his mouth for his trouble. Eleven days after the fight, *Life* magazine featured a full-page photograph of Dr. Alexander Schiff sewing up the new lightweight champion's badly damaged mouth. Bandages were over both of Henry's eyes as well.

"His lip is so badly mangled that it looks as if it had been pounded with a rough-edged steak hammer. After the fight he became very ill from the quart and a half of blood he had swallowed," Schiff told the magazine.²⁷⁹

Six years later, a writer for Henry's hometown paper, the *St. Louis Post-Dispatch*, asked him, "What was the hardest fight of your career?" Without a moment's hesitation, Henry gave his answer: winning the lightweight championship from skilled and rugged Lou Ambers.[280]

## Armstrong, Face Badly Battered, Looks Forward to Long Vacation

### Declares Ambers Is 'Pretty Tough Boy,' but Insists Lou Never Hurt Him—Beaten Fighter Eager for Return Bout

*New York Times*, August 18, 1938

# 12.
# Triple Crown

**Henry Armstrong, three-division champion**

Henry returned to Los Angeles as a conquering hero yet again, celebrated and toasted by Hollywood's royalty and his fans. Stepping off his train at the Santa Fe station sporting a new blue linen suit and pearl gray fedora, he was immediately surrounded by reporters.

"I want to take things easy for a while," he told the reporters. "I've won three titles in the past ten months and have had little leisure."[281]

He felt he had earned it. No fighter had moved so quickly forward in the esteem of boxing's critics. There had been men who had won championships in three divisions before. The legendary Bob Fitzsimmons had been the first, gathering the belts at middleweight, heavyweight, and then light heavyweight decades earlier during a career that spanned 29 years. More recently, Tony Canzoneri and Barney Ross had both claimed three championships, but only if one recognized the "junior" weight divisions that had popped up recently and were not yet universally accepted.

By contrast, Henry had won titles in three of the universally recognized eight weight classes, which only Fitzsimmons had done. It took Fitz many years to do so; Henry had matched the feat in just months. All three others had either lost or relinquished at least one of their previous division titles before picking up their third title. No fighter in history had ever worn their three crowns simultaneously.

Eddie Mead gave Henry a three-month break from the ring. He signed a deal with Mike Jacobs to have Armstrong back in action on November 2 for the first defense of his welterweight laurels, but not before. That meant Henry would not need to return to training until October. He enjoyed his leisure time. Perhaps a bit too much.

After a brief trip to New York to participate in a charity event called "Parade of the Stars" (along with Jack Dempsey, Babe Ruth, Benny Leonard, and Bill "Bojangles" Robinson) in front of eighty thousand fans at Yankee Stadium, he took his wife and daughter on vacation to Hawaii. Everywhere he went, he heard praise; from fans, sportswriters, celebrities, and random folks walking down the street. There were free drinks and free women, yet he still found ways to spend his money: the best clothes, the best car, and some wagers at the racetrack that were anything but the best.

By November of 1938, Henry had fought just twice in over seven months, which was by far the least active he had been in the ring since mounting his boxing career in earnest in California six years earlier. On September 12, Mike Jacobs announced that Henry would relinquish his featherweight championship to concentrate on defending his lightweight and welterweight honors. According to Jacobs, Henry could still make featherweight if he wanted to, but he felt there were no viable challengers to draw a sufficient gate for that title. The fact that Henry had fought at featherweight just once in nearly two years probably meant that getting down to 126 pounds to defend his championship would have been too draining, and he and his team likely decided to relinquish that belt rather than hurt his marketability by losing it on the scales or losing it in the ring.

"I'll toss it in and let Chalky Wright and the others fight for it," Henry told the press.[282]

There were those who criticized Henry's monopoly of nearly half the sport's championships. The retired former heavyweight champion Gene Tunney was among these. Tunney felt that a fighter should not be able to jump between divisions and immediately gather up championships without first proving themselves in those divisions. It hurt public interest in the sport, he said.

However, Tunney's objection to Henry's multi-division championships may have been racially motivated. "With five of the seven major boxing championships held by Negro fighters (Armstrong, Louis and John Henry Lewis, light heavy) the interest in the fighting sport is at low ebb," Tunney, who never once faced a Black opponent in the ring, commented to the Associated Press. "It is time to develop new contenders for the sake of public interest," he concluded. The assumption was that these new contenders and the public interested in them would be white.[283]

Henry's first challenger for his welterweight championship was not white. He was Ciprano "Ceferino" Garcia, a sturdy, rugged puncher from the Philippines who had been a welterweight and middleweight contender for years. A first-grade dropout and a feared street fighter as a youth, Garcia was working as a baker in Cebu City when he met a boxing promoter who got him his start in pro fighting at just fifteen years old in 1923. He earned the equivalent of seventy-five cents for his first bout.

**Ceferino Garcia**

Under his father's management, Ceferino won the so-called "Welterweight Championship of the Orient," traveled to the States in 1932, and, basing himself in California, tried out for the U.S. Olympic team in the same year Henry did. Losing a disputed decision in the trials, Garcia turned pro and almost immediately took on world-class opposition. His past opponents included Freddie Steele, Young Corbett III, Sammy Angott, Barney Ross, and Henry's friend Young Peter Jackson. Sometimes he won, sometimes he didn't, but he was always dangerous.[284]

Garcia was most famous for his "bolo" right uppercut, a punch which he would wind up in an underhanded looping circle not unlike a softball pitch before he crashed it home on an unfortunate opponent. He claimed he developed the movement while cutting sugar cane as a youngster, hence his naming it bolo after the cutting instrument used in the fields outside Manila. It was a punch designed to catch the eyes of judges and fans as much as it was to hurt opponents. Garcia was slow of foot and cared little for defense, but he could give and take as well as anybody. At a time when Joe Louis was in his prime, some still considered Garcia "the most murderous hitter in the game."[285]

Between February 1936 and July 1937, Garcia put together fourteen wins against one loss and one draw, leading to a challenge for Ross's welterweight belt on Mike Jacobs's historic "Carnival of Champions" card. Though he nearly scored a knockout over the star Chicagoan, his stamina failed him, and he lost a fifteen-round decision. But Ross broke his hand pounding on the durable contender, and some said it had been Garcia who had softened Ross up for Armstrong. Since then, Garcia had won ten straight fights as a middleweight, nine of them by knockout, before Jacobs scheduled him for a November 2 fight with Henry in the Garden.[286]

While wrapping up his training for the Garcia fight (scheduled for November 1 in New York's Hippodrome), Henry claimed a bad fall resulted in debilitating back pains. Eddie Mead told the press it was a back sprain and asked the commission for a postponement.

Syndicated columnist Dan Parker questioned the story after hearing stories of Henry carousing and bowling late at night instead of training. He was right. Many years later, Henry confessed to intentionally falling and faking the injury. They had heard that Garcia was having trouble staying under the 147-pound welterweight limit and figured a delay would weaken him. With help from a bribed doctor and his bandages, the ruse worked. They got the bout postponed to November 25.[287]

On the morning of the fight, betting odds favored Henry only slightly over Garcia. His supporters felt that Henry's come-forward style would smother his challenger's ability to get momentum behind his feared right uppercut. Meanwhile, those who favored Garcia felt that the middleweight's size and punching power would be too much for the ex-featherweight to handle, momentum or not. The right uppercut was also the best weapon that both Barney Ross and Lou Ambers used against Hurricane Henry.

When they weighed in on November 25, Henry, twenty-nine years old (though everyone, including Henry, believed him to be twenty-six), weighed just 134 pounds. Garcia, twenty-eight years old, had made 146 ½ pounds, a half-pound under the welterweight limit. He had a half-inch height advantage over the champion.[288]

Just short of thirteen thousand people turned out to the Garden, a significantly lower number than the capacity crowd Mike Jacobs had expected. Henry did ten rounds of shadowboxing in his dressing room.

The size difference in the opponents was evident from the start of round one when the compactly muscled Henry charged into his broad-shouldered challenger. In boxing vernacular, it became a "phone booth" fight. In other words, the men stood toe to toe, trading short, chopping blows; it was the kind of fight that could happen in the limited interior of a phone booth. It was the kind of fight fans loved, and cheers echoed through the arena. Referee Arthur Donovan took the third round from Henry with a penalty for a low blow.

At the start of round four, Garcia tried to switch tactics. He leaped off his stool and bounced, shooting his jab out to keep some distance between himself and the smaller man. Before long, the bobbing, weaving Henry was back on the inside working away, and Garcia had no choice but to trade in kind. By round five, Henry he was landing at least two punches to every one he took.

Garcia dealt a vicious beating to the body with his heavy hands in round six, and he once caught Henry with his signature bolo punch as the champion lunged in at him. That drew a gasp from the crowd.

Taking control back beginning in round seven, Henry mauled away through the next five rounds. The blood-spattered challenger remained upright, but only his size advantage kept him from going down. Donovan penalized Garcia for a low punch in the eighth frame.

In round twelve, an adrenaline-fueled Henry came out of his corner, forgetting his mouthpiece. At one point, Henry missed with a big right and almost fell behind the momentum of it. Taking advantage, Garcia landed a crashing right uppercut that staggered his foe. Henry would later call this the hardest blow he ever took years later. "There was a roar in my ears like a runaway showerbath," he told an interviewer. "I saw whole curtains of live flame and my head seemed to float into the air and bob up and down like a fishing cork." Blood sprang from Henry's lips.

His confidence boosted, Garcia began bouncing on his toes and throwing shots from the outside, but Henry dodged virtually all of them. "Had Ceferino known how badly I was hurt, he could have knocked me out easily," Armstrong later confessed.[289]

Rounds thirteen through fifteen bore witness to a relentless body assault from Armstrong, who had recovered his senses. At the bell to end the fight, Garcia stumbled into a neutral corner and only returned to his stool with help from his cornermen.

Donovan and both judges unanimously chose Armstrong as the winner. At the announcement that Henry Armstrong was still the world's welterweight champion, the crowd booed vociferously, as they had at the Ambers fight. Again, Henry and the press were astonished. Ted Carroll of *The Ring* recognized the victory for what it was. "Few fighters in history would have been capable of conceding this terrific hitter twelve pounds as Armstrong did," he pointed out.[290]

Amazingly, after his punishing battle with Garcia, Henry was back in the ring eleven days later to defend his welterweight championship against another naturally larger man. The opponent was Al Manfredo of San Francisco. They headlined a Cleveland Christmas charity event before 12,274 onlookers. *The Ring* did not rank Manfredo among the division's top ten at the time, but he had shared a ring with Ceferino Garcia, Fritzie Zivic, and Barney Ross in the past and even owned two wins over Garcia. Henry weighed 134 ¾ pounds to Manfredo's 146. Despite his weight advantage, Manfredo had to be saved by the referee in round three, as Henry teed off while the helpless challenger's arms hung limply at his sides. On the undercard were two familiar faces. Lou Ambers and Petey Sarron both won their matches.[291]

The Manfredo win capped off a glorious 1938 for Henry Armstrong, consisting of thirteen victories, nine of them by knockout. That ran his total win streak to forty-one victories without a loss between 1937 and 1938. He had won two division championships at welterweight and lightweight from two excellent champions and made two successful defenses of his welterweight crown.

When *The Ring* handed out its year-end award for Most Valuable Boxer of 1938, a tie in votes of fans and experts came in between Henry and his friend Joe Louis. Nat Fleischer decided to step in and cast the deciding vote for Louis because his historic, dominant, and meaningful defeat of Max Schmeling to defend the heavyweight championship outshined all sports stories of the decade, if not the century. It did not help Henry that, on the day Fleischer was to decide, November 1, word had come that Henry had requested to postpone his bout with Garcia. Even so, the magazine put Henry's smiling face beside Joe's on its cover.[292]

In an article celebrating the accomplishments of both men, Carroll, *The Ring*'s first Black staff writer, wrote:

> Hustlin' Henry has clearly earned the right to be ranked along with the greatest men his race has produced. After years of trial and tribulation his career reached a crashing crescendo in 1938 and he is a cinch to go down in history as one of the most amazing men who ever followed a ring career.[293]

Also of note for 1938, Eddie Mead had finally paid back his loans from actors Al Jolson and George Raft. It happened before the lucrative Ross fight, which made Jolson none too happy. He felt entitled to a piece of Henry, as he saw the five thousand dollars he gave Mead not as a loan but as an investment, a buy into the kid's future. Jolson complained that he did not get a percentage of the take from the title fight, but they drew up no contracts, so there was little he could do. Mead was the only man with a contract with Henry Armstrong and planned to make the best of it.

As usual, Henry Armstrong returned to Los Angeles to celebrate Christmas with his family. He was exhausted. He may have had plenty of time between bouts in the summer and fall of 1938, but those fights with Ross, Ambers, and Garcia were all hard-fought. All came with the considerable pressure and attention of major title fights. All required extensive preparation. All had bruised him or cut him or both. All had required that he give everything he had for fifteen rounds.

At the start of 1939, *The Ring* rated the welterweight contenders over which Henry Armstrong now ruled were rated thusly:

World's Champion – Henry Armstrong
Contenders:
1 – Ernie Roderick
2 – Ceferino Garcia
3 – Fritzie Zivic
4 – Charley Burley
5 – Saverio Turiello
6 – Sammy Luftspring
7 – Steve Mamakos
8 – Marcel Cerdan
9 – Jake Kilrain
10 – Norman Snow

The magazine rated the lightweights over whom Henry also reigned as follows:

World's Champion – Henry Armstrong
Contenders:
1 – Lou Ambers
2 – Pedro Montanez
3 – Davey Day
4 – Baby Arizmendi
5 – Sammy Angott
6 – Petey Sarron
7 – Tippy Larkin
8 – Aldo Spoldi
9 – Maxie Berger
10 – Eric Boon[294]

Henry had faced some of those names at lightweight before, but at number four was Alberto "Baby" Arizmendi, his old Mexican foe. Their rivalry stood at two wins apiece and begged for a settling of the score. Since their last fight, won by Armstrong, Arizmendi had won five of his six bouts, the lone outlier being a ten-round draw in a non-title affair with Lou Ambers when Ambers was still the lightweight champ. Henry admired Arizmendi's toughness. He and Eddie decided that it was long past due that the Baby got his genuine shot at a title. Both fighters could draw a gate at home in Los Angeles; thus, it was a promotional no-brainer. He would grant Arizmendi a shot at the welterweight championship.

Henry was in training as of New Year's Day at the Main Street Gym, with Eddie Mead and Harry Armstrong overseeing his preparation. His sparring partners were Herschel Joyner, a recent transplant to L.A. from Dubuque, Iowa; Bennie O'Neal, "a very classy little fellow" with more experience than Joyner; Tony Navarro, an upstart from San Francisco who had been appearing in the Olympic as of late. Members of the press noticed that Henry's sparring partners were outworking him and that he seemed exhausted after just a few rounds of work. Eddie Mead did not like his fighter's apparent lack of motivation and conditioning, and he unsuccessfully tried to have the fight postponed.[295]

The fight took place on January 10, 1939, at the Olympic. It was the first world championship match ever staged at the venue, and a capacity crowd of 10,500 turned out, paying $23,936 to see the two local favorites go at it once again. "If they repaid courage in dollars, Baby Arizmendi would be as rich as any man in the world," suggested Bill Henry of the *Los Angeles Times*. The Mexican warrior endured a horrific beating from bell to bell. As usual, it was a rough, physical fight with elbows and heads doing as much damage as their fists, but it was far from competitive. The judges gave Arizmendi just one round out of the ten, with eight going to Armstrong and one even. At the final bell, lumps and gore covered the Baby's face. Henry bled from the mouth again but was otherwise unmarked.[296]

That was the fifth and final time that Henry Armstrong and Baby Arizmendi would exchange leather. The only man Henry faced as often in the ring was Perfecto Lopez, but the best Lopez had managed as a pro were two draws against Armstrong very early in his career. Arizmendi had managed two wins, even if Henry claimed those scorecards were spiced with some Mexican cooking. Henry always knew he was in for a savage fight when facing his longtime rival.

"They had similar styles, in close without clinching, nonstop attack from two resolute little bulls," remembered author and screenwriter Budd Schulberg of witnessing the pair in action firsthand. Later, Henry admitted that Arizmendi "was the most durable, tough, and generally tenacious fighter that [I] met."[297]

Arizmendi fought on for years to come but was no longer the same fighter he had been before this last encounter with Armstrong. He lost his next bout when Lou Ambers stopped him on cuts in the eleventh round, and he continued to lose more frequently against topflight opposition like Sammy Angott and California Jackie Wilson. After suffering additional losses against lesser opponents, he finally hung up his gloves in 1942, a veteran of 129 professional fights at just twenty-eight years old. He enlisted in the United States Navy for service in the Second World War. "Beware Axis, Arizmendi Joins U.S. Navy!" read the *Los Angeles Times* headline. [298]

After returning to the States, he worked as a boxing manager and restaurateur. Never the most disciplined of men, he lost control of his health and weight. By the late 1950s, the resultant diabetes required hospitalization, and he passed away on December 31, 1963, of natural causes at age forty-nine. For being arguably the first Mexican boxing star to crossover in a major way into the U.S. market, for his wins over the likes of Armstrong, Fidel LaBarba, Freddie Miller, and Chalky Wright, and for fighting at a world-class level at every weight from featherweight to middleweight, Alberto "Baby" Arizmendi was posthumously inducted into the International Boxing Hall of Fame in 2004.

A few days after the fifth Arizmendi fight, Eddie Mead announced that Henry would have to postpone a scheduled exhibition tour of the Midwest and South in late January. Mead's reasoning varied. It was due to a bout of gastritis in some newspaper accounts, and in others, it was a sore nose incurred in the battle with Arizmendi.

Whatever the cause of the delay, Henry recovered and began the brief tour before the month was out. He fought in Louisville, Columbus, Cincinnati, Milwaukee, Racine, Baltimore, and Washington, D.C., sometimes on back-to-back nights, boxing for four rounds each night. Sometimes he faced two or three men at a single event, dividing the rounds between them. He fought in at least seven cities in eighteen days between January 30 and February 16.

While Henry was in Louisville, Kentucky, his chauffeur got into an auto accident and left the scene, breaking a Kentucky law. By the time police started looking for him, Henry had departed for Ohio. In Cincinnati, fans mobbed him at a restaurant shortly after his arrival, forcing the owner to close his establishment for the day.

Two weeks after the tour ended, Henry took his first trip out of the United States, landing in Havana, Cuba, to defend his welterweight belt against Bobby Pacho on March 4 in the Tropical Stadium. Pacho was a tough competitor, "like a hunk of granite," with at least 114 wins on his record, but was not rated among the top contenders by *The Ring* at the time.

Ten thousand fans arrived to watch the fight, and their referee was the recently retired former heavyweight champion, James J. Braddock. Coming in at a thirteen-pound weight advantage, Pacho boxed well at the opening of the first, but Henry dropped him twice by the round's close. The challenger wisely switched tactics in rounds two and three and slugged his way back into the fight, standing shoulder-to-shoulder with Armstrong to exchange blows on mostly even terms. Eventually, like most everyone else, Pacho's energy waned under Armstrong's unrelenting attack. Sensing an opportunity, Henry poured on the leather and backed his challenger to the ropes. Under a bombardment of lefts and rights, Pacho lost consciousness, his arms falling to his sides. Asleep, he slid down against the ropes at his back as more blows pummeled him, keeping him upright. Referee Braddock stepped in to push Henry away, and the beaten man toppled to the floor. Braddock dragged him to his corner.[299]

Back in the States just twelve days later, Armstrong put both his lightweight and welterweight championships up simultaneously against Brooklyn's Lew Feldman, another experienced ring veteran who was not among the top ten contenders in either division. Henry had beaten Feldman once before in 1938, just before the Barney Ross fight, finishing him off in the fifth. He had also served as Henry's sparring partner before the Ambers match.

The Feldman contest was Henry's first in St. Louis since his disqualification loss to Tony Chavez in 1936. Henry wanted to look good for his 9,816 hometown fans, and he did. He put Feldman down twice and knocked him out in just two minutes and twelve seconds. On the undercard, middleweight contender Archie Moore, another of Henry's old sparring partners and the future light heavyweight champion of the world, scored a ten-round decision over Marty Simmons.[300]

Davey Day, "The Human String Bean"

On the last day of March, Henry defended his welterweight belt against Davey Day, considered by some to be the best opponent he had faced, at least since Lou Ambers, maybe Barney Ross. Day had been an accomplished amateur out of Iowa via Chicago. As a pro, he was part of Sam Pian's management stable. Standing 5'9" tall, he never weighed more than 140 pounds in the ring, giving him a skeletal appearance. It might have looked as though a slight breeze off Lake Michigan could carry the wisp of a man into the atmosphere, but he was a sturdy combatant with dangerous punching power.

Day had assembled fifteen victories since losing a disputed decision to Ambers in 1937, bringing his win count to 56 against five defeats and four draws. *The Ring* rated him the number three contender at lightweight, just below Ambers and Sammy Angott. Nonetheless, Henry was a heavy favorite going in.

At Madison Square Garden on Friday, March 31, before a crowd of 10,028 fans cheering his every success, the challenger put up a valiant fight but was eventually broken down by the champion's assault. The *Times* reported that "each of the almost innumerable blows took its toll of his strength and prepared the way for his ultimate downfall." In the twelfth round, an Armstrong right to the body folded Day in half, leaving him cringing and crumpled on the canvas. Referee Billy Cavanaugh immediately stopped the fight and carried the broken challenger to his corner.[301]

While Henry was preparing for the Day fight, Eddie Mead arranged for him to defend his lightweight belt in a rematch with Lou Ambers set for August 9 in Yankee Stadium.

Mead had also been negotiating with British promoter Sydney Hulls to bring Henry to the U.K. with various potential opponents considered. Eventually, Liverpool's Ernie Roderick, the national welterweight champ, was picked. *The Ring* rated him the second-best contender for Armstrong's welterweight title behind Puerto Rico's Pedro Montanez. Editor Fleischer felt that Roderick would likely win the title from Armstrong by disqualification in the relatively more restrained and polite British boxing environment.

"The first low blow Henry lands in his London bout, regardless of the circumstances, will bring about his disqualification and the crowning of a British boy as new welter king," predicted Fleischer. Others felt that Roderick's superb left jab might give Henry trouble.[302]

As Henry had broken the index finger of his left hand against Day, Eddie postponed the fight but not the trip. On Friday, April 7, Henry, Eddie, Willa Mae, Lanetta, Harry, and Chalky Wright boarded the *Queen Mary* bound for England.

Ben Bennison, a writer for the *London Evening Standard*, caught up with Henry aboard the *Queen Mary* after it stopped in Cherbourg, France. Henry told Bennison that he was enjoying his trip ("a round of wonder," he called it), and his hand was healing well. While on the voyage, the cast came off, and Henry used electric treatments to hasten healing. The fighter reminisced about the difficulties of his upbringing in America and his struggles as a young fighter. Eddie Mead added that, following the Ambers rematch, Henry would have enough in the bank to take care of himself for the rest of his life.[303]

Bennison asked the champion what he planned to do after his boxing career was over.

"I have no fixed notions," replied Henry. "Maybe I shall go into the Church. I am that way inclined." He hoped to retire at the end of 1940, he said. When asked, he told Bennison that he had engaged in over three hundred boxing matches in his lifetime.[304]

Henry impressed Bennison as unassuming and engaging, "without sham or pretense." The reporter did not expect the self-assurance with which Henry regarded himself as a Black man from America. "He has all the pride of a deep-thinking, intelligent man in his race; he belongs to his own people, and would be no different." Henry's vocabulary, knowledge of subjects outside of boxing, and peaceful manner challenged Bennison's preconceptions about prizefighters. "I have found it difficult in the talks I have with Armstrong, to reconcile him with the ruthless, merciless man I know him to be in the ring."[305]

A tremendous welcome party of fans and reporters awaited Henry when he stepped off the *Queen Mary* at Southampton on Thursday, April 12, after a little less than a week of travel. Henry seemed humbled by the attention, coming across as genuinely surprised and embarrassed by so many eyes and cameras. Because the Easter holiday had held up the processing of his work permit, authorities initially detained the Armstrong party on the gangway. Only after some delay were they allowed to step onto the dock, from whence they proceeded to the train station for a trip to London.

Henry became the "talk of the pubs" during his stay in England. By virtue of either his race or profession or both, some white fans were astonished by his pleasant diction, good personal hygiene, and polite manners. "They didn't know what to make of him at first," reported a correspondent for the Associated Press, "but they like him now."

"Armstrong is the finest character I have ever met in boxing," observed one U.K. sportswriter. "He is a credit to his race and to his country."[306]

On January 15, Henry was the guest of honor at a dinner given by the distinctly upper-class London Sporting Club. Decked out in a tuxedo, he became the first Black man inducted as an honorary member of the Club, breaking an age-old rule that forbade membership to anyone but whites.

The Armstrong team set up a training camp at Clacton-on-Sea, a resort town on England's eastern shore in Essex. Sportswriters reported that Henry seemed to be taking it easy in training, apparently wanting to give his left hand a break but also frustrated that he could not work out as avidly as he would like. Though he did spar, his overall training schedule was relatively light, and Henry spent much of the time relaxing, enjoying the fresh air, and reading. British sportswriters who visited Henry's camp found his wide range of interests compelling. They reported on his reading books on philosophy and his interests in poetry and music.

On the day of the fight, May 25, odds had Henry a six to four favorite to retain his crown. A disappointing crowd of roughly seven thousand people turned out to see the match at the Harringay Arena. Henry came into the ring weighing just 135 pounds. His challenger outweighed him by ten and three-quarters pounds.

"I have not seen a better contest in many years," James Butler of the *London Daily Herald* would write the next day. As expected, Roderick made excellent use of his precision left jab. Henry astonished onlookers by not bothering to dodge them; he simply walked straight through them. By the second round, it was clear that Henry had little respect for Roderick's power, and he battered his opponent mercilessly. The Englishman seemed especially susceptible to Henry's dangerous right hooks. The challenger attempted rallies on occasion, bringing the crowd to its feet whenever he did so, but his punches did not affect the champion. By the seventh round, Roderick's eyes were beginning to close, but he continued to give everything he had in futilely trying to keep Henry off him.[307]

**Ernie Roderick**

By the eighth, the exhausted Englishman was nothing more than "a punching bag for this American machine." Henry was again bleeding from the mouth, as he had in almost every fight since facing Ambers, and his left eye was bruised, but he showed no other wear or tear from the fight. Armstrong's stamina amazed the British sportswriters, as did Roderick's fighting heart. They slugged it out on mostly even terms in round eleven, with both men landing damaging blows. It was the first time Roderick gave as good as he got, and Butler called the round "one of the most thrilling seen for years."[308]

Henry drew a warning from the referee after the twelfth for using his head too much when the fighters mixed it up. The thirteenth was a thriller. Armstrong decided to finish off his opponent rather than risk a disqualification. "Hammerin' Hank" bore in more aggressively than at any previous point, throwing haymakers to the body to end things then and there. With the champion abandoning all defense, Roderick fought back hard, again giving as good as he got, if not better.

**Willa Mae and sleeping Lanetta at the Roderick Fight**

In the fifteenth and final round, an exhausted Roderick did well to stay upright under an unrelenting attack, but he could no longer hold up his hands to defend himself. While enduring tremendous punishment, he impressed many by surviving on guts alone to the final bell. The decision went to Henry Armstrong, who earned a £10,000 payday, the largest ever purse in the history of the British prize ring to that point.[309]

Johnny Sharpe, the British correspondent to *The Ring*, expressed the approval of his fellow Englishmen when he wrote, "No longer shall we scoff at the reports of Henry's greatness. No longer shall we feel that the American scribes have overrated a young boy whose deeds have been compared to that of other amazing Negro fighters, the incomparable Joe Gans, George Dixon and Joe Walcott. We saw and we were satisfied." Sharpe was beyond thrilled by Armstrong's performance but also praised Roderick as "one of the gamest losers I have ever seen."[310]

"He was a fine, game boy," Armstrong concurred after the fight. "I'm sorry I couldn't put up a better fight, but both my hands are sore and bruised." A subsequent x-ray revealed that he had split a bone in his left thumb, requiring another cast. The Ambers rematch would ultimately be postponed to August 22 to give the hand time to heal fully.[311]

While in Europe, Henry received offers to fight the European Boxing Union's continental welterweight champ, Saverio Turiello of Italy, or France's Marcel Cerdan, who had recently beaten Turiello in a non-title fight. The payday was supposed to be an incredible sixty thousand in American dollars.

Plans were made for Henry to travel to Paris and sign to face Cerdan. In telling this story years later, Henry claimed that, though he traveled to Paris, concerns over Germany's increased militarism and the possibility of an invasion prevented the contract signing. Turiello and Cerdan then fought a rematch on June 3 instead, Cerdan taking the EBU title via a fifteen-round decision. Years later, the Frenchman would win the world's middleweight championship from Tony Zale, lose it to Jake LaMotta, and tragically die in a plane crash in 1949.[312]

While in England, Henry found time for loving as well as fighting. He met Joan Jackman, a beautiful young white woman, and became infatuated with her. Before he departed, Henry intended to propose marriage to Joan, but she ended things, and Henry returned to America with his wife and daughter.[313]

After two months away, the *Queen Mary* delivered Henry and his family to New York on Monday, June 5. No sooner did he step off the gangplank than Mike Jacobs shoved a contract to fight Lou Ambers for fifty thousand dollars at him. Henry signed the paper, then stayed in the Big Apple through the week to watch a boxing match between welterweight contender Al "Bummy" Davis and opponent Eddie Brink (Davis won a ten-round decision) at Madison Square Garden before heading for Los Angeles and home.[314]

On June 13, Nat Fleischer officially presented Henry with his custom welterweight championship belt from *The Ring* at the magazine's offices, along with another "extra-special" custom belt recognizing his unprecedented feat of being a simultaneous three-division champ.

Since Henry had taken his title, Lou Ambers and his vociferous manager Al Weill had been howling for a rematch. In the meantime, Lou kept as busy as Henry. He put together nine consecutive victories against opponents of varying quality. Perhaps the most impressive was a dominant thrashing of Baby Arizmendi, whose skin tore to ribbons under the Herkimer Hurricane's slashing combinations, forcing an eleventh-round stoppage in the Garden on February 24, 1939. When he received confirmation that he would get his rematch with Henry Armstrong, Ambers was taking a much-needed vacation at a Hot Springs, Arkansas resort. That summer, he went into training in Rockridge, New York.

Henry took in a little relaxation himself in Little Rock, Arkansas, at the Hot Springs Resort before he began training, arriving at the familiar Pompton Lakes camp in late July. There, a commission doctor pronounced Henry's left hand completely healed.

While both fighters went about their preparations, their two hot-tempered managers, Eddie Mead and Al Weill, met up in Rockridge and got into a heated conversation about what titles would be at stake in the fight. Mead proclaimed that, should Ambers win the fight, he and Weill could only claim lightweight honors and not make any claims to Henry's welterweight championship. Weill refused the agreement in no uncertain terms; both crowns should be on the line, he persisted. After exchanging colorful language, they brought the matter before the NYSAC. On August 1, the Commission ruled that only lightweight recognition would be on the line, and Mead and Weill, along with Mike Jacobs, signed a contract agreeing to this. The documents also included an agreement that, should Ambers regain the lightweight championship, he would be granted a third bout with the welterweight belt on the line.

The *New York Times* sports section gave almost daily updates on Henry's training and weight leading up to the fight. It reported that Henry was having trouble getting his weight down to the 135-pound lightweight limit, and he looked sluggish in action against sparring partner Lew Feldman.

Eddie Mead commented that he might advise Henry to voluntarily give up his lightweight belt after the Ambers fight and concentrate solely on the welterweight division. The concern was significant enough that Mead told the press that he was considering instructing Henry not to bother trying to cut any more weight, that they could instead put the welterweight championship on the line for Ambers. Mead would later claim that the weight concerns were all a publicity stunt he devised to make fans believe Henry's title was in real jeopardy.[315]

Meanwhile, those who visited the Ambers camp had nothing but praise. Lou's conditioning impressed middleweight champion Fred Apostoli, while Jack Dempsey professed certainty of an Ambers win.

"Oh, I know Armstrong is a fine fighter – his record proves that," conceded Dempsey. "But this boy Ambers has the valuable knack of turning the table on fellows who whipped him in earlier fights. Don't be surprised if he does." Jack's assessment was not wholly accurate. Lou had won every rematch in which he had taken part, but only one was avenging a prior loss.[316]

On the afternoon of Wednesday, August 16, Henry took a break from his hard training to join Dempsey and eight thousand enthusiastic boxing fans at New York's World's Fair for an event to honor the newly crowned light heavyweight champion of the world, the immensely likable Billy Conn of Pittsburgh.

Ambers and Armstrong square off at the weigh-in

By Tuesday, August 22, the day of his title defense against Lou Ambers, Henry Armstrong was a two-to-one favorite to retain his lightweight championship. The main event began at Yankee Stadium at 10 p.m. 28,088 fans paid $137,025 to watch the rematch between Hurricane Henry and the Herkimer Hurricane. The battle was as dramatic and thrilling as the first, if not more so. James P. Dawson of the *Times* wrote of the rematch, "In advance it had figured to be a primitive, savage, furious slug-fest. It was all of that."[317]

Henry came to the weigh-in at 136 pounds and had to shed an extra pound with a vigorous workout that morning before hopping back on the scales and making the required 135, evidence that Mead's tales of struggles with weight were not all fabrication. The challenger weighed just one-half pound less.

Ambers surprised many by meeting boxing's most feared slugger toe-to-toe in the first fight, and he did the same in the second. He landed the opening punches, aggressively plunging left hooks into Henry's ribs while holding Henry with his right. Henry returned the body blows in kind, and his punishment already had Lou's skin turning red with welts just seconds in. Henry threw body punches through most of the opening frame while Lou focused on left and right uppercuts to the face. Ambers sometimes tried to dance backward or hold his opponent to stem Armstrong's punishing attack. Henry ended the round with a series of shots both upstairs and downstairs that rocked the challenger and had the crowd roaring.

Henry later remembered round two as having the most vicious fighting of the bout, recalling that Ambers fought him with demonic fury. At one point, Henry landed a stiff left hook to Lou's jaw but caught a left and right to his chin in return. That combination stunned the champion and sent his mouthpiece flying. Worse yet, blood started streaming from his right eye, and the same eye was quickly swelling shut. Henry believed it had been caused by Ambers thumbing him, but if it was, referee Arthur Donovan did not call it. He did penalize Henry for a low blow, though.[318]

Henry continued pressing the fight in the third, chasing after his backpedaling challenger. With Lou's back to the ropes, a perfectly timed Armstrong right hook to his temple brought a groan from the crowd, but the challenger managed to push the battle back to ring center.

**Armstrong lands low on Ambers**

In round four, Armstrong's right hand to the body sent Ambers stumbling backward to the ropes, where he fell into them, and his head went outside the ring. Armstrong pursued and attacked, forcing frantic return fire and then a clinch from Ambers. Ambers was in such a hasty retreat that he slipped to one knee. When he got up, he found Henry almost immediately in his chest, pounding away with both hands at his short ribs. After absorbing four solid blows to his chin, the Herkimer Hurricane fought back with a flurry of hooks from all angles. The fans went wild, but the rally was hardly enough to win back the round.

A thudding Ambers left hook rocked Henry in round five, but he stayed upright. At about the midpoint of the round, Ambers landed a terrific right uppercut – always an excellent punch against Armstrong's constantly bobbing and weaving head – that sent his mouthpiece sailing through the air once again. Blood began to flow from inside Henry's mouth as it had in nearly all of Henry's fights since their first encounter. From there, Lou's confidence soared, and he landed all kinds of punches to both the head and midsection. When Henry tried to retaliate, one of his punches strayed low, and the referee penalized him again. When the fighters returned to their stools, Ambers had a cut streaming blood over his left eye, and Henry had one near each eye. His right eye was completely shut.

Ambers's repeated left jabs and left hooks won him the sixth. Henry's corner worked on mending his cuts between rounds but to no avail. He came out of his corner shaking and blinking, trying to clear the bloody "red mist" out of the vision of his one open eye. He walked into a right uppercut from Ambers at the start of the seventh. A follow-up punch staggered Henry. Recovering, he went toe-to-toe with Ambers through the rest of one of the most thrilling rounds of the fight.

Another punch from the blinded champion strayed low. A frustrated Donovan took another round away.

"Henry, you're throwing it away on these low blows. Keep 'em up!" he shouted.[319]

**Armstrong lands low again**

Henry was getting angry. After losing so many rounds to low blows, many other fighters would no longer go to the body. However, body punching is known to sap an opponent's stamina, particularly clever movers like Lou Ambers, so Armstrong went right back at the mid-section in round eight. In true Henry Armstrong fashion, he won the round by keeping Ambers in retreat or pinned to the ropes for all three minutes.[320]

In the middle of a wild exchange in the ninth, Henry shot a left that caught Ambers on the beltline, and referee Donovan stepped in and took another round away. Henry later said he was essentially blind and unable to determine where Lou's belt line was. He had Ambers trapped on the ropes for the entirety of the round. Had it not been for the ref's foul call, the round likely would have gone Henry's way.

Desperate to salvage a fight almost sure to be lost to penalties, Henry Armstrong poured on the leather in round ten, blind or not. The brave challenger fought back but was exhausted and spent much of the round leaning against the ropes in a neutral corner.

Henry got off to a good start in the eleventh, but Ambers came on in the middle of the round, landing accurately and in bunches. A left and right rocked Armstrong, but he maintained his footing and landed his chopping right clean to the challenger's chin. They then slugged it out on even terms until the bell ended the round. Amid all the punching, Donovan again took a competitive round from Henry for a low blow.

Throughout much of the twelfth and thirteenth, it seemed as though neither fighter could get an advantage over the other. Henry continued to punish the body while his opponent targeted the head.

Knowing he had two rounds left to prove his right to retain his championship, Armstrong dug deep inside himself to find the fury that had overwhelmed his tough opponents of the past. To those watching, he "seemed like a man gone crazy" when he came out for round fourteen. The champion seemed to be looking to put Ambers away as he unleashed wild punches from every angle, with almost nothing coming back in return. Ambers could not hold his arms up to defend himself and took a beating but showed tremendous resolve in staying on his feet. Nat Fleischer later called the fourteenth "by far the best round of the defending champion." [321]

Going into the fifteenth and final round, the champion and challenger shook hands to commemorate an impressive effort by both. The formality over with, Henry pounced on Ambers and immediately drove him back into the ropes. Lou bravely but ineffectually tried to fight back. The round ended with Henry in his "Human Buzz-Saw" mode, slashing away right up to the final bell. When it rang, Henry bounced to his corner. Lou followed and gave him a pat on the back. Henry gave the tough New Yorker a nod of acknowledgment.

Though not regarded as the classic thriller that their first encounter had been, the mutilated faces of the participants testified to the fiercely competitive nature of the fight. Both were almost unrecognizable, Henry's eyes shut and bleeding from two massive gashes, Lou's face a monstrosity of lumps and blood.

Both referee Arthur Donovan and judge Frank Fullam scored eight rounds for Ambers and seven for Armstrong. Judge Bill Healy scored eleven for Ambers, three for Armstrong, and one even. Lou Ambers had regained the lightweight championship by unanimous decision, making him only the second man (Tony Canzoneri was the first) ever to regain the division title.

The decision may have been unanimous among the officials, but neither the crowd nor the press agreed. The New York crowd seemed to appreciate Henry's effort for the first time in years. Many booed the decision when it was announced, and arguments could be heard everywhere as fans filed out of the stadium.

One of those arguments erupted between the managers. Mead and Weill, red in the face and shouting curses at one another, nearly broke into another foul-filled brawl before calmer heads separated them. "You'll get kilt," the notoriously hot-headed Weill screamed. The NYSAC would later slap Al with a four-month suspension for the threat.[322]

Even with Weil out of sight, Mead was on fire. "Ambers didn't land a legal blow throughout the fifteen rounds," insisted the manager while accusing Donovan of bias and the judges of robbery in no uncertain terms. "Three weeks ago, I knew this was going to happen. We couldn't win. They had it framed against us. Donovan went out of his way to hamper Armstrong while he let Ambers violate every rule in the book."

Despite the signed contract demanding a third meeting, Mead insisted he would refuse to let Henry fight Ambers again, saying he feared that judges would also rob Henry of his welterweight title.

Meanwhile, his fighter rested mutely on a nearby table, his face nothing short of mutilated from the evening's combat. While Mead raved, Armstrong silently contemplated his first loss in forty-seven contests. Pressed to offer a few words, Henry complimented Ambers's conditioning but agreed (in much more polite vocabulary) with Mead that Ambers fought dirty with impunity from the referee.[323]

Ambers was his typically jolly self in his dressing room, despite his swollen right eye and the cut above his left. He said, "the fight was a good one, and I thought I won decisively. Henry hurt me once or twice, but I got over it and I think I hurt him too." He then serenaded the reporters with a song until they retreated from the room.[324]

Lou wore a patch over his right eye as the people of Herkimer gave him a hero's welcome home. Six weeks later, he married his childhood sweetheart.

Of the twenty-seven sportswriters in attendance for the second Armstrong and Ambers battle, fourteen felt the decision was just, while thirteen argued Henry Armstrong deserved the victory. Opinions about the action and the decision varied wildly, prompting columnist Dan Parker to consider the following:

If the Ambers-Armstrong contest accomplished nothing else worth while, it proved at least how frail we boxing experts be. In the backwash of the brawl at Yankee Stadium, one finds a bewildering mass of conflicting opinions, that must convince the average reader that we're a bunch of opinionated idiots.

One young man thought the fight was a fake. Another called it the dullest on record. A third said it was the most savage lightweight battle in years. One said Ambers was the stronger at the finish. Another said Armstrong was in better shape at the end. There were several who thought Armstrong was robbed. One was of the opinion that Henry deliberately fouled Ambers repeatedly to get rid of the title. As for me, who predicted that Armstrong would win by a knockout, I've ordered an extra-long padded cell warmed up for myself.[325]

The day after the fight, *Times* writer James P. Dawson criticized Donovan for being over-zealous in taking away rounds for borderline low blows and felt that, even with the penalties, the judges got it wrong. He scored eight rounds for Armstrong and seven for Ambers, four of which he awarded because of Donovan's calls of foul.[326]

In the lead article for *The Ring*, the cover of which featured a painted portrait of a smiling Ambers placing a king's crown on his head, Nat Fleischer felt that Donovan's scorecard was correct, considering the penalties. He also felt that the referee had been too hard on Henry in taking away rounds for punches that landed on, not below, the beltline. Fleischer also criticized Frank Fullam for scoring the fourteenth for Ambers. As Fleischer saw it, Henry deserved to win all the last four rounds.

"Had Donovan ignored that belt line punch in the seventh which he should have done, and had Fullum seen the 14th... then Armstrong would have wound up the winner by a two to one tally, eight rounds to seven," Fleischer pointed out. He praised Armstrong for his relentless aggression and thought that Ambers looked like a beaten man at the fight's close. However, he also acknowledged that Ambers "did the best job of his career. He was a fighting demon."[327]

Interviewed about the Ambers rematch years later, Henry Armstrong always criticized referee Donovan's foul calls. "Lou's a fellow who bobs around the ring," Henry explained to an interviewer in 1940. "When I'd go after him he'd do his bobbing and weaving. Naturally some of my punches may have connected around the waistline, but Ambers was never in distress, and for that reason I feel that Mr. Donovan was too severe in taking away those five rounds." The foul calls, he said, were "the biggest lie in the world." He felt that promoter Jacobs took the lightweight title from him to avoid an investigation by the government for monopolizing boxing's championships.[328]

Criticism of bias on the part of Donovan reached a crescendo in 1939. Twice that year, he appeared before the NYSAC to face accusers. Promoter and manager Jimmy Johnston became so emotional in his reproach of the referee that he got suspended instead of Donovan. One witness specifically brought up the Armstrong and Ambers rematch, pointing out Donovan's habit of "deliberately" standing only behind Ambers as if intending only to watch Armstrong's every move and not those of Ambers. Others pointed out that Armstrong "was not permitted to punch Lou Ambers when he put him against the rope." At least one accusation of racial prejudice on Donovan's part was raised. In the end, he was not suspended.[329]

# 13.
# Keep Punching

Asked about his immediate plans after the Ambers loss, Henry said he would rest for a week and then move forward with a motion picture in the works with him as the lead. A year earlier, Joe Louis starred in a movie loosely based on his life, *The Spirit of Youth*. Mostly panned by critics, the film was popular enough to remain in theaters for a decade. Noting this, Eddie Mead thought it only appropriate that Henry star in his own version of *The Spirit of Youth*. Shot in Harlem and completed in September, *Keep Punching* premiered on December 5, 1939, at Harlem's Apollo Theater. John Clein directed, and Eddie Mead produced, though five thousand dollars of the funding came from Henry's pocket. Initial plans for Jolson to co-star never materialized.[330]

The role was hardly a stretch for Henry. He was Henry Jackson, a promising young Golden Gloves fighter on whom rested the hopes of his local Black community. Though his middle-class parents intended him to become a lawyer, Henry scandalizes them by turning to professional boxing and chasing the big money, high living, and fast women that come with being a boxing star. That chase gets him into trouble when his old school chum Frank, now a local racketeer, sets him up with a seductress who is supposed to drug him before his big title fight so that Frank's gangster friends can make a killing betting against him. Of course, Henry avoids the fate planned for him, wins his fight, gives up boxing, and the bad guy gets his comeuppance.

The plot was simple, the budget meager, and the editing sloppy. Henry did not deliver his lines as well as he delivered punches, but critics tended to give him the benefit of the doubt, and he certainly showed more acting ability than Louis. The climatic (if it could be called that) fight scene was a disorienting mix of staged sparring staged and archival footage of the brutal Armstrong-Ross fight. It was not a good movie, but it did respectable business as a "race" film, the term applied then to films made by and marketed to Black people.

The film was not without its historical value. After its release, the innovative swing dance moves incorporated into the several music numbers in the picture proved immensely influential in dance halls throughout the country.

The other lasting quality of the picture was its role in introducing three performers who would have notable careers by the standards for Black actors of the era. Most successful was Arthur "Dooley" Wilson, who played a vociferous local politician in *Keep Punching* but would gain silver-screen immortality three years later as piano-playing Sam in *Casablanca*. Wilson would star in fifteen Hollywood productions after debuting in *Keep Punching*.

**Henry and Mae E. Johnson in *Keep Punching***

Beautiful Mae E. Johnson, who played femme fatale Jerry opposite Henry, was already a popular singer at the Cotton Club when Clein cast her in *Keep Punching*. Known as the "Black Mae West," she would join a cast of stars including Lena Horne, Bill "Bojangles" Robinson, Cab Calloway, and Fats Waller in the historic 1943 film *Stormy Weather*.

Henry likely related to the third rising star most of all. His birth name was Leonard Canigata, but he was best known as Canada Lee. Lee was a somewhat restless character who had already attempted various careers before becoming a prizefighter in his late teens. After a brief time as a horse jockey, he was a ranked welterweight contender in the 1920s but suffered a detached retina in his right eye in 1929. He fought on, but his record deteriorated in unison with his vision until his eye went completely blind, and he eventually retired from the ring in 1933.

Hard up for work in the Great Depression, Lee found his way into stage acting and won the notice of the polymathic egomaniac of stage and radio, Orson Welles. Welles cast Lee in his version of *Macbeth*, and then Lee starred as Bigger Thomas in the play adaptation of Richard Wright's powerful novel

*Native Son*. He befriended Langston Hughes, who developed a strong social consciousness and left-leaning political beliefs in Lee, particularly concerning the oppression of Black people in America.

**Canada Lee as Bigger Thomas in the stage adaptation of *Native Son***

In his first motion picture role, Lee was wisely cast as Henry's grizzled trainer Speedy, who is wary of the nightlife his young charge has fallen into. Just as Speedy is protective of Henry Jackson and gives him advice inside and outside the ring, Lee hung around boxing gyms mentoring younger fighters. One wonders what conversations he and Henry Armstrong enjoyed between shooting scenes. They remained friends for the rest of Lee's life.

After his film debut, Lee continued in motion pictures, most notably appearing in Alfred Hitchcock's *Lifeboat* and Robert Rossen's *Body and Soul*. Henry once asked him how he successfully transitioned from the ring to the stage and screen. The actor replied that he could not put it into words except to say that he "thoroughly lives and feels the part."[331]

Lee was very vocal about the lack of roles of substance available to Black actors in Hollywood, and this, combined with his association with leftists like poet Hughes, screenwriter Abe Polonsky, and actor John Garfield, made him a target of the U.S. Senate's anti-communist witch hunts in the 1950s.

Blacklisted from working, Lee died of kidney disease at age forty-five on May 9, 1952.

Henry attended *Keep Punching*'s Chicago opening on January 27, 1940. It did well with Black audiences. Perhaps because most Black-focussed theaters were in the Jim Crow South, these films seem to go to great lengths to avoid the topics of racial oppression or inequality. Henry beat a white man in the ring as part of the movie's climax, but there was no attempt to frame his story as a fight against racial injustice. The villains of the story are Black. There is no white oppressor or message of standing up for one's rights in the face of bigotry. Systematic racism seems not to exist within the film's universe, even though it was a constant presence in the lives of Armstrong and his Black fans.

There is instead an unsubtle message in *Keep Punching* of moral uplift, inspiring one's community in times of trouble, and representing one's race with dignity, all of which are non-threatening to the white power structure and would have still appealed to Black audiences during the Great Depression. At the film's conclusion, realizing the folly in becoming a boxer and chasing wealth and women, Henry Jackson tells his doe-eyed virginal sweetheart from back home, "Soon there will be no more fighting. Soon there will be more schooling, and, if fate is kind, maybe I'll become a lawyer."[332]

The film also has a heavy theme of Christian salvation, another message that would have played well with middle-class Blacks and appeased Jim Crow whites. The cast sings hymns throughout, and the character of Jerry abandons her life of sin after hearing a preacher's sermon. Through prayer, she sees Henry's success in the ring as confirmation of God's approval of her repentance.

Henry toured the country with the picture, appearing at the local premiers in major cities. If his fictional counterpart had given up high living for the traditional values of home, religion, and clean living, Henry Armstrong had no intention of doing so. He made no attempt to avoid the nightlife of each town he passed through.

Eddie Mead was not the positive influence on Armstrong that the fictional Henry Jackson had found in his manager and trainer. Mead was in a jam the morning after the second Ambers fight. Expecting a big payday, he had borrowed ten thousand dollars from Mike Jacobs, a sum he quickly bet and lost at the horse track. At the time, Eddie thought nothing of it. He figured he would pay Mike back out of his share of Henry's purse from the fight. Yet, somehow, Henry's take from the fight only totaled eleven thousand dollars, which Jacobs duly handed to Mead to pay his fighter. Mead's salary, along with that of Harry Armstrong, not to mention other expenses, was supposed to come out of that eleven grand. Unwilling to steal Henry's entire payday for fear of the fighter leaving him, Mead reached out to a mob guy he knew and asked a favor. The gangster came through with the ten thousand for Jacobs and paid Henry's expenses.

The following day, word reached Henry, and he reprimanded his manager, but not for borrowing and gambling away their winnings.

"You shouldn't have done that, Mr. Mead," Henry said. "You should have known that no matter what happened, I would never leave you." Even with word that his manager had nearly lost him a championship purse, Henry failed to recognize the danger of spending and losing vast amounts of cash and trusting others to handle his finances. Instead, he was upset that Mead thought Henry would fire him and had gone elsewhere to recover the funds.

A short time later, when the New York State Athletic Commission suspended Mead for claiming the second Ambers fight was fixed, Mead offered to let Henry out of his contract so as not to hinder his career. Henry refused.[333]

Henry certainly could not blame his dwindling bank account entirely on Eddie. He had become a chronic loser at the racetracks himself. That and the financial drains of his boozing, womanizing, and love of high-end cars and fashion continued to siphon away his purses as quickly as they came without his manager's help.

He loved keeping company (and keeping up) with the wealthy Hollywood party set. Al Jolson and George Raft liked to show him off as their black boxer mascot to their friends. "I was a celebrity, owned by celebrities," he said. But their taste for the high life and the nightlife rubbed off on him. Jolson liked to throw expensive, all-night parties. The always opulent Mae West had a lifelong attraction to boxers and liked to keep Henry around, too. Henry later said West was "not at all like she seemed on the stage. That woman had a heart of gold."[334]

Henry's celebrity friends dressed to the nines, and he emulated their wallet-draining taste in fine clothing. Reporters commented on his tailor-made suits, imported cravat, and the huge diamond rings he wore.

At least one family member later claimed that Henry had romantic relationships with Lena Horne and Dorothy Dandridge and a six-week affair with Josephine Baker. These were arguably the three most sought-after female Black American entertainers of the era, but there is no evidence of any of these relationships beyond rumor.[335]

Decades later, from the vantage point of a middle-aged man, he commented, "I fought hard and I lived just as hard. I drank like a demon and I gambled, and if I didn't chase women, it's because I didn't have to. They chased me."[336]

Even Joe Louis, a notorious big spender and womanizer with little business sense himself, felt compelled to warn Armstrong. "Slow down," the heavyweight champion cautioned him. "Nobody's money goes as far as you stretch it."[337]

Though Henry frittered away most of his earnings, he also made attempts at lucrative financial investments. He purchased a ranch in Fontana, California, and was the landlord of three homes for rent in the Los Angeles area. In late August, Henry told reporters that he planned to retire by the end of 1939 and live off the money from these investments, some annuities, and a few more fight purses.[338]

With his bank account already dwindling, it was time for Henry to get back in the ring. The featherweight and lightweight championships were no longer his, but he still had the welterweight title. As of his loss to Ambers, *The Ring* ranked the top ten welterweight contenders over which Henry Armstrong ruled as follows:

> World's Champion – Henry Armstrong
> Contenders:
> 1 – Charley Burley
> 2 – Ernie Roderick
> 3 – Fritzie Zivic
> 4 – Pedro Montanez
> 5 – Sammy Luftspring
> 6 – Jimmy Leto
> 7 – Marcel Cerdan
> 8 – Kenny La Salle
> 9 – Milt Aron
> 10 – Mike Kaplan[339]

**Charley Burley**

At number one was Charley Burley, a Pittsburgh fighter who had twice whipped hometown rival Zivic and owned a victory over Leto. Born on

September 16, 1917, he was the son of a coal miner from Bessemer, Pennsylvania. His father died of black lung disease when he was twelve, and that same year the family moved to the Hill District in Pittsburgh, the center of commerce, culture, and residence for the city's Black people. Like Henry, Burley got his start as a street scrapper. He found his way into a boxing gym and amateur fights before he turned thirteen. In his first amateur bout, he beat an older boy, setting a pattern of whipping bigger opponents that would last the rest of his boxing life. After winning multiple amateur welterweight championships, he was considered for the 1936 Berlin Olympics but passed on the opportunity to attend the "Counter Olympics" held in Barcelona. Though he traveled to Madrid, that tournament never happened because it coincided with the opening shots of the Spanish Civil War. Returning safely stateside, Charley turned pro on September 29, 1936. Just under a year later, he fought on the undercard of the Henry Armstrong-Charley Burns fight at Hickey Park, losing a questionable decision to Connecticut's Eddie Dolan.

In 1938, Burley won the "Colored Welterweight Championship" from Louis "Cocoa Kid" Arroyo, knocking the Kid down thrice. *The Ring* sponsored the championship and the gold belt that came with it. In the 1930s, many superb Black fighters were still being "ducked" by white champions and even fellow Black champions, mainly because there existed little pressure from a prejudiced white public (the public who had the money to buy tickets) to cheer Black champions. "Colored" championships, which had been going in and out of vogue since the turn of the century, were an attempt to partially correct that wrong. The fact that the true champion of the division Henry Armstrong was himself "colored" made the title redundant, but the recognition nonetheless carried some weight.

Burley was an all-around special fighter: strong, quick, hard-hitting, rugged, and skillful. Veteran boxing trainer Ray Arcel, considered by some to be the best trainer in the sport's history, already saw Burley as the best fighter alive. "This guy can fight Joe Louis," he told middleweight Billy Soose after Soose met defeat at the hands of the Pittsburgh star. Arcel wasn't alone in this estimation. Decades later, Eddie Futch, one of the few trainers whose legacy rivals Arcel's, said he considered Burley the finest fighter he ever saw with his own eyes.[340]

If Henry Armstrong can be said to have "ducked" any fighter in his career, it is Charley Burley. At 5'9" tall, and already growing out of the welterweight division, Charley would have had a tremendous size advantage over Henry, and he was significantly younger. Those advantages and his outstanding skill and talent would have made him a real threat to lift the welterweight crown. Even if Armstrong did win the match, Burley could make him look bad while doing it. He was Henry's number-one contender for months and deserved a title shot.

The story goes that when Burley's people approached Eddie Mead in 1939, Mead insisted that Armstrong would first defend his welterweight crown in a third match with Lou Ambers and then return to the lightweight division permanently. Henry would no longer defend his welterweight championship and would abdicate the crown soon, he promised. Burley just needed to wait, and he could then fight for the vacated title. That lie stalled the Burley fight long enough for Charley to outgrow the welterweight division and begin campaigning permanently as a middleweight.

Charley Burley would spend his fourteen-year pro career chasing and never receiving a title shot. Wins over Soose, Cocoa Kid, Fritzie Zivic, Georgie Abrams, Jimmy Bivins, Holman Williams, Jack Chase, and Archie Moore did no good, even though all were world-class boxers, and several are now in the Hall of Fame. Zivic was so desperate never to meet Burley in the ring again that he allegedly bought Charley's managerial contract to create a conflict of interest forbidding the fight. Even the great Sugar Ray Robinson, who faced more world champions and Hall of Famers than any other fighter in history, supposedly jumped through all kinds of hoops to avoid meeting Burley in the ring.

For decent paydays, Burley would even take on heavyweights. Weighing just 151 ½ pounds himself, he turned the face of 219 ½ pound, six-foot-three-inch Jay D Turner "to raw beefsteak" in 1942.[341]

Arguably the greatest fighter to have never won a world championship, Charley Burley retired in 1950 with a record of 83 wins (50 by knockout), 12 losses, and two draws and took a job working for the city of Pittsburgh sanitation department. In June 1992, he was inducted into the International Boxing Hall of Fame. At long last receiving official recognition for his outstanding achievements, Charley Burley passed away just four months later, on October 16, 1992, at age seventy-five.

Eddie was not entirely lying when stalling Burley. There had been an agreement that Ambers's win for the lightweight championship guaranteed him a shot at Armstrong's welterweight laurels. That part was true. The plan called for the rubber match with Ambers on November 1. However, with Lou pending nuptials scheduled for October 5, Al Weill postponed the fight.

Mead decided the best way to make money in the interim was to take his champion on another barnstorming tour around the U.S. collecting quick paydays fighting lesser opponents once or twice a week, offering up the title as he did so. Weill predicted Ambers would be ready for another fight by December, which meant Henry could close out 1939 and his career with a big championship payday.

Thus, Henry's return to the ring after losing the lightweight belt came on short notice. On October 9, 1939, he fought a rematch against San Francisco's Al Manfredo, who was not ranked in the top ten in any division but was an experienced ring veteran. Henry had stopped Manfredo in the third round the prior year.

The second fight occurred in Des Moines, Iowa, of all places. The NBA declared that they would not recognize it as a title fight because of Manfredo's not being ranked among the organization's top three contenders. This was a dubious ruling, especially considering that the organization recognized Henry's other defenses against men not in their top three. Fifty-five hundred spectators filed into the Des Moines Coliseum to watch Henry, 141 ½ pounds, drown Manfredo, 146 ½ pounds, in a "shower of leather" until referee Alex Fidler stopped the fight in the fourth with Manfredo helplessly sagging into the ropes.[342]

Just four days later, Henry was in Minneapolis, Minnesota, facing another overmatched opponent in Howard Scott, an Okie based in Washington, DC, with forty-five losses on his record. Scott had been fighting for a decade and had multiple wins over former featherweight champ Battling Battalino on his resumé, not to mention Frankie Klick and Eddie Zivic. That was all in the past, though. When he entered the ring with Henry Armstrong, Scott had lost his previous six matches, two of those to Pedro Montanez, who was much more deserving of a title shot. Somehow, the NBA voiced no objections to recognizing this matchup for the welterweight honors.

On Friday the thirteenth, Henry put Scott on the floor twice inside two rounds, and the challenger could not rise the second time. Henry suffered a cut over his right eye during the fight, which may have prompted him to put his opponent away quickly. Feeling they did not get their money's worth, members of the crowd booed the quick knockout. Scott fought just once more and retired before the close of the year.

The day after the Scott win, Henry packed his bags for Seattle. It was Ritchie Fontaine's turn. Fontaine held a decision win over Henry from way back in 1936, but Henry had avenged that within weeks. Since then, Fontaine had been inconsistent. He had beaten Tony Chavez and California Jackie Wilson but also lost to both. There were more losses to Baby Arizmendi, Leo Rodak, and others. He challenged Henry for the title on October 20 in Seattle's Civic Auditorium. After watching Fontaine hit the deck seven times inside three rounds, referee Tony Clark saved him from further unnecessary punishment. The writer for the *Seattle Star* quipped that Henry "can be put down as the nation's leading exponent of shorter and shorter working hours."[343]

Again, Henry was on the road the very next day. This time his destination was home. A fight was scheduled in Los Angeles for ten rounds against Jimmy Garrison, the man many fans and writers called the most capable of Armstrong's tour. Raised in Kansas City but popular in the L.A. area, Garrison had a spotty record but had lasted ten rounds against Lou Ambers and had twice beaten Tony Chavez. Fight experts pointed out that Henry was a sucker for the uppercut and that "there is no finer exponent of that effective punch, anywhere in the world, than fighting Jimmy Garrison."[344]

Live underdog or not, Garrison's challenge of Henry Armstrong failed to draw out the champion's hometown fans. Many of the seats at the Olympic were empty when the fighters entered the ring on the evening of Saturday, October 24. Armstrong weighed 138 ½ pounds; Garrison was a pound heavier.

The reporter for the *Los Angeles Times* felt Henry seemed to be Dr. Jekyll and Mr. Hyde that night in the ring. For the first five rounds, he boxed cautiously against Garrison, who tried his best but barely laid a glove on him. Perhaps the champion was wary of the challenger's reputation, or perhaps he wanted to give his hometown fans a longer show than the quick knockouts he had been collecting of late. Whatever the reason, the famous fury of "Hurricane Henry" was nowhere in sight for the early frames but suddenly appeared in round six and stuck around until the final bell. Garrison showed bravery in getting up from a knockdown in the eighth round and surviving to the end, but never threatened to take away the title. Henry Armstrong walked away with a unanimous decision.[345]

On October 30, the champion squeezed in one more defense before the month's close, taking on Cleveland's Bobby Pacho, a man he had stopped in four rounds earlier in the year. Pacho went out inside of four rounds again in his second try at Henry's title at the Municipal Auditorium in Denver.[346]

That made for four successful title defenses inside one month, five if one counts the Al Manfredo bout, regardless of what the NBA decided. Joe Louis was considered a remarkably active champion for knocking over one challenger every thirty days or so. Henry's activity was putting the famous Brown Bomber to shame.

In November, Henry and Lou Ambers jointly fired the opening shots of New York's annual bicycle race at Madison Square Garden. Their appearance was a promotion for an expected third battle between the pair scheduled for December 1, with the welterweight championship on the line. However, Eddie eventually claimed that Henry had caught a cold, and called off the fight. The third meeting between Armstrong and Ambers would never materialize. Al Weill believed Henry simply did not want such a tough fight again, and he told Ambers so.[347]

To cap off the year that he had intended to be his last as a prizefighter, the champ squeezed in one more title defense, a rematch with Jimmy Garrison on December 11, this time in Cleveland. Henry, weighing 138 ¼ pounds, got off to a quicker start this time than in their first bout, bloodying and knocking out Garrison, 141 pounds, inside seven rounds. Even so, many in the press declared that he did not look like the "Human Buzz Saw" of old; some blamed the cold, and others saw it as a sign that his best years were behind him.

The Garrison bout was his eleventh successful title defense in 1939 and his one-hundredth professional win overall. A day later, Henry celebrated his thirtieth birthday but also received the news that the New York State Athletic Commission was considering suspending him for taking the fight with Garrison while claiming to be too sick to face Ambers.[348]

Despite the controversial loss of his lightweight title to Ambers, Henry had enjoyed an excellent year as a welterweight champion and movie star. *The Ring* recognized Joe Louis as Fighter of the Year for the second year in a row, but it had also been remarkable for Henry. He came in sixth place in the voting, one notch even above Ambers, who had taken the lightweight title from him that same year.

Nat Fleischer noted Henry's multiple defenses of the title but also pointed out that, only Davey Day and Ernie Roderick represented any genuine challenge to Armstrong, who Fleischer described as "without a peer." Even so, Nat wrote that Henry appeared to have lost a step both in punching power and speed through 1939 compared to the dynamo who had trounced Barney Ross the prior year. Whether he was a fading champion or not, *The Ring* still put Henry's face on its painted cover for its year-end issue, alongside those of the sport's other big-name stars of 1939, Joe Louis, Billy Conn, Lou Ambers, Al Hostak, and Ceferino Garcia.[349]

Henry returned to California to celebrate Christmas with his family in the second half of December. He felt ready for and entitled to retirement after such a successful and physically trying series of years between 1937 and 1939. His body was telling him so, too. He had broken knuckles and fingers on multiple occasions, and they were getting brittle. He bled in almost every fight now. Scar tissue crisscrossed his eyelids and lips. In his dressing room after the win over Pacho on October 30, he told reporters, "When I go in there, I go in to win of course, but I just don't enjoy it like I once did – not after 10 years. I suppose it's like any other job, it gets monotonous."[350]

In the end, the need for money outweighed retirement. Eddie Mead was engaged to a chorus girl and had a wedding and honeymoon to pay for. Henry also wanted to retire with a one hundred-thousand-dollar annuity, and at year's end, he found he was short twenty-five grand.

On the day after Christmas, word hit the papers that Henry would fight a white boxer named Joe Gnouly on January 4 in St. Louis. Missouri had finally legalized interracial fights. Gnouly was not a ranked contender so far as *The Ring* was concerned, probably because Freddie Miller, Benny Bass, Barney Ross, Kid Chocolate, Tony Canzoneri, and Lew Feldman had all beaten him up already. But he was a ten-year ring veteran who had only been stopped once in 101 outings, and that fact won him respect from the fans and the press in his hometown of St. Louis. For promoter Tom Packs, it was a no-brainer. The match between two local boxing stars for the world championship promised to draw a large hometown crowd.[351]

The Gnouly fight, held in the St. Louis Auditorium in front of 3,035 fans, was as much of a wipeout as one would expect. Down three times in the first three minutes, the challenger managed to survive the first round but was so out of it when he returned to his corner that his chief second had to administer "enough smelling salts to revive King Tut" between rounds. Amazingly, Gnouly made it as far as the fifth when a series of lefts put him down for the count. Henry received $2,228 of the $6,359 gate. Gnouly received $403.[352]

By mid-January, the NYSAC had gotten over their displeasure with the champion and decided against suspension. So, it was off to New York for Henry's first fight in Madison Square Garden in ten months against his most dangerous opponent since Ambers, Puerto Rican slugger Pedro Montanez.

Boasting a record of 91 wins against six defeats and four draws, Montanez had been fighting professionally since he was sixteen and had never once tasted the canvas. Nicknamed "El Torito" ("Little Bull"), he briefly held the Puerto Rican lightweight championship in 1933. Montanez was a world traveler. Bouts in Venezuela, Spain, France, England, and Italy were on his record before he came to New York City sometime in the late summer of 1935.[353]

**Pedro Montanez, "El Torito"**

In the Big Apple, the knockout artist Montanez became a sensation, the new favorite fighter of the city's growing Puerto Rican populace. However, Jimmy Johnston, then in charge at Madison Square Garden, refused to give Montanez a title shot, afraid he would take his championship abroad and out of Johnston's promotional jurisdiction should he win. This inspired Montanez to go undefeated in a string of fifty bouts between September 1933 and September 1937, essentially wiping out any viable alternatives for lightweight champion Lou Ambers to face. He even beat Ambers in a non-title affair on April 5, 1937. He was part of the talented crop of fighters Mike Jacobs signed as part of the wily promoter's coup to take over the Garden. Jacobs matched him with Ambers for the title in his "Carnival of Champions" that Autumn. He lost a majority decision (one judge scored it a draw) to the resourceful "Herkimer Hurricane." Many believed that the challenger had badly weakened himself to make weight.

Not to be denied another title shot, Montanez set his sights on Armstrong's crown and went undefeated in his next twenty-two bouts as a welterweight, beating the likes of Kid Berg, Howard Scott, Phil Furr, Young Peter Jackson, and others to establish himself as the number one contender in *The Ring* Ratings by May of 1939. However, an eighth-round stoppage loss to natural lightweight Davey Day that month not only knocked him off the number one spot but out of the magazine's top ten contenders altogether. Pittsburgh's Fritzie Zivic was now the outstanding welterweight contender as far as the magazine was concerned. Still, Pedro remained a big-time boxing star, especially in New York City, and the Garden nearly sold out in anticipation of his long-awaited shot at the welterweight title and the return of Henry Armstrong. "Many experienced followers of the punching business expect Montanez to furnish an upset," reported James P. Dawson in the *Times*.[354]

Henry began training on January 15 in the Roxy Gymnasium in New York. Fighters named Jackie Murray, Cal Holmes, Joe Law, Sammy Jackson, Gene Johnson, and Bobby Ruffin all served as his sparring partners. Noting that Henry was more flat-footed in training, some onlookers believed that the champ might have lost a step in his speed and was instead focusing on increased punching power. Others insisted that Hurricane Henry was as much a raging whirlwind as ever. His sparring partners frequently quit before the end of their scheduled sessions, and Eddie Mead told reporters that Henry was training the hardest he had since the Petey Sarron match. When Henry tried to sneak in another sparring session the day before the fight, promoter Jacobs nixed it, afraid the champion might get injured.[355]

Montanez trained first in Saratoga, New York, then in Lakewood, New Jersey, and finished up at Stillman's Gym. He was said to be more determined in his preparations than at any previous time in his career.

On Wednesday, January 24, a near-sellout crowd of 19,157 fans paid $59,575 to see Henry take on his most capable challenger in many months for the year's debut boxing show at the Garden. Henry would receive a payday of $17,694, Montanez $10,111. At fight time, Henry was the betting favorite by odds of about five or six to one, though Montanez was by far the sentimental favorite for the New York crowd. Armstrong weighed 139 ¾ pounds to Montanez's 144 ½.

The fans were treated to rousing back-and-forth action during the two opening frames and showed their appreciation by filling the vast venue with a steady roar. Armstrong threw more punches, but Montanez's blows seemed to be the harder of the two. On more than one occasion in the opening two frames, the Puerto Rican fighter's hard right uppercuts to Henry's face rocked him off balance. Likewise, Montanez could not seem to get out of the way of Henry's slashing left hook. The early going was close, but by the end of round two, the challenger was visibly exhausted by the champion's overwhelming pace.[356]

Pedro bravely fought on, but in round four, Armstrong pummeled him with a volley of "trip-hammer blows," and the bloodied Torito hit the deck for the first time in his career. He was up at five but was soon down again for a count of seven. At this, a fight broke out between fans in the boxed seats.[357]

In a desperate bid to turn the momentum of the action, Montanez summoned what remained of his strength and lived up to his "Little Bull" reputation by charging headlong at the champion in the fifth. He managed to survive through the next few rounds. As the two battlers slugged it out, a cut over the challenger's eye widened and bled terribly.

Montanez's cornermen tried to convince him to call it quits after the seventh, but he protested. "They say I yellow! No yellow! I fight!" he cried, shoving them aside. He bolted out of his corner at the bell before the cornermen could signal to the referee. Montanez had nothing left but his pride. Henry knew it, and he meant to end the Puerto Rican fighter's suffering in the eighth.

"So terrific was Henry's pace and so powerful were his punches then that Montanez virtually stood through that round a helpless creature," reported Nat Fleischer in *The Ring*. Toward the end of the round, an Armstrong right spun Montanez around in a circle, and Henry then sent home a left-right-left combination that put the challenger on the floor for a third time. The bell saved him, and after carrying him to their corner, his team reluctantly revived him for the ninth. Pedro made it a few feet out of his corner before Henry was on top of him, crashing home vicious blows with both hands on the defenseless challenger. Nearly every punch hit its target. As Montanez crumpled down against the ropes, referee Billy Cavanaugh stepped in and mercifully called a halt to the slaughter.[358]

James P. Dawson praised Montanez's gallant effort as the best of the Puerto Rican hero's New York performances despite the loss, but he wrote that Henry Armstrong was unbeatable. "No welterweight, no man near Armstrong's inches or poundage could have survived the blistering fire of blows the doughty Los Angeles Negro unleashed," he insisted.[359]

Ted Carroll of *The Ring* called the fight "one of the most slashing slugfests ever seen in the Madison Square Garden ring" and attributed Henry's win to the "durability of his never ceasing attack and his ability to wear down almost any opponent." He also praised Montanez's bravery and said that the Puerto Rican fighter was Armstrong's absolute equal in everything but stamina during the fight. Editor Fleischer considered the fight Henry's best performance since he took the welterweight title from Barney Ross in 1938.[360]

Ross had been ringside for the fight. He likely empathized with the challenger's valiant but hopeless effort against the relentless Armstrong assault. "No yellow," indeed. Montanez's bravery so moved Ross that he visited his dressing room after the fight to congratulate him on his effort, but the bloodied, swollen Pedro was inconsolable.

A group of reporters swarmed around Barney on his way out the door, wanting to know what he thought of Henry Armstrong's performance.

"Armstrong is terrific," he told them. "He wears you down by the round. You can nail him with everything you've got but he shakes them off."[361]

Before the fight, *The Ring* did not rate Pedro among its top ten welterweight contenders. Afterward, they installed him as seventh-ranked man in the division in recognition of his brave showing against the dominant world champion. Dubuque's Milt Aron was Henry's number-one contender thanks to his December knockout of Fritzie Zivic.[362]

Pedro Montanez fought just once more and retired. In retirement, he became a successful trainer and businessman and remained a beloved hero on his native island, where a sports stadium and baseball team were named after him. He passed away on June 26, 1996, at age 82 and was posthumously inducted into the International Boxing Hall of Fame in 2007. His Hall of Fame biography describes him as "one of the all-time great boxers from Puerto Rico," an island with a rich tradition of fistic icons.[363]

# 14.
# A Fourth Title?

Henry now had fourteen welterweight title defenses behind him, more than any other champ in division history. But once again, the monotony of one fight after another was setting in. He enjoyed the big paychecks and the lifestyle they brought him, but Henry told reporters he was growing weary of the grind. Without a goal before him, he always felt aimless.

So, Henry and Eddie came up with their next big plan. He had already tied the record for the most division championships with three, but now Henry would break the record and conquer a fourth by annexing the world's middleweight championship.

At the time, boxing's major sanctioning bodies differed in their recognition of middleweight championship. Filipino Ceferino Garcia held recognition by the NYSAC and was the lineal ("the man who beat the man") champion by virtue of his win over Fred Apostoli. The NBA, meanwhile, through circumstances happening both in and out of the ring, recognized Al Hostak, the "Savage Slav" from Minneapolis, as their champion. When the largely unknown Tony Zale of Gary, Indiana, beat him in Chicago on January 29, 1940, he became the NBA's new titleholder. All the while, *The Ring* didn't recognize any of them, declaring their championship vacant.

For some time, talk circulated that Henry intended to invade the middleweight division on a one-fight basis and challenge for his fourth title against Garcia, a man he had already beaten in defense of his welterweight honors back in 1938. Henry expressed eagerness to take on Garcia again and set a new record, but when Garcia refused to come down to 150 pounds to fight him, most figured the fight would not happen.

By January 26, the papers carried the unexpected news that Eddie Mead had signed a contract with Garcia's people for a ten-round fight in Los Angeles to be held on February 22. Mead and Armstrong withdrew the weight stipulation, and Garcia signed the contract. Even so, constant controversy plagued the Armstrong-Garcia fight.

The deal was made, but Henry was upset with the Hollywood Legion, the fight's promoters. They had a rule against promoting events featuring Black fighters but announced they would make an exception for this one lucrative matchup. Relying on Mead and attorney Hugh McBeth to work out the details, Henry insisted that he would only sign with them if they permanently removed the racial barrier. *The Chicago Defender*, the nation's leading Black newspaper, sent its attorney, Dan Shaw, to aid Henry's cause. West Coast boxing manager and promoter George Moore also threw his influence behind Henry. There were threats to boycott the fight.

The pressure Henry and others put on the Hollywood Legion made headlines nationwide. Pioneering Black actor Clarence Muse, a Hollywood resident, shared his thoughts on the matter with the readers of *The Defender*. He called Henry's push against the Legion's racist policy an inspiration. "Men fight side by side for DEMOCRACY, and then turn their backs when it comes to clean sport," he complained of the hypocrisy. Muse wrote that several movie stars aided Henry in pressuring the Legion to change its rules.[364]

Eventually, the California Athletic Commission got involved. On January 26, a crowd of Black residents arrived at the Commission offices to support Henry's stance. While the Commission was in recess to consider the case, the Legion voluntarily rescinded its policy rather than face the bad press of being ordered to do so. It was a rare instance of Henry using his prominence to expose and combat racism. McBeth, Moore, Muse, and others sent Henry a telegram to announce the victory and suggest Henry allow the Legion to promote the Garcia fight. Arriving by plane from Chicago on January 31, he did just that.

The Legion's policies were not the only promotional problem. Mead was having trouble getting permission from Mike Jacobs, who had no interest in promoting in California and owned exclusive promotional rights to Garcia and Armstrong. Uncle Mike threatened an injunction against the fight. Eddie stayed in New York to keep working on Jacobs.

Another roadblock to the fight came when L.A.'s Wrigley Field, the intended site of the event, was potentially taken off the table by construction and renovation projects on the ballpark, forcing Hollywood Legion representatives to consider new venues with just weeks to go. Eventually, Gilmore Stadium was chosen as the tentative replacement venue because it had seating for forty thousand.

Despite threats from Jacobs, Eddie Mead informed the Legion that Armstrong would show up for the fight, whatever the legal repercussions. Jacobs threatened Mead - by way of the *Hollywood Post*'s Charley MacDonald - that he intended to use all his extensive legal and financial resources to put a stop to the fight.

The California State Athletic Commission, now chaired by Henry's former manager Tom Cox, soon got involved. Based on the agreements of both fighters with the Hollywood Legion, the Commission announced that should the fight not happen in California, it would reprimand both fighters and request a federal investigation into the Twentieth Century Sporting Club's alleged monopoly over boxing. Jacobs backed off.

As if the fight needed more controversy, protests soon arose from residents of the Hollywood neighborhoods surrounding Gilmore Stadium, who objected to the noise and traffic expected with the most significant fight California had seen in years.

Henry arrived via airplane in rainy Burbank, California, on Wednesday, January 31. A large welcome wagon of fans, boxing personalities, reporters, and of course, Willa Mae and four-year-old Lanetta greeted him. That Friday, he watched a bout between two familiar names, Jimmy Garrison and Tony Chavez, who hoped for a shot at his title. Garrison won a ten-round decision.

Afterward, Henry sequestered himself into training at the Main Street Gym in L.A. His sparring partners in preparation for Garcia were middleweights Otto Blackwell and Nat Bor, along with welterweight Melvin Crisp.

While New York boxing fans and critics favored the welterweight champ to take his fourth division title, most sportswriters in California were not so sure. Garcia had been so weight-drained in challenging Armstrong for welterweight honors in 1938, said Ned Cronin of the *Los Angeles Daily News*, that he "needed only a pair of diapers to double for Mahatma Gandhi." Cronin pointed out that Garcia had lasted the full fifteen rounds with Henry in that meeting, insinuating that a well-nourished Garcia, the champion this time around, would perform even better in the rematch.

Dick Hyland of the *Los Angeles Times* wrote that "Mr. Armstrong is due to get himself tagged sufficiently to awaken from his dream of possessing four world championships in one lifetime," adding that "in the final rounds a tired Negro boy is going to find a bull-like Filipino much stronger, much more ferocious, not unlikely to knock him right on his back." Bob Ray, also of *The Times*, did pick Armstrong, but he was in the minority among the "experts" of his city.

Among ex-champions polled, former lightweight king Benny Leonard picked Armstrong to win, but the press pointed out Benny's horrible record of predicting outcomes. Barney Ross, who had shared the ring with both men, picked Garcia, as did Baby Arizmendi.[365]

In later life, Henry claimed that gangsters tried to bribe him to throw the fight. He had been training in the mountains of Pasadena because his home was being remodeled. Harry woke him up one morning and asked him to come to the Main Street Gym in L.A. for an unexpected meeting. Eddie was waiting for them with several cigar-smoking men he did not recognize. One of the strangers tossed a large stack of hundred-dollar bills on the table between them and spread it out "like a deck of cards." Henry estimated the amount at fifteen thousand dollars (Another source says seventy-five thousand).[366]

"Take it," the money man insisted. "It's all yours."

Naturally, Henry asked what the money was for. The man hesitated at first but eventually explained.

"Listen, Champ. I don't know just how to give you this, but – that money's yours if you'll let Garcia put you down in three rounds." In another version of the tale, the bag man told him it was only a down payment and he would get double the money once he took the dive. He said Henry could fake an injury, giving Garcia a technical knockout win.[367]

Shocked, Henry looked over at Eddie and Harry. They both looked back at him with pleading eyes, and he could tell they were in on it. They wanted the money. Henry thought of all the friends and fans risking their money on him and felt a surge of rage. He told the men he would not take a dive for a million dollars. He said he would fire Mead and report the fixers to the FBI if they returned. Retrieving their money from the table, the group departed, and Henry never saw them again. An acquaintance later told him they had represented Benjamin "Bugsy" Siegel, the New York City thug turned Los Angeles celebrity gangster, a lifelong pal of Henry's backer George Raft.[368]

Then a rope burn caused an infection in Garcia's leg. It seemed the fight was cursed. The champion's manager, George Parnassus, pulled him from training and announced that his fighter could not meet the February 22 date. Combat was rescheduled for March 1.

"The delay made it worse for me," Henry told sports columnist Prescott Sullivan years later. "I was under that much more strain, wondering what might happen to me because I wouldn't go through with the deal."[369]

**Henry Armstrong, Dr. Lloyd Mace, and Ceferino Garcia**

Henry may have turned down the money, but that was no guarantee he could beat Garcia at middleweight. He later recounted that he only weighed 131 ½ pounds on the day of the fight, not nearly enough to qualify to fight as a middleweight at the weigh-in before the boxing commission. Henry later said that Mead found some string that matched Henry's skin tone, sewed lead shotgun slugs into the string, and then tied the string around Henry's waist underneath his boxing trunks. He soaked the towel around Henry's waist in water to add weight. Henry then chugged all the water he could minutes before it was time to step on the scale. He still came in at just 142 pounds, eighteen pounds under the middleweight limit. Garcia was 153 ½.[370]

The sky was clear, and the night air was cool on Friday, March 1. Henry entered the open-air Gilmore Stadium ring wearing five-ounce gloves. At the same time, the champion sported six-ounce gloves because of a technicality in the California State Athletic Commission's rules that designated different glove sizes for boxers over 145 pounds and those under. George Parnassus pleaded with Tom Cox to make an exception, but Cox was unmoved. Both fighters arrived wrapped in thick bathrobes to keep warm.

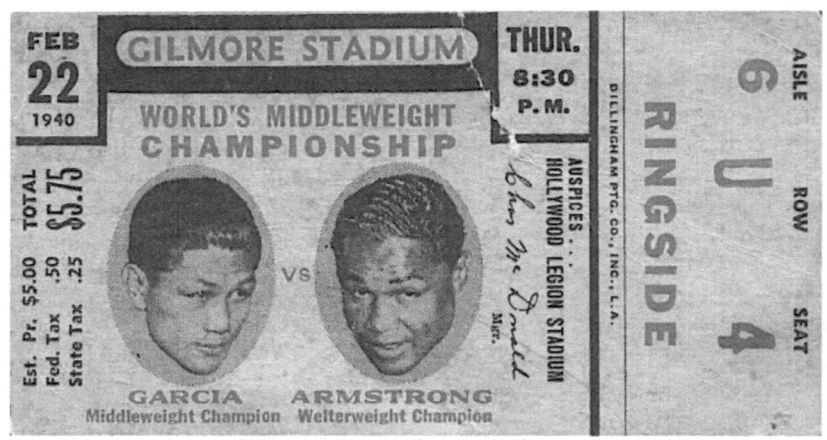

A ringside ticket to Armstrong-Garcia II

Twenty-five thousand fans paid $69,953.45 to watch the long-awaited ten-round fight. The gate disappointed the Hollywood Legion's expectations.[371]

More important to Henry, his ailing father made a rare appearance at ringside. Years of manual labor, alcoholism, and illness were taking their toll on Henry Jackson Senior's health, but he made it to the stadium to see his son make history.

Once round one got under way, both fighters immediately met shoulder-to-shoulder at ring center. They began shoving against each other, fighting for physical command of the ring real estate. Though he was only a half inch taller than Henry, Ceferino's much larger frame dwarfed his challenger. Henry could already feel the difference in the well-fed Garcia's physical strength and punching power. A huge bolo uppercut nearly dropped Henry, but he recovered quickly and poured back in with his ceaseless attack. The fight was a constant shoving match between the two sluggers. Henry ran back to his corner at the sound of the bell to end round one. Garcia returned to his corner bleeding from a cut above his left eye.

Through much of round two, Garcia threw terrific uppercuts that had Armstrong ducking and weaving for cover while returning too few punches of his own. Garcia's reputation as the hardest puncher in the sport was on full display. Referee George Blake, also serving as the sole judge for the fight, penalized Henry this round due to repeated use of his forearms and elbows as weapons. The round likely already belonged to Garcia based on his dominance of the early minutes.

By bringing his gloves underneath his chin in round three, Henry could block many of the uppercuts that had been so successful the prior round. He stayed in the champion's chest, taking the best Garcia could throw by blocking or moving his head. Again, the fighters shoved and wrestled for real estate. Garcia always wound up pressed into the ropes taking hooks and uppercuts from his challenger. When Henry returned to his corner, the old scar inside his mouth from the first Ambers bout had opened and was bleeding.

The next several rounds followed the same pattern as round three: As in every one of his fights, Henry was the aggressor, and he threw far more punches than his opponent. There were fewer of his signature looping overhand rights to the head as he focused instead on short uppercuts and hooks. Garcia stayed shoulder-to-shoulder with him but was usually pressed backward by the smaller man. Still, punching power is the great equalizer in boxing, and Garcia was landing the harder blows. Henry's right eye began swelling early. Blake penalized Henry for butting and an alleged low blow in round five, taking away a round that Armstrong would have likely won otherwise.

By round seven, Henry's right eye was completely shut and swollen to the size of a baseball, but Garcia's blows were at last losing steam. Henry was tearing him up with hooks to the head when that round ended. After an impressive rally in round eight, Garcia seemed to have no more energy left to land anything of consequence. Still, he bravely fought on, enduring terrific punishment from Armstrong, who seemed to be in a frenzy. "It became an acute problem of fighting back or jumping out of the ring and Garcia accepted the prerogative of meeting him blow for blow," reported *The Ring*'s Eddie Borden. [372]

Henry's powerful overhand right finally made repeated appearances in the tenth and final round, and Garcia could do little to defend against it. In his signature crouch, the challenger repeatedly thrust his head like a battering ram into the champion's chest as though he were trying to crash through his sternum. Garcia tried to tie Henry up for the first time, but the challenger was relentless. He slipped into his "Homicide Hank" persona and unleashed all his weaponry with white-hot fury. After the final bell, Blake had to pull the still-punching Armstrong off the trapped Garcia.

With the fight over, Garcia's face was puffy and bled from two cuts above his right eye. Gruesome swellings stuck out from each temple "like hardboiled eggs." Henry did not look much better. Cal Whorton of the *Los Angeles Times* thought he "looked like the result of some big accident."[373]

Referee Blake, the sole judge, held up the hands of both fighters, indicating his verdict of a draw. This meant that the reigning champion would keep his crown. Before the crowd could absorb the news, the referee "dashed down the aisle and disappeared out of the gate." A chorus of boos then erupted throughout the stadium.[374]

Debate raged throughout the stadium and in the newspapers after the fight. Who, if anyone, deserved the win? The *Los Angeles Daily News*'s Ned Cronin, who had initially predicted a Garcia victory, thought the draw appropriate. Gordon Macker of the same paper recorded that most of press row felt Henry was robbed. Paul Zimmerman of the *Los Angeles Times* felt that a verdict for either fighter would have been a better decision than a draw, so far as the fans were concerned. Jules Covey of the State Commission agreed with Zimmerman. The *New York Times* correspondent reported that the crowd was divided, but many thought Garcia deserved the victory because of his effective "bolo" uppercuts. Eddie Brietz of the Associated Press and Henry McLemore of the United Press thought the draw verdict appropriate.

"Many ring-siders thought Garcia earned it with his uppercuts to the head that twice had the Negro reeling backward, but just as many gave the fight to Armstrong for his usual ever-punching aggressiveness," wrote Brietz.

Borden thought Armstrong deserved the fight by two rounds when considering the foul deductions, by more if it were not for the penalties. *The Ring* would later name the hard-fought bout its "Fight of the Year" for 1940.[375]

In his dressing room after the fight, through badly swollen lips, Henry said he felt he won the fight but had no complaints about Blake's decision. He apologized to his fans for letting them down. Surprisingly, Eddie Mead had no complaints, either.

"I have all the trust in the world in George Blake," Eddie said. Blake was a "fine official" and "one of the most honest men in the game," he added.[376]

In Garcia's dressing room, George Parnassus said that a second, new leg infection had slowed his fighter. Garcia pointed to a red boil on Ceferino's leg and said the sore prevented him from keeping his distance.

"I had to stand and punch with him up close," admitted Garcia. His right hand was severely swollen from an injury he said happened in the fourth round.[377]

Regarding the decision, the champion had no comment, but his manager was more than willing to speak for him. Parnassus erupted in rage at the mention of Armstrong's rough tactics. He criticized the referee for not penalizing Henry enough. "Why don't we take a baseball bat in there?" he shouted at the reporters.[378]

Told of Parnassus's accusations by the press, Eddie Mead responded, "What did they expect my fighter to do? Did they want him to stop and wait for the red lights and go sign?" He then pointed out that the referee could have just as well penalized Garcia for repeated blows to Henry's kidneys.[379]

Henry Jackson Senior walked into the room and looked concernedly over his bruised, bloodied, and bandaged son. Henry wordlessly looked at his father and signaled that he was alright. Even so, the elder Henry wanted reassurance from the doctor, who promised his son would be fine.

To Whorton, Henry seemed more concerned with keeping his team in good spirits than with the referee's decision. He maintained a forced smile as he rose from a rubbing table and began to get dressed.[380]

Macker was sentimental in his second-person account of the same scene. "Before you leave you take one final look at the boy on the table. Guess you'd call it a reverent look. Because you feel tonight you've seen the greatest fighter in action you'll ever see in your lifetime."[381]

In over eighty years since the Garcia versus Armstrong middleweight championship fight, part of the Armstrong legend has always included that Blake's draw verdict amounted to robbery. Watching the fight film and reading the contemporary newspaper accounts of the battle, the result of a draw is not necessarily egregious. Several noteworthy writers either thought that Garcia won, thought a draw was correct, or recorded the sentiments of fans who thought Garcia deserved the win. Round one was fiercely competitive. Garcia undoubtedly took round two and arguably round eight. If one includes the two foul penalties, it is not unfathomable that Garcia would have ended up with five of the ten rounds.

Still, Borden noted that plenty of people thought Armstrong deserved the win at the time, as he dominated most of the action in the second half of the fight. It was a highly competitive fight with momentum changes. One man landed more punches while the other landed the harder blows. Such bouts often end up with controversial but not necessarily corrupt decisions.

The accusations of dishonesty on Blake's part are difficult to accept, considering his reputation. Eddie Mead was not the only man to regard him as a paragon of honesty. Damon Runyon, one of the most respected sportswriters of the era, thought him "the 18-karat mark of square dealing." Blake was a respected trainer and manager as well as a referee. He had guided Fidel LaBarba's prosperous ring career, and LaBarba testified to his honesty. "We never had a contract in thirteen years," the onetime flyweight champ recalled. "I had to argue him into taking the regular manager's cut of one third." He hardly sounds like a man who would compromise his reputation for money.[382]

George Blake had been refereeing fights for over thirty years when he took the Garcia-Armstrong assignment. His only other significantly controversial call before it was stopping the heavyweight championship match between Max Schmeling and Young Stribling. Some felt the stoppage was premature.[383]

Whenever reporters asked about his draw call saving Garcia's title, Blake would only respond, "Armstrong fouled himself out of the championship." He never refereed another fight and died at age seventy-three on December 20, 1952.[384]

Henry insisted he got a raw deal from Blake for the rest of his life. He said that he once confronted the referee about the match and that Blake admitted the fight was fixed. "They told him if he gave that fight to me, he'd never get out of that ring alive."[385]

"Maybe it's better they called it a draw, though, because if I'd won, before long they'd be matching me with Joe Louis!" Henry once quipped.[386]

Following his draw with Armstrong, Garcia lost the middleweight championship in his next defense to Norfolk, Virginia's Ken Overlin, a huge upset. He then went 5-4-1 in his next ten bouts and retired from boxing with a pro record of 121 wins (77 by knockout), 30 losses, and 14 draws.

He had a few bit parts in the movies through the rest of the 1940s and took Chalky Wright's position as Mae West's driver. Remaining a resident of Los Angeles for the rest of his life, Garcia died on New Year's Day, 1981, at age seventy-four. He still holds the record for most career victories of any Filipino boxer and is the only man from his nation to win the world middleweight championship. Though he was an inductee into *The Ring* Hall of Fame and the World Boxing Hall of Fame, both are now defunct, and he has yet to be enshrined in the International Boxing Hall of Fame, though he deserves the honor.[387]

After the Garcia fight, Henry's face was a mess for his doctor Alexander Schiff to patch up. But Henry mostly complained about pain in his left arm. Dr. Schiff discovered a bad hemorrhage in the bicep. He also told the press that Henry had broken his left hand again. Still the undisputed welterweight champion of the world, Henry would take the next seven weeks off to heal before defending his title. It was one of the longest layoffs of his career so far.

Facial scars, injured limbs, fragile hands, and slowing reflexes; Henry knew his body was beginning to break down on him, and his main goal remained retirement. During his break, he told reporters that he had put away ninety thousand of his intended one hundred-thousand-dollar annuity, which would start paying out in 1945.[388]

Eddie Mead's goal for Henry for the rest of 1940 seems to have been to collect as many paydays as possible against easy opposition and then end the year with a big fight against a top name. As of mid-August, *The Ring*'s top five contenders at welterweight, in order, were Cocoa Kid, Holman Williams, Izzy Jannazzo, Milt Aron, and Fritzie Zivic. There was also still a possibility of a third fight with Ambers, this time with welterweight honors on the line. He would face one of them before hanging up the gloves at the end of the year, but until then, it would be relatively easy pickings.[389]

On April 26, 1940, Henry returned to action defending his welterweight championship against Paul Junior, a veteran of nearly two hundred fights out of Lewiston, Maine. Junior had lost twice to Ambers in 1939 but had efficiently put together a twenty-two-fight winning streak afterward. Though stopped before, he had never taken a full ten count.

Junior was not in *The Ring*'s top ten welterweights (He was number seven at lightweight), but he was a big draw in Maine and western Massachusetts, and that was just the kind of non-threatening payday Henry and Eddie were looking for. Taking place in Boston Gardens, it was the first title fight to come off in that city in five years, another fact sure to draw out the area's starved boxing fans.[390]

The NBA did not think the challenger worthy, and they refused to sanction the fifteen-round affair as a title fight, but that mattered little to Armstrong, Junior, the press, or the crowd of 16,469 that flocked to the Gardens that Friday night. The turnout had Mike Jacobs "clicking his bargain counter teeth in a merry melody." Armstrong weighed 139 ½ pounds, Junior 141.

The challenger certainly fought like the championship was up for the taking, aggressively ripping hooks and uppercuts at Henry. "Junior was an agonizing kind of fighter," Henry complimented his challenger. "For a while I found it hard to hit him. He didn't hit me with anything that really hurt, but he started the blood coming from my left eye in the first round. It was the same cut I got in the Garcia fight."

As with all of Armstrong's welterweight challengers, Paul could not handle Henry's pace and eventually wilted. After watching the challenger go down five times, referee Johnny Martin stopped the fight.

Nat Fleischer was happy to take the rare trip to Boston. After the fight, he reported, "Hank has gone down considerably since he won his first world title by beating Petey Sarron in New York, but he still is kingpin among the welterweights."[391]

When asked if he would return to Boston in the future while in his dressing room after the fight, Henry replied, "Sure, with a house like this one, I sure would."

Having waited five years since hosting its previous championship match, Boston only needed to wait weeks to host another. Henry took on Ralph "The Ripper" Zannelli of Providence, Rhode Island, again at the Garden on May 24, 1940.[392]

Zannelli had a record of 44 wins (21 by knockout), eight losses, and three draws behind him when he challenged Henry for the welterweight title. A natural welterweight who had gotten his start in 1936, he had beaten the former junior lightweight champion Johnny Jadick and contender Young Peter Jackson early on but had been inconsistent since and was not rated in the top ten by *The Ring*. Henry weighed in at 140 ½ pounds on the morning of the fight, his challenger 145 ½. The day before the fight, oddsmakers had Henry a ten to three favorite.[393]

Before the fight, Hy Hurwitz of the *Boston Globe* predicted Zannelli would pull off a shocking upset. The next day, he ate a breakfast of his own words. "Little Sir Buzz-Saw made a red mess of Zannelli's swarthy face, flooring the Providence Powerhouse four times for counts of nine before referee Johnny Martin called an armistice one minute and 30 seconds after the fifth round began," Hurwitz was sad to report. Zannelli landed some good shots with both hands and a few low blows and elbows for good measure, but by Hurwitz's estimation, he received twelve punches for every one he landed, and it was mostly easy work for Henry Armstrong.[394]

On June 21, Henry demolished Paul Junior in a rematch. Held in Portland, Maine, it was the state's first title fight but drew a dismal $6,876 gate. Henry put Junior on the canvas four times in round three alone, forcing Johnny Martin to stop the contest. Junior retired at the end of the year.

# 15.
# The Sweetwater Swatter

Just as Henry Armstrong was running out of name opponents, a new and exciting figure arrived on the scene with punching power and personality to spare. He'd risen like a whirlwind out of Texas and run right over the Herkimer Hurricane.

For nine months after regaining the lightweight crown, Lou Ambers put his title on ice in favor of less risky, less trying non-title bouts above his division's weight limit. Victories over Jimmy Vaughn, Norment Quarles, and two over Wally Hally did not provide much of a challenge but did bring steady paydays. A non-title affair with Al "Bummy" Davis, an undefeated scrapper out of the Brownsville section of New York in February of 1940, posed some potential problems, but Lou ultimately came out alright with a unanimous decision victory.

In the meantime, his manager Al Weill was hard at work trying to line up a couple of big-name options for the lightweight champ. A third go at Henry Armstrong for Henry's welterweight belt was the target, but Eddie Mead was non-committal, to say the least. As far as Weill was concerned, stalling was a more apt word. There was also the possibility of a match with Sammy Angott. The NBA had stripped Lou of recognition as champion for taking so long to defend the title, and Angott had won their belt with a decision over Davey Day. Meanwhile, the NYSAC and *The Ring* continued to recognize Lou as the true, lineal lightweight champion of the world. Still, everyone knew that the champ was due for a big-name opponent in a championship fight.

*So why am I in here with this bum from Texas?* Lou Ambers must have been thinking to himself as he stood in the Madison Square Garden ring on May 10, 1940, with the championship finally on the line in front of a mediocre crowd of 13,186. Across the ring from him was not Armstrong or Angott or even the formidable Davis. Instead, a brittle-looking toothpick of a lightweight body topped with a noggin fit for a heavyweight stood in the opposite corner. Scars crisscrossed the face of this Johnny-come-lately out of a Texas backwater with fifteen losses on his record. Even more ridiculous, the word was that a woman managed the kid. His wife, no less.

The kid's name was Lew Jenkins, and less than a minute after the opening bell, he had Ambers on the seat of his pants, dazedly staring up at the Texas toothpick who had put him there and vaguely registering referee Billy Cavanaugh's count. He made it to his feet, a strange grin on his face.

"Now, what's a man grin in the ring for?" said Jenkins after the fight. "I said, 'Oh-oh, he's through!' because that grinnin' means he was hurt." Jenkins chased after the champion, but Ambers kept his left jab in his face to buy time until he could make it to the safety of his corner at the round's end.[395]

Ambers stormed out for the second round looking to avenge the embarrassing knockdown. Just as the champion seemed to be getting back in his groove and convincing himself and his astonished fans that the first round must have been a fluke, a surprise left hook dumped Ambers on the floor yet again. He was up at five and angry. The Herkimer Hurricane furiously waded in and traded left hooks with Jenkins until a devastating right found the champ's jaw and dazed him just as the bell tolled to end the round. Ignoring the toll, Jenkins kept blasting away at the stunned champ until the referee separated them. In his dressing room after the fight, Jenkins told the press that the screams of the shocked fans drowned out the sound of the bell. However, years later, he admitted that was a lie. "When they start to go, they got to go," he reasoned.[396]

A much meeker Ambers warily crept out of his corner to start round three, and Jenkins pounced on him, crushing him to the canvas a third time. Rising, Lou Ambers seemed to be the only person in the arena who did not know by now that he was finished. He willingly entered an exchange with his challenger and paid the price with a fourth knockdown. This time he barely beat the ref's count. Jenkins shrugged off the champion's feeble attempt to hold, lashed out with brutal lefts and rights, and convinced Al Weill to throw in the towel. Cavanaugh stopped the fight.[397]

It had been a tremendous upset, upending the odds of four to one in Ambers's favor. That it ended by technical knockout after the rugged Ambers had tasted the canvas four times in less than three rounds was unfathomable. The Herkimer Hurricane, who had taken the best punches that heavy hitters like Jimmy McLarnin, Ceferino Garcia, Bummy Davis, and Henry Armstrong had to offer and had never been stopped or knocked out, was candid in defeat.

"I've been hit by many good punchers," he said, "but none of them ever hurt me or did the things this Jenkins kid did. He punched harder than a lot of them put together."[398]

Weill insisted that Lou would now campaign exclusively as a welterweight and go after Henry Armstrong's belt. That third fight never materialized. Ambers then begged Weil for a second fight with Jenkins and received a shot at becoming a three-time lightweight champ on February 28, 1941. This time he made it into the seventh before being stopped.

Following the second stoppage loss to Lew Jenkins, Lou Ambers retired with a known record of ninety victories (thirty of them by knockout), eight defeats, and six draws, with possibly dozens more "smoker" battles unaccounted for.

Once America entered the Second World War, he enlisted in the Coast Guard and served under Lieutenant Jack Dempsey in a unit designed to train recruits in self-defense and bolster public support for the war. In peacetime, he and his growing family moved to Phoenix, Arizona. His post-military life saw him involved in various business and boxing ventures, from hotelier to trainer to public relations figure. Lou remained visible in and around the boxing world into his seventies. In his later years, he received various sports-related honors in recognition of his accomplishments in the ring, most notably induction into the International Boxing Hall of Fame in 1992. The man born Luigi D'Ambrosio but once famous as Lou Ambers, passed away following a stroke on April 25, 1995, at age 81.[399]

> I did a lot of things. All the rules you could break, I broke. Screwing, the whole goddamn thing.... I didn't go for that training. I seldom ever trained. Just like I told you, actually I was never in shape in my life, never in condition. I'd go out and run a little bit and sit down, smoke a cigarette, rest for a while. I had bottles in the corner and everything else. People have to seen it to believe the way I fought.[400]

These were the words of Verlin "Lew" Jenkins, the scrawny wild man out of Sweetwater, Texas, whose murderous punching power could make up for his absolute abhorrence of discipline.

Born on December 4, 1916, near Milburn, Texas, Lew was the third of seven kids. Though he had the advantage of being white, the poverty in which he grew up makes Henry's childhood appear luxurious by comparison. He traveled with his family in a covered wagon pulled by mules. They were itinerant laborers searching desperately for work throughout Texas before and during the Great Depression. Most often, they picked cotton, working fourteen-hour days, the children included. When the wagon had no room, he slept in a tent by the roadside. Soup was his primary source of nourishment; he owned a single pair of overalls for clothing; cardboard patches covered holes in his shoes. He did not enter school until his teens after the family finally settled in Sweetwater. When he got held back because his work in the fields demanded too many absences, he dropped out.

Like Henry Armstrong, Barney Ross, Ceferino Garcia, and so many others, Lew was an avid streetfighter as a kid. Some adults in Sweetwater took notice and began matching him with other poor kids, offering a pie as a reward for the winner. After his father died in 1932, fifteen-year-old Lew decided it would be better for his family if he were paid in cash rather than pies. He commanded between twenty-five and fifty cents per win. Some of that money went to an already-developing alcohol habit.

In 1934, Jenkins hooked up with T.J. Tidwell's traveling carnival. Tagging along through Texas, he earned between a dollar and a dollar and a half per day as a skinny teenager by offering to box any local tough who felt like showing off. Most takers were adults, some outweighing him by over one hundred pounds. He denied no one and fought between one to four times a day. Most of the time, he won.

After the carnival went on hiatus in January 1936, Lew returned to the cotton fields, taking paid fights when he could get them. With no formal instruction, very little food in his belly, and no discipline for training, his start in professional boxing was as rocky as Henry's. He lost four of his first eleven recorded fights. But he had a hell of a right-hand punch, and experience gradually taught him how to land it with increasing accuracy and impact.

In 1936, he joined the U.S. Army for what wound up being the first of three tenures in the service through his lifetime. Stationed at Fort Bliss, Texas, he met a gorgeous, pint-sized redhead named Katie Jenkins (no relation) after one of his fights. Hot-tempered and adventurous, Katie had been the paramour of Bonnie and Clyde associate Fred Hamilton at the time of Hamilton's capture and execution in 1935. She was also a death-defying midget race car driver. On their first date, Lew watched her roll her car over three times and still win her race.

Conveniently, Katie did not need to change her last name when they married in 1938. She thereafter became Lew's manager, possibly the first woman to ever manage a top-flight boxer. Though many men in the fight business refused to work with her or even allow her to set foot in a boxing gym, Katie's fearless attitude, fierce loyalty to Lew, and foul-mouthed temper usually won out against boxing's entrenched "no girls allowed" mentality.

The couple traveled all over the southwest in pursuit of fight purses, eating when they could and often sleeping in their car. By 1938, he was garnering occasional matches with well-known lightweights like Lew Feldman and Wesley Ramey, though he did not always win. He picked up the lightweight championship of Texas along the way and made a few appearances as far away as Chicago and Mexico. Still, the Jenkinses knew that real money came with fighting in New York City and winning a world championship.

Lew and Katie had fifty dollars between them when their beat-up jalopy rumbled into the Big Apple sometime in June or July 1939. Lew auditioned for trainer Willie Ketchum at the famous Stillman's Gym, and Willie agreed to train him. Initially, Lou Stillman refused to let Katie in the doors of his gym until "a withering barrage of salty language from Katie" convinced him otherwise. They ran into the same problem with the NYSAC, who forbade female fight managers, so they eventually hired Howling Hymie Caplin as a frontman. It did not take long for Katie and Hymie to start butting heads for control of Lew's career, but Caplin remained the manager of record.[401]

Fighting initially in low-paying shows in Long Island and the Bronx, Lew won eight straight in New York before his first fight with Ambers. Able to enjoy full-course meals for the first time since his Army days, Lew finally experienced consistent success in the ring. After he stopped Mike Belloise in seven rounds, Mike Jacobs set him up for his Madison Square Garden debut on December 15, 1939, against Billy Marquart, who went out in three rounds. Four months later, highly regarded Tippy Larkin went out in less than a round. Going into the fight with Ambers, Lew was on a seven-fight knockout streak.

This ten-month run from no-name hayseed to top contender status was among the most unexpected in boxing history, and his victory over a rugged, multi-talented veteran like Ambers was even more shocking. Ambers claimed that the struggle to make the lightweight limit weakened him. However, no one, especially not Ambers, could deny that the hard-drinking Texas gunslinger packed a fearsome punch.

The only things Jenkins went through quicker than knockout victims were whiskey and women. His alcohol intake and late-night carousing made even Henry Armstrong appear a celibate teetotaler by comparison. Hopping from bar to bar every day and night, he stayed drunk before his fights, during them, and after them. Among his favorite drinking buddies were actor Humphrey Bogart and boxer Chalky Wright, who were also rampaging alcoholics and womanizers. Things only got worse once he won the title.

"I just drank myself down," he later told Peter Heller. "I never did go to sleep, never did eat right, never did train at all hardly." He spent his winnings in record time, not just on booze and ladies. "Cadillacs, I had about nine of them in 1940, four motorcycles, an airplane, and two racehorses." To Lew, who had grown up starving in a tent with only a pair of mules for transportation and almost no formal education, his New York fight paydays seemed too big to be used up. "I never really worried about it," he explained to Heller. "I thought I was enjoying it. I probably wasn't but I thought I was. Anything I wanted, I had it."[402]

In his dressing room after winning the lightweight championship of the world, brimming with confidence, Lew told the reporters, "Henry Armstrong is the one I'd like to fight next. He couldn't knock out in thirty rounds the boy I knocked out in three rounds, so I ought to do all right with Henry."

Mike Jacobs worked out preparations for a Jenkins-Armstrong showdown on July 17, 1940, at the Polo Grounds in New York. Because the NYSAC now forbade any fighter to hold two championships, and neither man was willing to abandon his belt to challenge for the other's, it would be a non-title affair fought in the welterweight division. Henry signed a contract agreeing not to weigh more than 140 pounds.

Henry trained at Greenwood Lake, New York. Jenkins's camp was at Grossinger's Resort in the Catskills, but little, if any, training was being done there.

"I wasn't training no way," Lew later admitted. "Staying up all night, all them women. I couldn't even do no roadwork. I wasn't getting no sleep. I'd get up about nine o'clock in the morning, run a half mile, or walk."

Four days before the fight, Katie Jenkins showed up in camp and, seeing her husband's condition, took him away from Grossinger's against trainer Willie Ketchum's wishes. The couple arrived at Stillman's Gym in the city, where she could keep a better eye on Lew. Hymie Kaplan showed up enraged, but Katie didn't budge. Her husband stayed at Stillman's.[403]

Asked by reporters if he was planning any unique strategy for taking on a hard-hitting counterpuncher in Jenkins, Henry Armstrong said, "I still have the same general ideas, and that's to keep 'em off balance. They have to be set to nail you hard, and I try to keep 'em from getting set. No fighter off balance is going to hurt you much. I know how hard Jenkins can hit.... But if you keep on crowding in and never stop, they can't take aim and let you have it."[404]

Henry offered his hand to Lew at the weigh-in on the morning of the fight, but the Texan refused to shake. In his trademark southern drawl, he said, "Henry, I ain't gonna shake hands with ya and I ain't gonna wish you luck. No Henry, I ain't gonna say that damn lie. I'm aimin' to give you a lickin' an' I know I can do it too."[405]

Henry looked the taller man hard in the eyes. "Okay, if that's the way you want it," he shrugged.[406]

"I can't say I hope you win but I do hope you make a lot of money," Lew offered in parting.[407]

A few hours later, it looked like no one would make any money. When Jenkins's team showed up at his hotel room to take him to the arena, they found no sign of him. While scouring the nearby streets, Ketchum was not surprised to discover him hiding in a bar downing drinks. He dragged a drunken Lew to the Polo Grounds.

Then, another obstacle to the fight presented itself. Ten minutes before the main event was supposed to get under way, a NYSAC official objected to how Harry had wrapped Henry's hands, saying there was too much bandage on the welterweight champion's hands. Eddie Mead refused to unwrap his fighter's hands and re-wrap them as requested by the official. He said that there had been a private agreement with Jenkins's camp on how to wrap the hands and that Jenkins's team wrapped their fighter's hands with the same extra bandaging. Learning of the delay, a fuming Mike Jacobs burst into Henry's dressing room and settled the matter, convincing the Commission to let the fight go on anyway. The Commission would afterward suspend Eddie for six days for his disobedience.[408]

Henry weighed 139 pounds. Jenkins came in at 135 ½. Oddsmakers had Henry as much as a two-to-one favorite.[409]

**Armstrong and Jenkins**

The matchup with Jenkins was one of the most talked-about of Henry's career. As Jenkins's biographer, Gene Pantalone, explains in his excellent *From Boxing Ring to Battlefield*:

> There was so much interest in the fight that more than five thousand fight fans, anxious to learn the results of the bout in New York, telephoned the *Philadelphia Inquirer* that night. The callers taxed the telephone system so much that additional operators were installed. The fans also swamped city police switchboards. The various radio stations were airing the Democratic Convention in Chicago and not broadcasting the fight.[410]

The switchboard operators at NBC and the *New York Times* experienced the same inundation of irritated callers.[411]

More than twenty-three thousand fans filed into the outdoor arena to watch the fight, paying $111,486 for the privilege. That was an enormous gate for a non-heavyweight non-title fight for the Great Depression, the largest of Henry's career thus far.

Jenkins came out aggressive for the opening round, and an onslaught of lefts and rights caught Henry coming in. Onlookers were perplexed to see Henry doing little to no punching on the inside, only bobbing, weaving, and holding. Outside of two lefts to the body, he landed nothing of significance. Jenkins kept punching away and clearly took the round.[412]

Round two saw Armstrong staggered by a one-two combination. Jenkins seemed to target Henry's left eye, and a well-aimed, solid right-hand blow caused it to close before the round was over. Late in the round, Lew slipped to the canvas but got up quickly. The Sweetwater Swatter caught Henry with a right to the face at the bell.

Henry was more active in round three but still struggled to land effectively. Round four was a thriller. Perhaps sensing Henry was coming on, Lew opened with careful jabs to keep his opponent at bay, but Henry bore in behind a left to the body. An Armstrong left hook swept into Jenkins's jaw and put the lightweight champ on the floor. Lew toppled down hard and curled into a fetal position. It appeared to be all over. Yet somehow, the lightweight champion rose. Lew made it upright just as the timekeeper counted ten, but referee Arthur Donovan gave him the benefit of the doubt and let him continue.

His confidence bolstered by the knockdown, Armstrong began landing two and three punches to every one from his opponent. Jenkins, blood dripping from his nose, tried to hold but was unsuccessful at smothering his foe. Then, out of nowhere but Lew's tremendous fighting heart, came a big right hand that caught Henry perfectly on the chin and flung his head back.

Henry could hear his corner shouting, "Don't get careless!" "Watch that right hand!" "Hit him in the belly!" Another left to the head wobbled Jenkins, but he fought back well. The lightweight champion returned to his corner with a cut over his left eye following a fast-paced exchange.[413]

Between rounds four and five, Eddie Mead reiterated his warnings from round four. He told Henry to be careful against a dangerous puncher like Lew, to stay low, and to attack the body. In the other corner, Hymie Caplan admonished his fighter not to get too excited and to avoid an inside slugfest. Lew was the bigger puncher of the pair, but he was a counterpuncher who did better when he patiently awaited the right moment to land a single, brain-numbing shot. A fast battle was Henry Armstrong's style and did not give Lew a chance to pick his shots. "You are not fighting your fight," Caplin shouted at Jenkins.[414]

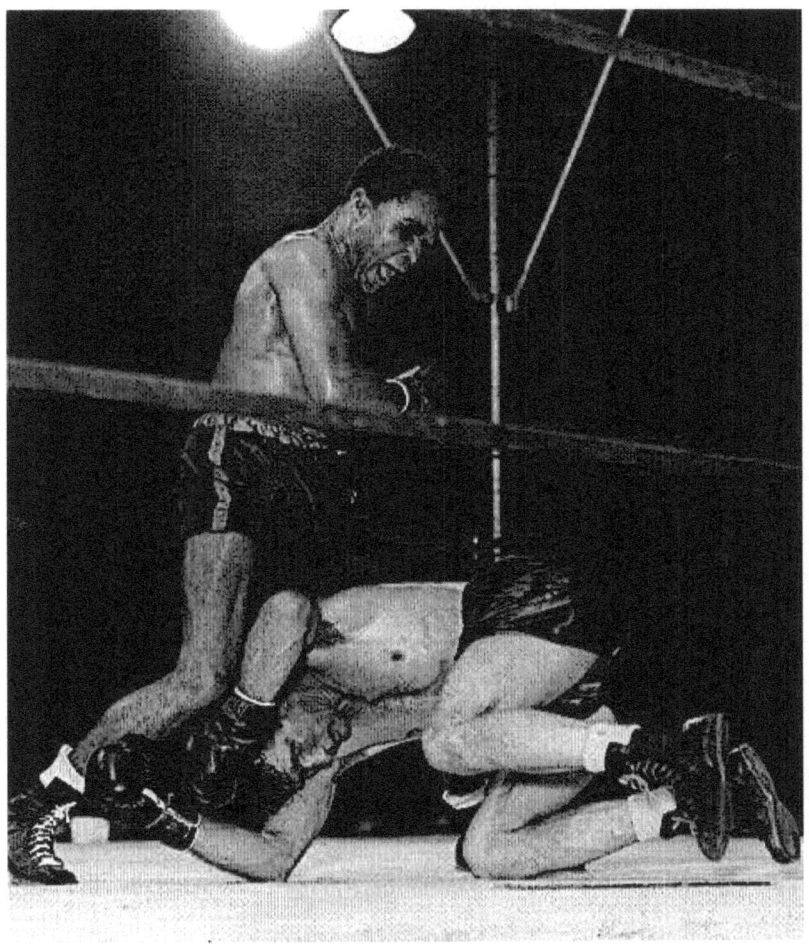

**Lew Jenkins hits the deck under an Armstrong assault**

Bloodied but still looking to win, Lew ignored his manager and attacked in round five, landing combinations "like a whirlwind" to Henry's face. A cut opened above the welterweight champion's right eye, but he never budged. Henry kept pushing forward, and Lew's feared right hand bounced off his head with no discernible effect. Shocked, "his face ashen pale," Lew glanced bewilderedly at his corner as if to ask them how a man could stand up to such blows.

It took a while, but Henry eventually started firing back, mainly at the body, while his opponent targeted his head. Jenkins retreated, and a pair of gut punches dropped him again. He shot up before Donovan could count to one, only to be dropped by a left into the ribs. Consumed with pain, the Texan "flopped like a roped steer" to the floor. He struggled up at the count of nine. Henry was slugging away at Lew's big, battered skull when the bell rang to end the round.[415]

Returning to the safety of his corner, Lew was disconsolate. He begged Caplin between gasps for breath, "By God, toss in the towel. Armstrong's beaten the hell out of me!" Somehow, his corner convinced him to give it another try.[416]

While Jenkins's cornermen wondered what to do, a doctor visited Henry's corner to look at his shut left eye and the bad cut over his right. The cornermen worked on Henry's face feverishly, doing what they could to obscure and stall the doctor's observation of the wounds. After taking a long time to get a good look, the doctor did not like what he saw. He turned to make his way over to Donovan and began shaking his head. Before he could say anything to the ref, the bell for round six rang, and Henry's corner practically tossed him into the center of the ring. Thanks to their stall tactic, the fight would continue.

Knowing he was in a do-or-die situation, Henry ripped back into the lightweight champion's mid-section at the start of round six. He could sense Lew weakening and caught him by surprise with a left hook to the face. Down went Jenkins for a fourth time. The rugged Texan made it up at the count of three, but Henry put him back down almost immediately for a count of nine. When Armstrong came in again, Jenkins hugged him, and Henry slipped to the floor. Lew went right back to hugging, but Henry refused to be smothered. He continued to attack the body. The bell rang to end the round, and Lew's handlers jumped into the ring to help their glassy-eyed, sleepwalking fighter make it to his corner.

When they reached the stool, Caplan screamed, "Are ya all right, Lew?" He received no answer. Jenkins suddenly fell forward off his stool. Caplin caught him, but Jenkins spun out of his arms and collapsed, causing his head to get caught on the bottom rope. His eyes were open, but he appeared delirious. Caplin picked him up and set him back on the stool.[417]

Donovan took a close look at the bruised and gasping Texan. The blood-spattered fighter was groaning and writhing around on his stool, repeatedly wheezing, "I need air." Donovan patted Lew on the shoulder. Turning to Caplin, he said with finality, "The fight's over."[418]

In a rare move for a referee, Donovan grabbed a microphone and addressed the disappointed crowd, who wanted to see a definitive knockout. "I stopped the bout before the bell rang to start the seventh round. There was no seventh round. I stopped it because Jenkins was in a dazed condition and not fit to continue," he told them. The bout would enter the record books as a seventh-round technical knockout.[419]

In his dressing room after the fight, Lew still had no idea where he was. With his cornermen still working on his wounds and reporters encircling them, Lew asked, "How'm I doing? What round is it?" Informed by Caplan that the referee had stopped the fight, Lew was enraged.

"You're crazy," he shouted. "I never was knocked out. I never was hurt." He continued to rage indignantly at Caplin and the others. When Caplin was able to get away, he told the reporters that his fighter had been too anxious for the fight, too set on knocking out Armstrong, and that the pressure and stress weakened Lew during the fight. Hymie also blamed Katie Jenkins for distracting his fighter with drama during preparations and interrupting the training process.[420]

Nat Fleischer would write in *The Ring* that Lew and his handlers had gotten too ambitious in thinking they stood a chance of beating Henry Armstrong. "Even champions can be overmatched," he wrote as if he were teaching the lightweight champion a valuable lesson.[421]

To Jenkins himself, looking back years later, it was not so much his ambitions that got the better of him but his lack of discipline. "I should have beat Armstrong," he told Joseph Heller. "I didn't train at all for that. I did no roadwork, nothing. I must have got hurt very early.... None of those guys could beat me if I trained the way they did."[422]

The press was unanimous in praising Henry Armstrong's skills, Lew Jenkins's bravery, and the fight overall. Jimmy Powers of the *New York Daily News* called it "one of the bloodiest and best among little fellows since the days of [Benny] Leonard and [Lew] Tendler."[423]

James P. Dawson of the *Times* wrote that Henry was "the best little piece of fighting machinery the ring has known since the days of [Joe] Wolcott [sic] and [Sam] Langford." Like Henry, Joe Walcott was a smallish Black man with a compactly muscled upper body. Hailing from Barbados, he was only the second Black man to win a world championship, holding the welterweight championship from 1901 to 1904. Despite his relatively diminutive size, he was known for giving light heavyweights and heavyweights hell.[424]

Sam Langford was a skilled Black fighter who fought from the turn of the century into the 1920s and had beaten many of the best men from the lightweight through the heavyweight divisions but was denied a shot at any championship. He and Walcott had fought to a draw back in 1904.

Fleischer echoed Dawson's sentiments almost exactly. He felt the Jenkins victory had solidified Henry Armstrong's legacy as the best pound-for-pound fighter of his generation. No matter what he did, retire or not, Fleischer felt Armstrong deserved "the honor of being the greatest fighter, weight for weight, since the days of the famous Joe Walcott, the Man Killer."[425]

"The little Negro gladiator whose flaying arms made Jenkins see a thousand gloves at one time, was a reminder of the great Walcott and Sam Langford. To those he will have to be compared when his last chapter is written," continued Fleischer.[426]

Barbados Joe Walcott, a great boxing hero to whom Armstrong was often compared

Lew Jenkins remained the lightweight champion because the bout had been a non-title affair. Despite being definitively trounced, he was eager for a second chance at Henry. Mike Jacobs arranged a non-title match scheduled to take place on September 27. As it turned out, Armstrong and Jenkins would not meet in the ring again for another two years.

Three weeks before Henry's win over Jenkins, his friend Joe Louis - still heavyweight champion of the world - belted out Chile's Arturo Godoy in defense of his title. Their victories continued to inspire their Black fans. Writing in the *Pittsburgh Courier*, a leading Black paper, the verbose Randy Dixon spoke for millions of others when he wrote:

> ...I say, and the chorus of amens will swell at my declaration, that at no time has the fistic orbit previously encompassed two gladiators comparable to Joe Louis and Henry Armstrong. Pound for pound, deed for deed, in or out of the ring, they rate as the best for the annals. Their accomplishments make one gaze at them and say with all sincerity "we've got all this and then a chance at heaven too."[427]

# 16.
# Zivic

Executing an extortion that could shock New York's most avaricious gangsters, the NYSAC ordered Mike Jacobs to withhold the purses of both Armstrong and Jenkins until they both signed agreements to make their next championship defenses in the State of New York and posted forfeits (two thousand dollars for Henry and fifteen hundred for Lew) guaranteeing such. Both fighters complied and received their paychecks. Rival commissioners from other states were livid.[428]

Henry and Eddie reviewed their options for the next defense of Henry's welterweight honors. According to *The Ring*, the division's top men following the victory over Jenkins were as follows:

World Champion: Henry Armstrong
1 – Cocoa Kid
2 – Milt Aron
3 – Charley Burley
4 – Holman Williams
5 – Fritzie Zivic
6 – Mike Kaplan
7 – Izzy Jannazzo
8 – Maxie Berger
9 – Phil Furr
10 – Young Kid McCoy[429]

It was a talented bunch (six of those names are now in the Hall of Fame). The number one contender, Herbert Lewis Hardwick, better known as Cocoa Kid, was born in Puerto Rico but got his start as a professional fighter in Atlanta, Georgia, in 1929, just a couple weeks after turning fifteen years old. Since then, he had sometimes held the colored welterweight championship and had beaten such notables as Kid Kaplan, Johnny Jadick, Holman Williams, Eddie Booker, and Chalky Wright. The papers were widely printing that the Kid was riding a forty-five-bout winning streak following a win over Phil Furr. It wasn't true. It was a seventeen-bout winning streak, but that was still impressive.

At 5'10 ½" tall, the lanky Kid knew how to use his height and reach to his advantage and possessed a dangerous straight right. As a Black Puerto Rican without roots in New York City, he was not a particularly large draw. His unique frame and abilities meant a lot of risk in exchange for little financial reward for Henry. Eddie Mead decided to look elsewhere for a challenger, as would future welterweight and middleweight champions. Like his hard-luck rivals, Charley Burley and Holman Williams, Cocoa Kid never got a shot at a world title. He retired in 1948 with 178 victories to his name, passed away in 1966, and was posthumously inducted into the International Boxing Hall of Fame in 2012.[430]

There was also the possibility of Jenkins's number one contender in the lightweight division, Sammy Angott. Angott came from Washington, Pennsylvania, not far south of Pittsburgh, but he had fought all over the eastern and midwestern states. His hit-and-hold style brought him victories over Freddie Miller, Aldo Spoldi, Petey Sarron, Baby Arizmendi, and Davey Day, against whom he won the NBA's version of the lightweight championship in May 1940. However, he was far from popular with the fans, who considered his frequent use of clinches a bore. Henry could not expect a spectacular payday against a man nicknamed "The Clutch."

The welterweight division boasted yet another star from the southwestern Pennsylvania area, one far more liked.

"There was something of Popeye-the-Sailor about Zivic's jutting jaw and his roughhouse manner," Robert Richards once wrote of Ferdinand "Fritzie" Zivic, the youngest and the best of the five fighting Zivic brothers out of Lawrenceville, also near Pittsburgh. Behind his trademark flattened nose and mischievous grin, Zivic possessed a self-deprecating wit that made good copy for sportswriters. That was part of what won him fans. The other part was his remorselessly dirty fighting style.

"I'd give 'em the head, choke 'em, hit 'em in the balls, but never in my life used my thumb because I wanted no one to use it on me," he admitted to Peter Heller years after his retirement. "I used to bang 'em pretty good. You're fighting, you're not playing the piano, you know." Fritzie also liked to point out that he never lost by disqualification in his life. He made a point to apologize after intentionally fouling a man. "Pardon me," he would say. Then he would head-butt them again.[431]

Frtizie also had a way of making his fouls look like they were the other fellow's fault. "Fritzie Zivic taught me more than anybody I ever fought," the great Sugar Ray Robinson once told writer W.C. Heinz. "He taught me that a man can make you butt open your own eye."[432]

Zivic could appear a world-beater one night and a poor excuse for a club fighter the next. He could break Lou Ambers's jaw or win a decision over Charley Burley but also lose seven fights in a row to mediocre opponents between 1935 and 1936. The papers had written him off as washed up more than once, only to have to report on a significant victory days later.

As of late, Fritzie had been on a good streak, posting five wins in a row, albeit against less-than-stellar competition. Twenty-seven years old and already the veteran of more than 125 fights, he was rated the fifth-best welterweight in the world by *The Ring*.[433]

On August 25, 1940, the United Press reported from Pittsburgh:

> The N.B.A. lightweight champion, Sammy Angott, and Fritzie Zivic, who meet in a 10-round non-title bout here Monday night, will be shooting for a chance at Henry Armstrong's welterweight crown. Co-promoter Art Rooney said that Manager Eddie Mead promised to pair Armstrong with the winner, provided the bout draws well, with the 147-pound title on the line.

The Zivic-Angott match was subsequently delayed three days, but Henry came along with Eddie to Pittsburgh to watch at Forbes Field, the home of the Pittsburgh Pirates baseball team, on Thursday, August 29. The pair of out-of-towners looked around them and were pleased with the turnout of 10,726 paying Pittsburghers to see the two hometown stars go at it. If they could draw that against one another, they could draw better against Henry for the title if the fight were in Pittsburgh.

Angott was the betting favorite, despite giving away more than six pounds to his opponent. He took an early lead by taking a Henry Armstrong approach, rushing out at round one and ripping into Zivic with ceaseless fury. Zivic was overwhelmed.

"Hooking hard to the head, sending short, snappy rights to the body and interspersing these with right uppercuts which had Fritzie's head bobbing, Sammy set sail early on what looked for sure like a kayo win," reported Regis M. Welsh of the *Pittsburgh Press*. Zivic failed to land a noteworthy punch in the first three rounds as Angott battered him from one end of the ring to the other.[434]

Zivic turned things around and surprised many onlookers by taking control of the fight in round six. First through a sustained body attack, and then by switching smoothly between brawling and boxing tactics, he so disoriented and exhausted Angott that the lightweight title holder looked "almost amateurish in his offense," reported Welsh. One minute, Sammy would be taking one clean shot after another to the chin and body, and the next, he would be desperately swinging at air as his attacker suddenly became a defensive mastermind. At multiple points in round nine, it looked as though Zivic was on the verge of winning by knockout, but Angott refused to go down. After ten rounds, both judges and referee Red Robinson gave the fight to Zivic via unanimous decision.[435]

It has always been a part of the Zivic legend that Eddie Mead left ringside after the fourth round with Zivic still in desperate trouble. The story goes that Mead caught a train to New York, where he told the Commission and Mike Jacobs that Armstrong would fight Zivic, who he saw as an easier mark. Someone informed him of Fritzie's come-from-behind victory, and the astonished manager realized he was trapped.[436]

The *Pittsburgh Press* published the day after the Angott-Zivic matchup proves this story bogus. Henry and Eddie were ringside for the entire fight, and they watched Zivic's remarkable comeback. Before the bout, the ring announcer introduced Henry to the crowd and told them that Henry had agreed to face the winner of the bout in a title fight in Pittsburgh. *The New York Times* reported that Henry had already signed a contract to face the winner before the fight, although the *Press* and *Pittsburgh Post-Gazette* contradicted this, saying Eddie Mead had promised to do so, but had not yet signed a contract as of fight time.[437]

As they watched Zivic close the show against Angott, the welterweight champ turned to his manager and said, "Boss, I better get in that gym. Maybe that Zivic is going to be tougher than we thought." Henry had ballooned to a lifetime high of 160 pounds in the month and a half since stopping Jenkins. The *Press* published a photo of an "amazingly fat" Henry looking concernedly up into the ring.[438]

Interviewed from ringside after the fight, Armstrong expressed how impressed he was with both men. "Zivic's a great little fighter and he beat a dead game guy," Henry remarked. He then went to the dressing rooms to congratulate both on an excellent fight.[439]

Art Rooney, Pittsburgh fight promoter and owner of the Pittsburgh Steelers football team, intended to stage the Armstrong-Zivic title fight at Forbes Field. Eddie Mead initially agreed but later had to tell Rooney there was a problem. Mike Jacobs had reminded Mead that Armstrong had signed an agreement with the NYSAC after the Jenkins fight to make a title defense in New York in October. Armstrong stood to forfeit his $2,500 deposit and incur a suspension should he break the agreement. Rooney was furious and burned up the telephone wires to the Big Apple for over two hours, berating Jacobs and NYSAC chairman John Phelan with a firestorm of verbal abuse.

Rooney angrily insisted that Mead do all he could to have Armstrong present in Pittsburgh on September 4 to sign to face Zivic. Mead said he would do everything he could. He wanted the big purse from the Pittsburgh crowd excited to watch their hometown hero challenge for the title. Rooney had initially offered an enormous twenty-five-thousand-dollar purse, but Mead opted for 37.5% of the expected gate, which promised to be a smart move if the fight would stay in Pittsburgh. Interest in Henry had faded in New York City, where audiences had seen him fight plenty. The Big Apple may have been the world's boxing capital, but this time the champion stood to make more money in the Steel City.[440]

Mead traveled to New York for a conference with Jacobs and Phelan. Ultimately, he lost his case, and the Zivic fight was scheduled for October 4 in Madison Square Garden. On September 27, Zivic and Mead (in Armstrong's stead) signed the contract to fight in New York.

In the meantime, Henry needed to get in shape and keep busy. On September 5, Mead signed for Henry to defend his title in a tune-up fight on September 23 against scrappy brawler Phil Furr in Furr's hometown of Washington, D.C. Ranked number nine in the welterweight division, Furr had almost as many losses on his record (thirty-three) as he did wins (forty-one). He had shared a ring with Ceferino Garcia, Fritzie Zivic, Jimmy Leto, Pedro Montanez, and Cocoa Kid, but he had lost to all of them.

The Furr fight took place at Griffith Stadium in front of a healthy crowd of fifteen thousand. The overmatched challenger, 147 pounds, came out bravely trading with the champion in the first couple of rounds but was ultimately "hacked to pieces." *Washington Evening Star* reporter Frances Stan condemned the mismatch as "prize fighting at its ugliest, bloodiest, most senseless." After going down four times in four rounds, the challenger was counted out while crawling around the ring on his hands and knees.[441]

The only problem Henry encountered against Furr was the opening of old scar tissue above an eye into yet another cut. "I can't see so well," he said afterward. "They're beginning to catch up with me."[442]

Again, the NYSAC and Mike Jacobs got riled up about Henry taking his title elsewhere. Jacobs was most worried about Henry risking injury before the showdown with Zivic at the Garden.

Eddie Mead had been managing Henry Armstrong's career since 1936, and he had lived almost exclusively off the income Henry provided (and loaned) him. Now Henry was looking to retire, and according to Fritzie Zivic, Eddie was looking to set up new sources of revenue.

As Zivic later told it, Mead only agreed to give Zivic a title shot if Zivic signed a deal promising the manager twenty-five percent of his purse from the fight and any future title defenses, should he emerge victorious. Hungry for his shot, Zivic felt he had no choice but to consent.

Four days before the fight, again according to Zivic, Mead asked Fritzie to "take it easy" on the champion, offering the Pittsburgh star fifteen thousand dollars cash to do so. Fritzie said he would think it over to get Eddie to leave and then never got back to him.[443]

Meanwhile, Mead told Henry, "You can knock this guy out, he's easy," while the champion prepared at Stillman's Gym. Henry told reporters that he was not taking Zivic lightly, but Mead seemed to encourage him to do so. Betting odds on fight day had Henry anything from a five-to-one to a three-to-one favorite, depending on the source. Jack Mahon of the *New York Daily News* figured Armstrong would cut up the challenger and force a stoppage by round eight.[444]

Friday, October 4, 1940, would be a historic night for boxing in more ways than one. In the opening fight on the card at Madison Square Garden, a young lightweight named Walker Smith, Jr. made his professional debut. Nobody then recognized that name, and few remember it today. But the fight posters, newspapers, and ring announcers called him by a different name, Sugar Ray Robinson. The man many would come to recognize as the greatest fist fighter who ever lived was already a Golden Gloves champion as an amateur, and there were great expectations for him as a pro; hence the rare honor of making his pro debut in the Garden on the undercard of a major championship match. He stopped Puerto Rico's Joe Echevarria in two rounds and then took his seat among the 12,079 other spectators to watch his hero Henry Armstrong do battle.

Henry entered the ring weighing 142 pounds, his opponent 145 ½. Zivic had about four and a half inches in height over him and four inches in reach. As usual for major title fights in the Garden, the referee was Arthur Donovan.[445]

At the opening bell, both fighters charged at one another and immediately set about punching away on the inside, each laying his head on the other's shoulder as if in agreement that the bout would be fought in a phone booth. Armstrong quickly proved the master on the inside against Zivic, who negated his height and reach advantages by willingly standing so close and trading blows in the first fifteen-round bout of his career against a champion who built his reputation on inside slugging and overwhelming stamina.

**Armstrong and Zivic at war**
*The Ring*, December 1940

"He punched the shit outta me," Zivic remembered later. "I'm grabbing, ducking, blocking, he kept coming, he'd throw a left hook, bang! hit you right in the eye." The second round went much the same way as the first, and Fritzie later called it the worst beating of his entire ring career.[446]

Rounds three through five found Armstrong delivering a heavy body attack. In his element, standing shoulder-to-shoulder with his challenger, he also put his head and elbows to work at mauling away at Zivic.

Zivic worried that his reputation as a dirty fighter would have the Donovan over-vigilant of any fouls on his part. He felt cheated that Armstrong's dirty tactics were not being penalized. As he later told Peter Heller:

> The first 5 rounds, he beat me up more than the next twenty guys. I got mad. He hit me low, choked me, give me the elbow, and everything else... I never complained... The first couple of rounds I was kind of confused because he was giving me the head and everything else. Donovan never warned him.[447]

By the end of round five, the champion had a commanding lead, and Zivic looked as if the fight's pace was drowning him. Henry was not unscathed; his left eye was puffed shut by the fourth round, the result of some precision Zivic punches. But he felt in charge.

Fritzie's right eye was closed going into the sixth. Furious at the illegal tactics of Armstrong, he began to deliver his own butts, low blows, and chokes. Each time he popped Henry below the belt line, Fritzie would offer his trademark apology, "Pardon me."[448]

For a time, the bout dissolved into a contest of dirty tactics, an ugly eye-for-an-eye brawl. Donovan stopped the action, separated the fighters, and gave each a stern look but ultimately gave in to the madness. He had gotten enough criticism for over-officiating Henry's second fight with Ambers to say the hell with it. "If you guys want to fight like this it's OK with me," he told them. That was all Fritzie Zivic needed to hear.[449]

"I pulled my trunks up and went to work on him," Zivic remembered later. He no longer felt any need to disguise the headbutts and elbows he used to rip open the champion's facial scars. A cut opened over Henry's right eye in the eighth. Henry was still getting the better of the punching, but he now intuitively knew that he would have to pull once more from that deep well of energy inside him and win a grueling war, as he had so many times before.

Despite the cut, the eighth had been Henry's best round. Landing with both hands, he seemed to have Zivic hurt repeatedly but could not put him away. Round nine also went to Henry, thanks to his ruthless attack, but that was the round where Zivic began to switch tactics. He started to stick and move, whipping his left jab at the champion's swollen and gashed eyes and then circling out of harm's way. Whenever Henry got in close, a butt or low blow stalled him. On the inside, Fritzie would rub the laces of his glove in Henry's cut to further dissuade the champion's aggression.

Observers differed as to round ten's action. Some saw Zivic boxing brilliantly on the outside and then staggering Armstrong with a body shot just before the bell rang. This blow left Armstrong gasping for air as he made his way to his corner. Others said round ten was an absolute toe-to-toe slugfest in which both men traded heavy blows to the head. To Joseph Nichols of the *New York Times*, it was the crowd that was left breathless after such a fantastic display of ring warfare.[450]

Many in the audience stayed on their feet through the final five rounds. Every prominent writer at ringside noted the cacophonous chaos of the crowd once Zivic began to work his way into the fight. "Seldom has Madison Square Garden been the scene of such wild acclaim as that exhibited by the fans," Nat Fleischer wrote. "The cheering was not all for Zivic," he surmised. "In fact, I believe that most of it was for the game, courageous little fighter who, unable to see from either eye after the tenth, fought desperately, taking all his opponent was sending his way, without giving any ground."[451]

The tide of battle had turned irrevocably to Zivic by round eleven. Zivic's jabs were wreaking havoc on Armstrong's eyes. The champion continued to rush blindly forward in his crouch, swinging his fists at blurs and shadows, but he was met with damaging right uppercuts anytime he got close.

If the eleventh brought a change in momentum, the twelfth was a massacre. Fritzie sent Henry reeling from one side of the ring to the other.

"Oh, if I could only see," Henry repeatedly complained between the late rounds of the fight.[452]

Sometime during this later stage, Eddie Mead told Henry he would throw in the towel and stop the fight. Henry pleaded with him not to, and Eddie reluctantly held onto his towel.[453]

Henry resumed his body attack in round thirteen but could not defend himself from the ferocious head blows and fouling tactics in return. He fought all of round fourteen with his eyes sealed shut but still lumbered forward, always forward. He could not see a thing as he rushed around the ring, trying to find his opponent by the sound of his footsteps.

At the opening of the final round, the challenger seemed confident of victory. He was careful and evasive, not wanting to walk into a lucky punch that could take everything away. Fritzie was a matador fighting a blind bull, but a bull was still a bull. Zivic landed precision jabs and uppercuts while the champion wandered ever forward into more punishment. Henry once fell under the momentum of a punch thrown at nothing.[454]

Late in the round, Fritzie wound Henry up in a clinch to glimpse the clock and saw it winding down. As he later put it, "I stepped on the gas." With about fourteen seconds to go, Henry lay helpless on the ropes, his opponent attacking from all angles like Henry had done to so many others in the past.

As Zivic battered him, Armstrong's head, neck, and shoulders became entangled in the ring ropes. Referee Donovan leaped between the boxers to shield the defenseless champion, and Fritzie stepped back. Henry unraveled himself and tried to catch his challenger off guard by immediately sending a wild punch soaring through the air. Simultaneously, Zivic hopped inside the punch and fired a picture-perfect right uppercut that slammed into Armstrong's face. Already off balance from the desperate momentum of his shot, Henry collapsed face-first onto the mat. A fraction of a second later, the final bell rang with Henry prostrate, every ounce of his legendary energy spent. He would have been counted out if the bell had not saved him.[455]

**Armstrong goes down**

As the cheers of thousands shook the walls of the Garden, the arena lights all inexplicably went out at once as if to signal the end of an era.

They came back on quickly, not that it mattered to Henry. He was blind. But he could hear. And what he heard as his cornermen guided him down the aisle toward his dressing room choked him with emotion. For the first time since he won the featherweight title in 1937, a Garden crowd loudly and unanimously chanted his name. Even as he sat exhausted, sore, and dejected inside his dressing room with his door closed, he could still hear them chanting away. Henry's heart swelled with bittersweet melancholy. He was happy that the fans appreciated his effort, but he had let everyone down.

As reporters crowded into Henry's dressing room, they found Dr. Alexander Schiff attending to him on his rubbing table and Eddie Mead standing off to the side, his big body quaking with emotion. Mead told the press that Henry was through. It would take six months for the eyes to heal, he said. By then, he would not be willing to ask Henry to get back into shape and fight again.[456]

Later, after the reporters moved on to compose their obituaries for his career, the sullen ex-champion heard the dressing room door swing open, and someone told him Fritzie Zivic had arrived. He felt Zivic grab his hand and shake it. "Henry, you're the greatest champion that ever lived!" the new champ told him, his voice quaking with feeling. Then, perhaps surprised and embarrassed by his own emotions, Fritzie fled the room almost before Henry managed to say thank you.

Henry received another memorable visitor that night. Ray Robinson, the youngster who had made his pro debut a couple of hours earlier, came into the room looking both star-struck and crushed. He had been eager to witness his hero Henry Armstrong in action for the first time, and he wept while watching Zivic take the title. Ray wiped away his tears before introducing himself to the former champion.

"Henry, you're my idol and someday I'm going to knock out Zivic for you," the youngster promised, determination chiseled into his handsome face. Henry managed a polite smile and some words of encouragement and gratitude through his battered and bloodied features before leaving the ambitious upstart to get some rest.[457]

As if he were writing Henry Armstrong's eulogy, Nat Fleischer closed his article on the Armstrong-Zivic fight by saying:

> During his days as a champion, Armstrong defended his welter title more often than any previous champion. He had taken the measure of many good boys, and some mediocre talent, but no one could blame him for not taking on only the tough ones. The only two sturdy contenders whom Hank failed to fight were Coco [sic] Kid and Charley Burley. He retires as champion with a proud record. He can point to his performances with pride.[458]

Fleischer was not the only sportswriter now writing of Henry's career in the past tense with a twinge of nostalgia for a lost prime. Caswell Adams of the *New York Herald* wrote that, with Henry's defeat, "one of the greatest chapters in fistic history was clapped shut." Then, as if Fritzie had killed Henry in battle, Adams closed with, "he went out the way the best do – fighting." The headline of the *Pittsburgh Press* sports page on March 6 was "Zivic's Win Likely Ends Henry's Career."[459]

In his widely read column in the *New York Journal-American*, Bill Corum raged against the dying of Henry's light. "Five years ago, the Robinsons, Beau Jacks and Bob Montgomerys couldn't have carried Henry Armstrong's gloves," he bitterly shouted onto the page, referring to a trio of up-and-coming talents in the sport.[460]

No one could blame the press for thinking Henry's career was over. He had been talking about retirement for over a year, and now Eddie Mead was telling them the time had come. At thirty-one years old, Henry had been fighting professionally for just short of a decade and incurred one kind of injury or another after almost every recent fight. After the Zivic fight, the opened scar tissue above his eyes required another thirteen stitches to close, and it promised to be even more tender in his next fight. There was always the risk of permanent injury. He claimed to have one hundred thousand dollars in the bank (The Zivic fight paid him another $9,659), no longer held any titles, and had just suffered his first definitive loss since becoming a marquee fighter.

Hanging up the gloves made a lot of sense to everyone who was not Henry Armstrong. However, the upset loss to Zivic, a man who was as much as a five-to-one underdog, hurt Henry's pride worse than his damaged eyes.

He was sure that, had his eyes not hindered him, and had he not underestimated the clever and tough scrapper from Pittsburgh, he would have won. He would win if he got another shot, he convinced himself.

Dr. Schiff had previously brought up the idea of surgery to remove the fragile scar tissue around his eyes. Henry always put the process off but now knew it would be essential for revenge against Zivic. He told Schiff to set a date and time for the procedure. Afterward, he would rest up at a resort like Hot Springs, Arkansas, and then be back in training by December for a fight in January.

On October 7, just three days after the fight, Mike Jacobs announced that both Armstrong and Zivic agreed to a rematch scheduled for January 17, 1941. In the meantime, Mike intended to keep the new champion busy by matching him with Brooklyn tough guy Al "Bummy" Davis in a non-title fight on November 17. Should Davis beat Zivic, then Davis would get his shot at the winner of the Armstrong-Zivic rematch with the title on the line.

Dr. Schiff successfully removed about an inch of scar tissue and cartilage from around Henry's left eye at Medical Arts Hospital on Tuesday, October 15. Schiff canceled the scheduled procedure for the right eye, deeming it unnecessary. Privately, he told his patient never to fight again, warning that a second operation on the left eye would not be possible and that further damage could leave him blind. But Henry had made up his mind, and the doctor went along with the plan. "He'll be as good as new for the return bout with Zivic," Dr. Schiff assured the press.[461]

While resting and healing in Hot Springs, Henry assured the Associated Press he was almost finished with boxing. Four more fights, he told them, and then he would hang up the gloves. "That's definite," he assured the reporter. "I'm not fooling myself. I'm like Old Black Joe – getting old." Asked what he intended to do in retirement, Henry said he intended to start a swing band.[462]

The day after Henry's surgery, he sent Harry to register him for the military draft in accordance with the newly instituted Selective Training and Service Act, the first such measure ever taken in peacetime.

That same day, Eddie Mead had a heart attack and joined Henry as a patient at the Medical Arts Hospital. On December 9, Mead returned to the hospital. His doctor forbade him from attending the corner of any fights for at least thirty days.[463]

On December 4, word came that the Boxing Writers Association of New York had unanimously voted Henry as the recipient of their third annual Edward J. Neil Memorial Award. The award honored boxers "who from the standpoint of activity, sportsmanship, and general behavior both in and out of the ring and influence on youth has brought special distinction to himself and boxing." It was the most prestigious honor in the sport outside of winning a championship or being named *The Ring*'s "Fighter of the Year."[464]

On January 9, 1941, Henry swung into New York to pick up his trophy during a special banquet dinner at Rupert's Brewery. Presented with the trophy by former New York City Mayor James J. Walker, Henry was visibly emotional and momentarily struggled to speak at the podium. Then he thought of Eddie Mead, whose faulty heart had barred him from attendance, and the words came to him as quickly as the tears came to his eyes.

"The real champion in this case is not me, it is not Henry Armstrong" he told the assemblage of boxing scribes below, "it is Eddie Mead, my manager," his voice cracked, "and my brother – Harry."[465]

Henry was glad to have Harry in attendance along with his friend Joe Louis, not to mention Lou Ambers and Fritzie Zivic, who had both turned up to pay tribute to their former opponent. Nat Fleischer served as toastmaster.

Fleischer's *The Ring* disagreed with the Boxing Writers Association in their choice for the outstanding boxer of the year. After tallying votes from two hundred experts, light heavyweight champion Billy Conn received their award. Armstrong finished third in the voting, under Conn and former heavyweight champ Max Baer.[466]

Henry stayed in New York to celebrate his thirty-first birthday in a Harlem nightclub, where boxing trainer Pee Wee Beale "shot off the big guns of entertainment" in his honor. He then returned to Los Angeles for several weeks' rest before heading for more recuperation in Hot Springs.[467]

On November 15, 1940, new welterweight champion Fritzie Zivic defended his title against Brownsville native Al "Bummy" Davis in Madison Square Garden. In what the *Times* branded "one of the most disgraceful exhibitions in the history of boxing in this state," Incensed by some of Zivic's notorious dirty tricks, Davis got himself disqualified after throwing no less than ten left hooks into Zivic's groin in the second round alone. When the referee stopped the fight, Davis kicked him and physically attacked Zivic, who was more than happy to fight back. A policeman had to drag the still-brawling Davis away.

Five weeks later, Zivic slugged to a draw with Lew Jenkins in a non-title affair in the Garden. He then headed to Miami for a vacation, intending to return by early January.[468]

Henry Armstrong arrived in New York City from Hot Springs on December 24 to celebrate Christmas with friends before heading to Greenwood Lake to prepare for his return shot at Zivic. Harry and Eddie wanted a new approach out of Henry for the rematch. They thought Henry might surprise Fritzie if he boxed instead of brawling this time around.

They brought in master trainer Ray Arcel. The child of Russian immigrants, Arcel was raised in Harlem and was one of the professors of Stillman's Gym, the most famous boxing gym in the nation. A.J. Liebling would later call it "The University of Eighth Avenue." Before he took on his assignment with Armstrong, Arcel had already worked the corners of greats Benny Leonard, Pancho Villa, and Barney Ross, among others.

Arcel's job was to help Harry Armstrong revamp Henry's all-out approach into that of a savvy master of ring science. With assistance from his protégé Al Silvani, he trained Henry to come out of his trademark crouch and instead stand up straight and use jabs and crosses against his trio of sparring partners.

Experienced Brooklyn welterweight Bernie Miller, Westchester welterweight upstart Randy Brown, and up-and-coming New York City lightweight Chester Rico comprised Henry's team of sparring partners. Mead and Arcel moved the camp to Stillman's as the fight grew closer.

Concerned over rumors that Henry was going blind, the NYSAC ordered three doctors to examine Armstrong extensively before the rematch. All three doctors confirmed Henry had 20-20 vision and cleared him to fight with "Generally good physical condition."[469]

Henry penned a piece for *The New York Age*, making his case for victory, reflecting on his career, and pondering retirement. "This is the twilight of my boxing career," it began.

> I know full well that this year, 1941, is likely to be my last in the ring. But it is my burning ambition to exit from this sport, not as just another fighter but as champion.
>
> Certainly, I have pride and lots of it. At one time, I held three titles, featherweight, lightweight, welterweight. Today, in my cupboard, there is no championship.
>
> Fritzie came out of Pittsburgh only a few months ago and took my last crown. Believe me when I tell you that my self-esteem was more battered than my features. In the Garden dressing room that night I made a vow to my manger Eddie Mead and to Harry Armstrong, who is my trainer, that when I retire from the ring I'll retire a champion.
>
> And after this Friday's fight with Zivic at the Garden, I'll be welterweight champion once more. This is not an idle boast but a firm purpose to fulfill a promise which I made to my dearest friends.
>
> As a pugilist, I also know that it takes more than words and promises to tangle with as dangerous a fighter as Fritzie Zivic. Long hours of strenuous training, a plan of battle, confidence, all are requisites to reach my goal.
>
> I have trained faithfully and worked harder for this fight than any other in my career. I have been doing road work for months and have amazed even my intimate friends with my adherence to even the dullest features of routine gym work.
>
> I must own up to one mistake, a mistake which I am not going to repeat. Frankly, I underrated Fritzie Zivic as a fighter. After all, Zivic has been fighting for lo these many years and has experience plus a great will to win.
>
> Today, my respect for Zivic has grown. But I also know how to fight him.
>
> How, well, Friday night, I'll write the conclusion to this literary effort with the aid of glove-encased fists.[470]

The *Pittsburgh Courier* polled "experts" as to who would win the rematch. Among them were nine sports editors from around the country (including Nat Fleischer), boxing manager Gus Greenlee, *New York Journal* boxing writer Hype Igoe, and six members of the *Courier* staff. The final tally had thirteen picking Armstrong and six picking Zivic.[471]

The oddsmakers initially agreed with the *Courier*'s panel. On the eve of battle, they had Henry around an eight to five favorite to regain the championship, but some blamed those odds on sentimental bettors. Late betting on Zivic brought the odds near even by fight time.[472]

The fight brought in the largest crowd in the history of Madison Square Garden on Friday, January 17, 1941. Mike Jacobs even sold standing room, packing the house with 23,190. Another five thousand were turned away. Gate receipts were $78,242, also a Garden record. When Henry entered the arena, a shockwave of applause erupted from the packed cheap seats. Those cheers forced him to hold back tears. He smiled at the feeling that all Harlem had come out to cheer him on. Their faith in him bolstered his confidence that he would regain his crown.[473]

In the corner before the opening bell, Ray Arcel and Al Silvani reminded Henry not to get carried away and to stick with the game plan and box. Instead, Henry, 140 ½ pounds, came out with his familiar aggression. Only this time, something not so familiar bothered him almost immediately. "The courage was there," Henry later remembered, "but this wasn't the old Hammerin' Hank; the speed, the blinding speed, was gone. Father Time had taken his toll."

Henry tried to follow his corner's plan of standing up straight and boxing at various points in the fight, but the change-up did not have the desired effect. Far from surprised by Armstrong's new strategy in round one, Zivic kept his left jab in his challenger's face. He had the longer reach, and he used it well. When Henry finally did press the champion to the ropes, he found himself taking hard hooks rather than landing them.[474]

Round two was nearly identical to the first, but in the third, Henry hurt Fritzie with a right hand to the jaw. Zivic retaliated with hard blows to the head and body, including a right that strayed low and drew boos from the crowd. Armstrong finally got in close, and the pair traded fearsome punches on mostly even terms until the round ended. When Henry returned to his corner, blood ran from above his right eye.

For every blow Henry landed, his fans made the walls of the Garden reverberate with their approval, but as the fight went on, they had fewer and fewer opportunities to cheer. Henry was able to get in close again at the start of the fourth, but both of his eyes were already starting to swell from the punishment of Zivic's jabs. Henry was still in punching range through the rest of the fourth and fifth rounds but seemed concerned primarily with bobbing and weaving out of the way of Zivic's quick and steady combinations.

**A headbutt from Zivic**

By the sixth, it was clear that Zivic was handling Armstrong "like a toy." The crowd gasped with every stiff cross that smacked his face. One of them started Henry's nose bleeding. A Zivic body shot caught him off balance and sent him to his knees, but referee Arthur Donovan called it a slip. Embarrassed, Henry got up immediately and tore into his opponent but found he could do nothing to stem the torrent of blows coming back at him.

Lunging out of his corner furiously to start round seven, Henry corraled Zivic into a corner, only to have his mouthpiece knocked out by a devastating right uppercut. Henry spat blood. Without wavering, he remained in Fritzie's chest for the rest of the round and did not have his mouthpiece put back in until he returned to his corner covered in his own blood at the end of the round.

The eighth round was perhaps the worst three minutes Henry had yet experienced in the ring. His face ballooned and blood-spattered, he did not land a single punch for the first minute. Zivic continued to stab away with his jab and land hard right crosses and uppercuts. Henry's mouthpiece went flying again. By the time he returned to his stool, the lids above both of his eyes were sliced open.

Round nine might as well have been a replay of the previous, down to another dislodging of his mouthpiece. For the first time, Henry appeared truly staggered. He was missing badly and failing to avoid the combinations that came back at him. Shouts began echoing down from the stands. They screamed the exact words that had accompanied Henry's assault of Barney Ross not even three years earlier: Stop the fight![475]

Struggling to see anything, Henry tried to go for Zivic's body in the tenth but walked into punches he could not see coming. Out came Henry's mouthpiece again. Unbeknownst to anyone but the champion himself, Zivic returned to his corner with a broken left hand.

Blinded once again, Henry heard Donovan talking to Ray Arcel and Harry Armstrong in his corner between rounds. The NYSAC's physician was with him.

"He's too game to quit, and he can't win," Donovan put it plainly. "The handwriting is on the wall. I'm not going to let him go beyond his limit."[476]

"Give me one more chance, Art," Henry begged. "If I can't do it in this round, you can do what you see fit."[477]

Donovan looked at Henry's unseeing face and reluctantly held up a single finger, a useless gesture to a blind man. Henry knew what it meant. He had just one more round to prove himself able to continue.

"There have been great thrills in sports before. But none has ever been or will be greater than that 11th round," Jack Smith wrote in the *New York Daily News* the next day. For three minutes, it looked as though Henry Armstrong had turned back the clock and would be champion of the world again. His cornermen had failed to stem the crimson waterfalls cascading from above each eye, but Henry seemed oblivious to anything but the need to dispatch his foe immediately. At the bell, he fired out of his corner as though it were the barrel of a gun, and he was the bullet. He plunged his head directly into Zivic's sternum and unleashed every punch any boxer had ever thought of, trapping the stunned champion in a neutral corner. The audience jolted to its collective feet.

"The flash of the fighting demon of old was on view every second of the first two minutes of that frame," Nat Fleischer later wrote. Still trying to hide the fact of his broken hand, Zivic could only cover up and backpedal from corner to corner. Armstrong was fighting "like a maniac," reported the *New York Times*. To Fleischer, he was "berserk." Henry tumbled to the mat more than once under the momentum of his own blows.

As the thrilling round came to its close, Zivic attempted to retaliate, but Henry refused to be denied. Relieved to hear the bell ending the round, Fritzie Zivic reeled clumsily to his stool. Sensing the sentimental favorite was ready to take back the title, the crowd remained in a frenzy of bloodthirsty delight for the full minute between rounds.[478]

The crowd was in pandemonium, and Donovan let the fight continue. Only Henry knew that he was finished. The eleventh had been a desperate final attempt to knock Zivic out and reclaim the belt. He had spent everything in those three minutes. Now his lungs were burning. Blood flooded his mouth and clogged his nose and throat. His legs shivered with fatigue. He felt as though there were a hundred-pound weight in each glove and spikes pinning his shoes to the floor. There were three cuts around his swollen right eye and another over his left; he could not see.[479]

It did not take long for Zivic to realize that his opponent had nothing left. Armstrong fell to the canvas after a missed punch again, this time less from the velocity of the blow than from his quaking legs. That was all Zivic needed to see. Once Henry righted himself, Fritzie battered him all over the ring. Donovan had at last seen enough. He stepped between the champion and his helpless target and threw his arms around the beaten challenger, signaling a stop to the fight.

The crowd politely applauded the champion as the ref lifted his hand. Moments later, as the loser's handlers aided him out of the ring and down the long walkway out of the arena, the place again shook with cheers for Henry Armstrong. Some in the crowd openly wept. It was a scene that reminded Fleischer of being at Yankee Stadium the night in 1927 that Joe Humphries announced the safe arrival of Charles Lindbergh and his *Spirit of St. Louis* in France.[480]

Applause or not, it was Henry's first stoppage loss since a starving featherweight with a broken rib named Melody Jackson got knocked out in the third round by another Pittsburgh fighter, Al Iovino, an entire decade and 130 fights earlier.

Henry sat on a bench in his stuffy, lonely locker room, resting his back against the lockers. The funereal silence made Henry feel the absence of verbose Eddie Mead, whose beleaguered heart demanded he sit that one out. Harry Armstrong attended lovingly and quietly to his bruised and disappointed charge, massaging the spent muscles and wiping off his cracked and swollen face. Henry could see the tears welling up in his typically stoic friend's eyes.

The stampeding footsteps of press row proceeding down the corridor outside broke the miserable silence, but Henry was in no mood for pictures and questions. Harry went to the door to head the reporters off. He spent fifteen minutes refusing them entry, but Henry eventually said to let them in. Harry insisted that the cameramen wait outside.

The new boxing strategy against Zivic had failed, leaving Ray Arcel to throw up his hands. "There wasn't a thing I could do," he told an inquiring writer. "Henry was dead set on going out fighting."[481]

Appearing every bit the washed-up wreck, Henry told them he was finished. "I know it had to come for me sometime, but I didn't expect it tonight," he admitted. "I don't want to expose my eyes to further danger. Guess they won't stand up any longer. I'm through."[482]

"It was a great fight." The words came meekly out of somewhere inside the crowd of newspapermen, a feeble offering of meager condolence. Henry nodded.

Someone whose vision must have been as impaired as his manners asked Henry how he felt. Forcing a pathetic grin, Henry told them he felt great. Not a soul believed it, including Henry. He was heartbroken.[483]

More questions came. Henry tried to answer them all, but his replies came slowly. Still seeing to his fighter's cuts, Harry fielded some of the questions for him, telling the writers that Henry intended to take a greater hand in the wine business he had started in California and put together a big band orchestra. For now, though, Henry needed a doctor. The reporters respectfully departed, and Henry went to the showers, where he sat motionless on the floor, contemplating the water swirling down the drain.

As Henry prepared to leave the arena, Fritzie Zivic approached him. Aside from his broken, swollen left hand, the champion was unmarked. He shook Henry's hand. "Henry, you're the greatest champ that ever lived," he said, repeating his compliment after their first meeting. The champ then took his leave to celebrate.[484]

As the crowd filed gloomily out of the Garden that night, fans' words of praise for the former champion filled the ears of listening reporters.

"They'll wait a long time see his equal."

"They'll never see another like him."

"A great little man, that Henry."[485]

Later that night, Henry and Harry arrived at Dr. Schiff's office to find Eddie Mead crying on the doctor's couch. They had listened to the fight on the radio. Speaking slowly and weakly, Eddie tried to console his fighter, telling him he'd never have to endure such punishment again. He was through boxing. He told Henry to go back to his family in California and rest.[486]

Schiff went to work on Henry, sewing up his eyes and the inside of his mouth. He told Henry he could remove more scar tissue, but his face was too swollen to operate. It would take at least five days for the swelling to dissipate. Schiff was relieved that Henry was hanging up the gloves. The doctor warned him to never get in the ring again if he wanted to save his eyesight. Hearing that, Harry Armstrong, usually so quiet and reserved, broke down sobbing and fled the room. Henry would not see him again for another four years.

Once again, the newspapermen composed obituaries for Henry's career. "Armstrong passed into the shadows a heroic figure," wrote Joe Williams in the *New York World-Telegram*. Henry's heart rushed with pride when he read that one. He clipped it and hung onto it for decades.[487]

# 17.
# "To Justify Being Alive"

Devastated by his second loss to Fritzie Zivic, Henry Armstrong found himself struggling to find any sense of forward motion outside the ring through the rest of 1941.

Two weeks after losing to Zivic, he was back in the Garden, but not to face an opponent. He stood beside ring announcer Harry Balogh, who introduced him to the eighteen thousand people in attendance for the heavyweight championship match between Joe Louis and Clarence "Red" Burman of Baltimore.

"Henry Armstrong, one of the greatest fighters of all time made his final ring appearance in this arena a few weeks ago. His great stand on that occasion will be remembered always as a gallant exit of a truly great titleholder. As a tribute to his glorious ring career, Promoter Mike Jacobs tonight presents him with a token emblematic of the well wishes of the boxing fans of America.

"Henry Armstrong, when you look upon this testimonial, may it always be a reminder of the many years of honorable service you have given the boxing world."[488]

Balogh then produced a diamond-encrusted gold watch and presented it to Henry, accompanied by the crowd's applause. Henry then sat down to watch Louis dispatch Burman easily in the fifth.

In February, ready to return to California, Henry went to Eddie Mead to collect his savings. He wanted to purchase a nice, new car as a retirement present to himself and drive home in style. Asked for the money, Mead blushed and told Henry the money was gone. To support his gambling habit, Mead had been borrowing from Henry's savings just as he had borrowed from Henry's purses and Mike Jacobs's pockets. With all the sincerity of an addict convinced he was in control, Mead promised Henry he would pay him back soon.

Though Henry later said he trusted that Mead would pay him back, it is hard to believe that there was not some resentment and anxiety gnawing at his brain as he cashed in some bonds to buy the car he wanted and started down the road for California.

On the trip back, Henry fantasized about life in retirement. He had a ranch and a wine business waiting for him, but the thought of being a businessman did not thrill him. He knew the drudgery of day-to-day administration and responsibility was not to his taste. He was more interested in remaining in entertainment and continuing the high life. While waiting for Mead to pay him back, Henry could live off the portion of his savings he had not entrusted to his manager. However, checking his accounts upon his return, he grew more concerned. There was not nearly as much there as he had assumed. Night clubs, women, huge tips, friends, cars, clothes, parties, surgeries, resorts, living expenses, gambling, and drinking had left him with little to show after a decade of putting his body on the line in the ring.

The wine business failed almost immediately, but Henry secretly felt relieved. He had by then hooked up with Chicago music manager Joe Glasser, the mob-connected man behind the great trumpeter and singer Louis Armstrong. Glasser had convinced Henry to come to Detroit and join up with Don Redman and his Orchestra. Henry, who had no music instruction and could not play an instrument, was told he could alternate between singing and conducting.

Glasser was putting together a stellar list of clients for his planned Associated Booking Corporation (ABC), which would wind up representing Billie Holiday, Benny Goodman, Duke Ellington, Lionel Hampton, and Redman.

Redman was a multi-instrumentalist child prodigy born in West Virginia in 1900. After graduating college in 1920, he participated in some of the pioneering jazz bands of the era, including the legendary Fletcher Henderson's big band, which was also an early proving ground for talents like Louis Armstrong and Coleman Hawkins. Jazz historians regard Redman as "a pivotal figure in the development of Swing," particularly for his arranging work for Henderson, Louis Armstrong, and Paul Whiteman.[489]

When a reporter told Count Basie of Henry's intentions, the famed big band leader was not impressed. He predicted that "Armstrong will discover the prize-fighting business is a push-over compared to the life of a swing bandsman."[490]

It proved a fair assessment. Henry's attempts to conduct a major, professional swing band proved disastrous, and he quit after a couple of weeks.

Dejected by losing his title and his aborted attempt at show business, Henry was downing beers in a Lenox Avenue joint in New York City when he first heard the name Beau Jack.

At a time when boxing was sometimes front-page news and every neighborhood in every major city had its gloved heroes, a well-known boxer, trainer, manager, or promoter spent much of his time being told by friends and acquaintances of this or that talented youngster who was sure to be the next Jack Dempsey. Inevitably, a request to mentor or otherwise help the kid was clumsily worked into the conversation. Naturally, the prospects who lived up to the hype were few and far between, and the professional would have to find a way to let them down politely. The ritual was a job prerequisite, a package deal with success in the ring.

This time, the recommended "next big thing" showed promise. Taking a stool next to Henry in the Lenox Avenue bar, Bowman Milligan, steward of the Augusta National Golf Club, started going on to Henry about a fighter he was bringing along. The kid had a syndicate of Augusta big shots behind him, including golf legend Bobby Jones. Would Henry be willing to look at him and give any pointers?

**Beau Jack**

Milligan was a friend, and with Jones's name dropped, Henry figured it could not hurt to give the youngster a few minutes' time.

Milligan introduced him to Sidney Walker, who fought under the moniker Beau Jack. Armstrong and Jack became fast friends. They had a lot in common. Eleven years younger, Beau could have passed as Henry's younger brother. A lightweight standing just an inch taller than Henry, he had the same massive shoulders and compact, muscular torso that boxing scribes mentioned in nearly every profile ever written about Henry Armstrong.

They likely bonded over their similar upbringings. Like young Henry Jackson, young Sidney Walker was raised primarily by his grandmother. It was she who gave him the nickname Beau Jack. Like Henry, he was reared on a farm in the Deep South and had spent many an afternoon shining shoes for pocket change. His earliest experiences with his fists came while defending his corner from kids looking to horn in on his business.

In his St. Louis days, Armstrong avoided participating in the battle royals wherein a group of young Black males was blindfolded and made to fight one another for the right to gather up tossed coins from the floor. As a teen in Augusta, Jack could not afford Henry's scruples. "The king of the battle royals," they called him. Years later, he would take some offense to those who criticized his participation in the racist spectacles. They were "fun," he said, pointing out that "it was that or pickin' cotton. Back then the money from battle royals bought me clothes, shoes and food. So, if that's what you call bad, well, keep it comin'."[491]

The Augusta National Golf Club was the site of the Masters Tournament, which had begun just a few years previous. The Club often sponsored battle royals, and Jack was a frequent star. He especially loved performing during the Masters because of all the big spenders the tournament attracted. Milligan was impressed with Jack and hired him as a bootblack, locker room attendant, and caddy at the Club.

Beau's fistic abilities also impressed Bobby Jones, winner of six amateur championships, four U.S. Opens, and three Open Championships, and co-founder of the Masters Tournament. There are multiple versions of how Jones became one of Jack's benefactors, but whatever the facts, Jones and some wealthy friends took up a collection to stake Beau in a boxing career in the North.

With Milligan as his manager, Jack took up residence at the Longmeadow Country Club in Springfield, Massachusetts, and began an intense training regimen. Throughout his career, he would be known for his enthusiasm for conditioning and training. He ran ten miles a day and sparred for hours, building up the kind of stamina the fight crowd had not seen since a young Henry Armstrong was ripping his way through three divisions.

The similarities between Jack and Armstrong were most evident in the ring. Jack bore into opponents with no evident concern for his safety. He was a fierce inside fighter whose primary weapons were hooks and his head. Like Henry, he rarely took a backward step and loved to slug with opponents, following his team's motto to "Rip 'em all the time."[492]

Beau reminded Henry of haymaker-tossing Ceferino Garcia more so than of himself. He was young and strong but too wild, thought Henry. Still, he saw the potential in the kid.

The two fighters got along and became roommates in a New York apartment. Everywhere Henry went, Beau tagged along after his idol, "thunderstruck." Henry kept his eye on Beau's sparring and offered pointers. He taught Beau to shorten his punches for accuracy and speed. Getting into the ring, he demonstrated how he used his shoulders to grind his way into an opponent's chest.[493]

Beau envied his hero's fine dress, fancy cars, and apparent mastery of the nightlife. This, he figured, was the life of a champion. He absorbed the master's lessons in and out of the ring with attention and imitated him when and where possible.

On April 22, 1941, Henry accompanied Beau to the Foot Guard Hall in Hartford, Connecticut, for Jack's fight with one Bob Reilly. The crowd cheered when they saw Armstrong giving Jack quick pre-fight instructions. Jack went on to stop Reilly in seven.

With the pointers from his hero and the attention that Armstrong's presence brought him, Jack's career would change for the better. Eventually, Henry said his goodbyes and returned to the West Coast, but their paths would cross again in the ring.

Back in L.A., Henry spent some time with another boxer. He made a brief cameo in the Republic Pictures film *The Pittsburgh Kid*, starring the famous light heavyweight champion Billy Conn. The film very loosely followed Billy's life story in a similar manner that *Keep Punching* had featured Henry. He had only recently failed to take the heavyweight title from Joe Louis but had put up a brave fight, and his fame was at its peak. Henry showed up to film a brief sparring session with Billy for the movie, which was released that summer. There is no record of what the producers paid him, but it probably was not much.

Back in his home in California, the Armstrong family struggled. Henry's father, who had moved in with Henry, Willa Mae, and Lanetta, was very ill. Henry worried for his father. He worried about bills. And he missed his old friend Harry.

Even after they became successful in boxing, Harry had lived next door to his "brother." Considered inseparable, they went to the same church and movie theater and often read the same books simultaneously. Yet, after that second loss to Zivic, a disconsolate Harry disappeared, leaving a distraught wife and a lonely friend in his wake.

In June 1941, Henry picked up a job traveling the West Coast as a referee for promoter Lee Lewis. That and the rent collected from some properties he owned kept the bills paid and food in the icebox, but Henry's spending habits demanded more. He later estimated that he lost five to six thousand dollars of what little remained of his savings in the three months following the second loss to Zivic.[494]

He missed the thrill of fistic combat and the roar of the crowd. He rarely saw his old friends Al Jolson, George Raft, and Mae West; they were all distracted by struggles with their own fading careers. Meanwhile, the championships, the parties, the celebrities, the women, and the adulation were gone. His wife was unhappy with him after years of Henry's absences, womanizing, and now failing finances.

Only the alcohol remained dependable, it seemed. With boredom, depression, and money woes setting in, beer was the last thing left that made Henry feel good. His weight ballooned thirty pounds in a few months.[495]

When Fritzie Zivic lost the welterweight championship to the underwhelming Freddie "Red" Cochrane in July, the temptation to return and take back his belt nagged at him. The next day, he received a telegram from Eddie Mead.

"Do you want your championship back?" the message read. Yes, he did. His self-esteem hungered for that validation, and his heart longed for forward motion.[496]

"I didn't mind not having money," Henry later told sportswriter Al Stump. "But I feared I'd be useless to myself and the world... I had to find some way to justify being alive."[497]

Then promoter Freddie Sommers came to Henry with some justification in the form of an exhibition tour. That would bring income, competition, and an audience. To Henry, it also meant testing the waters for a more serious comeback. Looking soft about the mid-section, Henry blasted out two overmatched local lightweights in Oklahoma City on September 17, 1941, in front of thirty-five hundred fans.[498]

Returning to the ring helped Henry feel alive and admired again. He felt a sense of purpose. Despite the lessons of the past, he spent his purse on a brand-new Buick to transport himself, Sommers, and a couple of other fighters between scheduled events.

Sometime in late September, Sommers lost control of the car near Warner, Oklahoma, on their way to a show in Little Rock. They shot off the road, turning over three times. In the tumbling, Henry spilled into the floorboard beneath the glove compartment. It proved a fortuitous fall, as the car's roof was crushed down to the dash. Luckily, no one was seriously hurt. Henry suffered the only injury, a broken pinky.

He felt so blessed to walk away from the wreck that he told the Little Rock crowd at ringside that night what had happened and credited God with saving him. As Henry professed his thanks to the Lord, the crowd became restless, so he eventually relented and went about beating his opponent for the evening, despite his broken finger.

While the pinky healed, he picked up paychecks refereeing fights in Texas and Alabama. He also began training and managing fighters, including Mike Delia, a nineteen-year-old white lightweight out of Oklahoma whose record included thirteen wins (eight by knockout) against one loss by the close of October 1941. However, Henry failed to sign contracts with these young men, believing a handshake was good enough. Sommers eventually stole Henry's fighters from under him, and Henry returned home to California feeling betrayed.[499]

In early November, he announced that he would not continue the Sommers-promoted exhibition tour and would retire for good. He said his finger had healed fine, but the injury had convinced him he was through. "I don't want to tear down with one poor fight the reputation I built up in 12 years," he said. Asked who stood out among the young crop of fighters coming up in the sport, he singled out one man: Ray Robinson, the slick and good-looking lightweight who had fought on the undercard of his first fight with Zivic. Living up to his promise to avenge Henry's defeat, Robinson won a ten-round decision over Zivic in a fight on October 31.[500]

# 18.
# The Comeback Trail

On the morning of Monday, December 8, 1941, Henry and the rest of Los Angeles opened the *Times* to read the headline, "JAPS OPEN WAR ON U.S. WITH BOMBING OF HAWAII." Like everyone else, he had heard the news streaming out of every radio in earshot for the entire prior day, since the early morning attack on the U.S. naval base at Pearl Harbor near Honolulu.

The City of Los Angeles, sitting on the California coast as it did, took the news with even more anxiety and offense than most of the rest of the country. City streets and telephone lines jammed all day Sunday, and mobs of people made their way downtown to newspaper offices and government buildings to catch the latest news and assess the danger. The extent of the damage to the Navy and the nature of the U.S. response were still unclear. Law enforcement mobilized, citizens' defense leagues surfaced immediately, and military men throughout the city rushed to their posts. The FBI was already out arresting Japanese "subversives" and had announced their intention to force the city's thousands of other Japanese Americans into "protective custody" camps as soon as Congress declared war. They issued orders to the press forbidding the publication of the names of those taken.

On Monday, Henry and the rest of the country listened to President Roosevelt memorialize December 7 as a "day of infamy" and ask Congress for a declaration of war. Four days later, Henry celebrated his thirty-second birthday.

In January, George Raft came calling from Hollywood. Raft had learned that new military recruits were upset about missing out on big boxing matches while in basic training. The actor was putting together a group of famous boxers to put on exhibition matches at Army camps throughout the country and the world, its purpose to increase morale among the troops. It would be called the George Raft Caravan, and he wanted Henry to join.

Like most young American men, many of boxing's elite talents, past and present, had signed up for U.S. military service after the attack. Joe Louis, Billy Conn, Ray Robinson, Al Hostak, and Jackie Wilson enlisted in the Army. Freddie "Red" Cochrane, the new welterweight champion, signed up for the Navy, as did Fred Apostoli, Georgie Abrams, Tony Zale, and Gene Tunney. Lou Ambers and Gus Lesnevich joined the Coast Guard. Barney Ross bravely insisted upon front-line duty in the Marines.

Henry never publicly addressed why he did not immediately sign up for military service. In 1944, he told the G.I.s at Fort George Meade in Maryland that the California Draft Board classified him as 1A, meaning he was fit for duty. If so, his notoriously bad eyes must not have prevented him from induction.

He did join the George Raft Caravan. Other former fistic stars who would participate were Jim Jeffries, Jack Johnson, Jimmy McLarnin, Tommy Ryan, Ceferino Garcia, Mushy Callahan, Willie Ritchie, Jack Root, and Fidel LaBarba. Several active fighters would participate in each event. Jackie Wilson, Chalky Wright, and Manuel Ortiz fought in exhibitions at one point or another on the tour. The retired fighters sometimes donned the gloves, but they were mostly around to make appearances while Raft and Callahan refereed the fights. Henry insisted on fighting in the exhibitions.

The George Raft Caravan - Back row: Al McCoy, James Jeffries, George Raft, unknown, Mushy Callahan, Ceferino Garcia, Jack Root, Maxie Rosenbloom, Jules Covay, Everett Sanders. Front row: Jerry Giesler, Henry Armstrong, Willie Ritchie, Jimmy McLarnin, Fidel LaBarba

The Caravan's first stop was at March Field, the Air Force base in Riverside County, California, and they continued to bases up and down the coast, making Raft "the idol of the doughboys." The tour proved more popular than the actor had anticipated, and as requests from more military officers came in, Raft continued to dip into his pockets to pay the expenses and the fighters. When military recruitment meant he was running out of active fighters to participate, he added pro wrestlers to the tour's attractions. By July, fifty thousand servicemen had seen Henry Armstrong and the others appear or perform in these exhibitions.[501]

The caravan brought a feeling of worth back to Henry's life, a sense that he was moving forward again. He was happy to have a reason to get back into shape. The fights themselves were easy, and the refereeing even easier. He enjoyed the applause and was happy to entertain the service members.

By the dawn of 1943, Raft's attention had drifted to the idea of assembling a troupe of female athletes guaranteed to entertain the young men of the military even more, and the Caravan fizzled out. As much as Henry liked it, it does not appear that he stayed with the tour to the end. The tour experience instilled in him the desire to mount a serious comeback by mid-1942. On May 6 of that year, he boxed a four-round exhibition for charity at Ocean Park, California, and rumors circulated that Henry would announce a comeback any day.

Henry was indeed entertaining thoughts of a return. He had promised never to return just months earlier, but the lure of competition, glory, and riches convinced him that he was still young, quick, and strong. He would regain the welterweight championship, he told himself.

A friend introduced Henry to a wealthy Texas sportsman in Los Angeles named Lucius Lomax, who agreed to finance some of Armstrong's training expenses in exchange for a piece of his purses. Estranged from Harry, Henry hired relatively inexperienced trainer Norman Sanders. Lomax set up a camp at a dude ranch in Victorville, California, for the duration of May. After word of this hit the papers, large crowds gathered at the ranch each weekend to watch him train and assess his chances. He looked good, reported the *California Eagle*, "still 'perpetual motion.'"[502]

On Monday, May 25, Henry signed a contract with promoter Babe Griffin to fight in his first pro bout in nearly seventeen months on June 1. He phoned Dr. Schiff in New York to tell him the news. He had already dashed off a short letter to Eddie Mead saying the same thing, he explained.

"Eddie just died," Schiff told him. "Heart attack. He scored on a big bet on a horse, and it was too much for his heart."[503]

Mead and his secretary had just left Schiff's office and had not made it far down the Fifty-fifth Street sidewalk. They intended to visit Mead's favorite New York spots, the bars, pool halls, bookies, and social clubs. He was in a good mood because a horse he had bet on, Liquid Lunch, had won its race, a rare victory for the unlucky gambler. When they got to Seventh Avenue, Eddie unexpectedly told his secretary that he would instead head back to his room at the Park Central Hotel to relax. His secretary asked him if he was all right.

"Sure, I feel fine," Mead responded before falling straight to the pavement like a felled tree.

Unable to wake Mead, the secretary sprinted back to Schiff's office to retrieve the doctor, but Eddie was dead by the time they returned. He was forty-nine years old.[504]

When reporters called, Henry told them he was shocked. "Eddie Mead was the swellest guy I ever met," he said and credited Mead with guiding him to his championships.[505]

The manager had never paid Henry back the tens of thousands (maybe hundreds of thousands) he had "borrowed" from him, but Henry did not mention that to the reporters. Even in later life, he was reluctant to speak ill about the manager he continued to see as one of his closest friends.

"I don't know how much he made off with. I loved that man," he told Barney Nagler in 1963.[506]

"I should have watched over my own money," he admitted to another writer, "but I didn't. That was my mistake.... I didn't know how to take care of money any more than Mead did. He ran through a couple fortunes of his own before he went through mine. Eddie felt bad. He didn't want to cheat me. It wasn't only me he cheated, but himself."

"Eddie Mead was a very good manager and I have no complaints," he told Ted Carroll in 1959. "I feel he meant well, but he just wasn't made to handle the kind of money we were getting."

He would at least admit that Mead's sudden passing without paying back the money he owed "left everything in such a tangle, it just couldn't be straightened out."[507]

Henry signed management contracts with Lucius Lomax and "a smart, gentle man" named George P. Moore. Lomax would provide the bulk of the financing while Moore would handle the business end of the fights as Henry's "road manager." Moore was a light-skinned, overweight Black man in his sixties. Before turning to the boxing business, he had been a hotelier. He had operated as a manager and promoter in the Pacific Northwest for over a quarter century and had strong connections in New York City.[508]

An orphan raised in a Catholic home in Independence, Texas, Moore may have been the "gentle man" that Henry said he was, but he had also been a hustler since childhood. In his teens, he drifted to Oklahoma City, where he got the funds to open a successful saloon. Then it was on to Portland, Oregon, where he bought the successful Golden West Hotel. The *Oregon Daily Journal* recognized him as "one of the wealthiest colored men in the city" and "the 'overseer' of the north end colored district."[509]

He owned the pool hall across the street from the hotel, too. On Moore's orders, the pool room put on boxing shows for twenty-five cent admission on Wednesday nights and eventually churned out a halfway decent fighter named Jack Taylor, the first fighter in Moore's managerial stable.

Moore had frequent run-ins with the law as the owner of the Golden West, which offered gambling and prostitution as attractions. Police raids were frequent, but Moore was never in a cell long. Most notably, police arrested him in Tacoma in 1913 after he allegedly made off with thousands of dollars in cash and jewelry following a split from his common-law wife, who also accused him of forcing her into prostitution.

Big Bill Tate, one of the best heavyweights of the 1920s, and Danny Edwards, a stellar bantamweight, were Moore's most famous charges in his early career. By the early 1920s, he was in New York with Edwards. He was instrumental in organizing the first legal mixed-race bout in New York City between Edwards, a Black man, and Irish Johnny Curtin on September 26, 1922, at the aptly named Pioneer Sporting Club.

As of Eddie Mead's death, Moore had been retired and living in California for about a decade until his work with Henry in breaking the color barrier at the Hollywood Legion sparked his passion for wheeling and dealing. He put in a call to Henry, and they signed a contract.

Six days after Eddie Mead's death, Henry was in a San Jose ring, ready to begin his comeback with Moore at his side. His opponent was initially to be Mexico's Cecilo Lozado, but Lozado failed the pre-fight medical exam, and promoters quickly recruited one Johnny Taylor of nearby Oakland as an alternate. Taylor had more losses and draws on his record than wins.

Though he weighed a career-high 148 pounds, Henry felt good that night. As was his custom, he began shadowboxing furiously in his dressing room, continued as he walked to the ring, and did not stop even during the referee's instructions. By then, he had shaken all the rust off his muscles and joints, and he just kept on punching until he stopped Taylor in four rounds.

Despite incurring a cauliflower ear, two cuts, and multiple bruises in the fight, Taylor was unimpressed by the comeback chances of the man he called his idol. "All ribbing on the square, I feel sorry for Armstrong," he told the press. "Because he has to keep on fighting tougher guys. I don't. We're both washed up. The only difference is I know it."[510]

If Henry did know it, he did not let on. "I felt good out there," he said. "I was missing a lot, but I boxed only two rounds in training. I was tickled that my eyes weren't cut even once. I guess that proves they're pretty well healed." Henry was paid $470 for the win.[511]

*The Ring*'s welterweight rankings as of Henry's return were as follows:

World's Champion – Freddie Cochrane
Contenders:
1 – Ray Robinson
2 – California Jackie Wilson
3 – Charley Burley
4 – Cocoa Kid
5 – Garvey Young
6 – Young Kid McCoy
7 – Marty Servo
8 – Reuben Shank
9 – Tony Motisi
10 – Freddie Archer[512]

On June 24, Henry won a hard-fought ten-round decision over Richard "Sheik" Rangel in Oakland Auditorium. "I thought I was in a glove factory, he hit me so often," Rangel later quipped. Nine days later, Henry lost one to up-and-coming contender Reuben Shank in Shank's native Colorado. It was Henry's first loss in a non-title outing since 1936, but he had scored the fight's only knockdown, and most ringside reporters felt he won the fight decisively.[513]

Nat Fleischer was not impressed with Henry's chances of regaining his past glory. He called the pursuit pathetic. "Hank still carries a wallop but any clever lad in the welter ranks who really goes after the former champ, who made 'perpetual motion' in boxing a national phrase, can take his measure."[514]

Undaunted, Henry continued fighting at the same clip that had been his trademark before his retirement. On July 20, he stopped overmatched Joe Ybarra in three rounds in Sacramento. In San Francisco on August 3, Aldo Spoldi, the former lightweight champion of Europe, hit the floor three times before the referee stopped the fight in the seventh round. Henry won a ten-round decision in a toe-to-toe brawl with veteran Utah welterweight Jackie Burke in Ogden on August 13. Mexico's Rodolfo Ramirez could take no more after eight rounds on August 26. That fight drew a record crowd to the Oakland Auditorium.[515]

Henry scored a third-round stoppage in a second meeting with Johnny Taylor on September 7 in Pittman, Nevada. Chicago's Leo Rodak was stopped on cuts in eight rounds in San Francisco one week later. On September 30, Henry returned to the Oakland Auditorium to face his first top-ten contender since losing to Shank and scored a fourth-round knockout over Earl Turner, who until then was ballyhooed by some as "the greatest welterweight in the world" (a now laughable assertion, considering that Ray Robinson, Henry Armstrong, Charley Burley, and Cocoa Kid were all prowling the division). Two weeks later, Henry finished off lightweight contender Juan Zurita in less than two rounds in Henry's triumphant return to the Olympic Auditorium. The arena sold out.[516]

Following the knockout of Turner, whom *The Ring* had recognized as the number nine welterweight, the magazine installed Henry in the number three contender spot behind champion Red Cochrane, "uncrowned champion" Sugar Ray Robinson, and former champ Fritzie Zivic. It was Henry's first return to the respected top ten since losing to Zivic for the second time nearly two years earlier. He was also named "Fighter of the Month."

"Hank seems to be moving along in fine style," commented the magazine's staff writer Meyer Ackerman.[517]

On October 1, San Francisco fight promoter Benny Ford announced that he had signed Henry Armstrong and Fritzie Zivic for a third fight, bragging that he had outbid Mike Jacobs. That was not entirely so. Jacobs desperately wanted to bring the fight to New York to repair his reputation after failing to make the much-anticipated heavyweight rematch between Joe Louis and Billy Conn happen. In late September, the embarrassed "Uncle Mike" assumptively told the New York papers he had Armstrong and Zivic all set up for early November. He then called George Moore with an offer. But Henry did not want to leave town. His father's condition had taken a turn for the worse, and no amount of money was worth being away from home.

Jacobs was beside himself. Probably thinking the refusal a bluff, he called Moore every day for five consecutive days, upping his offer until it hit an incredible fifty thousand dollars. Still, he could not get the fighter and manager to change their minds. The best he got was a promise that Henry would fight for Mike sometime in the next year. Armstrong signed with Foord, who afterward received a confirmation telegram from Pittsburgh saying that Zivic would come to California for the match. Foord scheduled the bout for October 26 at Frisco's Civic Auditorium.[518]

In the fifteen months since he lost the welterweight championship to Cochrane, Zivic's own comeback campaign had not been as swift or consistent as Armstrong's. He had put together fifteen wins but lost five fights and drawn another. Two of those defeats had come against undefeated rising star Sugar Ray Robinson. The others were to the capable but significantly less impressive trio of Tony Motisi, Reuben Shank, and Norman Rubio. The draw was with ranked contender Adam Pianga, better known as Young Kid McCoy. In September, Fritzie won a ten-round unanimous decision over Cochrane in a highly attended non-title rematch in Madison Square Garden, rocketing himself from unranked to the number two contender spot behind only Robinson in *The Ring*'s rankings.[519]

The Armstrong and Zivic rubber match was the biggest boxing event to hit San Francisco in years. From the day of its announcement, *San Francisco Examiner* sports columnist Eddie Muller wrote daily of expert opinions and news of the fight.

"If memory serves," wrote Muller, "Armstrong didn't draw as much boxing in this State when he was champion as he is drawing in his present comeback."[520]

Henry insisted that the eye surgeries and his rest from the ring would make the difference in this third fight and promised to turn the tables on Zivic. Fritzie predicted a third win, of course, relying on the old axiom that styles made fights. "His style of bobbing and weaving is made to order for me," he said. West Coast gamblers wagered heavily on Henry, but money from the East flooded in late to even the odds by October 23.[521]

Before a capacity crowd of 10,200 in the Civic Auditorium that Monday night, Armstrong entered the ring at 142 ½ pounds to Zivic's 146 ½. Navy man and world champion Cochrane was at ringside. Other West Coast boxing stars like Max Baer, Maxie Rosenbloom, John Henry Lewis, Eddie Booker, and Lloyd Marshall were in attendance.[522]

With the clanging of the opening bell, both combatants met at ring center, ready for war. By the second round, they had fallen into their familiar tactics. Henry bobbed and wove his way inside and targeted the body. Fritzie counterpunched, most effectively with hard uppercuts to the face. Zivic's jab was consistent and accurate, but Armstrong continued to bore in like the "Hammerin' Hank" of old. Henry staggered Fritzie multiple times, but the scrappy Pittsburgher never went down. The referee warned Zivic for low blows and headlocks. By round seven, Fritzie was showing signs of fatigue. Wanting to slow down the pace of the combat, he was holding and retreating. After catching several hard hooks to the face in round nine, Henry intentionally spit out his mouthpiece to suck wind but fought on and took the round. Henry let off the gas a bit in the tenth and final round, but he had fought most of the battle at a punishing tempo. Both men did damage, but Henry felt confident he had won.

When it was all over, referee Billy Burke and both judges awarded their decision unanimously to Henry by a comfortable margin. Muller of the *Examiner* scored six rounds for Henry, two for Fritzie, and two even. The United Press had seven for Henry, one for Fritzie, and two even.[523]

It would have been difficult to pick a winner based solely on the visage of each boxer. Fritzie was uncut, but his head was a swollen mass of bruises. Though nowhere near as bloody as in their first two encounters, Henry was displeased that a scar over his left eye had opened, and both eyes were nearly swollen shut. Facial damage aside, the long-awaited revenge against Zivic brought Henry a sense of vindication.

"Zivic was just nasty, Bad!" he told Bill Libby of *Boxing Illustrated* magazine decades later, a rare admission of dislike toward an opponent. "He couldn't punch, and he ran. But he could box, and he could cut you up... and he could fight dirty. He used to admit he tried to thumb everybody." He told Peter Heller that he carried Fritzie to the end, not out of respect, but to continue punishing his foe.[524]

The win also brought Henry professional relevance for the first time since returning. Where boxing scribes had once dismissed his return as pathetic, they now obsessed over his success, stopping just short of writing epic poems in his honor. Just months earlier, experts were writing him off as a sad figure. Now, the newspapers hailed him as "The Man of Destiny," "the jinx smasher," "pound for pound the greatest fighting man in all ring history," and "Toast of the Fighting World."[525]

Less ecstatic but still impressed was Nat Fleischer, who rated Henry "far from being the dynamic, two-fisted battler of his prime, but as the boxing game goes today, he rates a top-notcher," before going on to predict that Henry "is likely to be the best money-maker during the winter season."[526]

A painting of Henry in a fighting pose graced the cover of the January 1943 issue of *The Ring*, released shortly after the Zivic fight. He took over Zivic's place as the number two contender for Cochrane's crown in *The Ring* rankings, right behind Robinson. Fleischer and his fellow sportswriters speculated on the possibility of an Armstrong and Robinson fight to come.[527]

The loss to Henry Armstrong marked the end of Fritzie Zivic's time at the pinnacle of the sport, but he would fight on. Famous throughout the country and a sports icon in Pittsburgh, he continued to draw bouts against big-name opponents throughout his remaining career but won fewer and fewer of those matches and never got another shot at a championship. There was a four-fight rivalry with the "Bronx Bull," future middleweight champion and Hall of Famer Jake LaMotta, but Fritzie won only one. In 1946, he went 6-10-2, then 0-2 in 1947. Two years later, he hung up the gloves for good, a ring veteran of more than seventeen years and an astonishing 231 professional bouts. A well-liked figure in retirement, he lost money as a boxing manager and promoter in Pittsburgh but earned a living primarily through public appearances, including television cameos. He passed away in Pittsburgh on May 16, 1984, a few days after his seventy-first birthday, and was posthumously inducted into the International Boxing Hall of Fame in 1993.[528]

Suddenly, Henry Armstrong was the most talked-about man in boxing again. While his fighter rested and healed at a nearby Hot Springs resort, manager Moore considered who the next opponent might be. With champion Red Cochrane on active duty in the Navy, a chance at the title was slim to none for the moment. Mike Jacobs offered them their choice of three dates in January for a fight in New York. Jacobs seemed most interested in a fourth go with Zivic. The press was salivating over a possible matchup with number one contender Sugar Ray Robinson, who had signed up for the Army but was still taking fights for the moment. Robinson was not keen on the idea, but Moore and Jacobs contacted Robinson's management about a possible bout in January.

A Washington, D.C. promoter offered Henry five thousand dollars to face Brooklyn scrapper Al "Bummy" Davis in the capital, but Moore had promised Jacobs to bring Armstrong out to New York after the New Year. The powerful "Uncle Mike" was already upset that they had taken the lucrative Zivic fight to California. To come East but steal away to D.C. might test the Machiavelli of Eight Avenue's patience beyond repair.

Numerous offers of West Coast fights flooded in before the end of 1942. These would allow Henry to stay close to home, earn money, and avoid alienating Jacobs by leaving enough time for a fight in New York sometime in early 1943.

Moore wanted Henry to fight in front of a big Los Angeles crowd at the Olympic Auditorium. In late November, he got a call from West Coast matchmaker Joe Waterman proposing Henry give ex-lightweight champ Lew Jenkins another go. Henry had stopped the power-punching Texan in a slugfest back in 1940, and the "Sweetwater Swatter" had not recovered well. His carefree lifestyle was ruining him. Tales of drunk driving arrests, car and motorcycle accidents, violent rows with his hot-tempered wife Katie, debilitating injuries, training camp absences, and drunken fights spread through gyms and newspapers in the early 1940s.

Eleven months after Sammy Angott took his title, Jenkins had lost nine of his last ten fights. He had become, as one writer put it, "a second-rate fighter with a first-rate punch." Booze, legal fees, houses, cars, and women depleted his bank accounts. Katie divorced him in April amid accusations of terrible physical abuse. After the most recent loss, Jenkins's trainer Willie Ketchum had quit. He begged Lew to do the same, but the fighter seemed hellbent on completing his self-destruction.[529]

Despite his tarnished reputation, lack of conditioning, and blemished record, Lew Jenkins could still punch anyone's lights out, and he remained a draw. Having already served in the Army before the War, he volunteered for the U.S. Coast Guard on October 27 but would remain on inactive duty long enough for another fight.

Confident of an easy win and a decent payday, Henry signed for the fight. Organizers scheduled the bout for December 4 at the Portland Auditorium in Oregon, a populated locale that boxers of such renown as Armstrong and Jenkins rarely visited. Moore - who had operated in Portland for most of his career and had many connections there - hoped this would draw out the local fans.

Military service had always been a stabilizing force for the otherwise undisciplined and self-destructive Jenkins. The routine, structure, and a sense of purpose seemed to bring out the best in him throughout his life. But the Coast Guard had not yet had the chance to have that effect, and Lew was up to his old habits before the rematch. "I was drunk for eighteen days. I never trained a minute," he later recalled of the weeks before facing Henry again. Henry arrived in Portland on Monday, November 30, and immediately began preparations.[530]

Friday, December 4, was Lew Jenkins's twenty-sixth birthday, and he celebrated it by enduring a brutal beating in front of 4,570 fans at the Portland Auditorium, the largest indoor fight crowd in the city's history to that point.

"Jenkins was some puncher for a skinny guy," Henry later remembered. "But I stayed on top of him, throwing his timing off, and he only hit me with glancing blows. He seemed cocky and overconfident, and he was out of shape and couldn't take a punch."[531]

Assaulting his opponent from the opening bell, Henry put his left hook to good use and dropped the "Sweetwater Swatter" eight times inside eight rounds before referee Tom Louttit decided he had seen enough. Jenkins's alcohol-thinned blood was all over both fighters and the ring floor. Afterward, he endured forty stitches to repair the damage to his face.

As it had done in the past, military service did subdue Lew's reckless personality and lifestyle. His drinking subsided. Deployed overseas in 1943, he participated in several major battles in Europe and Africa, serving as a coxswain aboard the landing craft. On June 6, 1944, D-Day, his Higgins boat brought British troops to the shores of Normandy, including a trip to Omaha Beach. Discharged in November 1945, he returned covered in medals from every theater of the war and resumed his boxing career.

Though he was now completely sober, he was also thirty years old, and his comeback proved disappointing. He re-enlisted in the Army in February 1946 as a sergeant. Discharged in November 1948, he moved to Philadelphia and began a second boxing comeback. Lew's war experiences, a second marriage, and fatherhood calmed his wild lifestyle. But the damage he had done to his body over the years and advancing age meant that his newfound discipline mattered little against younger, fresher opponents. After losing four straight in 1950, Jenkins retired for good at age thirty-three.

Following the U.S. invasion of South Korea, Sergeant Jenkins re-enlisted in the Army, his third stint. As Barney Ross had done as a Marine in Guadalcanal during World War II, Lew Jenkins showed uncommon bravery as a soldier during the Korean War. The stories of the tremendous courage he displayed are worth recounting here.

In August 1951, he oversaw a platoon ordered to take Hill 773 with the rest of George Company at what would later be known as Bloody Ridge. Twenty-three men in Lew's platoon died on that mission, all victims of enemy landmines. Pressing on through the fog and mud at the front of the platoon, he inspired his men to continue even as they watched their comrades obliterated by mines, and he was the second man to reach the top.

When the North Koreans arrived to retake Bloody Ridge, "things went from bad to worse," he later remembered. Surrounded and divided, the George and Fox Companies, Lew's platoon included, went into retreat under heavy fire. He ran down the hill amid his comrades' fallen and falling bodies. Along with the sixteen other survivors from both companies, he took cover underwater in a creek, forced to hold his breath for as long as possible. Any man who lifted his head for oxygen risked being shot by the enemy, and many were.[532]

Emerging from the creek after a couple of South Korean soldiers arrived for protection, Lew discovered that some of his men were dead or severely injured. One distraught young man committed suicide in front of him. Exhausted but uninjured, Jenkins gathered those still able to fight into an impromptu squad composed of both Americans and South Koreans, the remnants of otherwise decimated platoons, and he led them away from the creek to a pass between the American lines and the cut-off Third Battalion on Hill 1179. Thinking they could bridge the gap, he ordered the men into defensive positions.

As expected, the enemy arrived in short order, looking to divide the American forces again. Under fire from an entire battalion for three days, Lew's beleaguered, disorganized, and fatigued squad held its position with just eight machine guns between them. Lew spent those days running back and forth between the men and an ammunition dump. He manned a gun himself when needed until reinforcements secured the position and the enemy retreated from the pass. He then joined those sent to cut off the enemy's retreat. After several more days of battle, the U.N. forces secured Bloody Ridge, though it cost them an estimated fifteen thousand casualties.

"I guess I didn't sleep eight hours in those twenty-one days," Lew remembered of his time there.[533]

In the aftermath, North Korean forces retreated to what the Americans called Heartbreak Ridge, so named because U.N. forces had already taken and lost the area seven times. After five days of "rest and rehabilitation," Sergeant Jenkins was ordered to Heartbreak Ridge as part of the Second Infantry Division under General Robert N. Young. They took part in an aggressive plan devised by Young called Operation Touchdown, which would meet fierce resistance and take heavy casualties. Re-strengthened after Bloody Ridge, George Company had just twenty-three living men after Heartbreak Ridge, Lew Jenkins among them.

President Harry Truman awarded Lew Jenkins the Silver Star for his actions in the pass at Bloody Ridge. The highly decorated General Young would later praise Lew as "one of the bravest and finest soldiers I have yet to have under my command."[534]

"Don't know why they gave me a medal," Lew commented. "The kids in my outfit did the work, and I got the glory." But a corporal in that pass at Bloody Ridge with him said that Lew had the most dangerous job of them all, spending three days running for ammunition under heavy fire while the rest of the men could stay low and take cover. Despite exhibiting bravery equal to that of Barney Ross at Guadalcanal, the military never gave Jenkins the kind of public relations ballyhoo Ross had received for some reason.[535]

Always open about his devotion and love for the Army infantry, Jenkins remained in the service until 1963, having first enlisted in 1936. Sober since the end of World War II, he moved with his wife and son to Concord,

California, where he drove a laundry truck and worked as a golf course greenskeeper. After years of heart trouble, Verlin "Lew" Jenkins, boxing champion and war hero, died on October 30, 1981, at age 64 and was buried at Arlington National Cemetery. He was posthumously inducted into the International Boxing Hall of Fame in 1999.

On the day before Henry's rematch with Jenkins, manager George Moore announced that Henry would be fighting his friend Sugar Ray Robinson for the "duration" welterweight championship, meant to determine an interim champion while the division's true champion served in the armed forces. That fight was tentatively scheduled for January 29 in New York City, fulfilling Moore's promise to promoter Mike Jacobs.

Far from excited over the showdown between the two best active men in the welterweight division, most of the press and boxing insiders thought the Robinson matchup a threat to Armstrong's health.

"Robinson, who combines the speed of a puma with the kick of a percheron, is a menace to a man with battered eyes like Henry's," warned the United Press, noting that "the seasoned boxing men who sit at the ringside for this fight, will be more concerned with the threat to Henry's eyes than with the possibilities of an Armstrong victory." Henry's hometown paper, the *Los Angeles Daily News*, predicted that he would take the worst beating of his career.[536]

In its February issue, *The Ring* named Sugar Ray Robinson its "Fighter of the Year" for 1941, crediting his fourteen consecutive victories, nine by knockout, that year. Henry came in fourth in the voting, writer Daniel M. Daniel noting that his "amazing comeback" had kept interest in boxing alive while many of the sport's champions went to war.[537]

By late December, word had arrived that the fight was off. Sugar Ray's manager, George Gainford, allegedly nixed the match, seeing no upside for his fighter. Robinson was only two years into his pro career. Facing a man of Henry's experience riding a ten-fight winning streak seemed like too much of a risk. Even if Ray won, Gainford figured the press and fans would see it as Ray beating up an over-the-hill, smaller man. When the newspapermen called, Robinson told them he did not want to hurt his idol.[538]

Instead, Robinson accepted a second fight with middleweight Jake LaMotta of the Bronx. He had beaten LaMotta in their previous match. In the February 4 rematch, the "Bronx Bull" charged Robinson through the ropes in the eighth round and took a unanimous decision, dealing Sugar Ray his first professional defeat. As a result, *The Ring* elevated Henry Armstrong to the number one welterweight contender's spot in its monthly rankings.[539]

Mike Jacobs announced intentions to match Henry with Al "Bummy" Davis, but those arrangements fell through, so the frustrated promoter lined up Henry's former roommate and protégé Beau Jack for the January 29 date.

In the meantime, George Moore kept Henry active. Two days after his thirty-third birthday, he closed out the year with a fourth-round technical knockout of Italy's Saverio Turiello, a veteran of nearly two hundred prize fights.

Henry opened his campaign for 1943 with a ten-round unanimous decision over Jimmy McDaniels on January 5. The press called McDaniels "a fearless son of Erin," but at four o'clock on the day of the fight, McDaniels suddenly discovered fear and announced to his team that he would not fight. He showed up in the ring only under badgering from promoter Cal Eaton.[540]

The McDaniels fight was Henry's long-awaited homecoming to the Olympic Auditorium in Los Angeles. Though not a sellout, the turnout was still sizable, paying a gate of $14,778.[541]

It was an unexpectedly tough one for Henry, partly because he had trouble breathing and swallowing. He kept having to spit his mouthpiece out as a result. A week later, a doctor informed him that he had tonsillitis. They required removal, but surgeons could not operate for another week. As a result, Moore had the Beau Jack fight postponed indefinitely. Mike Jacobs must have been exasperated.

**Willie Joyce**

While Henry took a month to recuperate from his tonsillectomy and then train back into condition, Moore lined up fights for his return. Another bout in the Olympic was scheduled for March 2, the opponent being lightweight contender Willie Joyce.

By February 24, Henry was preparing for Joyce at the Main Street Gym. He still followed the tradition he set with Eddie Mead of drinking beer with his meals while in training. However, when his post-op stitches began to hemorrhage, he was advised by his doctors to give up the beer for this training camp, and he did. As a result, he dropped to his lightest weight in years, 137 ½ pounds.

Born in Georgia but fighting out of Gary, Indiana, the 5'6" Joyce was ranked as the number five contender at lightweight by *The Ring*. The NBA and NYSAC ranked him as the outstanding contender for their crowns, which Sammy Angott and Beau Jack held, respectively. He had picked up two wins and a draw against Lew Jenkins in 1939, boasted a record of 46-6-7, and had never been stopped or knocked out. Most recently, he scored a sensational win over the previously undefeated John Thomas at the Olympic in early February.

Nicknamed "Wee Willie" and "The Wrecker" by sportswriters, Joyce usually relied on an aggressive, pressure-fighting style and a blistering body attack that had drawn comparisons with Armstrong. Able to box when called for, he possessed a superb jab and impressive hand speed, but he was not thought to carry Henry's punching power. By the day of the fight, the odds were three to one in Armstrong's favor, but some saw Joyce as a live underdog. They correctly surmised that he was the most dangerous opponent of Henry's comeback thus far.[542]

The Armstrong-Joyce matchup on Tuesday, March 2, 1943, drew the Olympic's largest crowd and gate ($26,835.95) since the start of the Great Depression, packing in 9,846 fans and forcing ticket sellers to turn thousands more away. When some persistent fans crashed through a back door, police were required to restore order.[543]

It was a big fight in L.A. Sergeant Joe Louis, still heavyweight champion of the world, was in attendance, as were Hollywood stars Johnny Weissmuller, John Garfield, Fred MacMurray, Ray Milland, Bill "Bojangles" Robinson, and the Marx brothers.

From the opening bell, Joyce used all his considerable boxing skills. Rather than bore in and trade as usual, he circled the ring to prevent Armstrong from planting his feet and force the older man to give chase. Offensively, Joyce threw swift combinations, occasionally lunging in with hard punches to the body.

Paul Lowry of the *Los Angeles Times* praised Joyce's skillful boxing and ring generalship, while Johnny Allen of the *Daily News* felt that "Jumpin' Joyce" danced too much and favored Henry's aggression, seeing Armstrong as the one who set the early pace. But both writers recognized that Joyce had gained control of the fight by round five.[544]

Henry pursued, looking to trade punches, but he often missed wildly against the "dancing, circling ebony dervish." In the eighth, he drew first blood with a right that hit just below the left ear. The punch broke Joyce's jaw, but the tough Indiana fighter remained focused. Joyce continued to give a boxing clinic against his tiring opponent. Armstrong spat out his mouthpiece multiple times, desperately trying to fill his lungs. Though round ten brought a strong Armstrong effort, it was too little too late. In the end, the referee and one of the two judges had Joyce comfortably ahead while the second judge scored the match a draw.

The crowd applauded the verdict in Willie's favor, and the press agreed. Lowry felt Joyce won all but the eighth and tenth rounds, while Allen had it much closer, but still for Joyce.[545]

"Guess I should have taken a warm-up bout before meeting Joyce," Henry admitted afterward. "You can't go from the operating room to the ring and expect to do a good job." He then complimented Joyce and said he intended to get revenge.[546]

"He's got a lot more than just a left hand, though you never get to see anything else when you box him because he keeps that left in your face all night," Henry said of Joyce's busy jab years later. "You can tell he throws a right occasionally because you can feel it land, but you can't see it coming because, no matter which way you turn, that left is playing tag with your nose."[547]

At the very least, Henry was happy that his eyes had held up against the loss with no cuts or swelling. Indeed, if facial appearances were the scorecards of a fight, Henry would have taken home a unanimous decision. The official victor bled from a cauliflower left ear. His jaw was broken, and his lips were swollen and bleeding. In his locker room, the dead-tired Joyce stared emotionlessly forward in a daze as congratulations and questions circled his head like chirping birds. He said little through his shattered jaw, offering only that he welcomed a rematch.

Lowry called it "the fistic upset of the year." "The local gambling set is in an uproar," reported Ned Cronin, the *Daily News* sports editor. "One group is shouting for joy and the other is hollering for aspirin in barrel lots."[548]

Loss or not, Henry had obligations to meet in the ring. Six days after the Joyce loss, he was back at it, this time in San Francisco's Civic Auditorium to face New Jersey's Antonio Pilleteri, better known to the fight crowd as Tippy Larkin. A 5'7" veteran of ninety-four professional bouts ranked among the best lightweights in the world, Larkin had bested Red Cochrane on three occasions. He was quick, skilled, and packed a solid punch in either hand. Unfortunately for him, his Achilles heel protruded from his chin. Lew Jenkins had decimated him inside of a round back in 1940, and Beau Jack took less than three rounds to do the same in a December 1942 fight for the NYSAC's lightweight belt.[549]

Oddsmakers had Henry as the two-to-one favorite. Nonetheless, Prescott Sullivan of the *San Francisco Examiner* picked Larkin to beat Armstrong. Sullivan's colleague Eddie Muller reported that many fight fans shared Sullivan's outlook. Larkin was younger, taller, and had four inches in reach on Henry. A capacity crowd packed the auditorium and produced a $15,000 gate with the idea that success or failure against Larkin would determine the future of Henry Armstrong's comeback.[550]

**Tippy Larkin, "The Garfield Gunner"**

Henry gave them their answer in devastating fashion. As the duo traded blows toe-to-toe in the second round, Henry landed a quick right hook that ruined the kid from Jersey. A left landed for good measure, but the damage was already done. Larkin's legs sprang out from under him, and the rest of him smacked the canvas with a thud. Heaving himself up to one knee as Joe Gorman counted over him, Larkin collapsed back to the floor before the count of ten, and the fight was over.

Tippy Larkin would go on to win the world's junior welterweight (140 pounds) championship against Willie Joyce in 1946 before voluntarily relinquishing that lightly regarded title in the same year. Fighting on until 1952, he struggled with alcoholism in later life. In 1958, his car swerved into oncoming traffic, smashing head-on into another vehicle, killing the other driver. Larkin served time for reckless driving. He passed away in his native New Jersey on December 10, 1991, at age seventy-four.[551]

In March 1943, Henry headed for Fort Huachuca in Arizona, home to the U.S. Army's all-Black 93rd division. He delivered a ten-minute speech, and the eight thousand soldiers present applauded him with a "rafter-trembling ovation."[552]

He then caught a train to Philadelphia for a fight with Al Tribuani, the first fight of his comeback in the East. Joe Gramby, the trainer of lightweight star Bob Montgomery, prepared him for the match. On March 22, before a crowd of 12,633 at Philly's Convention Hall, including Montgomery and Al Weill, Armstrong and Tribuani engaged in a fierce slugfest. Henry did not get the clear upper hand until the tenth and final round but managed to walk away with the decision win. Though the decision had its detractors, Montgomery and Weill commented that Armstrong looked good enough to whip Beau Jack in a highly anticipated showdown scheduled for April 2 in New York.[553]

Of late, Jack was showing that he had absorbed the lessons Henry Armstrong had taught him well, and after a rocky start, he was now one of the brightest stars on the fistic horizon. 1942 brought thirteen consecutive victories, culminating with collecting the NYSAC's lightweight belt with his third-round demolition of Larkin on December 18. Two decisions over Fritzie Zivic followed early the next year. By then, Jack was a significant ticket-seller for Mike Jacobs and Madison Square Garden, and sports columnists could not resist comparisons to his one-time mentor.

The Armstrong and Jack fight would take place above the lightweight limit of 135 pounds, so Jack's title was not on the line. Should Henry win, sportswriters predicted that Jack would have to grant him a title shot.

Henry had some reservations about taking the fight, although he did clarify that fighting a friend was not a concern. That part was strictly business, he told Arthur Daley of the *New York Times*. The concern must have been with Jack's fighting abilities, then. After all, the way the boxing press put it, Henry would be in there against a mirror image of his indefatigable younger self.

"I guess that meeting Beau Jack is the price of coming back," he admitted to journalist Bob Considine, mustering a brief chuckle to mask his legitimate worry.[554]

Just in case Beau had any qualms about giving his all in a fight with a friend, Henry shot him a telegram explaining that boxing was a business, and they were businessmen with a duty to entertain their paying customers with the best fight they could give.

Though Jack publicly professed a reluctance to face his friend and hero in the ring, he could not have been too reticent, given that he once knocked out his brother in a battle royal match. His manager, Chick Wergeles, insisted that the teacher-student story about Armstrong and Jack was overblown. He told Harold Parrott of the *Brooklyn Daily Eagle* that Henry and Beau had met and sparred once and that Henry had pronounced Jack "strong as a bull." He insisted that the lone meeting was the full extent of the "friendship" between the fighters.[555]

Arriving from Philadelphia, Henry set up his New York camp in Stillman's Gym, and preparations began on March 25. Baltimore welterweight Sammy Daniels served as his sparring partner. Jack was also training in the same famed facility, and huge crowds packed the building to watch the duo prepare to fight one another. Both camps wrapped up on April 1, the day before the fight. It was also Jack's twenty-second birthday.

Two doctors removed the last potential obstacle to the matchup on Tuesday, March 30, when they cleared Henry to fight. There had been some doubt as to whether his eyes would pass inspection by the commission's medical representatives, but he was pronounced fit for battle.

The fight crowd buzzed all over the country with predictions of what promised to be a thrilling showdown between the sport's two most exciting sluggers. Requests for press row tickets nearly equaled those of a Joe Louis heavyweight title fight but with fewer seats available.

Oddsmakers had Jack as the favorite by odds of around two to one as of Friday, April 2, the day of the bout. After all, Jack was only twenty-two years old compared to his thirty-year-old opponent (Henry was thirty-three, of course, but no one knew it).

John A. Cluney, a columnist for the *Waterbury Democrat*, saw Jack as "the strongest 'small' boxer I have seen in any ring in 25 years." Nat Fleischer admitted a sentimental fondness for Armstrong but conceded that Jack had all the advantages and was the most likely to win. But lightweight contender Bob Montgomery and manager Al Weill both picked Armstrong. So did *New York Age* columnist Buster Miller. Benny Leonard, the former lightweight champion of the world, also picked Henry, calling him "one of the smartest boxers I've ever seen [with] the most killing pace, I believe, the ring has ever known." Promoter Benny Foord joined their ranks, declaring himself "an Armstrong man from start to finish." Fritzie Zivic, who had been in the ring with both men, picked Armstrong.[556]

Henry was thrilled for his first bout in the Garden since his second loss to Zivic more than two years earlier. Despite pouring rain, a capacity crowd of 19,986 paid $104,976. Another five thousand were turned away. It was the largest indoor gate for a non-heavyweight, non-title bout in a decade and the largest boxing gate overall of 1943, a sign not only that the hard economic times of the Great Depression were a thing of the past for many but that fight fans expected Armstrong and Jack to deliver fireworks.[557]

Both men stood 5'5" tall. Armstrong weighed 138 pounds to Jack's 135 ¾ pounds.

"The fight was a bitter, nerve-tingling one in which neither gladiator bothered, even if he could, to display the faintest trace of ring science," reported Joseph C. Nichols of the *Times*. "They merely sailed into each other, put their heads together and proceeded to batter away, each operating on the theory that the other must drop sooner or later."[558]

Neither man would drop in the ten rounds it lasted, despite the grueling violence they endured. Henry showed rejuvenated hand speed and impressive punching power in his attack, but Jack repeatedly stopped him in his tracks with bolo right uppercuts.

While both men fought with fury in the opening two rounds, the younger man had the edge. Beau's punches came almost from the floor, yet Henry was either unable to or unwilling to get out of their way. He persistently bore in with his own ceaseless punches, mostly missing his target.

**Armstrong and Jack, friends turned rivals**

In the third, Jack twice reeled to the ropes under Armstrong's attack. At one point, it seemed to Nat Fleischer that Jack was ready to go down, but Armstrong could not land the *coup de grace*.

The middle rounds belonged clearly to Beau Jack and his uppercuts that "threatened to snap [Henry's] head off." Fleischer counted twenty-one uppercuts and eleven left jabs landing for Jack without an answer in the fourth. Jack also landed at will through the fifth until a big Armstrong right in the last twelve seconds blasted him backward. Only the ropes held him up, but referee Billy Cavanaugh neglected to call it a knockdown. Henry pummeled Beau with punches from all angles until the bell sounded, but the younger man remained upright.

In the sixth, the crowd jeered Beau for the sin of taking a backward step and once clinching Henry, but Fleischer felt that Jack "wasn't simply back-pedaling. He was connecting with good blows while in retreat." The United Press agreed, calling the sixth Jack's best round of the fight.[559]

Henry found a second wind in the seventh, his quick and powerful left hook finding a home in Beau's face and ribs. He had the lightweight champ on his heels from then until the closing of round ten. The rally continued into the eighth and ninth, as Armstrong's feared looping right repeatedly stunned and staggered Jack in those rounds. In those moments, the crowd reflexively sprang to its feet and howled for Henry. The tenth was all Henry Armstrong as Jack danced and held to burn out the clock. A heavy right dazed Jack, and Armstrong leaped on him with a desperate body attack, but the bell saved the Georgian.

With the fight over, referee Cavanaugh's scorecard had Beau Jack the winner by five rounds to three, with two even. Judge Bill Healy gave it to Jack by a score of eight to two, and judge George LeCron made the decision unanimous for Jack by a margin of seven to two, with one even.

For nearly a half hour after the announcement, the Garden shook with catcalls and boos from an audience that had rooted for Armstrong throughout the contest. Nichols and Dick McCann (of the *Daily News*) both felt that the decision was sound. So did Bill Corum of the *New York Evening Journal*, who called the fight for the evening's radio broadcast. Fleischer scored seven to two in Jack's favor, with one even. Jack Cuddy of the United Press scored the fight a draw but admitted that if he were forced to decide for either fighter, he would have picked Armstrong based on his aggression. He went so far as to compare the judges to the "three blind mice." In the definite minority among those at press row, the writer for the Associated Press scored the fight for Armstrong by a single round.[560]

In his dressing room after the fight, a frustrated Armstrong criticized Jack for running too much. Later, he granted that Jack was "a good boy... strictly a top notcher," but insisted that "if I ever won a fight in my life it was the one with Beau Jack." Jack praised Henry as a great fighter and admitted that he had been hurt once or twice in the battle, but his manager brushed off any possibility of a title shot for Henry.[561]

More than two decades later, Henry remembered of the Jack fight, "He didn't hit too hard, and he was wild, but he was difficult to fight, especially for an old guy like me. He had a hard skull, too. Once I hit him one of my hardest punches, and it didn't faze him a bit. But I was old, and maybe it wasn't as hard a punch as I thought."[562]

There was talk of a rematch, but Beau's management did not think it a good idea. They may have felt lucky to get away with a win in the first fight, but they told columnist Dan Parker that they feared that Beau might hurt Henry too severely.

Jack would headline more main events (twenty-one) in Madison Square Garden than any other fighter in history. He fought there three times in March of 1944 alone, drawing over 336,000 fans and $1,579,000 in just that month. His four-fight saga with skilled contender and future Hall of Famer Bob Montgomery was one of the best of the era, as the duo traded the NYSAC title back and forth. One of their battles garnered nearly thirty-six million dollars for a War Bond drive. It not only set a record gate by a long shot but also set a record for the highest-priced ringside seat ($100,000) that still stands today. When the pair finished their hard-fought rivalry, the end tally was two for Jack and two for Montgomery, but Montgomery ended the series with the belt.[563]

Jack continued to be a big draw after losing a bout with the other great lightweight of the era, Ike Williams, in 1948. He retired in 1951 after crooked managers and a fondness for high living had already depleted his bank account. After a draw and a loss with Williams in a comeback attempt, he hung up the gloves again and returned to shining shoes to eke out a living. Elected to the International Boxing Hall of Fame in 1991, he passed away on February 9, 2000, at age seventy-eight.

# 19.
# Sugar Ray

Henry was $24,158.17 richer after his thrilling battle with Beau Jack. It was the biggest payday of his comeback so far. Still, this third loss of his comeback meant a drop in the welterweight rankings. *The Ring* lowered him to the number two contender's place, underneath Sugar Ray Robinson. Reclaiming the top spot meant a showdown with the young and dangerous new star.[564]

Some fans decried the Jack decision as a fix afterward, but most impartial observers felt Jack won the fight handily. The best that Armstrong and Moore could claim is that Henry was, as always, continually the aggressor and that he had Jack badly hurt in the later rounds. They told reporters Henry wanted a rematch as soon as possible.

Jack Cuddy of the United Press and Nat Fleischer of *The Ring* both wrote that Henry had earned a shot at Jack's lightweight title. "Armstrong lost the decision, but he recaptured the affection of the fans," wrote Cuddy, "and now Hammering Henry must be given a title shot at Beau Jack, or… fans will want to know the reason why."[565]

Mike Jacobs wanted a second purse like the record-setting one that now lined his pockets. He told the Associated Press that he wanted to arrange a second meeting for June, this time over fifteen rounds, but admitted he could not compel Jack to put his belt on the line. Jack was already scheduled to defend it against Bob Montgomery in May and did not intend to defend again for at least another six months. Jacobs's enthusiasm notwithstanding, Jack's management was uninterested in a second go with Armstrong.

Unable to get a commitment from Jack's people, Jacobs offered a contract to Henry, promising he would face either Jack, Montgomery, or former lightweight champ Sammy Angott on June 11 in the Garden. Henry willingly signed, glad to sign up for another large payday and keep his comeback in motion. He told the press he preferred redemption against Jack.

On April 4, while still in New York, Henry stopped at St. Alban's Hospital to visit Barney Ross's sick bed. The champion-turned-Marine had recently returned from his Silver-Star-winning heroics at Guadalcanal. In March, Ross collapsed in his hotel room from exhaustion, malaria, and the lingering effects of his war wounds. After the visit, Henry took a rest of his own in Hot Springs, Arkansas.

A few weeks later, he was back in action, picking up some quick paydays in the ring before June's fight in the Garden. He stopped Saverio Turiello in a rematch in Washington D.C. on May 1, knocked out Tommy Jessup in the first round "before a glove could be laid on him" in Boston a week later, and then stopped Maxie Shapiro in seven in Philadelphia on May 24.

The day after the Shapiro win, Moore told the press that former lightweight champ Sammy Angott was up next for Henry. "There doesn't seem to be anyone else to fight Henry," he reasoned. Robinson was in the Army, and Jack was avoiding a rematch. Bob Montgomery, the new lightweight champion after a victory over Jack, was not likely to put his title on the line so quickly. But Henry had signed a contract agreeing to fight for Mike Jacobs at the Garden on June 11, and they needed a name big enough to draw a worthwhile gate there. That left Angott.[566]

"The Clutch" Angott was never a beloved fighter. But he was well-known and respected. Though he was a rough-edged inside fighter, fans and sportswriters considered him a bore for clinching his opponents too often. Boring or not, Angott was a tough, skilled, and highly accomplished fighter who had never been knocked out.

Born Salvatore Engotti, he had turned pro in 1935 at twenty years of age. He was part of that incredible crop of talents from the Western Pennsylvania region during the Depression (Angott, the Zivics, Billy Conn, Charley Burley, Jackie Wilson, Teddy Yarosz, and others). Unlike most of the others, he was not a great draw at home, so he mostly fought on the road. In his first three years as a pro, when most fighters would build their reputation at home, Sammy fought in New York, D.C., Louisville, Chicago, Milwaukee, Dallas, and New Orleans, and only occasionally Pittsburgh. Handsome and personable, he would eventually settle in Hollywood and befriend several movie stars.

Fighting on the road proved tricky for the novice Angott, and he picked up ten losses in his first twenty-six bouts. But he turned things around in 1938, going 12-1 and beating several top fighters. 1939 brought victories over a list of names all too familiar to Henry, including Aldo Spoldi, Petey Sarron, Davey Day, and Baby Arizmendi. Sammy then picked up the NBA's lightweight belt with a decision over Day on May 3, 1940.

Between 1940 and 1941, Angott lost just twice, to Zivic and Robinson, both in non-title fights. On December 19, 1941, twelve days after the bombing of Pearl Harbor, he comprehensively outboxed NYSAC champion Lew Jenkins in a lackluster affair in Madison Square Garden to become the undisputed champ. In the words of Pittsburgh sportswriter Roy McHugh, Sammy "wrapped [Jenkins] up like a Christmas present."[567]

Angott shocked the boxing world by announcing his retirement in November 1942. It was not that boxing writers and fans would miss "The Clutch." It was just that he closed shop at the height of his career. After all, he was only twenty-seven. Claiming an injured hand, he went to work in a steel mill.

After just a few months away, Angott was back in a ring on March 19, 1943, and not just any ring. It was the Madison Square Garden ring. His opponent was no overmatched pug set up to help Sammy chip the rust of the mill from his joints. He was the underdog against Willie Pep, the dazzlingly quick and skilled world featherweight champion who had assembled a phenomenal 62-0 record. Lucky for Pep, it was a non-title fight because Angott dominated the fight in his yawn-inducing manner. That tremendous upset put Sammy back in the running to regain the lightweight championship he had recently relinquished.[568]

The NBA pushed Bob Montgomery to defend his belt against Angott, who had beaten Montgomery on three prior occasions. But the champion needed time to rest after his fight with Jack. That left Angott and Henry Armstrong to face one another.

Both fighters trained at Stillman's Gym. Henry's sparring partner was a California welterweight named Terry Gibson, who had only been fighting a year and was preparing to make his all-important Garden debut against Saverio Turiello on the undercard of Armstrong-Angott.

As of fight time on June 11, oddsmakers had Angott the favorite at eight to five odds, but Henry vowed to the New York sportswriters that he would retire if he lost to Sammy. He entered the ring weighing 140 ¾ pounds. Angott weighed 138 ¼ pounds. More than thirteen thousand fans assembled in the Garden, paying $55,502. Most were Henry Armstrong fans, and they cheered their man boisterously.[569]

They were stunned to see their man outfought in the opening round. Standing toe-to-toe, Angott roughed him up on the inside. In the ring with "Hurricane Henry," not even Sammy Angott could be boring. His best punch was the right uppercut, which had always been Henry's weakness, and Angott used it throughout the fight. At times, Henry appeared genuinely stunned by his opponent's willingness to mix it up on the inside. It was not until the last half of the second round that Henry gave his fans something to cheer for. He started to outpunch Sammy and caught him with a hard left hook that forced Sammy to hold while his head cleared.

It was a closely fought inside battle the rest of the way. Dick McCann of the *Daily News* wrote that most of the fight could have happened "in a jeep's rumble seat."

"There was hardly a left jab thrown," observed Joseph C. Nichols of the *Times*. "The rivals were content to sail into each other with left hooks to the head, then shift the attack to the body in the hope that the other would fall." Angott hit the floor in the seventh, but the referee correctly ruled it a slip.[570]

By the end of the seventh, Henry seemed to have a tenuous edge in the fight. In the eighth, he landed a punishing right just under the heart. Nichols called it the best punch of the fight. The crowd rose while Angott doubled over in pain, but his fighting instincts would not let him go down. His arms reached out and pulled Armstrong close to avoid collapsing to the canvas in agony. Henry punished Sammy's body as "The Clutch" desperately grappled. Angott returned to his stool with a cut near his left eye. Meanwhile, both of Henry's eyes were quickly swelling.

Henry had found his target. He zeroed in on the body for the rest of the fight while Angott alternated between boxing and holding. Two of Henry's blows strayed low in the ninth, but referee Eddie Joseph issued no penalty. The weakened Angott slipped to the canvas again in the ninth. At the start of the next round, Henry stormed out of his corner, looking for a knockout.

He recklessly ran into multiple right uppercuts. Neither man gave ground as the fight drew to its close, and they were trading frantically at the sound of the bell.

**Angott and Armstrong maul on the inside**

It had been a tough fight for Henry, but referee Joseph scored it six rounds to four in his favor. Judge Jimmy Gearns scored it five rounds for Armstrong, four for Angott, and one draw. Judge Bill Healy scored it six rounds for Armstrong, three for Angott, and one even, awarding Henry a unanimous decision.[571]

Both Nichols and McCann scored the bout a draw. They agreed that it was Henry's most significant win thus far in his comeback.[572]

"Angott has the most unorthodox style of anybody in the ring," was Henry's assessment of Sammy a few months later. "You can't tell what he'll do next.... You can't hurt the guy."[573]

After the fight, Dr. Schiff stitched Henry's lacerated lip with eight stitches and ordered Henry to give the wound eight weeks before trading leather in the ring again. Henry agreed, and George Moore postponed a highly anticipated rematch with Willie Joyce.[574]

A badly injured right hand temporarily sidelined Angott after the fight. Four months after facing Armstrong, he regained the NBA's vacant lightweight belt with a decision over Luther "Slugger" White but lost it a short time later to Juan Zurita, a man Henry had twice knocked out. Angott continued to face big names for a time but gradually fell from the limelight as age and ring wear caught up with him. After multiple retirements and comebacks, he hung up the gloves for good in 1950 at age thirty-five. Impressively, he suffered only one knockout loss (to Beau Jack in 1946) in 131 professional bouts and had beaten seven future Hall of Famers.[575]

After an unsuccessful career as a boxing manager, Angott worked in an Ohio manufacturing plant and was active in various charities. He died from a blood clot in his brain on October 22, 1980, at age sixty-five. One of the great unsung boxing champions, he was posthumously inducted into the International Boxing Hall of Fame ten years later.

On the Sunday following the Angott win, Henry was the guest of honor at a Negro National League baseball doubleheader. Cheering his hometown St. Louis Stars, he watched them lose to the New York Black Yankees and then defeat the Philadelphia Stars.

Like almost everything else in the country, baseball was segregated, and the "separate but equal" line was as false in the sport as it was in all other cases. Black ballplayers were not paid nearly as much as their white counterparts. Their accommodations, arenas, and equipment were inferior as well. It was only one aspect of American life that confirmed the subjugation of Black Americans as second-class citizens.

While Henry recuperated from the Angott fight, George Moore worked on an idea he and Henry had conceived: the first boxing match benefitting the struggles of Black people in the United States. Weeks before the Angott fight, Moore met with a panel of Harlem sportswriters on Henry's behalf and told them he was working on the idea but asked them not to print any details yet, as he had not yet spoken to Mike Jacobs.

After Henry beat Angott, Moore talked to Jacobs, and the pair outlined a plan to have five percent of the gate receipts of a long-awaited showdown between Henry Armstrong and Sugar Ray Robinson go to a group of ten agencies working to improve Black lives in America. Moore and Judge Herbert Delaney would pick the groups and organize the distribution of funds.

During the three years since a young Robinson introduced himself to his hero, the two fighters developed a friendship. Even when Robinson was at the height of his fame, touring about in his famous pink Cadillac, "you'd often see Sugar Ray pull over and stop upon spotting Henry Armstrong, climbing out of his car to chat," writes Robinson biographer Wil Haygood.[576]

Moore and Jacobs felt Henry would have the best shot at convincing his friend to agree to the fight. They asked him to place the call, and he did.

"Ray, we'd make a good match," Henry began. "We'd draw a lot of money."

"I could never fight you, Henry," Ray responded. "You were my boyhood idol." He pointed out that he was still in the Army. It would be difficult to get approved leave to fight.

When Henry reported Robinson's refusal to Jacobs, the promoter picked up the phone and called Ray back. He asked the enlisted fighter when he had some leave coming.

"In August," the fighter responded, already knowing where the conversation was going.

"Good, how would you like Armstrong?" Ray responded that he would not. Expecting that, Uncle Mike knew exactly what to say.

"It'll do a lot of money, and it won't be a tough fight for you – Armstrong is making a comeback. He needs the money more than you do." Jacobs stopped and listened. Ray was silent, a sign Jacobs knew meant that Robinson was taking the bait. Jacobs only needed to reel him in. "He can make more money with you than with anybody else."

Jacobs landed the deal. Ray decided he would take the fight not for himself but for Armstrong because "if I didn't fight him, I'd be costing him money."[577]

Details of the planned benefit fight hit the press on June 26. Jacobs intended it for a yet-to-be-named outdoor arena in New York City in August and expected it to draw between two and three hundred thousand dollars. Beneficiaries would include the National Alliance for the Advancement of Colored People (NAACP), Young Men's Christian Association (YMCA), Council on African Affairs, National Urban League, and other groups.[578]

Meanwhile, Jacobs pressed Henry to stay in New York City. He could get him a fight with Bob Montgomery, he said. Henry insisted he needed to return to California for his promised rematch with Willie Joyce. The California Commission threatened to suspend his boxing license if he did not show a clear intention to make the match. They wanted a date set. George Moore was already packing his bags, and Henry planned to follow as soon as his mouth healed.

On June 22, Armstrong and Moore met with the California Commission and ironed out the details of the fight with Joyce. It would happen on July 24 at Gilmore Stadium in Los Angeles. That gave Henry less than the eight weeks Dr. Schiff had ordered to let his mouth heal, but Moore told the press his fighter would be ready.

Henry had been gone from home for three months fighting in Philadelphia, New York, Washington, and Boston. He was making money again and came back with full pockets, but things were difficult at home. Henry Senior's health continued to fail. Lanetta was now school-age, and Henry had left Willa Mae alone to care for their daughter and his dying father. The resulting arguments put a strain on their marriage. Henry's continued heavy drinking and womanizing could not have helped matters.

The Internal Revenue Service was after him, too. He was astonished at the enormous percentages they wanted of his purses. The IRS and his big-spender lifestyle once again meant he was putting little away for the future. A few weeks after he met with the California Commission, Henry was spotted prowling around Mike Jacobs's office in Manhattan, looking to borrow five hundred dollars from "Uncle Mike." Robinson and Joe Louis watched as Jacobs hid from the perpetually cash-strapped ex-champion.

"Did you see what Mike Jacobs did to Henry Armstrong?" Ray asked Joe on their way out of the building. He was astonished at the disrespect shown to a living legend of boxing. "Did you see how he treated him?"[579]

Henry's left eye was another cause of worry. He had been experiencing moments of blurred vision, and he visited Dr. Simon Jesberg in Hollywood to have it looked at. After an examination, Jesberg stressed to Henry that he should forget about boxing if he wanted to keep his vision. Dr. Schiff may have long since taken care of the scar tissue outside Henry's eyes, Jesberg told him, but scars were forming inside the eye itself.

Despite the dire warning, there were bills to be paid and a promise to fight the rematch with Joyce. Henry was slow on his feet on Saturday, July 24, but a late rally won him a narrow unanimous decision victory in a thriller. In the fifth, he broke Joyce's jaw for a second time, which turned the tide of battle in his favor, though Willie's team and a portion of the crowd voiced their displeasure with the decision. Fifteen thousand fans, including Governor Earl Warren, watched Henry avenge his March loss to Joyce.[580]

Much to Willa Mae's displeasure, Henry left home again in August, heading north for two fights. On August 6, he won a decision over Jimmy Garrison in Portland, Oregon, and another over Joey Silva in Spokane, Washington, on August 14. Then it was off to New York again to finally face Sugar Ray Robinson.

Robinson had been born Walker Smith, Jr. in Detroit on May 3, 1921, and raised in the run-down Black Bottom neighborhood ("Black because we lived there, Bottom because that's where we were at," he pointed out). He was known at home and in the streets as Junior.[581]

To keep her son from getting into trouble in those streets, Junior's mother, Leila, gave him a quarter each month to attend the nearby Brewster Center, a recreation center where kids learned to play sports. Children there pointed out to him another of the Center's attendees, their idol, Joe Barrow. A successful amateur boxer, Barrow was seven years older than Junior. They lived a couple of blocks from each other; Joe went to high school with Junior's older sister. Junior learned his hero's training schedule and planned his visits to the Center accordingly. Meeting Joe at the door, he excitedly and proudly carried the older boy's bag into the locker room for him. Seeing Joe in action inspired Junior to lace on the gloves and train at boxing. Within a few years, Joe Barrow was Joe Louis, and Junior Smith was Sugar Ray Robinson.

In 1932, to find work at the height of the Great Depression, the Smiths moved to New York City, settling first in Hell's Kitchen and later in Harlem. The kids in Harlem called him Smitty. At 15, he found his way to the Salem-Crescent Athletic Club and met boxing manager George Gainford, who "ruled amateur boxing in Harlem."[582]

Respecting Leila Smith's wishes, Gainford did not initially let Smitty box. He allowed the kid to hang around the club just to stay out of trouble. One night at a bootleg boxing show in Kingston, New York, a promoter came to Gainford saying he needed a flyweight for the night's event.

"Flyweight? I don't have a flyweight with me tonight," responded the trainer.

"Sure you do," Smitty spoke up, "I'm a flyweight."[583]

Because Smitty had no official AAU card authorizing him to fight, Gainford pulled out the card of another kid he happened to have on him and handed it to the promoter. It was the name of a kid who had recently quit, a kid named Ray Robinson. The new Ray Robinson won his first amateur fight by unanimous decision that night.

Despite his mother's objections, the young fighter embarked upon a stellar amateur career using his falsified AAU card. He was skinny but swift and quickly absorbed the techniques that Gainford and others imparted. After one of his many knockout victories as an amateur, sportswriter Jack Case commented to Gainford, "That's a sweet fighter you've got there."

A woman in earshot spoke up. "As sweet as sugar!"[584]

The next day, Case wrote a story about Sugar Ray Robinson.

Between October 1938 and September 1940, Robinson went undefeated in fifty-four amateur contests, including a win over future Hall of Famer Willie Pep. He won the New York Golden Gloves featherweight championship in 1940 and turned pro on October 4 of that year at Madison Square Garden on the undercard of the first Armstrong-Zivic fight.

Being granted one's pro debut at the Garden was an extremely rare recognition, but promoters and sportswriters already regarded Robinson as a special case. At only nineteen years old, he already seemed a destined champion. By the end of his first year as a pro, some experts already declared him the finest fighter they had ever seen.

After Armstrong lost the welterweight title to Zivic, boxing needed a new sensation in the lighter weight divisions. Robinson fit the bill perfectly. Quick of both hand and foot, he was equally dominant boxing on the outside or slugging away inside with an opponent. He had knockout power in both hands and a solid chin. His defense and timing were on point, and he was a good-looking kid. His unquantifiable star power allowed him to become one of the rare Black athletes who crossed over with some success to white ticket buyers. That made Mike Jacobs a big Sugar Ray Robinson fan.

By the time of his fight with Henry Armstrong, Robinson had filled out with muscle into a welterweight and, except for one brief intermission, had been *The Ring*'s number one contender in the division since his back-to-back victories over Fritzie Zivic in October 1941 and January 1942. Champion Red Cochrane had been avoiding him ever since, and the press called Ray the "uncrowned champion" of the division. He boasted a record of forty-four wins (thirty by knockout) and a lone defeat to future middleweight champion Jake LaMotta, who outweighed him by sixteen pounds. Among the top names he had beaten to this point were Zivic, LaMotta, Sammy Angott, and Izzy Jannazzo, and he had beaten them all twice. Most recently, he had outboxed one of Henry's old title challengers, Ralph Zannelli, in Boston on July 1.[585]

Sugar Ray Robinson was already a cultural icon in predominantly Black Harlem. Unlike Henry Armstrong and Joe Louis, who the neighborhood residents also loved, Robinson had the added advantage of being a resident. Proud Harlemites cheered him, shook his hand, and asked for his autograph as he passed down the street in a shining Cadillac. He may have grown up in Detroit, but as far as Harlem was concerned, he was one of their own.

**Sugar Ray Robinson**

In early August, New York City was one of several major urban centers throughout the nation that experienced violent "race riots" during the sweltering summer of 1943. As temperatures and wartime economic tensions escalated, Henry's home of Los Angeles had kicked things off with the now infamous Zoot Suit Riots months earlier. Now Robinson's home became the scene of looting and bloodshed after a white police officer shot a Black soldier.

"5,000 policemen and squads of soldiers were brought into the community to maintain order," reported the *New York Times*. Two days of rioting left six people dead and nearly five hundred wounded. Millions of dollars in property damage ruined Harlem structures and businesses. Police made five hundred arrests.[586]

Weeks later, racial tensions remained high in Harlem. A heavy police presence and fear of more violence kept people indoors. A week before the Armstrong-Robinson fight, Jacobs begrudgingly took it out of the outdoor Polo Grounds and inside Madison Square Garden, citing predictions of rain. At least some in the press speculated that the true reason was the tense Harlem atmosphere stifling ticket sales. Interest in the fight remained high, but Jacobs and his team worried when advance ticket sales lagged.

During a conversation with Robinson and Gainford, *New York Journal-American* writer Hype Igoe wondered aloud if Sugar Ray's affinity for Armstrong might make him pull his punches, giving the always-willing Armstrong a chance to upset the odds.

"You know this is business, Hype," Robinson told him a couple of days before the fight. "When the bell rings, Henry Armstrong will be there for only one purpose – to whip me. If he didn't think he could, he wouldn't be in there. He won't care that I've always admired him."

Igoe acknowledged Henry's mission but questioned Ray's commitment to giving his all. Ray hesitated. Privately, he did plan to go easy on Henry. Noticing his fighter falling silent, George Gainford interrupted, insisting Robinson intended to fight his best. "No room in this business for friendship," he said as much to Robinson as Igoe.[587]

On Friday, August 27, the day of the fight, oddsmakers had Robinson as a five-to-one favorite to beat Henry. Some experts felt that ring rust on the part of Robinson, who had been in the Army, combined with Henry's undying will to win, meant that the odds should be closer, but most recognized that Ray had every physical advantage. He stood a half foot taller than Henry and had more than five inches in reach on him. Ray was only twenty-two years old, eleven years younger than Henry.[588]

On Friday morning, Robinson weighed in at a trim 145 pounds. The muscle-bound Armstrong scaled 140 pounds for the fourth consecutive fight. It was an uneventful ceremony, and both men warmly shook hands before departing.[589]

Fifteen thousand three hundred seventy-one spectators ignored the nighttime rain to file into the Garden. It was not the sell-out crowd Jacobs had predicted. The fear of violence, high ticket prices, predictions of a one-sided fight, and finally, the rain had ensured that. Ticket sales generated $60,789, a good gate but much less than predictions. That meant the ten Black charities set to receive five percent of the proceeds would have to split a little more than three thousand dollars. The Jacobs publicity machine had ballyhooed the fight, but not everyone thought Henry had much chance. Those who saved their money expecting a cringe-worthy mismatch made a wise choice.

Henry left his corner for round one ready to trade leather but lacked the reflexes, footwork, and size necessary to keep up with a young, complete boxer of Robinson's caliber. Time and again, Henry would plant his feet to lash out with a hook only to eat a left jab. Robinson threw little else but weak jabs all night. That was all he needed to win.[590]

After seeing Henry sag as though he were already about to go down from a body shot in round one, Sugar Ray decided he did not want to embarrass his hero and would have to go even easier on Henry. Every jab rocked Henry's head back and froze him in his tracks. "He really was an old man. I couldn't hurt an old man," Robinson remembered in his autobiography.[591]

Henry sensed that Ray was holding back. Normally, he would expect a hard right hand or combination of punches to come behind a jolting jab, but none came. Henry became upset, but not at losing. He was mad because Robinson was not giving his all, and he knew it. He felt disrespected.

In rounds three and five, Henry closed the gap and landed a few solid shots – or Robinson let him. The United Press was kind enough to give him those rounds, and those rounds only. Henry would later claim to have Robinson ready to go in round three, but none of the ringside press saw it that way.

Flat-footed and off-balance, Henry's aging, weary legs creaked along after his foe. Meanwhile, Robinson glided effortlessly around the ring doing as he pleased, "as fleet on his feet as a gazelle," said the *Los Angeles Daily News*.[592]

**Armstrong was unable to get inside against Robinson**

Boos reverberated down from the stands. Henry continued to try to press the fight, but each time he got in close, Sugar Ray easily darted out of range and stabbed him with a jab. Robinson had not wanted to embarrass him, but to Henry, the slow death of a drawn-out, one-sided fight was more embarrassing than being knocked out by a younger, bigger man. Worse yet, the fans were not getting their money's worth. Henry had heard boos before but never for being in a dull fight.

"They must be booing you," he called out to Ray and told him to fight for real.[593]

"If you can catch me, catch me," Robinson replied. "I'm going to try and win this fight on decision."[594]

Soon enough, the press caught on that Robinson could put away Armstrong any time he wanted but was carrying his hero to the finish line. Joseph C. Nichols of the *New York Times* noticed that Ray was missing his right-hand crosses by "calculated margins."[595]

Occasionally, Robinson would forget himself and land a big punch, particularly the right uppercut to which Henry was so susceptible. Seeing Henry waver under his punching power, a regretful Ray would initiate a clinch so that he could help Henry stay upright.

By the opening of the tenth and final round, Henry was spent, his mouth bleeding and his vision troubling him. To those watching, he was a depressing sight, helplessly following Robinson around the ring, unable to land anything of consequence, not even a shadow of his relentless, awe-inspiring prime.

"The man who rose to fistic fame and glory with three championships through the piston-like fury of his two-handed attack could not lay a glove on Robinson," wrote Jesse Abramson in the *New York Herald Tribune*. "He tried to spear him with a leaping left and always missed. When he got in close, Robinson tossed him around like an empty barrel."[596]

The fight over, Henry stood tall, stuck out his chest, held his head up, and strode purposefully back to his corner to show pride in who he was and the fact that he had given it his all, and to ease the hurt of his fans. It was also to mask his embarrassment and disgust.

As a foregone conclusion, the judges awarded their unanimous decision to Robinson. While the United Press gave Robinson seven rounds, Armstrong two, and scored one a draw, the writers for the *New York Times*, *The Ring*, and the Associated Press unanimously scored the fight a shut out for Robinson.[597]

Looking and sounding every bit the worn-down fighter in his dressing room, Henry told the newspapermen he was through. "I'm smart enough to know I'm getting old," he told them, "and I've already made enough to pay my taxes." He spoke of his left eye's troubles and Dr. Jesberg's warnings never to fight again. "I don't want to gamble with it," he reasoned. As for immediate plans, he said he intended to look after some fighters he was managing, some of whom had upcoming fights in New York.[598]

One nostalgic reporter mentioned that Robinson would not have stood a chance with Armstrong had Henry been in his prime. The beaten man replied, "No, I couldn't have handled Robinson on the best night I ever had."[599]

The night of August 27, 1943 remained an embarrassing and painful memory for Henry for years to come. Even looking back from the vantage point of decades, Henry once told *Boxing Illustrated*, "People say he carried me.... I really can't deny it." In another interview, he would only speak sparingly of the Robinson bout, calling it "a disgusting fight."[600]

Sugar Ray Robinson would go on to build arguably the most illustrious career in the history of boxing. After an honorable discharge from the Army in 1944, he resumed his boxing career and dominated the welterweight division. It was not until 1947 that he finally got his shot at the welterweight title, and of course, he won it. On February 14, 1951, he took the middleweight championship by first outboxing and then thrashing reigning champ Jake LaMotta to a thirteenth-round stoppage in a fight the press dubbed "The St. Valentine's Day Massacre."

At one point in Robinson's career, he boasted an astonishing 129-1-2 record. By then, boxing experts worldwide recognized him as the greatest fighter who had ever lived, pound-for-pound. Failing in a bid to wrest the light heavyweight crown from Joey Maxim in 1952, he retired to become an entertainer and entrepreneur. Both ambitions failed, and he returned to the ring in 1955.

Though not as brilliant as he once was, Robinson was still arguably the best fighter in the sport through the mid-to-late 1950s and is the only man ever to win the middleweight championship five times. Expensive tastes, irresponsibility, and bad business investments kept him fighting until 1965, a quarter century after his debut on the undercard of the Armstrong-Zivic fight.[601]

In his post-boxing life, Robinson remained a visible celebrity, making TV appearances, taking bit parts in movies, publishing an autobiography, and founding a youth foundation during the 1960s and 1970s. But the early onset of dementia eventually eroded the eloquence, charisma, and cleverness for which he was once known, and he disappeared from public view. Walker Smith, Jr., the man the world knew as Sugar Ray Robinson, died on April 12, 1989, at age sixty-seven.

He was naturally among the original names inducted into the International Boxing Hall of Fame a little over a year later. After all, he won more fights against lineal world champions and Hall of Famers (twenty-five) than any other fighter to this day.

# 20.
# "Tired of Fighting"

"The Armstrong-Robinson bout is now a closed book," proclaimed Nat Fleischer a few weeks after the fight. "Hank closed his 12th year with the kind of 'fight' that must eventually come to all who persist in engaging in ring contests long after their prime." He praised Henry's decision to retire and not to listen to George Moore's insistence that he fight on. He congratulated the California Athletic Commission for refusing to permit Henry's next fight with Luther "Slugger" White. "In the long run, the one-time triple champion will thank those who saved him from becoming a physical wreck."[602]

Despite Fleischer's relief at Henry's retirement, *The Ring* hedged its bets on whether it would stick by continuing to rank him the number five contender in the welterweight division in the same issue. Great champions were notorious for reneging on promises to retire after a brief rest, finding their self-esteem and bank accounts emptier than anticipated. Henry had already adhered to that trend when he emerged from one retirement for a comeback, and now he had Moore breathing down his neck.

Moore told the press that Armstrong would still fight White, but White's manager refused to go through with the fight, insisting he would never put his fighter in against "a blind man." Moore continued to insist that both fighters fulfill their contract.

After recuperating in Hot Springs, Henry appeared before the California Commission and insisted that nothing was wrong with his eyes. He explained that the press had either misheard or misconstrued his statements about vision problems. But he still did not want to continue against White or anyone else. "I'm just tired of fighting," he sighed.[603]

After the Commission announced they would not allow the Armstrong-White bout, Moore sought to protect his meal ticket. "Does that mean Henry can never fight again if he changes his mind?" he asked. To his relief, the commissioners assured him that the injunction was against the one fight only and that Henry could fight again in the future, pending medical examination and Commission approval of the bout.

Moore continued to tell reporters that Henry would fight again. The fighter owed too much in taxes, he said, and had not made as much from the Robinson fight as anticipated. Moore insisted that doctors had examined Henry's eyes since his return to California, and he was pronounced "100 percent perfect."[604]

During a return visit to St. Louis with Moore, Henry told a reporter he had made more than a quarter million dollars in his boxing career.

"Where is it?" asked the interviewer.

Henry's lips broadened into a cynical smile, and he turned to look at Moore.

"Where is it?" Henry asked rhetorically. Moore gave no reply.[605]

When Moore first came on as Henry's manager, he told the press that he was helping Henry put money away. He claimed to have acted as Henry's advisor in purchasing real estate investments. He promised Henry would take half of his ring earnings and put it into a savings account.

"The sooner he gets his stake the better," Moore said then. "After all, he's not getting any younger." However, Moore knew his fighter's habits well. "Henry can't go into a shell and live a close-figured life," he noted. "He's just not built that way. He has his friends, and he likes to entertain."[606]

The manager was right. Henry complained that half of the money made in his comeback had gone into paying back taxes, and he still owed another twenty grand.

Not everything went into Uncle Sam's pocket. He was now spending money he did not have to keep up appearances with his various hangers-on and famous friends. Pianist Earl Hines had introduced Henry to a young white woman from Texas, and Henry was in love with her. Once again, he was thinking of leaving Willa Mae for another woman. His new lady accompanied him in his yellow convertible, carousing the popular L.A. nightclubs. Henry always picked up the checks for the friends who joined them.[607]

To help keep his tabs open, Henry began managing fighters, the most promising of which was a thirteen-year-old white amateur out of Utah named Keith Nutall. The boy initially came to his attention in a letter that Keith's father, Morris Nutall, wrote him, raving about the youngster's potential. Morris asked that Henry manage the kid, but Henry had received many such letters and felt no urgent need to head for Utah. Instead, he wrote Mr. Nutall back, explaining that he would take a gander at Keith the next time he came to Salt Lake City.

As fate would have it, that next time was only a few months later. Henry was in the area as a manager for a boxer named Gene Johnson. During a conversation with Henry, a local sports editor began to go on about a local boy named Keith Nutall, reminding Henry of his promise. The editor introduced Henry to Morris that evening. Morris told Henry that Jack Dempsey and other Eastern promoters were already offering ten thousand dollars for options on young Keith when he came of age. Armstrong responded that he did not have that kind of money, but Morris wanted his son to have Henry's guidance. The Nuttals came out to Los Angeles.[608]

Considering Nutall a "cinch champion," Henry presented the ninety-seven-pound youth to the troops at California military bases. The G.I.s were impressed. Nutall was a "keen little fighter with a lightning left and a professional-like talent for not getting hit," in the assessment of one private. But the kid was still an amateur; he was an investment, not yet significant income. In 1946, the investment looked even more promising after Keith won the Golden Gloves flyweight title in Chicago.

Henry also had a pro welterweight out of Missouri named Cecil Hudson under contract, but Hudson lost nearly as many as he won. Ditto for Kansas City middleweight Roy Miller.

Henry's percentage of Hudson's and Miller's purses and occasional paydays as a referee would not keep the lights on, pay his bar tab, and pay the tax man. He moved his family out of the home he had bought when a rising contender and moved them to a smaller one on W 55th Street in L.A.

Henry still owned some rental properties, which brought in a modest five thousand dollars a year. He also lent his name to a Hollywood nightclub at 228 E. First Street for a fee from the owner, but that did not fare well. It opened in November 1944 but closed its doors within six months after police arrested its owner for stealing a safe from the ration board's office.[609]

An aging champion's return to the ring is rarely only about money. A large part of Henry certainly wanted to stay retired; training had long since become a chore. But he found it hard to give up the intoxicating cheers of the crowd and the thrill of competition. In the decades after Henry Armstrong's career, Sugar Ray Robinson and Sugar Ray Leonard were the most popular non-heavyweight boxing attractions of their times. Like Henry, they built their reputations collecting championships in multiple weight divisions and fighting the biggest non-heavyweight stars of their eras. Both found it difficult to give up that glory.

"To be honest, I wish I were still having big fights," Robinson confessed in his autobiography not long after closing out a career that had lasted a quarter century. "Once you've had acclaim as a world champion, once you move into that sphere, you never want to move out."[610]

In his autobiography, Leonard candidly described the allure of the comeback for a retired boxing champion. "Life after boxing can be rewarding in many ways, but nothing comes close to the sound of applause, and any ex-fighter who claims he doesn't miss it is lying," he writes. "Only fighters know what it feels like to yearn for that place we go to when preparing for battle," he suggests later in the book. "There is no place like it."[611]

"I missed having a place to release my anger," Leonard admitted. An old man in boxing can still be a young man outside of the ring. After a few months in retirement, he will still feel fit and energetic after the sore joints and muscles heal. He not only misses the money, the competition, and the spotlight, he misses the outlet for his youthful energy. For years, society rewarded him for unleashing his anxieties and frustration through violence against a fellow human. Afterward, he struggles to find a socially acceptable way to replace that outlet.

In an interview with writer Tris Dixon, Joe Calzaghe, another retired multi-division champion, said of his early retirement period, "You miss the euphoria, the buzz, the adrenaline, that was my escapism. That was my self-worth, that's who I was, to me." Many ex-boxers, even ex-champions, spiral into crime and addictive substances to cope with their pent-up insecurities, aggression, and the absent adrenaline high.[612]

Caught up in the same need for praise and combat that would drive both Sugar Rays back to the ring multiple times after announcing retirements and desperate for income, Henry Armstrong agreed to George Moore's plans for another comeback.

On January 14, 1944, thirty-four-year-old Henry was back in the ring, knocking out Aldo Spoldi in three rounds of a bout to benefit the Infantile Paralysis Fund. To avoid problems with the California Athletic Commission and California promoters, Moore had taken Henry to Portland, Oregon.

Initial reports were that the Spoldi win was a one-time comeback fight, but Moore immediately put him on another breakneck barnstorming schedule. There were two fights in January, four in February, three in March, one in April, and two in May. These were in Portland, Kansas City, Washington, Des Moines, Miami, Boston, and Los Angeles. That made for eleven bouts in five months in seven cities. All were wins (seven by knockout), some against credible opponents like Jimmy Garrison and Ralph Zannelli. Four of the wins were over ranked top ten contenders. By the opening of June, *The Ring* rated Henry the number one contender in the division (Robinson was removed for inactivity while in the Army).

Because Cochrane and Robinson were both in the service, some state commissions recognized Henry as the "duration" welterweight champion pending Cochrane's return to civilian life. In April, the California Athletic Commission granted Henry permission to fight again after a medical exam reported he had perfect vision.[613]

On June 2, Henry was on the wrong side of a controversial decision following an action-packed rubber match with Willie Joyce in Chicago Stadium. Two weeks later, he dealt Al "Bummy" Davis a two-round thrashing in the Garden in New York. Davis's wildly aggressive style was made to order for Armstrong. In the few minutes the fight lasted, the Brownsville native hit the deck three times before Henry knocked him out cold, and the ref stopped the fight.

Two days after the Davis bout, Henry was among the many celebrities (including William Holden, Paul Whiteman, Eddie Albert, Oscar Levant, Johnny Dundee, and others) to appear at a "sports carnival" war bonds rally at the Polo Grounds. Thirty thousand spectators attended, and $5,773,700 in war bonds were sold.[614]

Henry was getting paid well again. The Joyce fight garnered him a $10,881 payday, and the Davis fight likely yielded something similar, given the total gate of $58,822. But he knew the success could only last so long for an aging fighter who had fought more than 160 professional ring battles. "It looked good. Actually, it wasn't," Henry later wrote of this period. "The old speed was gone."[615]

David Lardner of the *New Yorker* saw the writing on the wall when he sat down with Henry before the Davis match, but he understood Henry's dilemma. "It's probably a fact that he ought to be in some less wearing trade by now, since he is thirty-one years old and has more scar tissue over his eyes than should be offered as a target," he wrote, "but it's another fact that when he's in the ring he makes good money and when he's anywhere else he loses it." Henry was more likely thirty-four years old.[616]

On June 21, Henry won a unanimous decision against overmatched Nick Latsios in Washington, D.C., but looked slow in trying to hunt down a man he likely would have obliterated a few years earlier. Latsios was considered such a pushover that the D.C. commission nearly nixed the fight.

Back home in Los Angeles for Independence Day, Henry lost a one-sided decision to lightweight contender John Thomas, a man he had beaten less than three months earlier; Thomas was ten years his junior. For accomplishing the noteworthy upset in easy fashion, *The Ring* named Thomas its "Fighter of the Month."

July 14 brought his long-awaited showdown with Luther "Slugger" White, who had recently lost a fight with Sammy Angott for the vacant NBA lightweight belt. True to his nickname, White was willing to meet him toe-to-toe in a wild melee; there was no need to chase him down. Both men relied upon hooks and uppercuts to do their damage inside, and neither man initiated a clinch throughout the match. Again, Henry's reflexes looked slow, but when he did land, his punches were harder than White's. When it was over, one judge had it for Armstrong, another chose White, and the third scored a draw. The fight was a draw. White retired not long after the punishing battle.

Henry fought on, closing out 1944 with victories over three familiar faces. He beat Willie Joyce, Aldo Spoldi, and Mike Belloise in succession, Spoldi and Belloise by knockout. But the careers of all three were now in varying degrees of decline.

Despite losing the last of his four bouts with Armstrong, Joyce still had a little left in the tank; he even picked up a big win here and there over the next couple of years. After failing in two 1946 title fights, he called it quits the following year.

Spoldi's fourth loss to Armstrong was part of a six-fight losing streak that would eventually lead to his retirement. Henry was delighted that he had scored the second-round knockout win in front of his hometown fans in St. Louis's Kiel Auditorium.

Knocking out Belloise inside four rounds also came with some sense of gratification. After all, Belloise had wiggled out of defending his featherweight title against Henry twice. But that had been years ago. The shopworn "Bronx Spider" hung in until 1947, retiring at age thirty-six. He passed away in 1969 at just fifty-eight years of age.[617]

Henry's wins over these name opponents and the fact that many of the sport's top talents were in the military placed him again as the top welterweight contender as the new year dawned.

Henry certainly did not look like he deserved the top contender spot against Chester Slider on January 18. Seven years earlier, Slider had been inspired to take up boxing after attending one of Henry's fights, and he patterned his fighting style of all-out punching after Henry's. Now he dominated his hero in a ten-round battle in Fresno; at least everyone in the area but referee and sole judge Jimmy Evans thought he did. Evans declared the fight a draw, prompting boos from the stands.

After outgunning young Genaro Rojo to a decision victory on February 5, Henry granted Slider a rematch slated for Valentine's Day. A near-capacity crowd numbering nine thousand piled into the Oakland Auditorium, the scene of so many of Henry's great early triumphs. Their hero gave them a chance to relive the glory of yesteryear when he dropped Slider with a series of uppercuts to the face in round three. Slider rose at the count of seven and began limping. He had sprained his ankle in his tumble to the canvas. But he refused to give in before his idol. Chester wanted to beat Henry Armstrong but also to impress him. In the end, referee Billy Burke, the fight's sole judge, awarded his decision to Slider. The crowd booed, feeling Henry deserved the win. The Associated Press had scored it for Henry, while the United Press thought a draw was appropriate.[618]

**Chester Slider**
*Fresno Bee*, **October 5, 1943**

Burke caused a minor scandal when he failed to produce his scorecard to commission officials after the fight. Right after the action concluded, Burke said his card must have been misplaced or stolen, but he was sure he had Slider up by five points. Asked which rounds had gone to which fighter, Burke said he could not recall the specifics and then fumbled nervously through further questioning. Not surprisingly, George Moore demanded a hearing before the California Athletic Commission to have the fight results thrown out.

Burke later insisted that the scorecard had been stolen from him by an audience member who dashed into the ring, grabbed the card, and split before anyone else caught sight of him. The Commission suspended him for negligence, but the decision remained an official win for Slider. As for Henry, he honestly agreed with the decision. Slider had won only thirty-seven of his prior sixty-seven fights, and the loss once again prompted thoughts of retirement in Henry, who was now thirty-five years old.

On the evening after his loss to Chester Slider, Henry attended a banquet in Oakland organized in his honor by matchmaker Joe Waterman. In the early days, Waterman used to pay Henry twenty dollars per fight as "a fill-in kid, a drifter." Now, he was hailing Henry as one of the greats. As he sat and listened to various boxing celebrities and businessmen sing his praises, Henry could not help feeling that the whole event functioned as an unsubtle message from his friends to retire.[619]

He had been considering his post-boxing prospects for some time, searching for a way forward in life. He often spoke of preaching with family, friends, and the press, saying he felt a strong draw to the pulpit anytime he attended church. "I was never destined to be a fighter. I feel that now, but I had to eat," he told sports columnist Bert Nakaji during a conversation in an empty gym in January 1945. "I'm going to preach, you know, in my father-in-law's pulpit in Los Angeles the Sunday before I go overseas next month."[620]

While pondering his future, Henry fulfilled a prior commitment to enlist in the Army and tour as part of a USO-sponsored unit intended to liven the spirits of American service members worldwide. He would referee boxing matches at the bases. The pay would be meager, but at least it would keep Henry in the spotlight and close to boxing.

Known as the Henry Armstrong Sports Unit No. 500, the group included other popular Black sports figures of the day, including UCLA All-American football player Kenny Washington, Oregon University football player Joe Lilliard, basketball's Billy Yancey, and sportswriter Dan Burley of the *Amsterdam News*. Draft boards thwarted the intentions of iconic track and field star Jesse Owens and Cornell All-American football star Jerome "Brud" Holland to join.

For the first couple of weeks, the unit toured stateside, allowing Henry to meet up with members of the fight crowd around the country that he had not seen in some time. Managers took him to the local gyms to have him assess the talents of their latest boxing prospects and slip him some cash for his time.

By mid-April, they were in India, where Henry served as a cornerman for welterweight Corporal Ernie Copeland as he won the China-Burma-India theater Allied Services championship. The poverty Henry witnessed in Calcutta devastated him. The level of starvation and desperation surpassed anything he had witnessed in America, either in the cotton fields of the segregated South or the Depression-ravaged cities of America. He saw children lying in gutters and on sidewalks dying of starvation. He later wrote of them as "a multitude of the living dead." His heart broke for the starving, but he felt helpless to aid them and overwhelmed by the anxiety that helplessness brought him. He spent his days in India in a daze of despair and his nights unable to sleep.[621]

**Henry visits with two boys during his tour of the India-Burma theater**
*New York Daily News*, May 14, 1945

Eventually, the troupe moved on to Guam, Saipan, and Casablanca, but Henry could not shake the depression that swept over him in Calcutta. When word arrived in Casablanca that Henry Jackson, Sr. had passed away back in California, Henry asked for and received permission to leave the tour and return home. He arrived in New York City on July 7 a dozen pounds lighter than when he left. He greeted reporters with words of praise for the fighting skills of the country's service members and then began his trip to California.

Despite its brief duration, the Henry Armstrong Sports Unit No. 500 had traveled sixty thousand miles and entertained over half a million service members.[622]

Henry was hurting when he returned stateside. His father was dead, and memories of Calcutta disturbed his sleep. His white mistress had returned to Texas, ending his plans to marry her. And he still saw no direction forward in life.

However, his return brought some solace in a reunion with Harry Armstrong. Henry was shocked to get a call from Harry while he was still in New York. They met in the Theresa Hotel bar and caught up over a steady stream of alcohol. Harry explained that he had been drifting around Mexico. Upon his return to California, his wife greeted him with divorce papers. He had since re-married, but the couple had fallen on hard times.

Henry told Harry about Keith Nutall, the promising teenage amateur out of Utah. He asked Harry to return to California with him and help train and manage Nutall. Harry accepted, and the Armstrong "brothers" were reunited.

Henry was not in the States four days before California promoter Jimmy Murray announced to the press that he and George Moore were planning a fight between Henry and the winner of the upcoming Chester Slider-Genaro Rojo bout. Meanwhile, Mike Jacobs tried to cook up a match between Henry and Harold Green, a rising Brooklyn welterweight. For his part, Henry told the *New York World-Telegram*'s Lester Bromberg he had no interest in resuming his career. The Slider loss may have been controversial to some, but he had noticed enough of a difference in himself to admit he was through.[623]

Henry never did return to the ring as a boxer. Before leaving on the USO tour, he told a reporter that he had not decided if he would retire from boxing and felt it was no business of the public. "But when I do I'll just do it, say nothing, and let the boys guess," he promised. That's just what he did. There was no announcement, no statement, no press release. Henry just stopped fighting.

Shortly after his return stateside, he picked up a small paycheck for appearing as one of several famous fighters in the low-budget film *Joe Palooka, Champ*, based on the popular comic strip character of the period. But if he was no longer going to box, he needed to find steady pay.

He returned to picking up the occasional referee gig and managing fighters out of Los Angeles. The best was probably the young Black welterweight Cecil Hudson from Missouri. He had talent but was once called "one of the 'dirtiest' boxers ever to enter a ring." Hudson turned pro in San Jose back in 1939 as a nineteen-year-old and had managed to go undefeated in his first thirty outings, making him a hot commodity in Hollywood's boxing scene for a bit. He was becoming a headliner at the Hollywood Legion Stadium and was in line to fight Henry until Hudson lost a decision to Jimmy Garrison in 1942.

Henry and Cecil likely met when both men were part of the George Raft Caravan shows in 1942. After that, Hudson fought on the undercard of some of Henry's fights. By August of 1943, the papers referred to Hudson as Armstrong's protégé, but he had already lost seven more times since the Garrison fight.[624]

**Cecil Hudson**

Hudson won six of his first seven bouts under Henry's guidance. On February 13, 1945, Henry was in Cecil's corner when he faced NYSAC lightweight titlist Bob Montgomery in Montgomery's West Coast debut at the Olympic. In a torrid thriller that saw the fighters repeatedly scrapping after the bell, Cecil gave a good account of himself in front of ten thousand cheering fans. His persistent left jab occasionally bothered the lightweight champ. But "The Bobcat" Montgomery was famed as a merciless pressure fighter. He ultimately dropped Cecil twice to take the decision in a bout the *Oakland Tribune* called "one of the roughest scraps seen here in months."[625]

Three months later, Henry had the satisfaction of watching his charge emerge victorious over Chester Slider. Then, on December 10, 1945, he accompanied Cecil into the ring at Madison Square Garden for a Mike Jacobs promotion. In the corner opposite them sat Fritzie Zivic, considered the most challenging test of Hudson's career yet. The judges awarded Cecil a wide unanimous decision. Harold Conrad, a writer for the *Brooklyn Daily Eagle* (and future boxing promoter extraordinaire), saw the result more as evidence of Zivic's decline than Hudson's potential. "Hudson never had him in any trouble and should have shown better against such mediocre opposition," opined the less-than-impressed reporter. For his part, Zivic blamed the defeat on the Army's refusal to give him time to train. Before meeting Cecil Hudson, Fritzie had lost eight of his prior nine bouts.[626]

In 1947, Hudson earned a stunning upset victory over future middleweight champ Jake LaMotta (Dan Parker of the *New York Mirror* decried it as a fix). By then, Cecil was losing more often than he was winning, and he and Henry had gone their separate ways. Hudson passed away at age fifty-two in 1972.

After splitting with Hudson, Henry switched his focus back to the white teenager from Brigham, Utah, Keith Nutall, who entered the professional ranks in June of 1947. "I'm going to stick with the boxing game until I make this boy a champion," Henry told the press in 1945. He raved to sportswriters about Nutall's punching power and all-around ability.[627]

A streamlined 5'7" tall with a 67" reach, seventeen-year-old Nutall was a rangy boxer. Initially, Keith could only train with Henry in Los Angeles during his summer breaks from school. After graduation, he was in L.A. full-time and became Henry's top prospect. His frame was filling out now, and Henry predicted that this featherweight would, like him, grow to accomplish great things at lightweight and maybe even welterweight. "Keith will wear a world's championship diadem within three years," Henry wrote in an article for the *Ogden Standard-Examiner* in 1947.[628]

**Keith Nutall and Henry Armstrong**

Henry and Harry Armstrong put the boy in sparring sessions with Chalky Wright and Harold Dade, both former world champions. Henry accompanied him into the ring in his pro debut on June 24, 1947, in Salt Lake City, an eight-round decision victory over one Joe Tambe. Thanks to the publicity of his 1946 Golden Gloves win and Henry's endorsements, the novice's professional debut was the night's main event.[629]

Together they traveled throughout Nutall's native region for bouts in Colorado, Kansas, and Idaho. By the end of August 1948, Nutall's record stood at twenty wins, three losses, and two draws. Notice from mainstream magazines like *Esquire* and *Time* was already coming his way.

Even as Henry professed great faith in the fighter's potential, Morris Nutall lost faith in his son's manager. More than Henry's managerial choices, the father objected to him as a role model for his impressionable son. Henry's drinking was on the rise, and he spent much of his time and money in the taverns and nightclubs of the towns they visited. The Mormon father complained about the stench of liquor on the manager's breath and questioned Henry's priorities.[630]

In January 1949, Morris announced that Henry would no longer manage his son. There was a brief reconciliation, but the Nutalls moved on without Henry later in the year.

Citing injury, Keith Nutall retired in 1952 with a respectable record of forty wins, ten losses, and six draws. However, the closest he ever got to the world title Henry had wanted for him was the intermountain regional lightweight championship, the same title his father once claimed. A successful restaurateur in later life, Keith passed away on April 27, 2012, in Utah at age eighty-one.[631]

More hurtful than the loss of his most promising prospect was the loss of Harry Armstrong, who disappeared again after things with the Nutalls fell through. Henry never saw him again, and so far as this author can tell, the final fate of Harry Armstrong is unknown.

Their friendship went back twenty years. Before Wirt Ross, Eddie Mead, Al Jolson, George Moore, and even his wife Willa Mae, Harry Armstrong had been Henry's manager, trainer, traveling companion, and best friend. They had shared boxcars and starved together before any wealth, fame, or championships. Harry saw greatness in Henry before anyone else did. His departure stung. But Henry continued to push forward, the only direction he had ever gone.

After all, Cecil Hudson and Keith Nutall were not the only fighters out there. Henry also had a piece of a promising light heavyweight out of Kansas City named Roy Miller. He first noticed the young fighter after he came to L.A. as an amateur around 1940 and was impressed enough to keep him in mind. Turning pro in 1944, Miller signed on with Henry Armstrong and George Moore, each presumably sharing half the manager's customary third of Miller's earnings. Miller fought on plenty of Henry Armstrong undercards during Henry's comeback and was touted as his protégé by Moore and the press.

Henry was initially excited about Miller's chances at making it to the top, and he did have talent. His aggressive style reminded some of Henry's. There was an undefeated streak of fifteen bouts between June 1945 and June 1946 and another of sixteen bouts between February 1947 and April 1948. But a less-than-granite chin betrayed him. He hit the canvas twice each in fights with Gaston Miller and Oakland Billy Smith and four times against Fitzie Fitzpatrick. Bobby Castro, who had more losses than he did wins, stopped him in five rounds, Fitzpatrick in six, and Carl "Bobo" Olson, a future middleweight champion, stopped him inside five rounds. By then, Miller had long since left Moore and Armstrong to sign on with Al Weill. In a matchup of former Armstrong proteges, Cecil Hudson won a ten-round decision over Roy Miller on February 23, 1950. After three more fights, all losses, Miller retired.[632]

Henry managed other fighters who showed flashes of promise in the 1940s. There was Ernie Copeland, Johnny Miller, Terry Byrd, Levi Southall, Oscar Williams, Billy Reed, Cleo Shans, Elijah "Smuggy" Hursey, and someone called Punching Punjab. But nothing panned out for them under Henry's or anyone else's guidance.

Being a successful boxing manager required a hard-nosed attitude at the negotiating table, a solid financial sense, and a willingness to make enemies. As mean and pugnacious as he could be inside the ropes, Henry possessed none of those attributes outside of it. He had little patience for business, trusted those he should not have, and loved to be liked. He may have been a gifted fighter, but he was not a gifted fight manager.

In late 1946, Henry invested in another nightclub, this time in New York City. He purchased the Melody Room near the Polo Grounds on 155th Street in Harlem. His friends Joe Louis and Sugar Ray Robinson (both soon after opened their own nightspots nearby) visited, and musical acts Ida James, Doles Dickens, Doc Wheeler, and the Dickson Quartet appeared. One Pee Wee Marquette was the "smooth as satin" emcee.[633]

"With Henry being busy with other activities, he always finds time to greet his friends at the Melody Room," reported the *New York Age*. Henry must have been a more attentive greeter than a businessman, for the place was under new ownership by 1948.[634]

He briefly flirted with the idea of becoming a promoter back in California, establishing Henry Armstrong Triple Champion Enterprises. But that eventually failed, too. In the Spring of 1949, Chicago radio station WMAQ ran a dramatized biography of Henry on its half-hour program *Destination Freedom* entitled "The Saga of Melody Jackson." It generated little sustained public interest in Henry's life after boxing.[635]

By 1949, Henry was no longer signing fighters and looking to find satisfaction elsewhere. He tried to put boxing behind him.

# 21.
# God's Ball of Fire

Sometime in 1943, not long after his loss to Sugar Ray Robinson, Henry Armstrong sat alone in a Philadelphia hotel room feeling directionless and alone. He thought of Christ's disciples when He had sent them away in a boat and they found themselves "in the middle of the sea, tossed by the waves," and he began to scribble the words to a poem.[636]

Thrown into a turbulent sea
Of sharks and whales,
But yet unharmed.
Put into a fiery furnace
But yet unburned.
The faith in God won't let His child go wrong
Somehow:
Because I meant to do good.[637]

Life after boxing had been challenging for many retired champions. Henry was already familiar with many of these: the limited income and the loss of material wealth that comes with it; watching the public's attention drift to younger, active fighters; the bruised ego; the loneliness; the boredom. These things and others had already lured him into multiple comebacks and later influenced him to remain close to the sport as a trainer and manager.

Shortly before Christmas 1946, Henry went to lunch in New York with columnist W.C. Heinz, who was astonished and disappointed that no one on the street or in the restaurant seemed to recognize a man who was mobbed in public a few short years earlier. It had only been months since Henry retired. Heinz asked Armstrong if the loss of his fame hurt.

"No," Henry replied, pointing to his head. "You see, it's all in the mind."[638]

In his mind or not, and whether he wanted to admit it or not, it still hurt. During the 1940s, as his career in the ring wound down and his shortcomings as a manager became obvious, Henry sought solace in the comfort of the bottle. Eddie Mead had started him drinking beer regularly to increase his weight in 1938, but by 1949 Henry had moved on to harder stuff. The drug of choice was now whiskey. The disappointments of his finances, boxing career, and personal life were dulled by the intoxication of what he would later refer to as being "whiskey-happy," a mask to disguise his depression.[639]

On the night of Friday, January 21, 1949, Henry made his usual rounds of the bars and nightclubs on Central Avenue in Los Angeles. The back-slapping boxing fans he found there ensured he rarely had to pay for a drink; he preferred spending his money on the jukebox.

The bar scene also came with those who liked to take cheap shots at a famous aging fighter. Henry had become a walking cliché, an overweight, drunk has-been playing the big shot, and some people told him so. Enough whiskey could sour Henry's temper, making him surly and bitter. After one such confrontation that Friday night, Henry stormed out of the bar and rocketed away in his yellow convertible.

Early Saturday morning, Los Angeles patrolmen R. R. Cooper and R. L. Russell responded to a call of a one-car accident on Main Street. Arriving on the scene, they found Henry still sitting at the wheel of his car, its front end jammed into a lamppost. He was conscious but obviously intoxicated. Ordered out of the vehicle and into the patrol car, Henry admitted he was drunk but angrily refused to go anywhere. "I'm Henry Armstrong, and I take orders from nobody," he shouted at the officers before hurling curses their way.[640]

Arrested and brought to the local station, Henry continued his diatribe. "Jail me and I'll put a curse on you, and you'll die in three hours," he threatened while being booked. The officers confiscated the twelve dollars from his pockets and locked him up.[641]

He awoke behind bars with only vague memories of how he got there. Familiar faces from the Central Avenue watering holes surrounded him in the drunk tank. They were all brought before Judge Ida May Adams at the Lincoln Heights Jail.

"Henry Armstrong, what are you doing here," asked Adams, disappointment in her voice. She and Henry had been schoolmates as children, and she was aware of his success in boxing. Ashamed, Henry could not look her in the eyes and did not respond.

"You're letting a million boys down," Adams said before ordering Henry to pay a ten-dollar fine and sentencing him to a two-day suspended sentence in jail. The verbal reprimand stung worse than the punishment.[642]

Henry returned home to spend the rest of the day miserable in bed, exhausted and hung over. The Judge's words refused to let him sleep. Henry headed back out for the bars that evening, his head spinning with despair and anxiety.

He downed three vodka-based Moscow mule cocktails. When friends tried to cut him off, he attacked them, staggered to the parking lot, crawled back in his battered convertible, and tore off aimlessly. For a time, he blacked out, only coming to while hurtling seventy-five miles per hour on the road along Malibu Beach, twenty-five miles from his home.

He immediately pulled over to catch his breath and regain his senses. He parked facing the beach, gazing into the dark in a depressed stupor. He couldn't shake the thought that he was going straight but in the wrong direction. As he later described it, while he stared drunkenly at the waves, he suddenly felt a concussive shock of pain as though someone had violently slapped him across the face. His head jolted to the side. Stunned, he looked around but saw no one. After sitting dazed in his car for a long time, he turned the steering wheel toward home.

As he absorbed the experience during the drive, Henry interpreted the slap as a wake-up call from God intended to change the direction of his life. After that, he said, he never drank nor wanted alcohol again. He had found his rock bottom and never wanted to return.

By the time he arrived at his house, the Sunday morning sun was rising. He entered his bedroom and opened the Bible on his bedside table.[643]

Henry spent the next several days reading the Bible and accepted an offer from the Reverend S.M. Malone (father-in-law to Joe Louis) to preach at his Baptist church in Long Beach. His first sermon was called "It's Later Than You Think."

"I was afraid people would laugh," Henry confided to sportswriter Al Stump a few years later, "the idea of a fighter preaching the Gospel sounds strange, of course." He was delighted when Malone asked him to return, and he graciously delivered a second sermon entitled, "Christ – Winner and Still Champion!"[644]

At last, Henry found a direction for his life that brought him a sense of purpose and public acclaim to replace boxing. At Malone's urging, he enrolled in theological school. Determined to succeed as a preacher, he dedicated himself to studying the Bible with the same dogged discipline he once famously applied to conditioning and sparring in the ring. He even called it "training."

However, Henry's new direction did not necessarily make him a better husband or father. In September 1949, Willa Mae sought to end their fifteen-year marriage, citing "extreme mental and physical cruelty." She brought a suit for half his assets (valued at $125,000), custody of twelve-year-old Lanetta, and $1,000 a month in alimony. After mediation with a judge, the couple reconciled, but their troubles persisted.[645]

**A brief reconciliation between husband and wife.**

As it had in the ring, Henry's diligence guided him through his tough times, lighting the way forward; only now, instead of training in a boxing ring, he trained by reading the Bible. In 1950, Willa Mae's father, W.L. Strauther, ordained Henry a minister at the Morning Star Church in Los Angeles.

Henry initially turned down the promoters who came to him with ideas of going on the road and making money as a free-lance evangelist. His experience with similar men in boxing convinced him to distrust such offers.

Realizing that some might question the authenticity of his faith and see him as using religion solely as a hustle, Henry focused on the sincerity of his words and delivery. After carefully studying the Bible, he would write a sermon, then diligently re-read it to himself until he memorized the entire speech. Then he would throw away the written pages to speak from his memory and his heart on the pulpit, improvising when needed to convince his audience of the immediacy and genuine faith in his message.[646]

Through this approach, Henry earned high regard for his passionate delivery. During his life in the ring, sportswriters regularly compared him to forces of nature, most often a hurricane. On the pulpit, he moved his followers with the same elemental intensity. Those who saw him began to call him "God's Ball of Fire."[647]

He told believers and reporters alike that he had calculated the exact year of the End of Days. He had concluded that the world would only exist for six thousand years and that, based on the traditional Jewish calendar's aging of Earth, the year 2239 A.D. would be humanity's last in the corporeal world.[648]

Despite the apocalyptic prophecy, Henry stressed to reporters that his sermons were not about brimstone and damnation. "I preach only one thing – faith in God," he told the *Arizona Republic*. "No politics. No theology. No denomination. I preach faith as opposed to fear. Fear will destroy. Faith will heal."[649]

Memories of the starving people he saw in India during his time touring for the war effort and of Judge Adams's reprimand ("You're letting a million boys down") stuck with Henry through these early years as a preacher. Eventually, they inspired him to put his words into action. He settled upon the idea of creating a boys club, a youth center to help disadvantaged children find a sense of faith and direction. Combating "juvenile delinquency" was a popular cause in the 1940s and 1950s, and Henry felt he could contribute.

With this idea in mind, Henry warmed up to suggestions that he become a traveling preacher. He visited California's major cities to give his "fiery oratory" at churches, luncheons, and rallies, raising funds for a Henry Armstrong Youth Foundation. His favorite speech was titled "Combating Delinquency Among Negro Juveniles." He spoke at a California juvenile detention center and, by his account, made a great impression on the inmates. He later told Bob Burnes that the visit was one of the great thrills of his life because it gave him a sense of achievement. By late 1951, the regional tour had broadened to a cross-country trek.[650]

To help with bringing publicity and raising funds, Henry enlisted the fighters and celebrities he knew. They represented an amazing cross-section of entertainment mediums and ethnicities. Barney Ross was named Vice President. Sugar Ray Robinson was a member of the Advisory Board. Robinson would donate at least one of his fight purses to Henry's plans. Baby Arizmendi was on the board, too, as were famous boxers Jack Dempsey, Mickey Walker, Jimmy McLarnin, and Fidel LaBarba. Chuck Dressen, Ty Cobb, and other famed baseball personalities were on the list, as were film actors Joe E. Brown and Phil Harris and vaudevillian Wallace Ford. In October 1951, renowned evangelist Billy Graham brought Henry to Minneapolis, where he spoke before twenty-five thousand of Graham's followers.[651]

Henry was especially proud of the mix of religions and races participating in his proposed program. However, many of the names on the so-called Advisory Board were donors more than they were active participants.

The Foundation, through Henry's collections and the donations of his friends, was able to help Bishop W.E. Holman purchase fifty acres of land near Vicksburg, Arizona, on which was planned a Youth Town modeled on the famed Boys Town of Father Flanagan in Nebraska. The construction was predicted to cost three million dollars, a fee they never would raise. But Henry kept trying for years[652]

To raise more financing, the poet laureate of Vashon High self-published a collection of poems written throughout his life. Entitled *20 Years of Poems, Moods, and Meditations*, the book was eighty pages and sold for one dollar, all proceeds going to Henry's foundation.

Henry continued to give interviews for television, newspapers, and magazines through the 1950s, always talking about his dual mission to spread the word of God and save America's youth. The ABC network's television series *The Comeback* featured Henry's crusade in its January 15, 1954 episode. All the interviewers harped on his boxing career. He was happy to oblige them so long as the stories concluded with his work for God.

Many of the people who interviewed Henry for magazine, newspaper, and television pieces were impressed with his continued positive outlook on life after the challenges and setbacks of his life. They marveled at his continued energy and his resilient ambitions for the future. They saw he attacked his goals with the same relentless aggression he once used to defeat his opponents in the ring.[653]

In 1954, *The Ring* included him among its inaugural class of inductees in its Hall of Fame. He accompanied heavyweight icons Jack Dempsey and Joe Louis as the only three boxers inducted in the "modern" (post-1919) category. A fighter's name had to appear on seventy-five percent of the ballots received to qualify for induction. Of the ninety-one journalists and sportscasters polled, seventy-four (eighty-one percent) included Henry in their ballot.[654]

On the evening of Saturday, June 2, 1956, Henry went into convulsions and collapsed in his home. His condition stabilized in the hospital, and doctors cleared him to leave in a day or two. Henry's doctors told reporters that the ex-fighter had been suffering of late from a "digestive disorder."[655]

The mysterious and sudden attack may have put the forty-six-year-old in a reflective mood. The prior year, former middleweight champion Rocky Graziano published his memoir, *Somebody Up There Likes Me*. The book sold well and became an Oscar-winning film of the same name starring a young Paul Newman the following year.

Likely inspired in part by Rocky's success and that of the film that followed – and maybe frightened by his seizure – Henry once again put his writing skills to use, this time in telling his life story, which he titled *Gloves, Glory and God*. Co-written with Eddie Burbridge of the Associated Negro Press, it was first published in hardcover on October 1, 1956, by the Fleming H. Revell Company and sold for $2.95. The proceeds went to the Henry Armstrong Youth Foundation.

Henry wrote of his life in the third person. Explaining his reasoning for doing so, he wrote, "I've found that when I sit down and try to bring back to mind what happened to me at a certain time in my life… I am really looking at my former self, or selves, as if they were outside of the person I am now."[656]

He dedicated the book to Willa Mae, Lanetta, and Henry's older sister Henrietta, the last sibling he remained in contact with by 1956.

Naturally, Henry begins with his birth in Mississippi in 1912 and spends most of its 256-page length discussing the period from when he first took up boxing to his winning his third championship in 1938. Only the last thirty-eight pages are devoted to the rest of his life, encompassing the loss of his titles, multiple comebacks, overseas tour, retirement, management career, arrest, religious awakening, and the Henry Armstrong Youth Foundation.

Reviews of the book mostly stuck to summarizing the story with limited praise for revealing the "seamy side of boxing." In it, Henry wrote humbly about his life and with minimal bias or discernable factual errors. His childhood memories of poverty and segregation in Mississippi are particularly vivid, as are the details of his trek as a hobo to California. His recollections of his fights with Baby Arizmendi, Barney Ross, and Lou Ambers are entertaining. He is candid about his alcohol addiction and struggles with retirement.

In 1957, things were beginning to look up for Henry. He had steady work as an evangelist for causes he believed in. His autobiography was receiving attention in nationwide newspapers. MGM purchased the rights to his story for a planned motion picture rumored to star one of the country's most popular entertainers, Sammy Davis, Jr., as Henry. He had serious money in his bank account for the first time in a long time.

He doubtless felt a great swell of pride when the Henry Armstrong Youth Foundation was able to purchase a 180-acre ranch in California's Santa Ynez mountains in the autumn of 1957. Henry intended to turn it into another boys town type of center like the one Bishop Holman still had planned for Arizona.

Despite these signs of hope, the good times would not last. Things had not improved between Henry and Willa Mae since their reconciliation. "He left me at home and went out alone," she later remembered of their marriage. "He never showed me any affection."

They separated in 1956, and Henry filed for divorce, charging cruelty. Willa Mae then filed a cross-complaint accusing Henry of cruelty and adultery with Gussie Henry, a woman who aided him in his boxing management business. There would be no reconciliation this time, and a judge granted the divorce in January 1959 after twenty-five years of marriage.[657]

The settlement gave Willa Mae full ownership of Henry's "extensive business building" at 713 E 55th Street in Los Angeles. They sold their home and four other properties, splitting the money between them. He also paid her $1,387 in community debts.[658]

Henry's time away from home over the years had not only meant the dissolution of his marriage. He was also effectively estranged from his daughter Lanetta. He had not spent much time with her when she was a child, and now, as an adult, she felt little connection to her father. He would see even less of her for the next several years than before.[659]

On Friday, January 31, 1958, George Moore, who had managed the last years of Henry's boxing career, passed away at age eighty-four. By then, Henry had returned to promoting and managing fighters to fund his projects. He had high expectations for an amateur named Sal Rivas. Henry told reporters that Rivas would be the first Mexican heavyweight champion of the world. But Henry's hopes for Rivas never panned out. So far as this author can tell, the Mexican heavyweight never turned pro.

In May 1959, Gussie Henry sued Armstrong for ten thousand dollars, producing a signed note from January promising to pay her the money for her help in his boxing management career. Henry appeared in court, arguing that he was broke following his divorce. To his great embarrassment, the story made the California papers.[660]

By the start of the next decade, Henry was part of an evangelical tour of California headlined by Jerry "Curley" Owen, a former boxer and UCLA college football star who had also turned to preaching. Owen had once been a sparring partner for heavyweight champion Max Baer.

He began training well-known light heavyweight Jesse Bowdry, a baby-faced twenty-two-year-old former Chicago Golden Gloves champ out of St. Louis. Though a heavy puncher, Bowdry preferred scarfing down food to the rigors of training camp. He soon fattened himself out of the division. After he suffered a second consecutive stoppage loss to middleweight Henry Hank in January 1960, Bowdry's frustrated handlers put Jesse's career on hold and hired Henry Armstrong to remodel their fighter's attitude and physique. At the time, Bowdry's record stood at a respectable but declining 26-5, with three of those losses coming in his past six fights.[661]

"Young fighters now don't have the urge, the incentive," Henry told the press after signing on with the Bowdry camp. "Everything has been too easy for them. Bowdry is only 22 and so I have hopes for him. He has power, strength and youth. I will try to channel properly his talents and direct him. The rest is up to him."662

Jesse told the sportswriters that Henry "isn't as tough as you might think. He's a good guy. He understands a fighter. He told me what he wanted to do and set my mind at ease. But he knew he couldn't do it for me."663

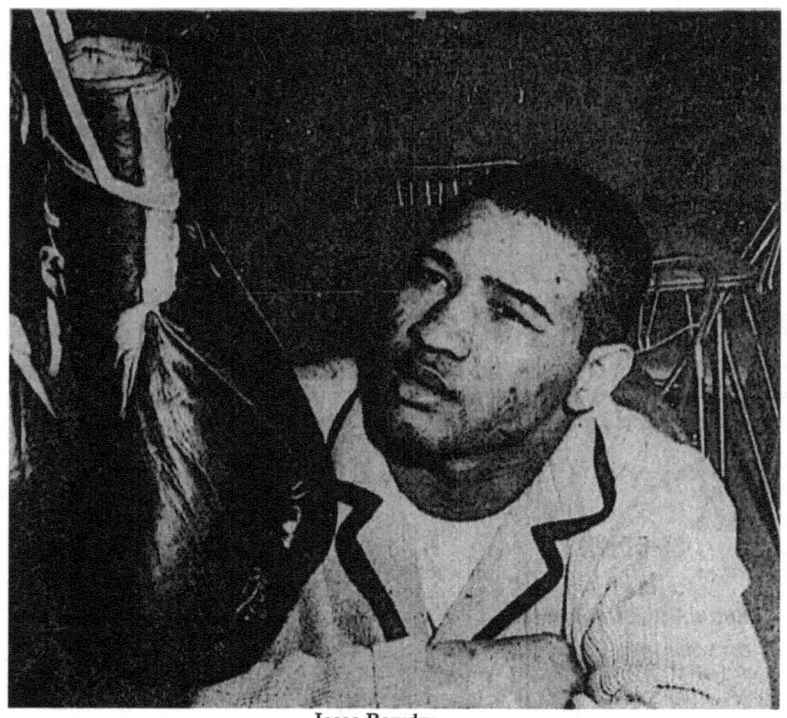

Jesse Bowdry
*Miami Herald*, February 6, 1961

The debut of the Armstrong-Bowdry partnership came on Wednesday, October 26, 1960, at the Miami Beach Auditorium. The opponent was local up-and-comer Freddy Blades, and they would fight just over the light heavyweight limit of 175 pounds. After five months of working together, Henry brought Jesse in at 178 pounds; Blades weighed 175 ¼ pounds.

During the opening five rounds, "the fighters were more hesitant than a vegetarian in a slaughterhouse," with Blades building a tenuous lead with his superior speed. The Floridian eventually tired, and Bowdry caught him with a good left hook in the ninth. Pouncing on his opponent, Bowdry pounded him with his full arsenal until the referee stopped the fight.664

"This is just the beginning," Henry told sportswriters.665

Florida promoter Chris Dundee wanted Bowdry back and booked him to face the slick top contender Willie Pastrano of New Orleans in the Miami Beach Auditorium on Tuesday, December 27. Pastrano had just been named in an NBA elimination tournament to determine a new light heavyweight champion following the abdication of Archie Moore. A win over him, thought Jesse and Henry, could also earn Jesse a spot in the tournament.

Pastrano was known as a "cutie," boxing parlance for a slick, defense-minded boxer. He was a three-to-one favorite at fight time, but Henry felt he had the right strategy to lead Bowdry to victory. He told the press that he would have Jesse charge at Pastrano as soon as the opening bell clanged – "Hurricane Henry" Armstrong style. But in private, he told Jesse this was just a ruse to make Pastrano and his trainer Angelo Dundee (brother to Chris) overconfident. Too much aggression would play into Pastrano's strengths, Henry told Jesse. Instead, Henry wanted his fighter to slow the fight's pace, using feints and timing to keep Pastrano uncomfortable and looking foolish.

By fight night, Henry got his fighter down to 172 pounds, three pounds under the light heavyweight limit, and Jesse followed his trainer's instructions perfectly. When he finally did turn aggressive in the third, he went for Willie's ribs and gut, pulverizing the body to slow his fleet-footed prey down. That was vintage Henry Armstrong.

In the fourth, Pastrano lowered his guard to protect his midsection. Spotting this, Bowdry slammed a series of overhand rights against his head. Pastrano was badly staggered but managed to stay on his feet. From there, Jesse was in complete control of the fight. By the eighth, a helpless Pastrano was fighting only to survive to the final bell. After ten rounds, the judges awarded Jesse Bowdry an upset unanimous decision. Interviewed after the fight, he gave all credit to Henry for developing the successful strategy.

On the undercard that evening, a young 1960 Olympic gold medalist out of Louisville, Kentucky, picked up his second professional win. Cassius Marcellus Clay, Jr. "quit being too cute and too clever long enough to polish off Herb Siler in one minute of the fourth round in the semi-final, scheduled for eight." Clay had previously been managed and trained by Henry's friend Archie Moore, but as of the Siler fight, Angelo Dundee had taken over that role. In 1964, Dundee would guide Clay to the world's heavyweight championship. Very shortly afterward, Cassius Clay became Muhammad Ali.[666]

As Henry hoped, Bowdry's win over Pastrano put him in line to fight for the vacant NBA light heavyweight title in February. His opponent would be the veteran contender Harold Johnson, a muscular, long-armed, skilled puncher out of Philadelphia. A pro since 1946, Johnson had been to war with former champ Moore on five occasions but had won just one of those matchups; Archie just seemed to have his number. When not in the ring with Moore, Johnson was a winner. Among the others beaten in his seventy trips to the ring so far were future Hall of Famers Jimmy Bivins and Ezzard Charles. Of late, he was riding a twelve-fight winning streak, including a win over contender Sonny Ray, who had beaten Bowdry three times.[667]

During the preparations for Johnson, Henry upset Bowdry's manager Eddie Yawitz by leaving camp for a court case in California. Still, he returned to continue training Bowdry weeks before fight time.

When approached by the press about his fighter's chances against the great Johnson, Henry was unusually noncommittal. "I've tried to show him how to make certain moves… and the way to punch," he explained, "but I don't trust him to do the things I could do instinctively in the ring."668

Henry led the training camp in the Dundee brothers' Fifth Street Gym, using veteran middleweight Sammy Stone and up-and-comer Willie Giles as sparring partners. As preparations concluded, the reporter for the *Miami Herald* felt that Henry had Jesse's timing and left jab both looking sharp.669

Johnson used the same facilities but on a different schedule and had Cassius Clay as his sparring partner. The *Miami Herald* felt he looked the best he ever had. Bettors had him a three-to-one favorite, most experts feeling his experience and cleverness would prevail against Bowdry's youth and power.670

The fight was on Tuesday, February 7, 1961, at the Convention Center. 4,017 fans – a record for a boxing event at the venue – produced a gate of $20,829.50. The going was slow in the early rounds, as in the Pastrano fight. Johnson was quick but on the defensive, using a precision left jab to avoid a slugfest with his younger opponent. Meanwhile, Bowdry was a "bobbing, weaving, bull-like fighter who kept trying to get in close only to run into his own frustrations."671

After four rounds of this, an infuriated Eddie Yawitz climbed into the ring and demanded Henry leave the corner. Henry stepped out, and Bowdry landed a couple of good shots in the sixth. Excited by his first real success in the fight, he came out of his crouch. As he did, Johnson clipped him with a left hook and collapsed Bowdry to the floor. Though he reached his feet, he was down again toward the end of the eighth round.

In the ninth, Johnson came out looking for the kill, and he got it with his third punch thrown. Bowdry rose from this third knockdown, but the end was a forgone conclusion. As Johnson swarmed all over his broken opponent, a member of Bowdry's corner stepped into the ring waving a white towel, the sign of surrender. The fight was over.

The end of Johnson vs. Bowdry
*St. Louis Post-Dispatch*, February 8, 1961

Yawitz forbade Henry entrance into the dressing room. "He's living in the past," ranted the manager. "All he wants to talk about is how great he was, instead of helping Jesse. I'm sick of hearing it."

Standing in the hallway outside, Henry told reporters, "Eddie gets awfully excited during a fight.... I worked with Bowdry because I felt I could help him. I'm a minister... I wouldn't be in boxing at all unless it meant so much to me. Now, I don't know."

"I told Jesse that he couldn't fight Johnson as he had Pastrano because Johnson is a harder puncher," Henry explained to another reporter. "I told Bowdry to fight out of a crouch and keep his chin covered with his forearm."

"That went along all right for four rounds," he continued. "Then somebody behind Eddie Yawitz was hollering that Jesse should jab Johnson. That's all Johnson wanted. When Bowdry pulled down his hands and started to jab, Johnson merely stepped aside and hit Bowdry with a left hand that dropped him the first time."[672]

A pensive Bowdry blamed only himself. "Sometimes in a fight you can make a lot of mistakes," he mused. "And nothing ever happens to you. But every time I made a mistake against Johnson, I was on the floor. I guess that's the mark of a great fighter."[673]

One Jun 1, 1963, Willie Pastrano would win a fifteen-round split decision over Harold Johnson to claim the light heavyweight championship. Both men are now inductees in the International Boxing Hall of Fame.

Bowdry fired Yawitz, not Armstrong, who stayed on to train him for his next bout with Allan Harman. But Jesse lost that one too, and it seems the pair went their separate ways. Jesse Bowdry won just two of his next ten bouts. His last was a six-round decision loss to Otha Brown on the undercard of the Sonny Liston and Cassius Clay heavyweight title fight in Miami on February 25, 1964. Clay won the championship, and boxing entered a new era. As boxing moved on without him, Henry tried to move on without boxing.

# 22.
# Tolling Ten

Just as things with Jesse Bowdry were falling apart, so too were Henry's careers in evangelism and boxing management. There were no preaching tours or promising fighters on the horizon.

Contributions to the Henry Armstrong Youth Foundation and his boys home projects dried up. The Sammy Davis picture never materialized. With little money coming in, Henry could no longer afford to live in Los Angeles.

On a visit to St. Louis, Henry became reacquainted with Velma Tart, the high school sweetheart who had broken up with him to marry another man before Henry left for Los Angeles in 1930. Velma was divorced now, and she and Henry began seeing each other again.

Sometime in 1960, they married, and he packed what little he owned and moved into the small brick duplex at 4815A Penrose Street in St. Louis that Velma shared with one of her two daughters and her daughter's family.

Henry worked for various youth-centered charities and programs in St. Louis, collecting whatever meager pay he could. But the couple lived mainly off the annuities Henry had managed to save during his boxing career, amounting to about four thousand dollars a year. He still had some rental properties left over after the divorce from Willa Mae. Those brought another two thousand a year. "And my wife has some money," he told *Boxing Illustrated* in 1963.[674]

Other than his new wife, the other great thing about his newfound downtime was the chance to reconnect with his daughter Lanetta. He was a grandfather now, spending more time with Lanetta – and her son, his first grandchild – than he ever had.

Los Angeles matchmaker Don Chargin knew Henry in these days and found the ex-fighter content. "He'd given up drinking by then," Chargin later reminisced to journalist and author Thomas Hauser. "He was very likable, very talkative, constantly quoting from the Bible. He talked a lot about how his drinking days and carousing days were behind him; that he hadn't been a very good husband or father when he was young, but that he was a much better person and much happier now that he'd found the Lord. I think he was sincere. He seemed to have peace of mind."[675]

He began writing a second autobiography titled *Now I Fight for God*, but he either never completed it, or it simply was never published. He told a local reporter that his goal was to have his own church in St. Louis, which he still planned to call the Triumph Church.

"When I have that church, I will be satisfied," he said. "My church will welcome all races, all kinds and manner of men. I've learned my lesson – that a man cannot live by bread alone, or by money, or the cheers of the crowd, or by going through life just knocking the other fellow down."[676]

In February of 1963, Henry briefly appeared in Albany, New York, to testify at hearings about whether boxing should be banned in the state. The in-ring death of former welterweight champion Benny "Kid" Paret had sparked a firestorm of backlash against the sport. "Boxing should never be abolished," Henry said before the State Senate. Instead, he argued for reform, saying that the sport needed "referees, managers, doctors, and others who know what they are doing."[677]

Henry was now in his fifties and feeling more irrelevant with each day, despite the coverage of his testimony. As a new generation of Americans grew up and found new sports heroes, fewer writers sought to interview or profile him for their magazines and newspapers. His name still popped up in the papers, but only on nostalgic anniversaries of his big fights and only to talk about what he once did, not what he was doing. The public was moving on.

One of the celebrities the public had moved on to was garrulous Cassius Clay, the young Olympian who would soon be known as Muhammad Ali. Handsome, boastful, and undefeated at age twenty-two, young Cassius was a magnet for sportswriters and television cameras. Promoters had matched the outrageous youngster with surly heavyweight champion Sonny Liston for the heavyweight title on February 25, 1964, in Miami, and most predicted an easy night for Liston.

Cassius was nearly as quick on his feet as he was with his tongue, but few gave him a shot against the crushing blows of Liston, who had lifted the heavyweight crown from the head of his predecessor in all of two minutes and six seconds. Liston was a massive betting favorite.

For his part, Henry knew that no fighter, not even Liston, was invincible. He had learned that himself the hard way and was among the minority who predicted a Clay victory.

"Liston is a good puncher," he told the writer for the United Press International news agency, "but Clay is young – he's a young strong boy and he's unusually fast for a big man." He compared the fight to his own against Sugar Ray Robinson when the flame of Henry's prime had burnt out, and Robinson's was still heating up.

"Clay is a worrisome puncher," he went on. "He jabs and runs and that is going to get Liston provoked. Liston will be in there with a man as strong as he is."[678]

As it turned out, Henry's assessment very closely resembled the action of the fight itself. Relying on his superior footwork, speed, and long-range punches, Clay frustrated Liston, who looked old and clumsy. Liston was indeed provoked but found no way to turn his motivation into success. Eventually, the motivation left him, too. He quit on his stool before round seven, claiming a shoulder injury. Cassius Clay was the new heavyweight champion of the world, to the astonishment of all but himself – and Henry Armstrong.

But Henry's prediction of the Clay victory did not mean he saw much promise in the youngster for becoming a great champion. "Strictly a flash in the pan, with a mouth too big for his talents," was the assessment he gave to Bill Libby of *Boxing Illustrated*.[679]

Libby was one of the few writers to bother penning a profile of the aging ex-champ in this period. To him, Henry looked younger than his age.

> His hair has lost its youthful traces of red. His flat, round face seems unmarked. Operations and plastic surgery have pared the scar tissue from around his eyes. He has a belly now, and carries 180 pounds, 50 above his best fighting weight, on his 5'5" frame. But he doesn't look fat.
>
> His mind and mouth are untouched from the ring wars. He is alert, intelligent and speaks beautifully, with occasional Biblical flourishes. He loves to talk about the old days. He could talk through a thousand nights about the old days. He remembers staggering detail. 'Would I like to live those days again?' He cocked his head wistfully, a smile as big as a slice of watermelon interrupting his expression. 'Oh yes, I would. I would dearly love to live them again.'
>
> He lowers his head, hunches his shoulders, cocks his two fists, lifts his legs up and down in a miniature prance, snorts in air through his nose, and for just a second he has taken you back and showed you the remarkable fighter he once was.[680]

Understandably, Henry missed the competition, youth, fame, and money of his fighting days. He also missed Los Angeles, where he felt more connected to the world's happenings.

He did what he could to bring a sense of meaning to his life in St. Louis. He volunteered as the athletic director at the Ringside Athletic Club on Easton Avenue. It was a unique facility dedicated to "the combined religious and athletic approach to youth." Members would train there during the week under Henry's tutelage, pounding away on the heavy bag or spar in its boxing ring. But on Sunday, they could receive religious instruction.

"It is my own idea," Henry told a writer for the *St. Louis Globe-Democrat*, "and much good may come of it. I am a sports figure, and I am trying to exert a good influence on youth in the sports field."[681]

Through this work, he discovered a young local talent to train and manage. The youngster's name was Adolph Pruitt. "I really think I have a future champion in the young man," he wrote to Harry Markson, boxing manager at Madison Square Garden in New York.[682]

Henry first became aware of Pruitt as an amateur. He appeared on some of the first boxing shows Henry organized at the Ringside Athletic Club. Adolph turned pro as a lightweight on December 29, 1961, but lost the match. Still, he was a natural talent and a skilled fighter. After slow going early in his career, he began to rebound, and Henry took him to Los Angeles in 1963. Together, they went undefeated in fourteen fights between September 1963 and October 1965.

Adolph Pruitt, Henry Armstrong, Barney Ross, and Tommy Garrison.
*New York Daily News,* June 3, 1965

In June of 1965, Henry took Adolph to New York City, which was still the center of the boxing universe. He had the youngster set to face Tommy Garrison, who happened to be Barney Ross's pupil. As part of the promotion, Henry and Barney posed in front of cameras wearing boxing gloves as though they were about to resume their 1938 hostilities. In the Madison Square Garden, where Armstrong had taken Ross's welterweight title, Pruitt won a ten-round unanimous decision over Garrison.

On December 11, 1965, future Hall of Famer Jose Napoles stopped Pruitt, who afterward took a year off to mend a separated shoulder. After that, it seems Henry and Adolph went their separate ways. Pruitt would challenge for world titles on three occasions but never won a championship before retiring in 1972. He passed away on January 13, 2019, at age seventy-nine.

After splitting with Pruitt, Henry became the associate pastor at the First Baptist Church and Assistant Director of the Herbert Hoover Boys Club, where he also served as a boxing coach. There was also the occasional payday refereeing fights or speaking at dinners and events.

The mainstream sports press would occasionally remember him and write an article or honor him at some gala. In 1964, some St. Louis citizens awarded Henry and Branch Rickey, the man who signed Jackie Robinson to the Brooklyn Dodgers, their annual Brotherhood Through Sports award for their contributions to racial equality. Two years later, a group of Missouri sportswriters and sportscasters inducted Henry into the Missouri Sports Hall of Fame with a dinner in his honor in Columbia, Missouri.

In 1968, he took a trip to Las Vegas to be handed a "world award" alongside fellow athletic greats Jesse Owens, Johnny Weissmuller, and Satchel Paige.

Henry and Velma Armstrong outside of the First Baptist Church in St. Louis

His most high-profile appearance was as one of a crowd of famous athletes appearing on a 1975 variety television special hosted by Muhammad Ali, but his role was only to shake Ali's hand and stand on the stage for a few minutes. By then, Henry acknowledged that Ali, who had recently won the heavyweight championship for a second time with a knockout of undefeated George Foreman, was no flash in the pan, as he had predicted back in the early 1960s. Ali, he would admit, belonged "with the great ones."[683]

During the mid-1970s, Velma began suffering from ill health. She was hospitalized with pneumonia but appeared to recover. Not long after she came home, on the evening of Tuesday, June 8, 1976, she complained to Henry of chest pains. Worried, he helped her to their car and sped off for Barnes Hospital. About halfway there, she turned to Henry and told him, "Stop the car and hold me." Moments later, she died in Henry's arms.[684]

After burying his wife, Henry devoted himself to his work at the Herbert Hoover Boys Club and delivering his sermons at the Mount Olive Baptist Church.

No one could blame him for wanting to relive the glory of his youth between his daily meals at the local Burger Chef and playing checkers with the children at the Boys Club. He liked to take the kids to a conference room and show them his old fight films, commentating all the while. "The kids just loved it," an acquaintance once remembered to writer Wil Haygood. "He shared his moments. He shared his life."[685]

He still longed to return to Los Angeles. "I have a very good job here in St. Louis working for the Boys club but my heart is in Los Angeles," he wrote in a letter to a California friend in 1979, asking for help securing employment in L.A.

"I believe somehow… that if I come back to Los Angeles, to live where I had great fortune in the early thirties in the Boxing world, I'll be favored again from God with those same blessings," he wrote in another letter to the same friend.686

Henry continued to believe that his life story would make an excellent film, and he thought that if he moved back to Los Angeles, he would have a better chance of getting Hollywood's attention.

Henry enjoyed his role at the Herbert Hoover Boys Club.

On August 30, 1979, sixty-nine-year-old Henry Armstrong married his third wife, Gussie Henry, a nurse's aide from St. Louis four years his junior. She had helped Henry in his management business, and Henry's first wife had accused them of an affair in her divorce filing. Gussie had once sued him for thousands of dollars, but the pair had reconciled.687

Sometime that year, Henry visited the old Papin Street neighborhood of his youth. Treading slowly along those same sidewalks, he recalled his parents, grandmother, and siblings, all now gone. He thought of his first fights, the neighborhood scraps that clued him in that he might be something special. He thought of the ups and downs of an eventful, often rewarding life.

As his thoughts took him to the past, he failed to notice two young men approaching. They beat him viciously. While he lay bleeding, they rummaged through his pockets and took his wallet. Then one of them grabbed the hands that had felled a hundred men and removed his Hall of Fame ring, the symbol of all that he once was.

When Bob Burnes, sports editor for the *St. Louis Globe-Democrat*, heard the news, he rushed to the hospital to visit his friend. Henry's face was swollen and bruised. His first words to Burnes were, "I would have taken them both out in a minute in my prime."[688]

Finally, there would be no more moving forward for Henry Armstrong. After the assault, Henry showed progressive signs of the condition known then as pugilistic dementia and now recognized as Chronic Traumatic Encephalopathy (CTE). Very common among former boxers and caused by trauma to the brain, CTE can come with some or all of a variety of symptoms. There is no cure or significant treatment for CTE, a progressive condition. Early on, it appears as trouble remembering things, headaches, slurred speech, confusion and disorientation, and drastic mood swings. In its advanced stages, symptoms include tremors, compromised equilibrium, diminished mental capacity, reduced motor skills, and muscular rigidity.

Someone with significant CTE can appear to be inebriated when they are completely sober, and thus the condition was commonly called "punch drunk" in Henry's time, and people incorrectly thought it only affected unskilled fighters, the assumption being they were inept at avoiding punches. Because of this, there was a stigma attached to the term, and many boxers tried to hide their symptoms; they would not admit to them or disappear from public view. Boxing insiders often denied or downplayed boxing-related brain damage. But plenty of the sport's all-time greats suffered from its symptoms, including men Henry had battled or befriended during his boxing career.

One of those was Joe Louis, who passed away at age sixty-six on April 12, 1981, after decades of failing mental and physical health. Henry traveled to Washington, D.C., to attend his old friend's funeral at Arlington National Cemetery. Former heavyweight champion Joe Frazier escorted Henry around the nation's capital in a black limousine. At the funeral, some young fans asked Muhammad Ali (who was by then also displaying early symptoms of CTE) for his autograph. "Why don't you ask the *real* champ," Ali responded, pointing them toward Henry.[689]

In March 1982, Henry and Gussie moved into a small, two-bedroom bungalow on East 55th Street in South Central Los Angeles together, though some of Henry's friends and family objected to the idea. Crime and gang activity was on a well-publicized rise in the area.

"His wife came one day to the boys club and took him away from there, with his briefcase and himself," Velma Armstrong's daughter Edna Nashville told a reporter of Henry's sudden departure. "None of his belongings, none of that. He had a lot of fantastic friends here."690

Edna said she tried to call her stepfather shortly after their move, and Gussie took the phone away from Henry, saying, "You know you're not allowed to use the phone."691

"We tried not to let him leave here," recalled a St. Louis friend of Henry's a few years later. "I know he was getting up in age, getting senile and forgetful, but he should have stayed. He had the kind of job where he basically didn't do anything and got paid for it. People were impressed just because of who he was. That was the way it was, but it was kind of sad."692

Whatever the couple hoped to find in Los Angeles never came their way. Henry's annuities had long ago run out, and the real estate properties were gone. Henry and Gussie subsisted on an eight-hundred-dollar monthly check from social security. Henry's trophies, medals, and belts were also gone; Gussie told reporters they had been stolen in another robbery.

Occasionally, he would appear at a big boxing event. In November 1982, promoter Bob Arum invited Henry to Miami for junior welterweight champion Aaron Pryor's much-anticipated showdown with three-division titlist Alexis Arguello. Pryor's quick hands, sturdy chin, and startling aggression were already drawing comparisons with a young Armstrong, and Arguello was fighting to break Henry's record of three division championships. Parading Henry before the fans gave the event a sense of legacy. Arguello said he was dedicating his upcoming performance to Armstrong.

Escorted from his hotel to Miami's Orange Bowl in a limousine with Gussie, he was proud that some fight fans still recognized him. They pointed him out to their children and friends, telling them that Henry Armstrong was still the only man ever to hold three division championships simultaneously. Reporters pulled him aside, hoping for a few good lines of copy.

"I don't do much anymore," Henry confessed to columnist Dave Anderson, "except make appearances like I'm doing for this fight." He had never seen either Pryor or Arguello fight before, but the two great fighters put on a scintillating battle for the ages that harkened back to the days of Armstrong and Ambers. Pryor, the betting underdog, stopped Arguello in the fourteenth round. Henry's record held.693

When he made another appearance ringside, a young Mike Tyson introduced himself. Tyson was the rampaging heavyweight knockout machine of the day and an amateur fight historian. Honored to take a picture next to one of his heroes, Tyson happily admitted that he patterned much of his famously aggressive style on Henry's.694

Henry Armstrong and Mike Tyson
*Los Angeles Times*, August 14, 1988

Throughout the 1980s, Henry's health deteriorated steadily. He developed a noticeable limp, favoring his left leg, a common symptom of CTE. He told people it came from a low blow suffered in the ring against Ceferino Garcia. In time, he would need a cane and, eventually, a wheelchair. In the latter half of the decade, the man who was once one of the premier athletes on the planet was no longer able to shave, bathe, or dress himself; Gussie was there to help with those tasks.

His family in St. Louis complained that they could not contact Henry and that Gussie prevented their visits. They asked Henry's friend Archie Moore to check in on him, and he reported that Gussie was not giving Henry proper care and that he looked weak and depressed. He belonged in a home, said Archie.[695]

In November 1987, an ophthalmologist discovered Henry was blind in his left eye due to a retinal detachment. No one could say how long that had been the case, not even Henry, for he was by then in the advanced stages of dementia. The ophthalmologist recommended surgery, but Gussie never brought him back for the procedure.

Between January and August of 1988, Century City Hospital staff admitted him six times for conditions such as anemia, dehydration, pneumonia, and dementia. Eventually, he refused to eat. His weight dropped to ninety-five pounds. After that, a feeding tube was inserted into his stomach.

Dr. Abe Green, the internal medicine and kidney specialist at Century, tried to establish a fund to pay for Henry's home care, as Gussie refused to move him into a nursing home. She was afraid of a reduction in her social security payments. "What can I do? I need something to live on," she told Thomas Bonk of the *Los Angeles Times*.

Bonk wrote a long story on Henry to draw attention to the dying fighter's plight. In it, Dr. Green revealed that the ex-champion's deterioration moved him personally as well as professionally:

It's difficult dealing with someone who was such a remarkable physical specimen who has ended up as one of the most debilitated persons I have ever had to deal with. At first it wasn't that emotionally trying because I had seen other people like that in county hospitals and veterans' hospitals. Then, suddenly having a picture thrown in my face and someone say, 'This is Henry 40 years ago,' it really sends shivers down my spine.[696]

Gussie drew upon her training as a nurse's aide to care for her husband at home the best she could, but he developed infections in his stomach and leg while in her care. When she brought him back to the hospital, his leg was bent and rigid. Medical staff were unable to straighten it.

Henry's gnarled body lay curled on his side in a hospital bed with flowers from Lanetta on a nearby table. So far as anyone could tell, he was no longer aware of his surroundings. His clouded eyes stared without registering anyone around him, only occasionally fluttering when someone opened the curtains to brighten his hospital room.

Two days after being sent home from yet another visit to the hospital, Henry was rushed to California Medical Center. In the early morning of Saturday, October 22, 1988 – fifty years and one week after he accomplished the impossible by winning his third simultaneous championship – the powerful heart that had tirelessly pushed him through so many difficult trials and fights finally gave out at age seventy-eight.

He was laid to rest a week later at Rosedale Cemetery in Los Angeles. Because Gussie could not afford the service and burial, Jerry Buss, the Los Angeles Lakers basketball team owner and a lifelong boxing fan, paid the four thousand dollars in expenses.[697]

That evening, undefeated champion Julio Cesar Chavez fought challenger Jose Luis Ramirez for the lightweight championship Henry Armstrong won fifty years earlier. The HBO premium cable television channel broadcast the event.

Boxing has a time-honored tradition of honoring the recently departed at events. Before the main bout, with Chavez, Ramirez, Mike Tyson, and Muhammad Ali standing nearby, ring announcer Chuck Hull took a moment to announce Henry's passing to the crowd. Speaking extemporaneously but briefly, he did his best to capture the importance of Henry Armstrong's life:

And now, ladies and gentlemen, if I may, I'd ask us to pause and reflect for just a moment on the passing of one of boxing's greatest… a man who freed himself from the ghettos of St. Louis, Missouri and went on to win three world titles at the same time in different weight divisions. He held the lightweight, the featherweight, and the welterweight championships all at the same time, the only man in history to accomplish that feat. After he retired from boxing, he became a member of the ministry and went to California to work with youth around the Long Beach, California area. He was not only an historical boxer; he was a great humanitarian. So, I would ask you now, all rise, please, as I ask our timekeeper Al Byzick to sound the ten count for one of boxing's greatest, Hammerin' Henry Armstrong.

The crowd quieted as the bell tolled away a final ten count for Henry Armstrong. Then Hull said simply, "May God rest his soul."

# Afterword

An afterword to the life of a great boxer should, I suppose, talk about his greatness. But if the preceding pages did not convince the reader of Henry Armstrong's ring prowess and legacy, then I have not done my job, and a few more paragraphs would not help.

For those wondering where he ranks among the sport's elite champions, one need only pull up any credible list of the all-time greats presented by one of the respected boxing websites or magazines. One can also read what trainers and boxers like Emmanuel Steward, Teddy Atlas, Ray Arcel, Jack Dempsey, Benny Leonard, and Mike Tyson have said about him.

In boxing literature, Henry's name regularly appears alongside those of Muhammad Ali, Sugar Ray Robinson, and Joe Louis as being among the sport's most elite practitioners. Robinson, Ali, and Louis have had at least a half dozen books written about each one of them over the years. Then there are the documentaries and feature films made about them. If Armstrong ranks among them, why has only one book (an autobiography) been published about him before this one?

There are some superficial answers to that. Ali and Louis were heavyweights – and extremely famous ones at that. Just as they did when Henry was fighting, the heavyweights can still steal the limelight from the smaller fellows; especially when they are great heavyweights.

Though not a heavyweight, Sugar Ray Robinson was a unique fighter, maybe the best of any day and indeed the flashiest and most charismatic boxing star of the generation immediately following Henry's. He benefited from the dawn of the television age and remains in living memory. You can still meet and talk to people who remember seeing Sugar Ray fight. The people who followed Henry Armstrong's career in real time could not do so via television. If they could not see him fight in person or could not afford the ticket to watch the fight films at the theater, they had to listen to radio broadcasts and read about him in newspapers. And almost all of them are gone now, no longer able to regale those of us still here with memories of the human dynamo who thrilled and inspired.

But does any of that mean that we should forget Henry Armstrong? For those who take it upon themselves to delve into the sport's annals, he remains one of the first figures they will learn about, but that should not be necessary. Boxing fanatics may mention him in the same breath as Ali or Robinson, but so should anyone who knows anything about American sports.

"Centuries from now they will talk about how he won three world titles," Henry's friend and fellow boxing Hall of Famer Ike Williams remarked upon hearing of Henry's death. They should, but will they?[698]

In 2005, film audiences and critics cheered the story of Jim Braddock and his unexpected rise to the heavyweight championship during the Depression in *Cinderella Man*. Henry's struggles and triumphs during the same era would have been just as intriguing on the big screen: rising out of the horrors of Jim Crow Mississippi; surviving the streets of St. Louis; starving and riding the rails during the early years of the Depression; battling racism along with his opponents; serving as a symbol of hope for millions of oppressed Black people; and still accomplishing things no other boxer had accomplished before or since. What a tale, one too few people know.

Of course, Braddock was a white heavyweight, and Armstrong was neither. Those traits alone would have changed the marketability of the film.

Though his ethnicity played an incalculable role in his life and career, Armstrong was no firebrand in the manner of later activist athletes like Ali. The society he lived in precluded his speaking out as much as he would have liked. But in pursuing success, he found small ways to combat racism outside of the ring and in it. He refused to participate in the demeaning battle royals. Because Jim Crow laws in Missouri forbade him from fighting white opponents, Henry Armstrong left the state. In California, he boycotted a segregated venue until its promoters caved and allowed him to participate in its first interracial bout. He financed and starred in a film with an all-Black cast that promoted self-respect and racial uplift and jump-started the careers of groundbreaking Black actors Dooley Wilson and Canada Lee. He hired George Moore, one of the pioneering Black boxing managers and promoters. He helped organize a benefit fight for the NAACP and similar organizations. And he was always aware of his symbolic importance for Black Americans.

Before Henry won his first championship in 1937, Black American boxing champions were few and far between. A decade later, there were four reigning Black champs (Louis, Ray Robinson, Ike Williams, and Bob Montgomery) and several more on the horizon. Black journalist and artist Ted Carroll acknowledged Henry's role in the ascendance of black fighters and in combatting racism in general. "A polished highly intelligent fellow, a poet of all things, well-spoken and educated, Henry formed with Louis a double play combination that sent many bigots back to the dugout from which they may never emerge," wrote Carroll in a 1947 article celebrating the rise of Black boxers to prominence.[699]

Of course, Henry saw his grandest triumph as his embrace of God, the Bible, and the pulpit. While proud of his ring accomplishments, he found greater satisfaction in getting young boys off the streets and saving souls. "Now I fight for God," he would say. It was a cause that brought him a sense of peace and purpose and began the work of his foundation.

Until the last decade, his life was one of constant motion, of barreling forward through the opposition (and the opposition was fierce) to attain his goals and ultimately find peace with himself. His story should be told, retold, and remembered by more than the ever-dwindling cult of boxing obsessives.

While interviewing Henry for a profile in the January 1955 issue of *Sport* magazine, Al Stump was humbled by Henry's presence. His words prove as fitting of a closing for the Henry Armstrong story as any I could write.

He put so much into what he set out to do with so little in his favor; against poverty, race discrimination, education, the double-dealing of those for whom he bled, mismanagement even through his great years, broken health, the bitter blows of bigger men. Whatever your own situation, you feel that Henry came from well back of that to set his records. Nobody ever will forget that record, not merely because he holds the only Triple Crown ever won by a fist fighter, but because at no time and nowhere did he ever back down one inch from life.

That's the lasting sermon of Reverend Henry Armstrong.

# Henry Armstrong's Verifiable Boxing Record

(A source key is at the end of the records section)

## Amateur: 18 wins (11 by KO), 7 losses (1 by KO)

| DATE | OPPONENT | RESULT | SOURCE |
|---|---|---|---|
| **1930** | | | |
| March 20 | James Burch | Win-TKO 1 | *SLPD* 3/21/1930 |
| (Wins AAU Western Colored Featherweight Championship) | | | |
| October 28 | James Burch | Win-KO 3 | *SLPD* 10/26/1930 |
| **1931** | | | |
| March 19 | Roy Johnson | Win-TKO 1 | *SLPD* 3/20/1931 |
| November 12 | Clarence Togan | Win-TKO 2 | *PP* 11/13/1931 |
| November 19 | Jimmie Garcia | Loss-KO 1 | *BDER* 11/20/1931 |
| November 26 | Leo Sentoya | Win 3 | *BDER* 11/27/1931 |
| December 10 | Henry Olsen | Win 3 | *BDER* 12/11/1931 |
| **1932** | | | |
| January 7 | Alfredo Ortiz | [unknown] | *LAEPR* 1/6/1932 |
| January 20 | Augie Solis | [unknown] | *LAEPR* 1/20/1932 |
| January 28 | Ace Bergerren | Win 3 | *LAECN* 1/29/1932 |
| (Wins AAU Southern California Featherweight Semi-Finals) | | | |
| January 28 | Perry Thompson | Win 3 | *LADN* 1/29/1932 |
| (Wins AAU Southern California Featherweight Championship) | | | |
| February 3 | Angelo Posedo | [unknown] | *LADN* 2/2/1932 |
| February 6 | Henry Hernandez | Win-TKO 3 | *LO* 3/7/1932 |
| February 13 | Eddie Ware | Win 3 | *LADN* 2/15/1932 |
| February 15 | Bobby Decker | Loss 3 | *LAT* 2/16/1932 |
| February 24 | Mickey Markin | Loss 3 | *LAEPR* 2/25/1932 |
| March 9 | Henry Seminola | Win-TKO 2 | *LADN* 3/10/1932 |
| March 12 | Perfecto Lopez | Loss 3 | *LAT* 3/14/1932 |
| March 22 | Augie Solis | Win-TKO 3 | *SAR* 3/23/1932 |
| April 4 | Babe Gonzalez | Win-KO 3 | *LAECN* 4/5/1932 |
| April 20 | Joe Carter | [unknown] | *LAT* 4/17/1932 |
| May 14 | Gene Dagupa | [unknown] | *LAEPR* 5/14/1932 |
| May 19 | Joe Grajade | Loss 3 | *SPNP* 5/20/1932 |
| May 21 | Manuel Hernandez | Win-TKO 1 | *LADN* 5/23/1932 |
| May 26 | Bill Espinosa | Win-KO 2 | *SPNP* 5/27/1932 |
| May 28 | Joe Barrera | Win-KO 1 | *LAEPR* 5/30/1932 |
| June 4 | Frankie Leon | Win 3 | *CE* 6/10/1932 |
| June 16 | Augie Soliz | Win 3 | *SPNP* 6/17/1932 |
| June 18 | Joe Grajade | [unknown] | *LEPR* 6/17/1932 |
| June 22 | Ralph Montoya | Win 3 | *VEV* 6/25/1932 |
| July 1 | Johnny Hines | Loss 3 | *SPNP* 7/2/1932 |
| (Los Angeles Olympic trials, featherweight final) | | | |
| July 20 | Frank Gallucci | Win-TKO 3 | *SFE* 7/21/1932 |
| (National Olympic trials, bantamweight, first round) | | | |
| July 21 | Jess La Barba | Loss 3 | *PPB* 7/22/1932 |
| (National Olympic trials, bantamweight, second round) | | | |

# Professional: 147 wins (98 by KO), 21 losses (2 by KO), 11 draws

Names in **bold** represent world champions and/or International Boxing Hall of Fame inductees.

Names with * represent fighters ranked in the Top 10 of any division by *The Ring* magazine at the time of the fight.

| DATE | OPPONENT | RESULT | SOURCE |
|---|---|---|---|
| **1931** | | | |
| July 27 | Al Iovino | Loss-KO 3 | *PPG* 7/28/1931 |
| July 31 | Sammy Burns | Win 6 | *PPG* 8/1/1931 |
| **1932** | | | |
| August 30 | Eddie Trujillo | Loss 4 | *LADN* 8/31/1932 |
| September 27 | Al Greenfield | Loss 4 | *LADN* 9/28/1932 |
| December 13 | Gene Espinosa | Win 4 | *LADN* 12/14/1932 |
| December 31 | Young Corpus | Win 4 | *SMT* 1/3/1933 |
| **1933** | | | |
| February 3 | Johnny Ryan | Win 6 | *VCS* 2/4/1933 |
| February 17 | Georgie Dundee | Win 6 | *VCS* 2/18/1933 |
| March 21 | Paul Wangley | Win-TKO 4 | *LAT* 3/22/1933 |
| April 28 | Perfecto Lopez | Win 6 | *VCS* 4/29/1933 |
| May 24 | Young Bud Taylor | Win-KO 2 | *NJ* 5/25/1933 |
| May 31 | Max Tarley | Draw 6 | *LADN* 6/1/1933 |
| June 7 | Ricky Hall | Win-KO 3 | *SMT* 6/8/1933 |
| June 28 | George Haberski | Win 4 | *WDPJ* 6/29/1933 |
| July 11 | Baby Manuel | Loss 6 | *LADN* 7/12/1933 |
| July 29 | Benny Pelz | Win 4 | *LO* 7/30/1933 |
| August 8 | Bobby Calmes | Win-KO 5 | *SPNP* 8/9/1933 |
| August 30 | Hoyt Jones | Draw 4 | *LAT* 8/31/1933 |
| September 5 | Perfecto Lopez | Draw 4 | *LAT* 9/6/1933 |
| October 11 | Perfecto Lopez | Draw 4 | *LADN* 10/12/1933 |
| October 19 | Johnny Granone | Win-TKO 6 | *SB* 10/20/1933 |
| November 3 | Kid Moro | Draw 10 | *LAECN* 11/7/1933 |
| November 23 | Kid Moro | Draw 10 | *SB* 11/23/1933 |
| December 14 | Gene Espinosa | Win-TKO 7 | *SB* 12/15/1933 |
| **1934** | | | |
| January 26 | Baby Manuel | Win 10 | *SB* 1/27/1934 |
| February 13 | Benny Pelz | Win 4 | *LADN* 2/14/1934 |
| March 27 | Young Danny | Win-KO 1 | *LAEPR* 3/28/1934 |
| May 4 | Kid Moro | Draw 10 | *SB* 5/5/1934 |
| May 22 | Johnny DeFoe | Win-KO 6 | *LADN* 5/23/1934 |
| June 5 | Vincente Torres | Win 6 | *LADN* 6/6/1934 |
| June 14 | Davey Abad | Win 10 | *SB* 6/15/1934 |
| July 17 | Perfecto Lopez | Win 6 | *LADN* 7/18/1934 |
| August 28 | Perfecto Lopez | Win-TKO 5 | *LAT* 8/29/1934 |
| September 7 | Joe Sanchez | Win-TKO 4 | *VCS* 9/8/1934 |
| September 13 | Max Tarley | Win-KO 3 | *LAECN* 9/14/1934 |
| September 28 | Perfecto Lopez | Win 8 | *VCS* 9/29/1934 |
| November 4 | **Baby Arizmendi*** | Loss 10 | *SB* 11/5/1934 |
| (For World Featherweight Championship as recognized by NYSAC, Mexico and CA) | | | |
| December 1 | Joe Conde* | Win-TKO 7 | *R* February 1935 |
| December 15 | Ventura Arana | Win-KO 5 | *LAT* 12/17/1934 |
| **1935** | | | |
| January 1 | **Baby Arizmendi*** | Loss 12 | *LAEPR* 1/2/1935 |
| February 16 | Baby Casanova* | Loss-DQ 4 | *HMJ* 2/17/1935 |
| March 19 | Sal Hernandez | Win-TKO 2 | *LAT* 3/20/1935 |
| March 30 | Davey Abad* | Loss 10 | *SLPD* 4/1/1935 |
| April 6 | Tully Corvo | Win-TKO 5 | *SB* 4/8/1935 |

| Date | Opponent | Result | Location/Date |
|---|---|---|---|
| April 16 | Kid Covelli* | Win 8 | SB 4/17/1935 |
| May 10 | Mark Diaz | Win 8 | VCS 5/11/1935 |
| May 28 | Davey Abad | Win 10 | SB 5/29/1935 |
| June 25 | Varias Milling | Win 10 | LAEPR 6/26/1935 |
| September 13 | Alton Black | Win-TKO 8 | NSJ 9/14/1935 |
| September 18 | Perfecto Lopez* | Draw 8 | SFE 9/19/1935 |
| October 21 | Lester Marston | Win-TKO 7 | OT 10/22/1935 |
| November 12 | Leo Lomelli | Win-TKO 6 | OT 11/13/1935 |
| November 27 | **Midget Wolgast*** | Win 10 | OT 11/29/1935 |
| December 6 | Alton Black | Win-TKO 8 | NSJ 12/7/1935 |

**1936**

| Date | Opponent | Result | Location/Date |
|---|---|---|---|
| January 1 | Joe Conde* | Loss 10 | R March 1936 |
| February 26 | Ritchie Fontaine | Loss 10 | OT 2/27/1936 |
| March 31 | Ritchie Fontaine* | Win 10 | LADN 4/1/1936 |
| May 19 | Pancho Leyvas* | Win-TKO 4 | LAT 5/20/1936 |
| June 22 | Johnny DeFoe | Win 10 | MS 6/24/1936 |
| August 4 | **Baby Arizmendi*** | Win 10 | LAT 8/5/1936 |
| **(Wins World Featherweight Championship as recognized by Mexico and CA)** | | | |
| August 18 | **Juan Zurita*** | Win-TKO 4 | LADN 8/19/1936 |
| September 3 | Buzz Brown | Win 10 | SB 9/4/1936 |
| September 8 | Tommy Ganzon | Win-KO 1 | SB 9/9/1936 |
| October 27 | **Mike Belloise*** | Win 10 | LAT 10/28/1936 |
| November 2 | Gene Espinosa | Win-KO 1 | LAT 11/3/1936 |
| November 17 | Joey Alcanter | Win-TKO 5 | SLGD 11/18/1936 |
| **(Wins Missouri State Lightweight Championship)** | | | |
| December 3 | Tony Chavez* | Loss-DQ 8 | SLGD 12/4/1936 |

**1937**

| Date | Opponent | Result | Location/Date |
|---|---|---|---|
| January 1 | Baby Casanova | Win-KO 3 | LAT 1/3/1937 |
| January 19 | Tony Chavez* | Win-KO 10 | LAT 1/20/1937 |
| February 3 | Moon Mullins | Win-TKO 2 | LAT 2/4/1937 |
| February 19 | Varias Milling | Win-KO 4 | LAT 2/20/1937 |
| March 2 | California Joe Rivers | Win-TKO 4 | LAT 3/3/1937 |
| March 13 | **Mike Belloise*** | Win-KO 4 | NYDN 3/14/1937 |
| March 19 | Aldo Spoldi* | Win 10 | NYT 3/20/1937 |
| April 6 | Pete DeGrassse* | Win-KO 10 | LAT 4/7/1937 |
| May 4 | **Frankie Klick** | Win-TKO 4 | LADN 5/5/1937 |
| May 28 | Wally Hally | Win-TKO 4 | LADN 5/29/1937 |
| June 9 | Mark Diaz | Win-KO 4 | PP 6/10/1937 |
| June 15 | Jackie Carter | Win-TKO 3 | LAT 6/16/1937 |
| July 8 | Alf Blatch | Win-TKO 3 | NYT 7/9/1937 |
| July 19 | Lew Massey | Win-TKO 4 | NYT 7/20/1937 |
| July 27 | **Benny Bass** | Win-KO 4 | PI 7/28/1937 |
| August 13 | Eddie Brink | Win-KO 3 | NYT 8/14/1937 |
| August 16 | Johnny Cabello | Win-TKO 1 | WES 8/17/1937 |
| August 31 | Orville Drouillard | Win-TKO 5 | SFP 9/1/1937 |
| September 9 | Charley Burns | Win-KO 4 | PSC 9/10/1937 |
| September 16 | Johnny DeFoe | Win-TKO 4 | NYT 9/17/1937 |
| September 22 | Bobby Dean | Win-KO 1 | OMBN 9/23/1937 |
| October 18 | Joe Marciente | Win-KO 3 | PI 10/19/1937 |
| October 29 | **Petey Sarron*** | Win-KO 6 | NYDN 10/30/1937 |
| **(Wins Undisputed World Featherweight Championship)** | | | |
| November 19 | Billy Beauhuld* | Win-TKO 5 | NYT 11/20/1937 |
| November 23 | Joey Brown | Win-KO 2 | NYT 11/24/1937 |
| December 6 | Tony Chavez* | Win-TKO 1 | NYT 12/7/1937 |
| December 12 | Johnny Jones | Win-KO 2 | NYT 12/13/1937 |

**1938**

| Date | Opponent | Result | Location/Date |
|---|---|---|---|
| January 12 | Enrico Venturi | Win-KO 6 | NYT 1/13/1937 |
| January 21 | Frankie Castillo | Win-TKO 3 | ADS 1/22/1938 |
| January 22 | Tommy Brown | Win-KO 2 | AR 1/23/1938 |
| February 1 | **Chalky Wright** | Win-TKO 3 | NYT 2/2/1938 |
| February 9 | Al Citrino | Win-TKO 4 | SFE 2/10/1938 |

| February 25 | Everett Rightmire* | Win-TKO 3 | CT 2/26/1938 |
| February 28 | Charley Burns | Win-TKO 2 | MSL 3/1/1938 |
| March 15 | **Baby Arizmendi** | Win 10 | LAT 3/16/1938 |
| March 25 | Eddie Zivic | Win-TKO 4 | NYT 3/26/1938 |
| March 30 | Lew Feldman | Win-KO 5 | NYT 3/31/1938 |
| May 31 | **Barney Ross*** | Win 15 | NYT 6/1/1938 |

(**Wins Undisputed** World Welterweight Championship)

| August 17 | **Lou Ambers*** | Win 15 | NYT 8/18/1938 |

(**Wins Undisputed** World Lightweight Championship)

| November 25 | **Ceferino Garcia*** | Win 15 | NYDN 11/26/1938 |

(**Retains Undisputed** World Welterweight Championship)

| December 6 | Al Manfredo | Win-TKO 3 | WES 12/7/1938 |

**1939**

| January 10 | **Baby Arizmendi*** | Win 10 | LAT 1/11/1939 |

(**Retains Undisputed** World Welterweight Championship)

| March 4 | Bobby Pacho | Win-TKO 4 | NYDN 3/5/1939 |

(**Retains Undisputed** World Welterweight Championship)

| March 16 | Lew Feldman | Win-KO 1 | NYT 3/17/1939 |

(**Retains Undisputed** World Welterweight & Lightweight Championships)

| March 31 | Davey Day* | Win-TKO 12 | NYT 4/1/1939 |

(**Retains Undisputed** World Welterweight Championship)

| May 25 | Eddie Roderick* | Win 15 | LDH 5/26/1939 |

(**Retains Undisputed** World Welterweight Championship)

| August 22 | **Lou Ambers*** | Loss 15 | NYT 8/23/1939 |

(**Loses Undisputed** World Lightweight Championship)

| October 9 | Al Manfredo | Win-TKO 4 | CRG 10/10/1939 |

(**Retains Undisputed** World Welterweight Championship)

| October 13 | Howard Scott | Win-KO 2 | MNS 10/14/1939 |

(**Retains Undisputed** World Welterweight Championship)

| October 20 | Ritchie Fontaine | Win-TKO 3 | SS 10/21/1939 |

(**Retains Undisputed** World Welterweight Championship)

| October 25 | Jimmy Garrison | Win 10 | LAT 10/25/1939 |

(**Retains Undisputed** World Welterweight Championship)

| October 30 | Bobby Pacho | Win-TKO 4 | FCC 10/31/1939 |

(**Retains Undisputed** World Welterweight Championship)

| December 11 | Jimmy Garrison | Win-KO 7 | DDN 12/12/1939 |

(**Retains Undisputed** World Welterweight Championship)

**1940**

| January 4 | Joe Gnouly | Win-KO 5 | SLPD 1/5/1940 |

(**Retains Undisputed** World Welterweight Championship)

| January 24 | **Pedro Montanez** | Win-TKO 9 | NYT 1/25/1940 |

(**Retains Undisputed** World Welterweight Championship)

| March 1 | **Ceferino Garcia*** | Draw 10 | LAT 3/2/1940 |

(**For NBA & Lineal** World Middleweight Championship)

| April 26 | Paul Junior* | Win-TKO 7 | BG 4/27/1940 |

(**Retains Undisputed** World Welterweight Championship)

| May 25 | Ralph Zannelli | Win-TKO 5 | BG 5/25/1940 |

(**Retains Undisputed** World Welterweight Championship)

| June 21 | Paul Junior | Win-TKO 3 | BDN 6/22/1940 |

(**Retains Undisputed** World Welterweight Championship)

| July 17 | **Lew Jenkins*** | Win-TKO 7 | NYT 7/17/1940 |
| September 24 | Phil Furr* | Win-KO 4 | WES 9/24/1940 |

(**Retains Undisputed** World Welterweight Championship)

| October 4 | **Fritzie Zivic*** | Loss 15 | NYT 10/5/1940 |

(**Loses Undisputed** World Welterweight Championship)

**1941**

| January 17 | **Fritzie Zivic*** | Loss-TKO 12 | NYT 1/18/1941 |

(**For Undisputed** World Welterweight Championship)

**1942**

| June 1 | Johnny Taylor | Win-TKO 3 | SRPD 6/2/1942 |

| Date | Opponent | Result | Source |
|---|---|---|---|
| June 24 | Sheik Rangel | Win 10 | SFE 6/25/1942 |
| July 3 | Reuben Shank* | Loss 10 | SB 7/4/1942 |
| July 20 | Joe Ybarra | Win-TKO 3 | SB 7/21/1942 |
| August 3 | Aldo Spoldi | Win-TKO 7 | HMJ 8/4/1942 |
| August 13 | Jackie Burke | Win 10 | OSE 8/14/1942 |
| August 26 | Rodolfo Ramirez | Win-KO 8 | OT 8/27/1942 |
| September 7 | Johnny Taylor | Win-TKO 3 | OT 9/8/1942 |
| September 14 | Leo Rodak | Win-TKO 8 | LAT 9/15/1942 |
| September 30 | Earl Turner* | Win-KO 4 | OT 10/1/1942 |
| October 13 | **Juan Zurita*** | Win-KO 2 | LAT 10/14/1942 |
| October 26 | **Fritzie Zivic*** | Win 10 | SFE 10/27/1942 |
| December 4 | **Lew Jenkins** | Win-TKO 8 | OT 12/5/1942 |
| December 14 | Severio Turiello | Win-TKO 4 | SFE 12/15/1942 |

**1943**

| Date | Opponent | Result | Source |
|---|---|---|---|
| January 5 | Jimmy McDaniels | Win 10 | LADN 1/6/1943 |
| March 2 | Wille Joyce* | Loss 10 | LAT 3/3/1943 |
| March 8 | **Tippy Larkin*** | Win-KO 2 | SFE 3/9/1943 |
| March 22 | Al Tribuani | Win 10 | PI 3/24/1943 |
| April 2 | **Beau Jack*** | Loss 10 | NYT 4/3/1943 |
| May 1 | Severio Turiello | Win-TKO 5 | LAT 5/1/1943 |
| May 7 | Tommy Jessup | Win-KO 1 | SFE 5/8/1943 |
| May 24 | Maxie Shapiro | Win-TKO 7 | OT 5/25/1943 |
| June 11 | **Sammy Angott*** | Win 10 | NYT 6/12/1943 |
| July 24 | Willie Joyce* | Win 10 | LAT 7/25/1943 |
| August 6 | Jimmy Garrison* | Win 10 | OT 8/7/1943 |
| August 14 | Joey Silva | Win 10 | SSR 8/15/1943 |
| August 27 | **Ray Robinson*** | Loss 10 | NYT 8/28/1943 |

**1944**

| Date | Opponent | Result | Source |
|---|---|---|---|
| January 14 | Aldo Spoldi | Win-KO 3 | LAT 1/15/1944 |
| January 25 | Severio Turiello | Win-KO 7 | KST 1/26/1944 |
| February 7 | Lew Hanbury | Win-KO 3 | NYDN 2/8/1944 |
| February 23 | Jimmy Garrison | Win-TKO 5 | KST 2/24/1944 |
| February 29 | Jackie Byrd | Win-KO 4 | DMR 3/1/1944 |
| March 14 | Johnny Jones | Win-KO 5 | MH 3/15/1944 |
| March 20 | Frankie Willis* | Win 10 | NYDN 3/21/1944 |
| March 25 | Ralph Zannelli* | Win 10 | BG 3/26/1944 |
| April 25 | John Thomas* | Win 10 | LAT 4/26/1944 |
| May 16 | Ralph Zannelli* | Win 10 | BG 5/16/1944 |
| May 22 | Aaron Perry | Win-TKO 6 | LAT 5/23/1944 |
| June 3 | Willie Joyce* | Loss 10 | CT 6/4/1944 |
| June 15 | Bummy Davis | Win-KO 2 | NYT 6/16/1944 |
| June 21 | Nick Latsios | Win 10 | PBP 6/22/1944 |
| July 4 | John Thomas* | Loss 10 | LAT 7/5/1944 |
| July 14 | Slugger White* | Draw 10 | SB 7/15/1944 |
| August 21 | Willie Joyce* | Win 10 | SFE 8/22/1944 |
| September 15 | Aldo Spoldi | Win-KO 2 | SSAT 9/16/1944 |
| November 4 | **Mike Belloise** | Win-KO 4 | MMT 11/5/1944 |

**1945**

| Date | Opponent | Result | Source |
|---|---|---|---|
| January 16 | Chester Slider* | Draw 10 | LADN 1/17/1945 |
| February 6 | Genaro Rojo | Win 10 | LAT 2/7/1945 |
| February 14 | Chester Slider* | Loss 10 | LADN 2/15/1945 |

*Source Key:*

*ADS* – Arizona Daily Star
*AR* – Arizona Republic
*BDER* – Burbank Daily Evening Review
*BDN* – Bangor Daily News
*BG* – Boston Globe
*CE* – California Eagle
*CE* – Chippewa Herald-Telegram
*CRG* – Cedar Rapids Gazette
*CT* – Chicago Tribune
*DDN* – Dayton Daily News
*DFP* – Detroit Free Press
*DMR* – Des Moines Register
*DO* – Daily Oklahoman
*FCC* – Fort Collins Coloradoan
*HMJ* – Hanford Morning Journal
*IS* – Indianapolis Star
*KN* – Kenosha News
*KST* – Kansas City Times
*LADN* – Los Angeles Daily News
*LAECN* – Los Angeles Evening Citizen News
*LAEE* – Los Angeles Evening Express
*LAEPR* – Los Angeles Evening Post-Record
*LAT* – Los Angeles Times
*LBS* – Long Beach Sun
*LDH* – Liverpool Daily Herald
*LO* – La Opinion
*MH* – Miami Herald
*MMT* – Medford Mail Tribune
*MNS* – Minneapolis Star
*MS* – Montana Standard
*NA* – Newark Advocate
*NJ* – Napa Journal
*NYDN* – New York Daily News
*NYT* – New York Times
*OMBN* – Omaha Morning Bee-News
*OSE* – Ogden Standard-Examiner
*OT* – Oakland Tribune
*PBP* – Pittsburgh Press
*PI* – Philadelphia Inquirer
*PP* – Pasadena Post
*PPB* – Pomona Progress Bulletin
*PPG* – Pittsburgh Post-Gazette
*R* – The Ring
*RNL* – Richmond News Leader
*SAR* – Santa Ana Register
*SB* – Sacramento Bee
*SFE* – San Francisco Examiner
*SLGD* – St. Louis Globe-Democrat
*SLPD* – St. Louis Post-Dispatch
*SMT* – Santa Maria Times
*SPNP* – San Pedro News-Pilot
*SRPD* – Santa Rosa Press Democrat
*SS* – Seattle Star
*SSAT* – St. Louis Star and Times
*SSR* – Spokane Spokesman-Review
*VCS* – Ventura County Star
*VEV* – Venice Evening Vanguard
*WDPJ* – Wilmington Daily Press Journal
*WES* – Washington Evening Star

# Bibliography & Sources

Ackerman, Meyer, "Armstrong, Fighter of the Month," *The Ring*, December 1942

"Another Colored Star." *The Ring*. November 1936.

Armstrong, Henry. *Gloves, Glory, and God*. Westwood: Fleming H. Revell. 1956.

Armstrong, Henry. "I Fought for Keeps." *Argosy*. October 1955.

Armstrong, Henry and Bill Libby. "Now I Fight for God." *Boxing Illustrated*. January 1964.

Ashe, Arthur, Jr. *A Hard Road to Glory: Boxing*. New York: Amistad. 1988.

Bak, Richard. *Joe Louis: The Great Black Hope*. New York: Da Capo. 1996.

Baker, Aaron. *Contesting Identities: Sports in American Film*. Urbana: University of Illinois Press. 2003.

Baker, Mark Allen. *Lou Ambers: A Biography of the World Lightweight Champion and Hall of Famer*. Jefferson: McFarland. 2021.

Borden, Eddie. "Henry Proves His Mettle." *The Ring*. May 1940.

Bromberg, Lester. "Armstrong Pilot Cracked Ban Here on Mixed Bouts." *The Knockout*. July 24, 1943.

Brown, David. "Henry Armstrong: Fighter for God." *Negro Digest*. January 1962.

Callis, Tracy and Chuck Johnston. *Boxing in the Los Angeles Area 1880-2005*. Victoria: Trafford. 2009.

Cannon, James. "Triple Champ." In H. Meyers (ed.) *The Big Fights* (pp. 120 – 122). New York: Avon. 1950.

Carroll, Ted. "Sable Sockers to the Fore." *The Ring*. March 1947

Carroll, Ted. "Sepian Sockers Supreme." *The Ring*. March 1939

Carroll, Ted. "Stamina – Is a Great Ring Asset," *The Ring* April 1940

Carroll, Ted. "Triple Champ Armstrong Has 'No Regrets'." *The Ring*. May 1959

Cavanagh, Douglas. *Pittsburgh Boxing: A Pictorial History*. Self-published. 2020.

Century, Douglas. *Barney Ross: The Life of a Jewish Fighter*. New York: nextbook. 2006.

Chafe, William H., Raymond Gavins, Robert Korstad, ed. *Remembering Jim Crow: African Americans Talk About Life in the Segregated South*. New York: The New Press. 2001.

Christie, Matt. "On This Day: Sugar Ray Robinson Beats a Shell of the Legendary Henry Armstrong." boxingnewsonline.net .

Cousins, Mark. *The Story of Film*. London: Pavilion. 2020.

Daley, Paul. "Henry Armstrong: The Story of the Hurricane." topclassboxing.com.

Daniel, Daniel M. "Armstrong Wins Ring's Most Valuable Award." *The Ring*. March 1938.

Daniel, Daniel M. "Hall of Fame." *The Ring*. October 1954.

Daniel, Daniel M. "Ring's Most Valuable Award to Louis." *The Ring*. March 1939.

Daniel, Daniel M. "Robinson Named The Fighter of the Year." *The Ring*. February 1942.

Dewey, Donald. *Ray Arcel: A Boxing Biography*. Jefferson: McFarland. 2012.

Dixon, Tris. *Damage: The Untold Story of Brain Trauma in Boxing*. Boston: Hamilcar. 2021.

Field, John and Earl Brown. "The Fight Racket." *Life*. June 17, 1946.

Dunphy, Don. *Don Dunphy at Ringside*. New York: Henry Holt. 1988.

Fitzgerald, Mike. *The Ageless Warrior: The Life of Boxing Legend Archie Moore*. Sports Publishing. 2004.

Fleischer, Nat. *50 Years at Ringside*. New York: Fleet. 1958.

Fleischer, Nat. "Armstrong at His Best." *The Ring*. April 1940.

Fleischer, Nat. "Armstrong's Feat Unique in Boxing." *The Ring*. August 1938.

Fleischer, Nat. *Black Dynamite, Vol. II: "Jolting Joe": The Amazing Story of Joe Louis and His Rise to the Heavyweight Title / "Homicide Hank": The Socking Saga of Henry Armstrong*. New York: Fleischer. 1938.

Fleischer, Nat. "Body Blows Whip Lew." *The Ring*. October 1940.

Fleischer, Nat. "Fighter of the Year Award Made to Billy Conn." *The Ring*. February 1941.

Fleischer, Nat. "Henry's Rally Too Late." *The Ring*. June 1943.

Fleischer, Nat. "History Repeats Itself." *The Ring*. November 1939.

Flesicher, Nat. "Louis Tops for 1939." *The Ring*. February 1940.

Fleischer, Nat. "Nat Fleischer Says." *The Ring*. May 1937.

Fleischer, Nat. "Nat Fleischer Says." *The Ring*, May 1939.

Fleischer, Nat. "Nat Fleischer Says." *The Ring*. July 1940.

Fleischer, Nat. "Nat Fleischer Says." *The Ring.* September 1942.
Fleischer, Nat. "Nat Fleischer Says." *The Ring.* January 1943.
Fleischer, Nat. "Nat Fleischer Says." *The Ring.* November 1943.
Fleischer, Nat. "Six World Championships Changed Hands in 1935." *The Ring.* February 1936.
Fleischer, Nat. "The Kid's Last Fight." *The Ring.* April 1941.
Fleischer, Nat. "Who Will Halt Henry?" *The Ring.* October 1938.
Fleischer, Nat. "Zivic's Novel Attack Wins." *The Ring.* December 1940.
Fleischer, Nat and Sam Andre. *An Illustrated History of Boxing.* 6th ed. New York: Citadel. 2001.
Frankenfield, W.C. "Rivers and Floods, May 1912," *Monthly Weather Review,* May 1912.
Fried, Ronald K. *Corner Men: Great Boxing Trainers.* New York: Four Walls Eight Windows.
Friedman, Jack and Lorenzo Benet. "Fifty Years After the Glory, Forgotten Legend Henry Armstrong Quietly Slips Out of the Ring." *People.* November 21, 1988.
Ganzel, Bill. "Riding the Rails." livinghistoryfarm.com.
Glass, Andrew. "Great Depression hits bottom, July 8, 1932." politico.com.
Graham, Frank. "They Called Him Hammerin' Hank." *Sport.* November 1952.
*Great Depression, The.* Captivating History. 2018.
Hauser, Thomas. "Henry Armstrong Revisited." *And the New: An Inside Look at Another Year in Boxing.* Fayetteville: University of Arkansas. 2012.
Haygood, Will. *Sweet Thunder: The Life and Times of Sugar Ray Robinson.* New York: Knopf. 2009.
Heinz, W.C. "The Greatest, Pound-for-Pound." *The Top of His Game: The Best Sportswriting of W.C. Heinz.* 2015.
Heller, Peter. *"In This Corner..!" 42 World Champions Tell Their Stories.* Cambridge: Da Capo. 1973.
Helliwell, Arthur. *The Private Lives of Famous Fighters.* Windsor Berks: Cedric Day. 1949.
Hietala, Thomas R. *The Fight of the Century: Jack Johnson, Joe Louis, and the Struggle for Racial Equality.* Armonk: M.E. Sharpe. 1994.
Horne, Gerald. *The Bittersweet Science: Racism, Racketeering, and the Political Economy of Boxing.* New York: International Publishers. 2021.
Kafka, Barney. "Scene in New York." *The Knockout.* June 26, 1943.
Lardner, David. "Notes on Sports." *The New Yorker,* June 10, 1944
Leonard, Sugar Ray and Michael Arkush. *The Big Fight: My Life In and Out of the Ring.* New York: Plume.
Liebling, A.J. and Harold Ross. "Training Camp." *The New Yorker.* August 30, 1935
Madden, Kevin. "Henry Armstrong." *Missouri Life.* January-February 1980.
Markson, Harry. "They Went Out Swinging." *The Ring.* April 1941.
McElvaine, Robert S. *The Great Depression: America 1929 – 1941.* New York: Three Rivers. 2009.
McHugh, Roy. *When Pittsburgh was a Fight Town.* Self-Published. 2019.
McNulty, John and Harold Ross. "Henry and Harry." *The New Yorker.* April 16, 1938.
Mee, Bob. *Boxing: Heroes and Champions.* Edison: Chartwell. 1997.
Mitchell, Kevin. *Jacobs Beach: The Mob, the Garden & the Golden Age of Boxing.* Boston: Hamilcar. 2009.
Monaco, James. *How to Read a Film: Movies, Media, and Beyond.* Oxford: Oxford University Press. 2009.
Moore, Archie. *Any Boy Can: The Archie Moore Story.* Englewood Cliffs; Prentice-Hall. 1971.
Moore, Archie. *The Archie Moore Story.* New York: McGraw-Hill. 1960.
Mullan, Harry. *The Big Book of Boxing.* New York: Crescent. 1987.
Mullins, Robert. *Beau Jack: The Boxing Life of Sidney Walker, Two-Time Lightweight Champion.* Jefferson: McFarland. 2020.
Mydans, Carl. "Speaking of Pictures…." *Life,* January 31, 1938
Nagler, Barney. "Hammerin' Henry Armstrong." *Sport.* June 1963.
Nash, Gary B., Cynthia J. Shelton, et al. *The Private Side of American Life: Since 1865.* San Diego: Harcourt. 1987.
"New Wonder of the Ring? Armstrong Lives Up to Name of 'Perpetual Motion.'" *Newsweek.* June 13, 1938.
Newland, Christina. "Jockey Fighter Actor Activist: The Short, Brilliant Life of Canada Lee." *Ringside Seat: Review.* 2021.
O'Toole, Andrew. *Sweet William: The Life of Billy Conn.* Urbana: University of Illinois. 2008.

"On This Day: One of Boxing's Absolute Greatest, Henry Armstrong, Died at the Age 75." boxingnewsonline.net

Pantalone, Gene. *From Boxing Ring to Battlefield: The Life of War Hero Lew Jenkins.* Lanham: Roman & Littlefield.

Richards, Robert R. "Homicide Hank." *Fight Stories.* Fall 1947.

Roberts, James B. and Alexander G. Skutt. *The Boxing Register: International Boxing Hall of Fame Record Book.* Ithaka: McBooks. 2006.

Roberts, Randy. *Joe Louis: Hard Times Man.* New Haven: Yale. 2010.

Robinson, Sugar Ray and Dave Anderson. *Sugar Ray.* Boston: Da Capo. 1970.

Robinson, T. and Harold Ross. "Comment." *The New Yorker.* July 19, 1940.

Rodney, Lester. "What They Forgot to Tell About Joe Louis." *Detroit Metro-Times.* June 11-25, 1981.

Romano, Frederick. *The Boxing Filmography: American Features, 1920 – 2003.* Jefferson: McFarland. 2004.

Rosenfeld, Allen S. *Charley Burley: The Life and Hard Times of an Uncrowned Champion.* Bloomington: 1st Books Library. 2003.

Ross, Barney and Martin Abramson. *No Man Stands Alone: The True Story of Barney Ross.* Philadelphia: J.B. Lipincott. 1957.

Ryan, James. "Boxer Henry Armstrong Dead at 75." upi.com

Schulberg, Budd. *Ringside: A Treasury of Boxing Reportage.* Chicago: Dee. 2006.

Sharpe, Johnny. "Hank's Greatness Proved to British." *The Ring.* August 1939

Shocket, "The Turbulent Life of Henry Armstrong. *The Big Book of Boxing*, January 1975

Silver, Mike. *The Arc of Boxing: The Rise and Decline of the Sweet Science.* Jefferson: McFarland. 2008.

Smith, Mona. *Becoming Something: The Story of Canada Lee.* New York: Farrar, Straus and Giroux. 2004.

Soderman, Robert. "Year 1936 Results (Aug3-Sep5)." *International Boxing Research Organization Journal,* December 21, 2001.

Stradley, Don. "Baby and the Babes: Arizmendi's Wild Life in the Ring and Beyond." *The Ring* March 2009.

Stump, Al. "Hammerin' Henry: The Last of the Triple Champions." *Sport.* January 1955.

Sugar, Bert Randolph. *Bert Sugar's Punchlines.* Guilford: Lyons. 2014.

Sugar, Bert Randolph. *Boxing's Greatest Fighters.* Guilford: Lyons. 2006.

Sugar, Bert Randolph. *The Great Fights.* New York: Gallery Books. 1981.

Sugar, Bert Randolph. *The Ring 1980 Record Book.* The Ring. 1980.

Sussman, Jeffrey. *Boxing and the Mob: The Notorious History of the Sweet Science.* Lanham: Rowman & Littlefield. 2019.

Sustar, Lee. "Blacks and the Great Depression." socialworker.org

Suster, Gerald. *Lightning Strikes: The Lives and Times of Boxing's Lightweight Heroes.* London: Robson. 1994.

Tereba, Tere. *Mickey Cohen: The Life and Crimes of L.A.'s Notorious Mobster.* Toronto: ECW. 2012.

Toledo, Springs. *The Gods of War.* Tora Book Publishing. 2014.

Tulley, Jim. *A Dozen and One.* Hollywood: Murray & Gee. 1943.

Van, Young. "Van-O-Grams." *The Knockout.* March 6, 1943.

Vogan, Travis. *The Boxing Film: A Cultural and Transmedia History.* New Brunswick: Rutgers. 2021.

Ward, Geoffrey C. *Unforgivable Blackness: The Rise and Fall of Jack Johnson.* New York: Knopf. 2004.

Wright, Richard. "High Tide in Harlem: Joe Louis as a Symbol of Freedom." *The Hurt Business.* London: Aurum.

**Periodicals Referenced:**

Argosy; Arizona Daily Star; Arizona Republic; Arizona Sun; Atlantic City Press; Baltimore Evening Sun; Bangor Daily News; Bartlesville Morning Examiner; Beatrice Daily Sun; Bennington Evening Banner; Berkshire Eagle; Big Book of Boxing; Boston Globe; Boxoffice; Boxing Illustrated; Brooklyn Daily Eagle; Buffalo Evening News; California Eagle; Chicago Bee; Chicago Defender; Chicago Tribune; Chippewa Herald-Telegram; Coos Bay World; Davenport Quad City Times; Detroit Free Press; Detroit Tribune; Evansville Courier and Press; Fight Stories; Hansford Sentinel; Harrisburg Sunday Courier; Hartford Courant; Hawaii Tribune-Herald; Hazelton Standard-Speaker; Hazleton Plain Speaker; Hill Top Times; Imperial Valley Press; International Boxing Research Organization Journal; Knockout; La Opinion; Leicester Evening Mail; Life; Liverpool Daily Post; London Evening Standard; London Guardian; Long Beach Sun; Long Beach Telegram; Longview News-Journal; Los Angeles Evening Citizen News; Los Angeles Evening Express; Los Angeles Evening Post Record; Los Angeles Herald-Examiner; Los Angeles Mirror; Los Angeles Times; Mason City Globe-Gazette; Medford Mail Tribune; Miami Herald; Miami News; Minneapolis Star; Missouri Life; Modesto Bee and News-Herald; Montana Helena Independent; Montana Standard; Napa Journal; New York Age; New York Daily News; New York Times; Newark Advocate; Newsweek; Oakland Tribune; Ogden Standard-Examiner; Omaha Morning Bee-News; Orlando Evening Star; Pomona Progress Bulletin; Pasadena Post; Passaic Herald-News; Paterson News; Petaluma Argus-Courier; Philadelphia Inquirer; Pittsburgh Courier; Pittsburgh Post-Gazette; Pittsburgh Press; Pottsville Evening Herald; Redding Record Searchlight; Richmond News Leader; Ridgewood Herald News; Ring, The; Ringside Seat; Rochester Democrat and Chronicle; Sacramento Bee; Salt Lake City Deseret News; San Francisco Examiner; San Luis Obispo Telegram-Tribune; San Pedro News-Pilot; Santa Ana Register; Santa Maria Times; Santa Rosa Press Democrat; Seattle Star; Shamokin News Dispatch; South Bend Tribune; South Florida Sun-Sentinel; Spokane Spokesman-Review; Sport; Springfield News-Leader; Springfield News-Sun; St. Louis Post-Dispatch; St. Louis Star and Times; Venice Evening Vanguard; Ventura County Star; Washington Evening Star; Waterford Democrat; Wilmington Daily Press Journal; Wilmington News-Journal; Winnipeg Tribune

**Websites Used:**

ancestry.com; baseball-almanac.com; bible.com; boxing360.com; boxrec.com; boxingnewsonline.net; britannica.com; census.gov; chroniclingamerica.loc.gov; cyberboxingzone.com; dglobe.com; books.google.com; henryarmstrongfoundation.org; history.com; ibhof.com; latimes.com; legacy.com; livinghistoryfarm.org; njboxinghof.org; news.google.com; newspapers.com; newyorker.com; nytimes.com; politico.com; pubmed.ncbi.nlm.nih.gov; sabr.org; shsmo.org; socialworker.org; sun-sentinel.com; time.com; topclassboxing.com; upi.com; youtube.com

# Index

1924 Paris Olympics · 86
1932 Los Angeles Olympics · 47
1932 Olympic trials · 44, 45, 46
1936 Berlin Olympics · 62, 82, 164
1939 New York World's Fair · 151
*20 Years of Poems, Moods, and Meditations*, book · 267
*42nd Street*, film · 66

Abad, Davey · 57, 67, 85, 289, 290
Abrams, Georgie · 165, 217
Abramson, Jesse · 116, 248
Abramson, Martin · 118
Ackerman, Meyer · 222
Adams, Caswell · 202
Adams, Ida May · 264, 266
Adonis, Joey · 68
Africa · 226
Akins, Virgil · 23
Alabama · 216
Albany, NY · 275
Albert, Eddie · 253
Alcanter, Joey · 73, 290
Alexander, Devon · 23
Ali, Muhammad · 8, 271, 275, 278, 280, 283-286
    Armstrong's opinions of · 275, 278
    vs. Sonny Liston · 273, 275
Allen, Johnny · 230
Amateur Athletic Union (AAU) · 32, 34, 43, 45, 243
Ambers, Lou · 77, 89, 102, 103, 124, 127, 132-134, 140-143, 145, 149, 150 - 158, 161, 163-168, 180, 182, 185, 194, 204, 217, 268, 291
    and death of Tony Scarpati · 126
    early life · 124
    fighting style · 126
    later life and death · 183
    vs. Henry Armstrong · 128-131, 151-156
    vs. Lew Jenkins · 182, 183
    vs. Pedro Montanez · 169
    vs. Tony Canzoneri · 126
American Broadcasting Company (ABC) · 267
American Federation of Labor · 25
*Amsterdam News* · 256
Anderson, Dave · 281
Angott, Sammy · 92, 138, 141, 143, 145, 182, 194, 195, 225, 230, 237, 238, 241, 244, 254, 292
    fighting style · 238
    later life and death · 241
    vs. Fritzie Zivic · 195
    vs. Henry Armstrong · 239, 240
    vs. Willie Pep · 238
Apollo Theater, New York City, NY · 158
Apostoli, Fred · 88, 150, 172, 217
Arana, Ventura · 55, 289
Arcel, Ray · 107, 108, 113, 115, 126, 164, 204, 285
    training of Henry Armstrong · 204, 206, 208, 209
Archer, Freddie · 221
Arguello, Alexis · 281
Arizmendi, Baby · 41, 53-57, 59, 62, 64, 65, 68, 70, 74, 76, 83, 99-101, 124, 126, 127, 141, 142, 150, 166, 174, 194, 238, 267, 268, 289-291
    later life · 143
    vs. Henry Armstrong · 53-57, 61, 99-101, 142, 143

Arizona · 232
*Arizona Republic* · 266
Arlington National Cemetery, Washington, DC · 228, 280
Armstrong, Gussie · 269, 280, 281, 283, 284
Armstrong, Harry · 31, 32, 34, 39-41, 43, 45, 51, 54, 55, 56, 61, 65, 73, 75, 78, 93, 98, 104, 130, 142, 145, 161, 174, 187, 204, 205, 208-210, 215, 219, 258, 260, 261
Armstrong, Henry
  alcoholism · 74, 215, 261, 263, 264
  amateur career · 32, 34, 41-44
  and George Raft Caravan · 218, 258
  and Henry Armstrong Sports Unit 500 · 256, 257
  and racism · 40, 80, 82
  as boxing trainer, manager, and promoter · 251, 252, 258-262, 269-274, 276, 277
  as hero to Black America · 10, 61, 62, 82, 93, 118, 119, 173, 192, 286
  as hobo · 40
  as husband · 53, 265, 269
  as preacher · 265, 266, 267, 274, 277, 278, 286
  autobiography · 268, 274
  birthdate confusion · 13
  childhood · 13, 14, 16, 18, 20, 21
  combating racism · 172, 286
  death · 284
  divorce · 269
  fighter of the year awards · 94, 203
  fighting style · 43, 61, 79, 95, 112, 119
  film roles · 158-161, 214, 258
  friendship with Beau Jack · 214, 233
  friendship with Joe Louis · 104, 120, 204
  friendship with Ray Robinson · 241, 246
  health issues · 267, 281, 283
  marries Gussie Henry · 280
  marries Velma Tart · 274
  marries Willa Mae Shandy · 53
  military service · 256, 257
  nervous breakdown · 98
  personality · 146, 286
  poetry · 105, 263, 267
  popularity · 8, 93, 99, 224
  religious experiences · 16, 118, 264
  vs. Al Iovino · 36
  vs. Al Manfredo · 165
  vs. Al Tribuani · 233
  vs. Aldo Spoldi · 253, 254
  vs. Alf Blatch · 83
  vs. Baby Arizmendi · 53-57, 61, 99-101, 142, 143
  vs. Baby Casanova · 76
  vs. Barney Ross · 111-115
  vs. Beau Jack · 234, 235
  vs. Benny Bass · 85
  vs. Bobby Pacho · 144
  vs. Bummy Davis · 253
  vs. Ceferino Garcia · 139, 176-178
  vs. Chalky Wright · 99
  vs. Chester Slider · 254, 255
  vs. Davey Day · 145
  vs. Eddie Trujillo · 49
  vs. Enrico Venturi · 96
  vs. Ernie Roderick · 147-149
  vs. Frankie Klick · 82
  vs. Fritzie Zivic · 197-200, 206-208, 223
  vs. Gene Espinosa · 49
  vs. Howard Scott · 166
  vs. Jimmy Garrison · 166, 167, 243, 253
  vs. Joe Gnouly · 168

vs. Joey Alcanter · 74
vs. Juan Zurita · 64
vs. Kid Moro · 50, 51
vs. Lew Feldman · 144
vs. Lew Jenkins · 188-190, 226
vs. Lou Ambers · 128-131, 151-156
vs. Midget Wolgast · 59
vs. Mike Belloise · 71, 78, 254
vs. Paul Junior · 180, 181
vs. Pedro Montanez · 170, 171
vs. Perfecto Lopez · 45, 49, 52
vs. Petey Sarron · 91
vs. Phil Furr · 197
vs. Ralph Zannelli · 253
vs. Ray Robinson · 246-248
vs. Ritchie Fontaine · 60, 166
vs. Sammy Angott · 239, 240
vs. Sammy Burns · 37
vs. Slugger White · 254
vs. Tippy Larkin · 232
vs. Tony Chavez · 74, 76, 94
vs. Wally Hally · 83
vs. Willie Joyce · 230, 231, 243, 253, 254
womanizing · 150, 162, 251, 269
Armstrong, Lanetta · 57, 73, 94, 145, 173, 215, 242, 265, 268, 269, 274, 283
Armstrong, Louis · 80, 121, 212
Armstrong, Velma · 31, 274, 278, 281
Armstrong, Willa Mae · 53, 55, 57, 73, 75, 93, 94, 119, 146, 173, 215, 242, 243, 251, 261, 265, 268, 269, 274
Aron, Milt · 163, 171, 180, 193
Arroyo, Louis · *See* Cocoa Kid
Arum, Bob · 281
Associated Booking Corporation (ABC) · 212
Associated Press · 47 ,72, 120, 127, 137, 147, 177, 203, 236, 237, 248
Atlanta, GA · 193
Atlantic City, NJ · 119
*Atlantic Monthly* · 35
Atlas, Teddy · 285
Attell, Abe · 107
Augusta National Golf Club, Augusta, GA · 212, 214
Augusta, GA · 213

Baer, Max · 8, 76, 88, 89, 103, 107, 204, 223, 269
Baker Bowl, Philadelphia, PA · 84
Baker, Josephine · 162
Balogh, Harry · 91, 211
Baltimore, MD · 143, 211, 233
Barcelona, Spain · 164
Barnes Hospital, St. Louis, MO · 278
Barnum and Bailey's Circus · 87
Barrera, Joe · 288
Barrow, Clyde · 185
Barrow, Joseph · *See* Louis, Joe
Bascon, Severo · *See* Kid Moro
baseball · 8, 10
Basie, Count · 121, 212
Bass, Benny · 84, 85, 94, 168, 290
Battaglia, Christopher · *See* Battalino, Battling
Battalino, Battling · 64, 166
battle royals · 32, 213, 214, 286
Battling Shaw · 54
Battling Siki · 29
Beale, Pee Wee · 204
Beauhold, Billy · 94, 290

Beck, Jules · 35, 37, 38, 85
Belloise, Mike · 54, 64, 65, 70-72, 77, 78, 79, 90, 93, 94, 185, 254, 290, 292
Bennison, Ben · 146
Berg, Jackie "Kid" · 169
Berger, Maxie · 141, 193
Bergerren, Ace · 43, 288
Beshore, Freddie · 69
Bessemer, PA · 163
Bier, Dr. Joseph · 104
Bimstein, Whitey · 126
Birmingham, AL · 86
*Birth of a Nation, The*, film · 17, 18, 19, 28
Bivins, Jimmy · 165, 271
Black Bottom, Detroit, MI · 243
Black, Alton · 59
Blackburn, Jack · 109, 120, 121
Blackwell, Otto · 174
Black, Alton · 290
Blades, Freddie · 270
Blake, George · 176-179
Blatch, Alf · 84, 290
Bloody Ridge, Korean War · 226, 227
*Body and Soul*, film · 118, 160
Bogart, Humphrey · 186
Bojangles · *See* Robinson, William "Bojangles"
Bolo Sluggers softball team · 120
Bonk, Thomas · 282
Booker, Eddie · 193, 223
Boon, Eric · 141
Bor, Nat · 174
Borden, Eddie · 177, 178
Boston Gardens, Boston, MA · 180, 181
*Boston Globe* · 181
Boston, MA · 180, 242, 253
Bowdry, Jesse · 269, 271-274
    vs. Freddy Blades · 270
    vs. Harold Johnson · 272
    vs. Willie Pastrano · 271
boxing · 9, 41, 42, 44, 86, 96, 107
    and racism · 9, 27, 32, 80, 81, 120
*Boxing Illustrated* · 224, 248, 276
Boxing Writers Association of New York · 203
Braddock, James · 76, 89, 103, 107, 110, 143, 144, 284
Bradley, Ruby · 57
Braverman, Al · 126
Brewster Center, Detroit, MI · 243
Brietz, Eddie · 177
Brigham, UT · 260
Brink, Eddie · 85, 150, 290
British Guiana · 122
Broadway, New York City, NY · 87
Bromberg, Lester · 258
Bronx, New York City, NY · 185, 228
*Brooklyn Daily Eagle* · 233, 259
Brooklyn Dodgers · 277
Brooklyn, New York City, NY · 144, 205, 225, 258
Brown, Buzz · 290
Brown, Earl · 87
Brown, Joe E. · 267
Brown, Joey · 94, 290
Brown, Newsboy · 54
Brown, Otha · 273
Brown, Randy · 205
Brown, Tommy · 96, 98, 290

Brownsville, New York City, NY · 182, 204, 253
Buckley, Robert "Jaimaica Kid" · 29
Buffalo Bill's Wild West Show · 87
Buffalo, NY · 94, 97
Buntag, Bunny · 36
Burbank, CA · 173
Burch, James "Jimmy" · 32, 34, 288
Burke, Billy · 223, 255
Burke, Jackie · 221, 292
Burley, Charley · 141, 163-165, 193, 194, 202, 221, 222, 238
Burley, Dan · 256
Burma · 256
Burman, Clarence "Red" · 84, 211
Burnes, Bob · 266, 280
Burns, Charley · 85, 100, 164, 290, 291
Burns, Sammy · 37, 289
Burns, Tommy · 27
Buss, Jerry · 283
Butler, James · 147, 148
Butte, MT · 100
Byrd, Jackie · 292
Byrd, Terry · 262
Byzick, Al · 284

Cabello, Johnny · 85, 290
Calcutta, India · 256, 258
California · 173, 174, 209, 211, 215, 217, 220, 222, 225, 239, 242, 253, 258, 262, 268, 269, 271, 284, 286
*California Eagle* · 219
California Medical Center, Los Angeles, CA · 283
California State Athletic Commission · 41, 51, 52, 58, 173, 175, 177, 242, 250, 253, 256
*California Voice* · 60
Callahan, Mushy · 218
Calloway, Cab · 121, 159
Calmes, Bobby · 289
Calzaghe, Joe · 252
Canigata, Leonard · *See* Lee, Canada
Cannon, Jimmy · 87, 121, 131, 132
Canzoneri, Tony · 54, 77, 84, 102, 107, 125-127, 136, 168
Caplin, Hymie · 185, 188, 190, 191
Capone, Al · 106
Carnera, Primo · 69, 76, 103, 104
Carondolet, MO · 26, 39
Carpentier, Georges · 88
Carroll, Ted · 140, 171, 220, 286
Carter, Jack · 83, 290
Carter, Joe · 288
*Casablanca*, film · 158
Casablanca, Morocco · 257
Casanova, Rodolfo "Baby" · 56, 76, 289, 290
Castillo, Frankie · 96, 290
Castro, Bobby · 261
Cavanaugh, Billy · 115, 129, 130, 145 171, 182, 235
Cebu City, Philippines · 137
Center Avenue YMCA, Pittsburgh, PA · 35
Century City Hospital, Los Angeles, CA · 282
Cerdan, Marcel · 141, 149, 163
Champion Dynamiters softball team · 120
Chaplin, Charlie · 65
Chargin, Don · 274
Charles, Ezzard · 69, 107, 271
Chase National Bank · 24
Chase, Jack · 165
Chatman, Henrietta · 13, 21, 23, 26, 30, 35, 38, 57
Chatman, Henry · 13

Chavez, Julio Cesar · 283
Chavez, Tony · 65, 74-76, 94, 144, 166, 174, 290
Cherbourg, France · 146
*Chicago Defender* · 34, 172
Chicago Stadium, Chicago, IL · 253
Chicago, IL · 38, 41, 88, 96, 100, 103, 105, 109, 117, 145, 154, 161, 185, 222, 238, 262
Chile · 192
China · 256
Chip, George · 35
Chronic Traumatic Encephalopathy (CTE) · 280, 283
Cincinnati, OH, USA · 143
*Cinderella Man*, film · 285
Cisneros, Chico · 38
Citrino, Al · 100, 290
Civic Auditorium, San Francisco, CA · 222, 223, 231
Civic Auditorium, Seattle, WA · 166
Clacton-on-Sea, UK · 146
Clark, Jeff · 29
Clark, Tony · 166
Clay, Cassius Jr. · *See* Ali, Muhammad
Clein, John · 158, 159
Cleveland, OH · 94, 97, 140, 167
Club Plantation, New York, NY · 93
Cluney, John A. · 234
Cobb, Ty · 267
Cochrane, Freddie "Red" · 215, 217, 221, 222, 224, 231, 244, 253
Cocoa Kid · 126, 164, 165, 180, 193, 196, 202, 221, 222
Cohen, Mickey · 67
Colorado · 221
Columbia, MO · 277
Columbus, MS · 19, 20
Columbus, OH · 143
Concord, CA · 227
Conde, Joe · 55, 59, 76, 289, 290
Coney Island, New York City, NY · 87
Conn, Billy · 151, 168, 204, 215, 217, 222, 238
Conrad, Harold · 259
Considine, Bob · 233
Convention Hall, Philadelphia, PA · 233
Coolidge, Calvin · 24
Cooper, Gary · 121
Cooper, R.R. · 264
Copeland, Ernie · 256, 262
Corbett, Dick · 65
Cornell University, Ithaca, NY · 256
Corpuz, Clarence "Young Corpus" · 49, 289
Corum, Bill · 202, 236
Corvo, Tully · 289
Cosmos Hotel, Mexico City, Mexico · 54
Costello, Frank · 68
Cotton Club, New York City, NY · 159
Council on African Affairs · 242
Cousins, Mark · 66
Covelli, Kid · 290
Covey, Jules · 177
Cox, Tom · 42, 43, 45, 46, 48, 173, 176
Crisp, Melvin · 174
Cronin, Ned · 174, 177, 231
Crowley, Dave · 71
Cuba · 144
Cuddy, Jack · 236, 237
Curtin, Johnny · 220

D'Ambrosio, Antonio · 124

D'Ambrosio, Luigi · *See* Ambers, Lou
Dade, Harold · 260
Dado, Speedy · 41, 50, 54, 57, 76
Dagupa, Gene · 288
Daley, Arthur · 233
Dallas, TX · 238
Dalton brothers · 47
Dandridge, Dorothy · 162
Daniel, Daniel M. · 94, 228
Daniels, Sammy · 233
Darcy, Les · 36
Davis, Al "Bummy" · 150, 182, 183, 203, 225, 228, 253, 292
    vs. Fritzie Zivic · 204
    vs. Henry Armstrong · 253
Davis, Sammy Jr. · 268, 274
Dawson, James · 96, 129, 151, 156, 169, 171, 191
Day, Davey · 141, 145, 167, 169, 182, 194, 238, 291
Dean, Bobby · 85, 290
Dearborn, MI · 46
Decker, Bobby · 288
DeFoe, Johnny · 85, 289, 290
DeGrasse, Pete · 82, 290
Delaney, Herbert · 241
Delia, Mike · 216
Dempsey, Jack · 8, 9, 26, 39, 51, 65, 76, 88, 89, 121, 123, 124, 136, 150, 151, 183, 212, 251, 267, 285
Des Moines Coliseum, Des Moines, IA · 165
Des Moines, IA · 165, 253
*Destination Freedom*, radio program · 262
Detroit, MI · 80, 85, 89, 97, 101, 243, 244
Dewey, Thomas E. · 121
Diaz, Mark · 83, 290
Dickens, Doles · 262
Dickmann, Bernard · 73
Dickson Quartet · 262
DiMaggio, Joe · 110, 121
Dixon, George · 90, 149
Dixon, Randy · 192
Dixon, Tris · 252
Dolan, Eddie · 164
Don Redman Orchestra · 212
Donald, Dick · 60
Donovan, Arthur · 91, 96, 110, 113-115, 121, 139, 140, 152-157, 188-190, 197, 199, 200, 207-209
Doyle, Jack · 60
Dragna, Jack · 68
Drake, Frances · 69
Dressen, Chuck · 267
Drouillard, Orville · 85, 290
Du Bois, W.E.B. · 10, 18
Du Valle, Jimmy · 36
Dublin, Ireland · 87
Dubuque, IA · 142
Dumer, Bill · 37
Dundee, Angelo · 271
Dundee, Chris · 270
Dundee, George · 49, 289
Dundee, Johnny · 253
Duran, Roberto · 107

East River, NY · 103
Eastside Arena, Los Angeles, CA · 73
Eaton, Cal · 229
Echevarria, Joe · 197
Echeverria, Fillo · 65
Edwards, Danny · 220

El Toreo de Cuatro Caminos, Mexico City, Mexico · 56
Ellington, Duke · 121, 212
England · 146, 147, 150, 168
Engotti, Salvatore · *See* Angott, Sammy
Erwin, Jimmy · 89
Escobar, Sixto · 88
Espinosa, Bill · 288
Espinosa, Gene · 49, 73, 289, 290
*Esquire* · 260
European Boxing Union (EBU) · 64, 150

Fairbanks, Douglas · 121
Federal Bureau of Investigation (FBI) · 68, 174, 217
Feldman, Lew · 101, 127, 144, 150, 168, 185, 291
Fidler, Alex · 166
Field, John · 87
Fields, Jackie · 41, 107
Fields, W.C. · 47
Fifth Avenue Fashion Show, New York, NY · 87
Fifth Street Gym, Miami, FL · 272
First Baptist Church, St. Louis, MO · 277
Fischer, Eddie · 118
Fitzpatrick, Fitzie · 261
Fitzsimmons, Bob · 136
Flanagan, Edward · 267
Fleischer, Nat · 7, 40, 49, 59, 64, 79, 86, 90, 94, 113, 115, 140, 145, 150, 154, 156, 167, 171, 180, 191, 200, 202, 204, 206, 208, 209, 221, 224, 234-237, 250
Fleming H. Revell Company · 268
Fontaine, Ritchie · 60, 166, 290, 291
Fontana, CA · 98, 162
Foord, Benny · 222, 234
*Footlight Parade*, film · 66
Forbes Field, Pittsburgh, PA · 195, 196
Ford, Wallace · 267
Foreman, George · 278
Fort Bliss, TX · 184
Fort George Meade, MD · 217
Fort Huachuca, AZ · 232
Foster, Eddie · 31, 32, 35, 36, 38, 39
France · 122, 149, 168, 209
Frazier, Joe · 280
Free Milk Fund for Babies · 88
Fresh Air Gym, Pittsburgh, PA · 36
Fresno, CA · 255
Frierson, Clarice · 14
Frierson's Chapel, Lowndes County, MS · 15
Frogley, Ken · 99
*From Boxing Ring to Battlefield*, book · 187
Fullam, Frank · 155, 156
Fuller, Sammy · 126
Furr, Phil · 169, 193, 196, 291
Futch, Eddie · 164

Gable, Clark · 54, 65, 121
Gainford, George · 228, 243, 246
Gains, Larry · 29
Gallucci, Frank · 46, 288
Gandhi, Mahatma · 174
Gans, Joe · 13, 32, 90, 149
Ganzon, Tommy · 290
Garcia, Ceferino · 50, 89, 103, 108, 120, 137, 141, 168, 172-175, 178, 179, 180, 183, 184, 196, 214, 218, 283, 291
  early life · 138
  later life and death · 179

    vs. Barney Ross · 138
    vs. Henry Armstrong · 139, 176-178
Garcia, Cipriano · *See* Garcia, Ceferino
Garcia, Jimmie · 42, 288
Garfield, John · 160, 230
Garrison, Jimmy · 166, 167, 173, 243, 253, 258, 291, 292
Garrison, Tommy · 277
Gary, IN · 172, 230
Gearns, Jimmy · 240
Germany · 120, 122, 149
Gherig, Lou · 8
Gibson, Terry · 239
Giles, Willie · 272
Gilmore Stadium, Hollywood, CA · 173, 175, 242
Gilmore, Fred · 51
Gish, Lillian · 17
Glasser, Joe · 212
*Gloves, Glory and God*, book · 7, 268
Gnouly, Joe · 168, 291
Godfrey, George · 29
Godon, Charley · 104
Godoy, Arturo · 192
Goebbels, Joseph · 120
*Gold Diggers of 1933*, film · 66
Golden West Hotel, Portland, OR · 220
Goldman, Charley · 103, 126
Gonzalez, Babe · 288
Goodman, Benny · 212
Gorman, Joe · 232
Graham, Billy · 267
Grajade, Joe · 45, 288
Gramby, Joe · 233
Granone, Johnny · 289
Grant, Archie · 42
Graziano, Rocky · 268
Great Depression · 8, 9, 10, 23, 24, 25, 26, 39, 41, 42, 46, 61, 80, 96, 107, 159, 161, 184, 188, 230, 234, 243, 285
Greb, Harry · 9, 35, 95
Green, Abe · 282
Green, Harold · 258
Greenburg, Benny · 73
Greenfield, Al · 49, 289
Greenlee, Gus · 38, 206
Greenwood Lake, NJ · 186, 204
Griffin, Babe · 219
Griffith Stadium, Washington, DC · 196
Griffith, D.W. · 17
Grossinger's Resort, Catskill, NY · 186
Grover, Red · 36
Guadalcanal, Philippines · 117, 226, 227, 237
Guam · 257

Haberski, George · 289
Hall, Freeman · 14
Hall, Ricky · 289
Hally, Wally · 83, 182, 290
Halsy, Pat · 79
Hamilton, Fred · 185
Hampton, Lionel · 212
Hanbury, Lew · 292
Hank, Henry · 269
Hankinson, Hank · 52
Hardwick, Herbert · *See* Cocoa Kid
Harlem, New York City, NY · 93, 107, 118, 122, 158, 204, 206, 241, 243, 244, 245, 262

Harman, Allan · 273
Harrell, Willie · 18
Harringay Arena, London, UK · 147
Harris, Phil · 267
Harris, William "Woogy" · 35
Hartford, CT · 214
Hauser, Thomas · 274
Havana, Cuba · 143
Hawaii · 136, 217
Hawkins, Burton · 85
Hawkins, Coleman · 212
Haygood, Wil · 241, 278
Healy, Bill · 155, 235, 240
Heartbreak Ridge, Korean War · 227
Hearst, William Randolph · 88
Heinz, W.C. · 194, 263
Hell's Kitchen, New York City, NY · 243
Heller, Joseph · 191
Heller, Peter · 78, 97, 130, 186, 194, 199, 224
Hemingway, Ernest · 121
Henderson, Fletcher · 212
Henry Armstrong Sports Unit No. 500 · *See* Armstrong, Henry
Henry Armstrong Youth Foundation · 266, 267, 268, 274
Henry, Bill · 72, 142
Henry, Gussie · *See* Armstrong, Gussie
Herbert Hoover Boys Club, St. Louis, MO · 277, 278, 279
Herkimer, NY, USA · 124
Hernandez, Henry · 49, 288
Hernandez, Manuel · 288
Hernandez, Sal · 57, 289
Hickey Park, Millvale, PA · 37, 85, 164
Hill District, Pittsburgh, PA · 37, 38, 163
Hines, Earl · 251
Hines, Johnny · 45, 288
Hippodrome, New York, NY · 88, 138
Hitchcock, Alfred · 160
Hitler, Adolf · 82, 120
Holden, William · 253
Holiday, Billie · 212
Holland, Jerome "Bud" · 256
Hollywood Legion · 172, 173, 176, 220
Hollywood Legion Stadium, Hollywood, CA · 54, 258
*Hollywood Post* · 173
Hollywood, CA · 66, 96, 118, 173, 217, 230, 238, 252, 279
Holman, W.E. · 267, 268
Holmes, Cal · 170
Holmes, Larry · 107
Holtzer, Maurice · 59, 64, 65
Home Box Office (HBO) · 283
Honolulu, HI · 57, 217
Hoover, Herbert · 24, 46
Hoover, J. Edgar · 121
Hope diamond · 121
Horne, Lena · 81, 159, 162
Hostak, Al · 168, 172, 217
Hot Springs Resort, Little Rock, AR · 150
Hot Springs, AR · 150, 203, 204, 237, 250
Hudkins, Ace · 41
Hudson, Cecil · 252, 258-262
Hughes, Langston · 65, 105, 160
Hull, Chuck · 283, 284
Hulls, Sydney · 145
Humphries, Joe · 209
Hursey, Elijah "Smuggy" · 262

Hurwitz, Hy · 181
Hyland, Dick · 174

Igoe, Hype · 206, 246
Independence, TX · 220
India · 256
Indiana · 231
Indianapolis, IN · 57
Infantile Paralysis Fund · 253
Internal Revenue Service (IRS) · 242
International Boxing Hall of Fame, Canastota, NY · 59, 85, 92, 100, 118, 165, 171, 179, 184, 193, 224, 228, 236, 241, 249
Iovino, Al · 36, 37, 85, 128, 209, 289
Italy · 77, 95, 149, 168, 228

Jack, Beau · 202, 212, 229-231, 233, 234, 236-239, 241, 292
    early life · 213
    fighting style · 214
    friendship with Henry Armstrong · 214, 233
    later life and death · 236
    rivalry with Bob Montgomery · 236
    vs. Henry Armstrong · 234, 235
Jackman, Joan · 150
Jackson, America · 14, 15, 19, 20
Jackson, Dynamite · 41
Jackson, Henrietta · 21, 25, 73, 75, 268
Jackson, Henry Jr. · *See* Armstrong, Henry
Jackson, Henry Sr. · 13, 19, 26, 57, 176, 178, 215, 242, 257
Jackson, Melody · *See* Armstrong, Henry
Jackson, Ollus · 14, 19
Jackson, Oscar · 19
Jackson, Sammy · 170
Jackson, Young Peter · 41, 47, 50, 138, 169, 181
Jacobs, Mike · 86-89, 93, 96, 97, 102, 103, 107-110, 117, 120, 124, 127, 132, 136, 139, 150, 156, 161, 170, 173, 180, 185-187, 191, 193, 195-197, 203, 206, 211, 222, 224, 228, 233, 237, 238, 241, 242, 244-246, 258, 259
    "Carnival of Champions" promotion · 88, 89, 126, 13
    early life and rise to power· 86-89
    personality · 87
Jadick, Johnny · 126, 181, 193
Jamaica · 122
James, Ida · 262
Jannazzo, Izzy ·108, 180, 193, 244
*Jazz Singer, The*, film · 65
Jeffra, Harry · 88
Jeffries Arena, Burbank, CA · 43
Jeffries, James · 28, 41, 88, 218
Jenkins, Katie · 185, 186, 191, 225
Jenkins, Lew · 185, 187, 191, 192, 193, 194, 204, 230, 231, 238, 291, 292
    early life · 184
    later life and death · 228
    military service · 184, 225-227
    reckless lifestyle · 185, 186, 225
    vs. Henry Armstrong · 188-190, 226
    vs. Lou Ambers · 182, 183
Jenkins, Verlin · *See* Jenkins, Lew
Jesberg, Simon · 242, 248
Jessup, Tommy · 237, 292
Jim Crow laws · 17-19, 31, 161, 286
*Joe Palooka, Champ*, film · 258
Johnson, Gene · 170, 251
Johnson, Harold · 271, 272
Johnson, Jack · 22, 27, 28, 30, 32, 81, 82, 88, 121, 123, 218
Johnson, Larry · 38

Johnson, Mae E. · 159
Johnson, Roy · 34, 288
Johnston, Jimmy · 88, 89, 156, 169
Jolson, Al · 65, 68-70, 72, 84, 90, 101, 140, 141, 162, 215, 261
Jones, Bobby · 212, 214
Jones, Hoyt · 289
Jones, Johnny · 94, 290, 292
Joseph, Eddie · 239, 240
Joyce, Willie · 229, 230-232, 240, 292
Joyner, Herschel · 142
Junior, Paul · 180, 181, 291

Kansas City, MO · 39, 73, 166, 252, 253, 261
Kaplan, Hymie · 186
Kaplan, Kid · 193
Kaplan, Mike · 163, 193
Keeler, Ruby · 66, 67
*Keep Punching*, film · 158, 159, 161, 215
Kennedy, Les · 41
Ketchum, Willie · 185, 186, 225
Kid Azteca · 76
Kid Chocolate · 10, 30, 35, 73, 76, 82, 85, 90, 93, 168
Kid Moro · 50, 51, 55, 289
Kiel Auditorium, St. Louis, MO · 254
Kiernan, John · 86
Kilrain, Jake · 141
King Solomon · 47
Klaus, Frank · 35
Klick, Frankie · 82, 94, 107, 126, 166, 290
Korean War · 226, 227
Ku Klux Klan · 17, 18

La Barba, Jess · 46, 288
La Morte, Willy · 57
La Salle, Kenny · 163
LaBarba, Fidel · 41, 54, 143, 179, 218, 267
LaGuardia, Fiorello · 121
Lakewood, NJ · 170
LaMotta, Jake · 150, 224, 228, 244, 260
Lancaster, PA · 59
Langford, Sam · 29, 191
Lardner, David · 253
Larkin, Tippy · 141, 185, 231-233, 292
Las Vegas, NV · 277
Latsios, Nick · 254, 292
Law, Joe · 170
Lawless, Thomas "Bucky" · 36
Lawrenceville, PA · 194
LeCron, George · 115, 131, 236
Lee, Canada · 159, 160, 286
Leon, Frankie · 288
Leonard, Benny · 9, 76, 107, 127, 136, 174, 191, 204, 234, 285
Leonard, Ray · 252
Lesnevich, Gus · 217
Leto, Jimmy · 126, 163, 196
Levant, Oscar · 253
Levinsky, Kingfish · 38
Lewis, John Henry · 10, 137, 223
Lewis, Lee · 215
Lewiston, ME · 180
Leyvas, Pancho · 290
Libby, Bill · 224, 276
Liebling, A.J. · 104, 204
*Life* magazine · 87, 95, 134

*Lifeboat*, film · 160
Lilliard, Joe · 256
Lincoln, Abraham · 21
Lindbergh, Charles · 209
Liston, Sonny · 273, 275
Little Rock, AR · 150, 216
Liverpool, UK · 145
Lomax, Lucius · 219, 220
Lomelli, Leo · 290
*London Daily Herald* · 147
*London Evening Standard* · 146
London Sporting Club, London, UK · 146
London, UK · 57, 146
Long Beach, CA · 265, 284
Long Island City, NY · 103
Long Island, New York, NY · 185
Longmeadow Country Club, Springfield, MA · 214
Lopez, Perfecto · 45, 49, 52, 53, 59, 142, 288-290
Los Angeles Athletic Club, Los Angeles, CA · 41
*Los Angeles Daily News* · 72, 174, 177, 228, 230, 231, 247
*Los Angeles Evening Express* · 42
Los Angeles Lakers · 283
*Los Angeles Times* · 29, 62, 72, 82, 142, 143, 166, 174, 177, 217, 230, 282
Los Angeles, CA · 40, 41, 44, 51, 54, 57, 67, 70, 75, 76, 94, 96-98, 100, 119, 122, 135, 141, 142, 150, 162, 166, 172, 174, 175, 179, 204, 214, 217, 219, 225, 229, 230, 245, 251, 253, 254, 256, 258, 260, 263, 269, 274, 276, 279, 280, 282, 283
Loscalzo, Joseph · *See* Wolgast, Midget
Loughran, Tommy · 77
Louis, Joe · 7, 8, 76, 80, 89, 94, 101, 104, 108-110, 120, 123, 126, 132, 137, 140, 162, 167, 179, 192, 211, 215, 217, 222, 230, 234, 242-244, 262, 265, 267, 285, 286
  as cultural icon · 10, 62, 80, 81, 120, 122
  as hero to Black America · 10, 192, 282
  death and funeral · 280
  friendship with Henry Armstrong · 120, 204
  imitation of Henry Armstrong · 120, 121
  vs. Max Schmeling · 81, 120-122
Louisville, KY · 143, 238, 271
Louttit, Tom · 226
Lowndes County, MS · 19
Lowry, Paul · 230, 231
Lozado, Cecilo · 220
Luftspring, Sammy · 141, 163
Lugon, Joe · 42
Lynch, Joe · 67

*Macbeth*, play · 159
MacDonald, Charley · 173
Mace, Lloyd · 175
Macker, Gordon · 177, 178
MacMurray, Fred · 230
Madden, Owney · 68
Madison Square Garden Bowl, Long Island City, NY · 103, 110, 119
Madison Square Garden Corporation · 88, 93, 119
Madison Square Garden, New York City, NY · 30, 76-79, 83, 85, 88-90, 93-95, 102, 103, 126, 132, 138, 139, 145, 150, 167, 168-171, 182, 185, 196, 200, 201, 204-206, 211, 223, 233, 234, 236, 237, 238, 244, 246, 253, 259, 276, 277
Mahon, Jack · 197
Main Street Gym, Los Angeles, CA · 41, 45, 61, 142, 174, 230
Maine · 180
Malibu Beach, Malibu, CA · 264
Malone, S.M. · 265
Mamakos, Steve · 141
Manfredo, Al · 140, 165, 167, 291
Manhattan Gym, Los Angeles, CA · 41

Manila, Philippines · 138
Manuel, Baby · 51, 289
Maplewood, MO · 23
March Field, CA · 218
Marciano, Rocky · 126
Marciente, Joe · 85, 290
Markin, Mickey · 288
Markson, Harry · 276
Marquart, Billy · 185
Marquette, Pee Wee · 262
Marshall, Lloyd · 223
Marston, Lester · 290
Martin, Johnny · 180, 181
Marx brothers · 230
Marx Brothers, the · 54
Massachusetts · 180
Massey, Lew · 84, 290
Masters golf tournament · 214
McBeth, Hugh · 172, 173
McCaffrey, Dominick · 35
McCann, Dick · 236, 239, 240
McClelland, Jack · 35
McConnell, Abe · 73
McCoy, Young Kid · 193, 221, 223
McDaniel, Hattie · 80
McDaniels, Jimmy · 229, 292
McGovern, Terry · 79
McGurn, Machine Gun Jack · 106
McHugh, Roy · 238
McLarnin, Jimmy · 77, 107, 183, 218, 267
McLean, Evalyn · 121
McLemore, Henry · 177
McNulty, John · 105
Mead, Eddie · 66, 67, 69, 70, 73, 76, 78, 84, 86, 89, 93, 95-98, 101-104, 110, 119-121, 127, 132, 136, 138, 140-142, 145, 145, 149, 150, 155, 158, 161, 164, 165, 168, 170, 172-175, 178-180, 182, 187, 188, 193-197, 200-205, 209-211, 215, 220, 230, 261, 263
    death · 219, 220
    early career · 67
    gambling · 67, 97, 211
    mishandling of Armstrong funds · 67, 161, 162, 211, 219
    personality · 67
    signs Armstrong · 69
Medical Arts Hospital, New York City, NY · 203
Mellon, Andrew · 24
Melody Room, New York City, NY · 262
Metro-Goldwyn-Mayer (MGM) · 268
Metropolitan Opera House, New York City, NY · 87
Mexican Boxing Commission · 54
Mexico · 53-55, 57, 62, 64, 185, 221, 258
Mexico City, Mexico · 54-57, 59
Miami Beach Auditorium, Miami, FL · 270
Miami Beach Convention Center, Miami, FL · 272
*Miami Herald* · 272
Miami, FL · 173, 204, 253, 275, 281
Milburn, TX · 184
Milland, Ray · 230
Miller, Bernie · 205
Miller, Buster · 234
Miller, Freddie · 49, 53-55, 59, 62, 64, 65, 76, 86, 143, 168, 194
Miller, Gaston · 261
Miller, Johnny · 262
Miller, Roy · 252, 261
Milligan, Bowman · 212, 214
Milling, Varias · 76, 290

Milwaukee, WI · 143, 238
Minneapolis, MN · 100, 166
Mississippi River · 25
Missouri · 252, 286
Missouri Sports Hall of Fame, Springfield, MO · 277
Missouri-Pacific Railroad · 26
Mitchell, Brassie · 45
Mobile River · 19
*Monkey on My Back*, film · 118
Monroe, Marty · 131
Montana, Small · 57
Montanez, Pedro · 89, 126, 141, 145, 163, 166, 168-171, 196, 291
    vs. Henry Armstrong · 170, 171
    vs. Lou Ambers · 169
Montgomery, Bob · 202, 233, 234, 236-239, 242, 259, 286
Montoya, Ralph · 288
Montreal, Canada · 57
Moore, Archie · 20, 22, 75, 144, 165, 270, 271, 283
Moore, George · 172, 173, 220, 222, 224, 225, 228, 237, 238, 240-242, 250, 253, 255, 258, 261, 286
    death · 269
    early life · 220
Moran, Bugs · 106
Moran, Frank · 35
Morning Star Church, Los Angeles, CA · 266
Morris, Bill · 59
Motisi, Tony · 221, 222
Mount Olive Baptist Church, St. Louis, MO · 278
Muller, Eddie · 223, 231
Mullins, Moon · 76, 290
Municipal Auditorium, St. Louis, MO · 74
Murray, Jack · 104
Murray, Jackie · 36, 170
Murray, Jimmy · 258
Muse, Clarence · 172, 173
Mydans, Carl · 95
Myers Bowl, North Braddock, PA · 35, 36
Myrdal, Gunnar · 10

Nagler, Barney · 219
Nakaji, Bert · 256
Napoles, Jose · 277
Nashville, Edna · 281
National Association for the Advancement of Colored People (NAACP) · 10, 18, 242, 286
National Boxing Association (NBA) · 64, 73, 74, 84, 93, 165, 166, 167, 172, 180, 182, 194, 230, 238, 239, 240, 254, 270, 271
National Broadcast Corpany (NBC) · 188
National Recovery Act · 25
National Stadium, Mexico City, Mexico · 55
National Urban League · 242
Navarro, Tony · 142
Negro National League · 241
New Jersey · 229, 231, 232
New Orleans, LA · 57, 94, 97, 238
*New York Age* · 234, 262
*New York American* · 131
New York Black Yankees · 241
New York City, NY · 9, 30, 54, 57, 65, 67, 76, 77, 86, 89, 94, 96, 97, 100, 101, 107, 109, 136, 150, 168, 169, 171, 173-175, 180, 182, 185, 186, 188, 193, 195, 196, 203-205, 219, 220, 222, 225, 233, 238, 239, 242, 243, 245, 248, 258, 262, 263, 277
*New York Daily News* · 139, 191, 197, 208, 239
*New York Evening Journal* · 236
*New York Herald* · 202
*New York Herald Tribune* · 248
*New York Journal* · 206

*New York Journal-American* · 132, 202, 246
*New York Mirror* · 260
*New York Post* · 132
New York State Athletic Commission (NYSAC) · 54, 57, 64, 70, 72, 77, 78, 90, 93, 96, 103, 110, 127, 150, 155, 156, 162, 167, 168, 172, 182, 185-187, 193, 195-197, 205, 208, 230, 231, 233, 236, 238, 259
*New York Times* · 25, 96, 127, 129, 132, 145, 150 - 152, 156, 177, 188, 191, 195, 199, 204, 208, 233, 234, 239, 245, 248
*New York Tribune* · 116
*New York World-Telegram* · 210, 258
New York Yankees · 110
*New Yorker* · 95, 105, 253
Newman, Paul · 268
*Newsweek* · 105, 119
Nichols, Joseph · 199, 234, 236, 239, 240, 248
*No Man Stands Alone*, book · 118
Nogales, AZ · 54
Norfolk, VA · 179
Normandy, France · 226
North Side YMCA, St. Louis, MO · 34
Nutall, Keith · 251, 258, 260, 261
Nutall, Morris · 251, 261


O'Neal, Bennie · 142
Oakland Auditorium, Oakland, CA · 59, 60, 221, 222, 255
*Oakland Tribune* · 259
Oakland, CA · 46, 57, 220, 256
Ocean Park, CA · 218
*Ogden Standard-Examiner* · 260
Ogden, UT · 221
Oklahoma City, OK · 216, 220
Olsen, Henry · 288
Olson, Carl "Bobo" · 261
Olympic Auditorium, Los Angeles, CA · 41, 43, 44, 50, 60, 67, 71, 76, 82, 99, 100, 142, 166, 222, 225, 229, 230, 259
Operation Touchdown · 227
Orange Bowl, Miami, FL · 281
*Oregon Daily Journal* · 220
Oregon University, Eugene, OR · 256
Ortiz, Alfredo · 288
Ortiz, Manuel · 218
Oswald, Lee Harvey · 118
Overlin, Ken · 179
Owen, Jerry "Curley" · 269
Owens, Jesse · 62, 82, 256, 277


Pacho, Bobby · 143, 144, 167, 168, 291
Packs, Tom · 168
Paige, Satchel · 277
Panama · 122
Pantalone, Gene · 187
Paradise, Otis · *See* Ambers, Lou
Paret, Benny "Kid" · 275
Paris, France · 57, 149
Parker, Bonnie · 185
Parker, Dan · 138, 155, 236, 260
Parnassus, George · 175, 176, 178
Parrott, Harold · 233
*Pasadena Post* · 72
Pasadena, CA · 42, 100, 174
Pastor, Bob · 83
Pastrano, Willie · 270, 272
Patrick, Tom · 52
Pearl Harbor, HI · 217, 238
Pelz, Benny · 289

Pep, Willie · 99, 238, 244
Perry, Aaron · 292
Peterson, Eddie · 69
Phelan, John · 110, 196
*Philadelphia Inquirer* · 188
Philadelphia Stars · 241
Philadelphia, PA · 57, 84, 85, 97, 226, 233, 237, 242, 263, 271
Philippines · 137
Phoenix, AZ · 97, 183
Pian, Sam · 103, 107, 112, 113, 144
Pianga, Adam · *See* McCoy, Young Kid
Pilleteri, Antonio · *See* Larkin, Tippy
Pine Street YMCA, St. Louis, MO · 31, 73, 75
Pioneer Sporting Club, New York, NY · 220
Pismo Beach Arena, Pismo Beach, CA · 50
Pittman, NV · 222
*Pittsburgh Courier* · 34, 35, 122, 192, 206
Pittsburgh Crawfords, the · 38
*Pittsburgh Kid, The*, film · 214
Pittsburgh Pirates · 195
*Pittsburgh Post-Gazette* · 195
*Pittsburgh Press* · 195, 202
Pittsburgh Steelers · 196
Pittsburgh, PA · 34-36, 41, 85, 97, 101, 151, 163, 165, 194, 195-197, 205, 209, 222, 224, 238
Poland · 122
Polo Grounds, New York City, NY · 30, 88, 103, 124, 128, 186, 187, 246, 253, 262
Polonsky, Abe · 160
Pompton Lakes, NJ · 104, 109, 120, 127
Portland Auditorium, Portland, OR · 225
Portland, ME · 181
Portland, OR · 46, 220, 243, 253
Posedo, Angelo · 288
Powers, Jimmy · 191
Providence, RI · 181
Pruitt, Adolph · 276, 277
Pryor, Aaron · 281
Puerto Rico · 145, 171, 193, 197
Punching Punjab · 262
Purficato, Gustave · 125

Quarles, Norment · 182
*Queen Mary*, boat · 145, 150
Queens, New York City, NY · 103

Racine, MI, USA · 143
Raft, George · 68, 69, 78, 101, 140, 162, 175, 215, 218
    George Raft Caravan · 217, 218, 258
Ramage, Lee · 80
Ramey, Lew · 185
Ramirez, Jose Luis · 283
Ramirez, Rodolfo · 221, 292
Rangel, Richard "Sheik" · 221, 292
Ray, Bob · 174
Ray, Sonny · 271
Redman, Don · 212
Reed, Billy · 262
Reilly, Bob · 214
Reilly, Pete · 72
*Remembering Jim Crow*, book · 18
Reno, NV · 59
Republic Pictures · 214
Rice, Grantland · 112, 115, 116, 121, 123, 133
Richards, Robert · 194
Rickard, Tex · 8, 76, 88, 103, 120

Rickey, Branch · 277
Rico, Chester · 205
Rightmire, Everett · 74, 100, 291
*Ring, The* · 7, 40, 49, 55, 59, 64, 70, 73, 77, 79, 80, 82, 86, 90, 93, 94, 117, 132, 134, 140, 140, 144-145, 149, 150, 156, 163, 164, 167-169, 171, 172, 177, 179-182, 191, 193, 194, 203, 204, 221-224, 228, 230, 237, 244, 248, 250, 254, 267
Ringside Athletic Club, St. Louis, MO · 276
Ringside Gym, Los Angeles, CA · 41
Ritchie, Willie · 218
Rivas, Sal · 269
Rivera, Diego · 65
Rivers, Joe · 76, 290
Roberts, Porter · 122
Robinson, Jackie · 277
Robinson, Ray · 87, 165, 194, 197, 201, 202, 216, 217, 221, 222, 224, 228, 237, 238, 241-244, 246, 248-250, 252, 253, 262, 263, 267, 275, 285, 286, 292
    early life · 243
    fighting style · 244
    friendship with Henry Armstrong · 241, 246
    later life and death · 249
    vs. Henry Armstrong · 246-248
Robinson, Red · 195
Robinson, William "Bojangles" · 80, 136, 159, 230
Rocha, Tony · 54
Rockridge, NY, USA · 150
Rodak, Leo · 166, 222, 292
Roderick, Ernie · 141, 145-149, 163, 167, 291
Rodgers, Jackie · 34
Rojo, Genaro · 255, 258, 292
Rooney, Art · 194, 196
Roosevelt, Franklin · 10, 25, 120, 217
Root, Jack · 218
Rosedale Cemetery, Los Angeles, CA · 283
Rosenbloom, Maxie · 77, 223
Rosofsky, Beryl · *See* Ross, Barney
Ross, Barney · 38, 77, 88, 103, 107, 108, 110, 112, 113, 123, 125, 127, 136, 138, 140, 141, 145, 160, 168, 171, 174, 184, 204, 207, 217, 226, 227, 237, 267, 268, 277, 291
    as idol to Jewish Americans · 107
    childhood · 105
    drug addiction · 118
    fighting style · 108, 116
    military service · 117
    post-war years · 118
    relationship with Jack Ruby · 118
    vs. Cerferino Garcia · 138
    vs. Henry Armstrong · 111-115
Ross, Harold · 105
Ross, Wirt · 47-49, 51-54, 56, 58-61, 65, 67-69, 98, 261
Rossen, Robert · 160
Roth, Abe · 72
Rowe, Billy · 123
Roxborough, John · 89
Roxy Gymnasium, New York City, NY · 170
Rubio, Norman · 222
Ruby, Jack · 118
Ruffin, Bobby · 170
Runyon, Damon · 121, 123, 124, 179
Rupert's Brewery, New York City, NY · 203
Russell, R.L. · 264
Ruth, Babe · 8, 136
Ryan, Johnny "Mickey" · 49, 289
Ryan, Tommy · 218

Sacramento, CA · 221

Saipan · 257
Salem-Crescent Athletic Club, New York City, NY · 243
Salt Lake City, UT · 260
San Bernardino, CA · 40
San Diego, CA · 43
*San Francisco Examiner* · 223, 231
San Francisco, CA · 41, 43-45, 82, 100, 140, 142, 165, 221-223, 231
San Jose, CA · 220, 258
San Pedro, CA · 43
Sanchez, Joe · 289
Sanders, Norman · 219
Santa Ynez mountains, CA · 268
Saratoga, NY · 170
Sardinas-Montalbo, Eligio · *See* Kid Chocolate
Sarron, Petey · 62, 64, 65, 73, 74, 85, 86, 89, 93, 94, 100, 140, 141, 170, 180, 194, 238, 290
*Scarface*, film · 68
Scarpati, Tony · 126
Schiff, Alexander · 134, 179, 201, 203, 210, 219, 240, 242
Schmeling, Max · 76, 81, 104, 110, 120, 121, 140, 179
Schulberg, Budd · 87, 143
Scott, Howard · 166, 169, 291
*Seattle Star* · 166
Seattle, WA · 166
Seminola, Henry · 288
Sentoya, Leo · 288
Servo, Marty · 221
Shandy, Willa Mae · *See* Armstrong, Willa Mae
Shank, Reuben · 221, 222, 292
Shans, Cleo · 262
Shapiro, Maxie · 237, 292
Sharkey, Jack · 76, 103
Sharpe, Johnny · 149
Shaw, Dan · 172
Shea, Eddie · 38
Shreveport, LA · 39
Shrine Auditorium, Los Angeles, CA · 54
Siegel, Benjamin "Bugsy" · 68, 175
Siler, Herb · 271
Silva, Joey · 243, 292
Silvani, Al · 204, 206
Simmons, Marty · 144
Singer, Al · 30, 107
Slider, Chester · 254, 256, 258, 259, 2929
Sloan, Haystack · 47
Small's Paradise, New York, NY · 118
Smith, Jack · 208
Smith, Leila · 243
Smith, Oakland Billy · 261
Smith, Walker Jr. · *See* Robinson, Ray
Smith, Willie · 65
Snow, Norman · 141
Soberanes, Bill · 83
Soliz (Solis), Augie · 45, 288
*Somebody Up There Likes Me*, book · 268
Sommers, Freddie · 119, 215, 216
Soose, Billy · 164, 165
South Africa · 86, 89, 122
South Korea · 226
Southall, Levi · 262
Spain · 168
Spanish Civil War · 164
Spinks, Leon · 23
Spinks, Michael · 23
*Spirit of St. Louis*, aircraft · 209

*Spirit of Youth, The*, film · 158
Spokane, WA · 243
Spoldi, Aldo · 77, 79, 93, 94, 141, 194, 221, 238, 253, 254, 290, 292
*Sport* magazine · 286
Springfield, MA · 214
St. Alban's Hospital, New York City, NY · 237
*St. Louis Argus* · 34
St. Louis Auditorium, St. Louis, MO · 168
*St. Louis Globe-Democrat* · 276, 280
*St. Louis Post-Dispatch* · 30, 34, 134
*St. Louis Star and Times* · 30
St. Louis Stars · 241
St. Louis Urban League · 25
St. Louis, MO · 19-21, 25, 26, 34, 36, 38, 40, 73, 74, 85, 122, 144, 168, 213, 250, 254, 269, 274, 276, 277, 281, 282, 284, 286
St. Valentine's Day Massacre · 106
Stan, Frances · 196
Steele, Freddie · 138
Steward, Emmanuel · 285
Stillman, Lou · 185
Stillman's Gym, New York City, NY · 170, 185, 186, 197, 204, 233, 239
*Stormy Weather*, film · 159
*Story of Film, The*, book · 66
Strauther, Walter L. · 53, 266
Stribling, Young · 179
Stump, Al · 215, 286, 287
Sugar, Bert Randolph · 107, 108
Sullivan, Prescott · 175, 231
Summit, NJ, USA · 127
"Swanee" song · 65
Swartz Athletic Club, St. Louis, MO · 34
Sweetwater, TX · 184
Swissvale, PA · 36, 128

Talbot, Gayle · 120, 124
Tambe, Joe · 260
Tarantino, Carmine · 96
Tarleton, Ned · 65
Tarley, Max · 289
Tate, Big Bill · 220
Taylor, Elizabeth · 118
Taylor, Jack · 220
Taylor, Johnny · 220, 222, 291, 292
Taylor, Young Bud · 49, 289
Tendler, Lew · 191
Texas · 182, 184, 216, 219, 251
*The Comeback*, TV series · 267
*The New York Age* · 205
Theresa Hotel, New York City, NY · 258
Thil, Marcel · 88
Thomas, Jimmy · 34, 38
Thomas, John · 230, 254, 292
Thompson, Perry · 43, 288
Tidwell, T.J. · 184
Tiger Flowers · 29
*Time* magazine · 260
Togan, Clarence · 288
Tombigbee River · 19
Torres, Vincente · 289
Toussaint L'Ouverture Grammar School, St. Louis, MO · 20
Tribuani, Al · 233, 292
Tropical Stadium, Havana, Cuba · 143
Trujillo, Eddie · 49, 289
Truman, Harry · 227

Tucson, AZ · 96, 97, 98
Tully, Jim · 62, 65, 68
Tunney, Gene · 8, 9, 76, 121, 136, 217
Turiello, Saverio · 141, 149, 228, 237, 239, 290
Turner, Earl · 222, 292
Turner, Jay D. · 165
Turnverein Hall, Los Angeles, CA · 41
Twentieth Century Sporting Club · 88, 89, 90, 102, 103, 107, 173
Tyson, Mike · 281, 282, 283, 285

U.S. Army · 184, 217, 226, 227, 232, 238, 246, 253, 260
U.S. Coast Guard · 217, 225
U.S. Marines · 117, 217
U.S. Navy · 143, 217, 224
United Press · 177, 194, 223, 228, 235-237, 247, 248, 255, 275
United Service Organizations (USO) · 256, 258
University of California, Los Angeles, CA (UCLA) · 256
Utah · 221, 251, 258

Valdes, Eladio "Black Bill" · 29
Vashon High School, St. Louis, MO · 23, 267
Vashon, John Boyer · 31
Vaughn, Jimmy · 182
Velma Tart · *See* Armstrong, Velma
Venezuela · 168
Venturi, Enrico · 95, 290
Veteran Boxers Association · 85
Vicksburg, AZ · 267
Victorville, CA · 219
Villa, Pancho · 50, 104, 204

Walcott, Joe · 149, 191
Walker, Eddie · 104
Walker, James J. · 203
Walker, Mickey · 76, 267
Walker, Sidney · *See* Jack, Beau
Waller, Fats · 159
Wangley, Paul · 50, 289
Ward, Alan · 58
Ward, William "Kid Norfolk" · 29
Ware, Eddie · 288
Warner Bros. · 65
Warner, OK · 216
Warren, Earl · 243
*Washington Evening Star* · 196
Washington, Booker T. · 10
Washington, DC · 46, 64, 97, 143, 166, 196, 225, 238, 253, 254, 281
Washington, Kenny · 256
Washington, PA · 194, 238, 242
*Waterbury Democrat* · 234
Waterman, Joe · 225, 256
Waters, Ethel · 80, 121
Weill, Al · 90, 102, 103, 124, 125, 132, 150, 155, 165, 167, 182, 183, 233, 234, 261
Weissmuller, Johnny · 230, 277
Welles, Orson · 159
Welsh, Regis · 195
Wergeles, Chick · 233
West, Mae · 45, 54, 58, 72, 99, 159, 162, 179, 215
Westchester, NY · 205
Wheeler, Doc · 262
White, Edward · 18
White, Luther "Slugger" · 240, 250, 254, 292
Whiteman, Paul · 212, 253
Whorton, Cal · 177, 178

Wiggin, Albert · 24
Willard, Jess · 28
Williams, Holman · 165, 180, 193
Williams, Ike · 236, 285, 286
Williams, Joe · 210
Williams, Oscar · 262
Wills, Harry · 29
Willis, Franke · 292
Wilson, Arthur "Dooley" · 158, 286
Wilson, California Jackie · 142, 166, 221
Wilson, Jackie · 35-37, 217, 218, 238
Wilson, Woodrow · 18
Winchell, Walter · 65
WMAQ, Chicago, IL · 262
Wolgast, Bobby · 57
Wolgast, Midget · 57, 59, 74, 290
World Boxing Hall of Fame · 179
World War II · 117, 183, 217, 226
Wright, Albert "Chalky" · 47, 98-100, 104, 127, 136, 143, 145, 179, 186, 193, 218, 260, 290
Wright, Richard · 121, 159
Wrigley Field, Los Angeles, CA · 41, 60, 62, 65, 66, 83, 173

Yancey, Billy · 256
Yankee Stadium, New York City, NY · 103, 120, 136, 145, 151, 156, 209
Yarosz family · 35
Yarosz, Teddy · 36, 107, 238
Yawitz, Eddie · 271, 272
Ybarra, Joe · 221, 292
Young Corbett III · 138
Young Corpus · *See* Corpuz, Clarence "Young Corpus"
Young Men's Christian Association (YMCA) · 242
Young, Garvey · 221
Young, Robert N. · 227
Youngstown, OH · 85, 97

Zale, Tony · 107, 150, 172, 217
Zannelli, Ralph · 181, 244, 253, 291
Zinnerman, Paul · 177
Zivic family · 35, 101, 238
Zivic, Eddie · 101, 166, 291
Zivic, Fritzie · 97, 126, 140, 141, 163, 165, 169, 171, 180, 193-197, 201, 202, 204, 205, 209-211, 215, 216, 222, 233, 234, 238, 244, 291, 292
   fighting style · 194, 224
   later life and death · 224
   vs. Bummy Davis · 204
   vs. Cecil Hudson · 259
   vs. Henry Armstrong · 197-200, 206-208, 223
   vs. Sammy Angott · 195
Zoot Suit Riots · 245
Zurita, Juan · 64, 76, 222, 240, 290, 292
Zwillman, Longy · 68

# Endnotes

**Foreword**
[1] Schaap, *Cinderella Man*, xi; baseball-almanac.com
[2] Silver, *The Arc of Boxing*, 35; boxrec.com
[3] Hauser, "Henry Armstrong Revisited," *And the New...*, 7
[4] Myrdal, 734 and 903; Sugar, "The History of Boxing: The Way Out," *Bert Sugar's Punchlines*, 175

**Chapter 1: A Sea of Cotton**
[5] Armstrong, 15; ancestry.com
[6] Margolick, 63; Year 1910 census, ancestry.com
[7] Year 1900 census, ancestry.com
[8] Armstrong, 15; Heller, 193; Stump, "Hammerin' Henry," *Sport*, January 1955; Armstrong, "Now I Fight for God," *Boxing Illustrated*, January 1964; ancestry.com
[9] Year 1910 census, ancestry.com; year 1900 census, ancestry.com
[10] Armstrong, 15
[11] Armstrong, 17
[12] Armstrong, 16; Heller, 194
[13] Armstrong, 19
[14] Armstrong, 19
[15] shsmo.org
[16] shsmo.org
[17] Armstrong, 18
[18] Cousins, 54; Monaco, 262
[19] Cousins, 56
[20] Frankenfield, "Rivers and Floods, May 1912," *Monthly Weather Review*, May 1912; census.gov
[21] Stump, "Hammerin' Henry," *Sport*, January 1955
[22] Armstrong, 25

**Chapter 2: You Ain't No Jack Johnson**
[23] Armstrong, 30
[24] Fitzgerald, 8
[25] Armstrong, 35; Heller, 194
[26] Missouri death certificates, 1910 – 1969, ancestry.com
[27] Moore, *The Archie Moore Story*, 15
[28] McElvaine, 28
[29] *Great Depression*, 8
[30] *Great Depression*, 11; loc.gov
[31] McElvaine, 30
[32] McElvaine, 29-30
[33] *New York Times*, September 27, 1931; history.com
[34] Sustar, "Blacks and the Great Depression," socialworker.org; britannica.com
[35] britannica.com
[36] Heller, 194
[37] McElvaine, 172
[38] Nash, 252
[39] Heller, 195
[40] Helliwell, 10; *Liverpool Daily Post*, April 13, 1939
[41] shsmo.org
[42] Armstrong, 52
[43] *Los Angeles Times*, July 6, 1910
[44] boxrec.com
[45] Armstrong, 52
[46] Heller, 196

**Chapter 3: Melody**
[47] Tully, 214
[48] Heller, 197
[49] Heller, 198
[50] Stump, "Hammerin' Henry: The Last of the Triple Champions," *Sport*, January 1955
[51] Heller, 199
[52] Armstrong, "Now I Fight for God," *Boxing Illustrated*, January 1964; *Pittsburgh Courier*, June 27, 1931
[53] Cavanagh, 191
[54] *Pittsburgh Courier*, July 18, 1931
[55] *Chicago Bee*, July 21, 1940
[56] Cavanagh, 121; *Pittsburgh Press*, May 27, 1968
[57] Cavanagh, 121; boxrec.com
[58] *Pittsburgh Post-Gazette*, July 28, 1931
[59] *Pittsburgh Sun-Telegraph*, October 17, 1941
[60] Heller, 199
[61] *Pittsburgh Courier*, August 1, 1931; *Pittsburgh Post-Gazette*, August 1, 1931
[62] Heller, 199; *Pittsburgh Courier*, August 8, 1931; boxrec.com
[63] *Minneapolis Journal*, February 12, 1938
[64] Ganzel, "Riding the Rails," livinghistoryfarm.com
[65] Heller, 202
[66] Armstrong, 91
[67] Fleischer, *Black Dynamite v. II*, 117
[68] Helliwell, 9

**Chapter 4: Becoming Henry Armstrong**
[69] Armstrong, 122
[70] Armstrong, 124; Stump, "Hammerin' Henry: The Last of the Triple Champions," *Sport*, January 1955; *Santa Maria Times*, October 4, 1957
[71] *Santa Maria Times*, October 4, 1957
[72] *Santa Maria Times*, October 4, 1957
[73] *San Pedro News Pilot*, January 29, 1932; *Los Angeles Daily News*, January 29, 1932; *Los Angeles Times*, February 14, 1932
[74] Armstrong, 127; Stump, "Hammerin' Henry: The Last of the Triple Champions," *Sport*, January 1955
[75] *San Pedro News-Pilot*, July 2, 1932
[76] Armstrong, 135
[77] Heller, 205
[78] Helller, 206
[79] Armstrong, 142
[80] Armstrong, 142; *The Missoula Missoulian*, July 21, 1932
[81] *San Francisco Examiner*, July 22, 1932
[82] Glass, "Great Depression hits bottom, July 8, 1932," politico.com
[83] *Longview News-Journal*, July 22, 1948
[84] *Longview News-Journal*, July 22, 1948
[85] Armstrong, 145
[86] "Another Colored Star," *The Ring*, November 1936
[87] Heller, 206
[88] boxrec.com
[89] *San Luis Obispo Tribune*, November 4, 1932
[90] Armstrong, "Now I Fight for God," *Boxing Illustrated*, January 1964
[91] *San Pedro News-Pilot*, June 28, 1933; *California Eagle*, March 4, 1934; *Ventura County Star*, September 4 and 6, 1934

**Chapter 5: Ups and Downs**
[92] California, birth, marriage, and death records, 1849 – 1980, ancestry.com
[93] Stradley, "Baby and the Babes," *The Ring*, March 2009
[94] Armstrong, 156
[95] Armstrong, 158
[96] Heller, 208
[97] *Fresno Bee*, November 5, 1934
[98] Tully, 217
[99] Armstrong, 167
[100] Armstrong, 167; *Chicago Bee*. July 21, 1940
[101] Heller, 209
[102] Tully, 218
[103] *Fresno Bee*, January 2, 1935
[104] Armstrong, 163
[105] ancestry.com
[106] boxrec.com
[107] *Oakland Tribune*, November 27, 1935
[108] *Oakland Tribune*, November 28, 1935
[109] Roberts, *Boxing Register*, 253; boxrec.com
[110] Fleischer, "Six World Championships Changed Hands in 1935," *The Ring*, February 1936
[111] *The Ring* February 1936
[112] *Oakland Tribune*, February 27, 1936
[113] *California Eagle*, March 6, 1936
[114] *Oakland Tribune*, June 1, 1938
[115] Armstrong, 173
[116] Armstrong, 174; *Los Angeles Daily News*, August 5, 1936
[117] Armstrong, 175
[118] Tully, 221
[119] *Pittsburgh Courier*, August 15, 1936
[120] *Los Angeles Times*, August 14, 1988

**Chapter 6: The Big Time**
[121] *Pittsburgh Courier*, August 15, 1936
[122] *The Ring*, November 1936
[123] Tully, 220
[124] Tully, 220
[125] Tully, 223
[126] Cousins, 120
[127] *San Francisco Examiner*, May 21, 1942
[128] *Orlando Evening Star*, June 21, 1939
[129] Stump, "Hammerin' Henry: The Last of the Triple Champions," *Sport*, January 1955
[130] Tully, 223
[131] Armstrong, 178
[132] Sussman, 51-52
[133] Heller, 210
[134] *The Ring*, March 1937; boxrec.com
[135] Armstrong, 179; *Los Angeles Times*, October 28, 1936
[136] *Los Angeles Daily News*, October 28, 1936; njboxinghof.com
[137] *St. Louis Post-Dispatch*, October 28, 1936; njboxinghof.com
[138] *Los Angeles Times*, October 28, 1936; *Los Angeles Daily News*, October 28, 1936; *Pasadena Post*, October 28, 1936; *St. Louis Post-Dispatch*, October 28, 1936
[139] *St. Louis Post-Dispatch*, October 28, 1936
[140] *Los Angeles Times*, October 28, 1936
[141] *Los Angeles Times*, November 3, 1936
[142] *Chicago Defender*, November 28, 1936
[143] Stump, "Hammerin' Henry: The Last of the Triple Champions," *Sport*, January 1955
[144] *St. Louis Globe-Democrat*, November 18, 1936; *Chicago Defender*, November 28, 1936
[145] *St. Louis Globe-Democrat*, November 22 and 26, 1936
[146] *St. Louis Globe-Democrat*, December 4, 1936

[147] Armstrong, 182
[148] Stump, "Hammerin' Henry: The Last of the Triple Champions," *Sport*, January 1955
[149] Armstrong, 184; *New York Daily News*, March 14, 1937; Carroll, Ted, "Triple Champ Armstrong Has 'No Regrets,'" *The Ring*, May 1959
[150] *New York Daily News*, March 14, 1937
[151] Stump, "Hammerin' Henry: The Last of the Triple Champions." *Sport*. January 1955.
[152] Heller, 211
[153] Carroll, "Triple Champ Armstrong Has 'No Regrets,'" *The Ring*, May 1959; Armstrong, 186; *New York Times*, March 20, 1937
[154] Fleischer, "Nat Fleischer says," *Ring*, May 1937; Stump, "Hammerin' Henry: The Last of the Triple Champions." *Sport*. January 1955.

### Chapter 7: "You Can't Jim Crow a Left Hook"
[155] Rodney, "What They Forgot to Tell About Joe Louis," *Detroit Metro Times*, June 11-25, 1981
[156] Margolick, 171-173
[157] Roberts, *Joe Louis*, 121; Vogan, 41
[158] boxrec.com; cyberboxingzone.com
[159] *Los Angeles Times*, May 3, 1937
[160] *Los Angeles Daily News*, May 5, 1937
[161] *Petaluma Argus-Courior*, May 29, 1982; boxrec.com
[162] *New York Times*, July 9, 1937
[163] *New York Times*, July 9 and 21, 1937; Stump, "Hammerin' Henry," *Sport*, January1955
[164] *Philadelphia Inquirer*, June 26, 1975; boxrec.com
[165] *Philadelphia Inquirer*, July 28, 1937
[166] *New York Times*, August 14, 1937; *Washington Evening Star*, August 17, 1937
[167] *Washington Evening Star*, August 17, 1937
[168] *Detroit Free Press*, September 1 and 2, 1937
[169] *Pittsburgh Sun-Telegraph*, September 10, 1937

### Chapter 8: Armstrong & Jacobs: Undisputed
[170] *New York Times*, October 29, 1937; boxrec.com
[171] Fleischer, *50 Years*, 139; Field and Brown, "The Boxing Racket," *Life*, June 17, 1946
[172] Field, "The Boxing Racket," *Life*, June 17, 1946
[173] Mitchell, 16; Field and Brown, "The Boxing Racket," *Life*, June 17, 1946
[174] Schulberg, 261 - 262
[175] Mitchell, 15
[176] Roberts, *Joe Louis*, 61-62; Sussman, 61
[177] Roberts, *Joe Louis*, 64
[178] Fleischer, *Black Dynamite v. II*, 133; Fleischer, *50 Years*, 142
[179] Flesicher, *Black Dynamite v. II*, 133; Fleischer, *50 Years*, 142
[180] Armstrong 191-192; *New York Daily News*, October 29, 1937
[181] Nagler, "Hammerin' Henry Armstrong," *Sport*, June 1963; *New York Daily News*, October 29, 1937
[182] Daley, "Henry Armstrong: The Story of the Hurricane," topclassboxing.com
[183] Armstrong, 195-196; Stump, "Hammerin' Henry: The Last of the Triple Champions," *Sport*, January 1955
[184] *New York Daily News*, October 30, 1937
[185] Fleischer, *Black*, 134
[186] *New York Daily News*, October 30, 1937
[187] *Los Angeles Times*, August 14, 1988
[188] Shocket, "The Turbulent Life of Henry Armstrong," *The Big Book of Boxing*, January 1975

### Chapter 9: Breakdown of a Champion
[189] Armstrong, 197
[190] Armstrong, 197
[191] *New York Times*, November 20 and December 7, 1937
[192] *The Ring Extra*, Vol. III, No. 1
[193] Daniel, "Armstrong Wins Ring's Most Valuable Award." *The Ring*. March 1938
[194] Anonymous, "Henry and Harry," *The New Yorker*, April 16, 1938; *St. Louis Star and Times*, January 4, 1940
[195] Home, 88; Armstrong, "I Fought for Keeps," *Argosy*, October 1955
[196] Armstrong, "I Fought for Keeps," *Argosy*, October 1955
[197] Mydans, "Speaking of Pictures...," *Life*, January 31, 1938
[198] Mydans, "Speaking of Pictures...," *Life*, January 31, 1938; *New York Times*, January 13 and 19, 1938
[199] Stump, "Hammerin' Henry" *Fight*, January 1955
[200] Heller, 251; boxrec.com
[201] *Los Angeles Daily News*, February 1, 1938; *Los Angeles Times*, February 1, 1938
[202] Roberts, *The Boxing Register*, 662-667; Heller, 215
[203] *San Francisco Examiner*, February 10, 1938; *Chicago Tribune*, February 26, 1938; *Minneapolis Star Tribune*, March 1, 1938
[204] *Los Angeles Times*, March 16, 1938; *Los Angeles Daily News*, March 16, 1938
[205] "On This Day: One of Boxing's Absolute Greatest, Henry Armstrong, Died at the Age 75," boxingnewsonline.net
[206] Heller, 211
[207] Dunphy, 245; *New York Times*, May 22, 1938

### Chapter 10: "To Live, Men Must Fight"
[208] Liebling, "Training Camp," *The New Yorker*, August 30, 1935
[209] McNulty, "Henry and Harry," *The New Yorker*, April 16, 1938
[210] "New Wonder of the Ring? Armstrong Lives Up to Name of 'Perpetual Motion,'" *Newsweek*, June 13, 1938
[211] Ross, 66-67
[212] Ross, 67; Century, 18-19

[213] Sugar, *The Great Fights*, 74
[214] Sugar, *Boxing's Greatest*, 64
[215] *New York Times*, May 22, 1938
[216] Carroll, "Triple Champ Armstrong Has 'No Regrets',", *The Ring*, May 1959
[217] Armstrong, 209
[218] Sugar, *The Great Fights*, 74; Shocket, "The Turbulent Life of Henry Armstrong," *The Big Book of Boxing*, January 1975
[219] Armstrong, 209; *New York Times*, May 30, 1938
[220] Carroll, "Triple Champ Armstrong Has No Regrets," *The Ring*, May 1959
[221] Armstrong, 210; *New York Daily News*, June 1, 1938

222 Richards, "Homicide Hank," *Fight Stories*, Fall 1947; *New York Times*, June 1, 1938
223 *Washington Evening Star*, June 1, 1938
224 *Washington Daily Star*, June 1, 1938
225 *Daily Oklahoman*, July 27, 1945
226 Ross, 164
227 Ross, 164
228 Ross, 164
229 Ross, 165
230 Ross, 165-166
231 Heller, 214; "New Wonder of the Ring? Armstrong Lives Up to Name of 'Perpetual Motion'," *Newsweek*, June 13, 1938
232 Ross, 166
233 *New York Daily News*, June 1, 1938
234 Dewey, 81
235 *New York Daily News*, June 1, 1938
236 Heller, 214; Fleischer, "Armstrong's Feat Unique in Boxing," *The Ring*, August 1938; *Washington Evening Star*, June 1, 1938
237 Fleischer, *Black*, 148; Fleischer, "Armstrong's Feat Unique in Boxing," *The Ring*, August 1938
; *New York Times*, June 1, 1938
238 Ross, 167; *The Ring Presents Special*, Vol. 2, No. 2
239 *Washington Daily Star*, June 1, 1938
240 *New York Times*, June 1, 1938
241 Ross, 168; *New York Times*, June 1, 1938; *Oakland Tribune*, June 1, 1938; *The Ring*, August 1938
242 Armstrong, 211; Shocket, "The Turbulent Life of Henry Armstrong," *The Big Book of Boxing*, January 1975
243 Century, 118-122
244 *Los Angeles Daily News*, February 25, 1943
245 Armstrong, 211
246 Armstrong, 211
247 *Oakland Tribune*, June 1, 1938
248 Baker, 140; "New Wonder of the Ring? Armstrong Lives Up to Name of 'Perpetual Motion'," *Newsweek*, June 13, 1938
249 Dunphy, 246
250 Wright, "High Tide in Harlem," *The Hurt Business*, 69-70
251 Ashe, 35
252 shsmo.org
253 *San Pedro News Pilot*, June 10, 1938
254 Wright, "High Tide in Harlem." *The Hurt Business*, 70.
255 Margolick, 314; *Pittsburgh Courier*, July 2, 1938

**Chapter 11: When Hurricanes Collide**
256 Tully, 225; *Washington Evening Star*, June 1, 1938; *Pittsburgh Courier*, June 11, 1938
257 *Buffalo News*, June 1, 1938
258 *Pittsburgh Sun-Telegraph*, June 6, 1938
259 *Kansas City Star*, December 25, 1946
260 *Oakland Tribune*, June 1, 1938
261 *New York Times*, August 7, 1938; *Oakland Tribune*, October 1, 1938
262 Pantalone, 36; Fried, 159-160, 190
263 Heller 181; Baker, 94
264 Rosenfeld, 122
265 Baker, 140; *New York Times*, August 4, 1938
266 Toledo, 186
267 *New York Times*, August 10, 1938
268 *New York Times*, August 18, 1938
269 Fleischer, "Who Will Halt Henry?" *The Ring*, October 1938; *New York Times*, August 18, 1938
270 Heller, 214-215
271 Fleischer, "Who Will Halt Henry?" October 1938; *New York Times*, August 18, 1938
272 Armstrong, "I Fought for Keeps," *Argosy*, October 1955
273 Cannon, *The Big Fights*, 121; *New York Times*, August 18, 1938
274 Fleischer, *Black*, 151; Fleischer, "Who Will Halt Henry?" *The Ring* October 1938; *New York Times*, August 18, 1938
275 Armstrong, "I Fought for Keeps," *Argosy*, October 1955
276 Cannon, *The Big Fights*, 122; *New York Times*, August 18, 1938
277 *New York Times*, August 18 and 19, 1938
278 Baker, 146; Rosenfeld, 70; *The Ring Extra*, Vol. III, No. 1; Richards, "Homicide Hank," *Fight Stories*," Fall 1947; *Los Angeles Daily News*, August 18, 1938
279 Nagler, "Hammerin' Henry Armstrong," *Sport*, June 1963; "Picture of the Week," *Life*, August 29, 1938
280 *St. Louis Post-Dispatch*, September 10, 1944

**Chapter 12: Triple Crown**
281 *New York Times*, August 18, 1938
282 *Los Angeles Times*, August 30, 1938
283 *New York Times*, August 23, 1998
284 *Los Angeles Daily News*, February 14, 1940; *California Daily Eagle*, February 22, 1940; boxrec.com; boxing360.com
285 Richard, "Homicide Hank," *Fight Stories* Fall 1947
286 boxrec.com
287 Armstrong, "I Fought for Keeps," *Argosy*, October 1955; Daniel, "Ring's Most Valuable Award to Louis," *The Ring* March 1939; *Rochester Democrat and Chronicle*, November 15, 1938; *New York Times*, November 25, 1938.
288 *New York Daily News*, November 26, 1938
289 Shocket, "The Turbulent Life of Henry Armstrong," *The Big Book of Boxing*, January 1975; *New York Daily News*, October 2, 1940
290 Carroll, "Sepian Sockers Supreme," *The Ring* March 1939; *New York Daily News*, November 25, 1938
291 *The Ring*, February 2022; *New York Daily News*, December 6, 1938; *Washington Evening Star*, December 6, 1938
292 Daniel, "Ring's Most Valuable Award to Louis," *The Ring* March 1939
293 Carroll, "Sepian Sockers Supreme," March 1939
294 *The Ring*, March 1939
295 *Los Angeles Daily News*, January 4, 1939; *Davenport Quad-City Times*, January 16, 1939
296 *Los Angeles Times*, January 11 and 12, 1939; *Los Angeles Daily News*, January 11, 1939
297 Stradley, "Baby and the Babes," *The Ring*, March 2009; Armstrong, 175

[298] Roberts, *Boxing Register*, 58; Stradley, "Baby and the Babes," *The Ring*, March 2009
[299] Richards, "Homicide Hank," *Fight Stories*, fall 1947; *New York Daily News*, March 5, 1939; boxrec.com
[300] *New York Times*, March 17, 1939; boxrec.com
[301] *The Ring*, July 1939; *New York Times*, April 1, 1939
[302] Fleischer, "Nat Fleischer Says," *The Ring*, May 1939; *The Ring*, July 1939; *Leicester Evening Mail*, April 1, 1939; *Liverpool Daily Post*, May 25, 1939
[303] *London Evening Standard*, April 12, 1939
[304] *London Evening Standard*, April 12, 1939; *Liverpool Daily Post*, April 13, 1939
[305] *London Evening Standard*, April 17, 1939
[306] *New York Times*, May 16, 1939
[307] *Liverpool Daily Post*, May 26, 1939; *London Guardian* May 26, 1939; *New York Times*, May 26, 1939; boxrec.com
[308] *Liverpool Daily Post*, May 26, 1939
[309] *New York Times*, May 26, 1939
[310] Sharpe, "Hank's Greatness Proved to British," *The Ring*, August 1939
[311] *New York Times*, May 26 and 27, 1939
[312] shsmo.org
[313] shsmo.org
[314] shsmo.org
[315] *New York Times*, August 3 and 9, 1939; Fleischer, "History Repeats Itself," *The Ring*, November 1939
[316] *New York Times*, August 3 and 16, 1939
[317] *New York Times*, August 23, 1939
[318] Armstrong, 221; *New York Times*, August 23, 1939
[319] Armstrong, 222; *New York Times*, August 23, 1939
[320] Armstrong, 222; *New York Times*, August 23, 1939
[321] Fleischer, "History Repeats Itself," *The Ring*, November 1939
[322] Nagler, "Hammerin' Henry Armstrong," *Sport*, June 1963
[323] *New York Times*, August 23, 1939; Nagler, "Hammerin' Henry Armstrong," *Sport*, June 1963
[324] *New York Times*, August 23, 1939
[325] *Pottsville Evening Herald*, August 29, 1939
[326] Fleischer, "History Repeats Itself," *The Ring*, November 1939; *New York Times*, August 23, 1939
[327] Fleischer, "History Repeats Itself," *The Ring*, November 1939
[328] Heller, 216; *St. Louis Star and Times*, January 4, 1940
[329] Horne, 89

**Chapter 13: Keeping Punching**
[330] Lardner, "Notes on Sports," *The New Yorker*, June 10, 1944; *Pittsburgh Courier*, June 11, 1938
[331] *Pittsburgh Sun-Telegraph*, April 26, 1941
[332] Baker, *Contesting*, 112; youtube.com
[333] Graham, "They Called Him Hammerin' Hank," *Sport*, November 1952; *Paterson News*, September 1, 1939
[334] Shocket, "The Turbulent Life of Henry Armstrong," *The Big Book of Boxing*, January 1975
[335] *Scranton Times-Tribune*, December 7, 1993; "Boxing's Little Giants," *In This Corner*, ESPN
[336] Armstrong, "Now I Fight for God," *Boxing Illustrated*, January 1964.
[337] Stump, "Hammerin' Henry," *Sport*, January 1955; *St. Louis Star and Times*, January 4, 1940
[338] *Berkshire Eagle*, September 1, 1939
[339] *The Ring*, November 1939
[340] Rosenfeld, 93-94; Roberts, *The Boxing Register*, 325
[341] boxrec.com
[342] *Waterloo Courier*, October 9, 1939; *Davenport Daily Times*, October 10, 1939; *Cedar Rapids Gazette*, October 10, 1939
[343] *Seattle Sear*, October 21, 1939; *Los Angeles Times*, October 21, 1939
[344] *Los Angeles Times*, October 23, 1939
[345] *Los Angeles Times*, October 25, 1939
[346] *Fort Collins Coloradoan*, October 31, 1939
[347] Baker, 165; Heller, 183
[348] *Dayton Daily News*, December 12, 1939; *Los Angeles Evening Citizen*, December 12, 1939
[349] Fleischer, "Louis Tops for 1939," *The Ring*, February 1940
[350] *Fort Collins Coloradoan*, October 31, 1939
[351] *St. Louis Post-Dispatch*, January 3, 1940; boxrec.com
[352] *St. Louis Post-Dispatch* January 5, 1940; *St. Louis Star and Times*, January 5, 1940
[353] *New York Times*, January 25, 1940; boxrec.com
[354] *The Ring*, July 1939 and March 1940; *New York Times*, January 21, 1940
[355] *St. Louis Globe Democrat*, January 24, 1940
[356] *New York Times*, January 25 and 26, 1940; boxrec.com
[357] *New York Times*, January 25, 1940
[358] Richards, "Homicide Hank," *Fight Stories*, Fall 1947; Flesicher, "Armstrong at His Best," *The Ring*, April 1940
[359] *New York Times*, January 25, 1940
[360] Carroll, "Stamina – Is a Great Ring Asset," *The Ring*, April 1940; Fleischer, "Armstrong at His Best," *The Ring*, April 1940
[361] Richards, "Homicide Hank," *Fight Stories*, Fall 1947
[362] *The Ring*, April 1940
[363] ibhof.com

**Chapter 14: A Fourth Title?**
[364] *Chicago Defender*, November 25, 1939
[365] *Los Angeles Daily News*, February 12, 1940; *Los Angeles Times*, February 13 and 24, 1940
[366] Armstrong, 225; Heller, 216; Horne, 88; Armstrong, "I Fought for Keeps," *Argosy*, October 1955; Madden, "Henry Armstrong," *Missouri Life*, January-February 1980; *San Francisco Examiner*, January 20, 1957; *St. Louis Post-Dispatch*, July 4, 1965
[367] Armstrong, 22; *San Francisco Examiner*, January 20, 1957
[368] *New York Daily News*, November 13, 1982; Armstrong, 225; Horne, 88
[369] *San Francisco Examiner*, January 20, 1957
[370] Richards, "Homicide Hank," *Fight Stories*, Fall 1947; boxrec.com
[371] *Los Angeles Times*, March 2, 1940; Borden, "Hank Proves His Mettle," *The Ring*, May 1940
[372] Borden, "Hank Proves His Mettle," *The Ring*, May 1940
[373] *Los Angeles Daily News*, March 2, 1940; *Los Angeles Times*, March 2, 1940
[374] *Los Angeles Times*, March 2, 1940

375 Borden, "Hank Proves His Mettle," *The Ring*, May 1940; *Los Angeles Daily News*, March 2, 1940; *Los Angeles Times*, March 2, 1940; *New York Times*, March 2 and 3, 1940
376 *Los Angeles Times*, March 2, 1940
377 *Los Angeles Times*, March 2, 1940
378 *Los Angeles Times*, March 2, 1940
379 *Los Angeles Times*, March 2, 1940
380 *Los Angeles Times*, March 2, 1940
381 *Los Angeles Daily News*, March 2, 1940
382 *San Francisco Examiner*, December 21, 1952
383 boxrec.com
384 *San Francisco Examiner*, December 21, 1952
385 Madden, "Henry Armstrong," *Missouri Life*, January-February 1980.
386 *Santa Maria Times*, October 5, 1957
387 boxrec.com; boxing360.com
388 *Boston Globe*, April 18, 1940
389 *The Ring*, June, 1940
390 *Boston Globe*, April 2 and 6, 1940
391 *Boston Globe*, April 27, 1940; Fleischer, "Nat Fleischer Says," *The Ring*, July 1940
392 *Boston Globe*, April 27, 1940
393 *Boston Globe*, May 23 and 24, 1940; boxrec.com
394 *Boston Globe*, May 25, 1940

## Chapter 15: The Sweetwater Swatter
395 Pantalone, 46
396 Pantalone, 47
397 Heller, 183; *New York Times*, May 11, 1940
398 Pantalone, 43
399 Baker, 162, 191, 203; Roberts, *Boxing Register*, 56-57
400 Heller, 233-234
401 Roberts, *Boxing Register*, 446
402 Heller, 234 – 235
403 Heller, 234; Pantalone, 53-54
404 Pantalone, 54-55
405 Richards, "Homicide Hank," *Fight Stories*, Fall 1947
406 Richards, "Homicide Hank," *Fight Stories*, Fall 1947
407 *New York Daily News*, July 18, 1940
408 *New York Times*, July 18, 1940; *New York Daily News*, July 20, 1940 Pantalone, 55 and 62
409 *New York Times*, July 18, 1940; *New York Daily News*, July 18, 1940
410 Pantalone, 57
411 Robinson, "Comment," *The New Yorker*, July 19, 1940
412 *New York Times*, July 18, 1940
413 Pantalone, 55; Fleischer, "Body Blows Whip Lew," *The Ring*, October 1940; *New York Times*, July 18, 1940
414 Pantalone, 56; *New York Daily News*, July 18, 1940
415 Fleischer, "Body Blows Whip Lew," *The Ring*, October 1940; *New York Times*, July 18, 1940
416 Roberts, "Homicide Hank," *Sport*, 1947
417 *New York Daily News*, July 18, 1940
418 *New York Daily News*, July 18, 1940; *New York Times*, July 18, 1940
419 *New York Times*, July 18, 1940
420 Pantalone, 58-60
421 Fleischer, "Body Blows Whip Lew," *The Ring*, October 1940
422 Heller, 234
423 *New York Daily News*, July 18, 1940
424 *New York Times*, July 18, 1940
425 Fleischer, "Body Blows Whip Lew," *The Ring*, October, 1940
426 Fleischer, "Body Blows Whip Lew," *The Ring*, October, 1940
427 *Pittsburgh Courier*, July 27, 1940

## Chapter 16: Zivic
428 *New York Daily News*, July 20, 2022
429 *The Ring*, October 1940
430 boxrec.com; ibhof.com
431 Heller, 246-247; McHugh, 100
432 Heinz, "The Greatest, Pound-for-Pound," *The Top of His Game*, 475
433 *The Ring*, October 1940; boxrec.com
434 *Pittsburgh Press*, August 30, 1940
435 *Pittsburgh Press*, August 30, 1940
436 McHugh, 140
437 *Pittsburgh Press*, August 30 and September 1, 1940; *New York Times*, August 30, 1940; *Pittsburgh Post-Gazette*, September 4, 1940
438 *Pittsburgh Press*, August 30, 1940
439 *Pittsburgh Press*, August 30, 1940
440 *Pittsburgh Post-Gazette*, September 4, 1940
441 *Washington Evening Star*, September 24, 1940; *New York Times*, September 24, 1940
442 *Winnipeg Tribune*, October 17, 1940
443 McHugh, 107
444 Heller, 217; *New York Daily News*, October 4, 1940; *New York Times*, October 4 and 5, 1940
445 *New York Times*, October 5, 1940; boxrec.com
446 Heller 243; McHugh, 107; *New York Times*, October 5, 1940; *New York Daily News*, October 5, 1940
447 Heller, 243
448 McHugh, 107; Heller, 243
449 Heller, 243
450 *New York Daily News*, October 5, 1940; *New York Times*, October 5, 1940
451 Fleischer, "Zivic's Novel Attack Wins," *The Ring* December 1940
452 *New York Daily News*, October 5, 1940
453 Fleischer, "Zivic's Novel Attack Wins," *The Ring*, December 1940

454 *New York Daily News*, October 5, 1940
455 Heller, 244; Fleischer, "Zivic's Novel Attack Wins," *The Ring*, December 1940
456 *Pittsburgh Press*, October 6, 1940
457 *Los Angeles Herald-Examiner*, November 9, 1982
458 Fleischer, "Zivic's Novel Attack Wins," *The Ring*, December 1940
459 Armstrong, 227; *Pittsburgh Press*, March 6, 1940
460 Stump, "Hammerin' Henry," *Sport*, January 1955
461 Armstrong, 232; *New York Daily News*, October 16, 1940; *South Bend Tribune*, October 24, 1940
462 *New York Daily News*, November 25, 1940
463 ancestry.com
464 *New York Times*, December 4, 1941
465 *New York Daily News*, January 16, 1941; *New York Age*, January 18, 1941
466 Fleischer, "Fighter of the Year Award Made to Billy Conn," *The Ring*, February 1941
467 *Pittsburgh Courier*, December 20, 1941
468 *New York Times*, November 16 and December 21 and 25, 1940; boxrec.com
469 *New York Times*, January 15, 1941
470 *New York Age*, January 18, 1941
471 *Pittsburgh Courier*, January 8, 1941
472 *New York Times*, January 16 and 17, 1941; *New York Age*, January 18, 1941
473 Armstrong, 228; *New York Daily News*, January 18, 1941; *New York Times*, January 18, 1941
474 *New York Daily News*, January 18, 1941
475 *New York Daily News*, January 18, 1941
476 *New York Daily News*, January 18, 1941
477 Heller, 217
478 Fleischer, "The Kid's Last Fight," *The Ring*, April 1941; *New York Times*, January 18, 1941
479 Heller, 217; Armstrong, "I Fought for Keeps," *Argosy*, October 1955
480 Fleischer, "The Kid's Last Fight," *The Ring*, April 1941
481 Fried, 88
482 *New York Times*, January 18, 1941
483 *New York Age*, January 25, 1941
484 Armstrong, 230
485 Fleischer, "The Kid's Last Fight," *The Ring*, April 1941
486 Armstrong, 230
487 Armstrong, "I Fought for Keeps," *Argosy*, October 1955

**Chapter 17: "To Justify Being Alive"**
488 Markson, "They Went Out Swinging," *The Ring*, April 1941
489 syncopatedtimes.com
490 *Wilmington News-Journal*, February 14, 1941
491 Mullins, 21
492 Sugar, 178
493 *San Francisco Examiner*, March 30, 1943
494 Lardner, "Notes on Sports," *The New Yorker*, November 10, 1944
495 *San Francisco Examiner*, March 30, 1943
496 Armstrong, 237
497 Stump, "Hammerin' Henry," *Sport*, January 1955
498 *Daily Oklahoman*, September 18, 1941
499 boxrec.com
500 *Buffalo Evening News*, November 6, 1941

**Chapter 18: The Comeback Trail**
501 *Shamokin News-Dispatch*, April 22, 1942; *Los Angeles Times*, April 25 and July 12, 1942
502 *California Eagle*, May 14, 1942
503 Nagler, "Hammin' Henry Armstrong," *Sport*, June 1963
504 *New York Times*, May 26, 1942
505 *San Francisco Examiner*, May 26, 1942
506 Nagler, "Hammerin' Henry Armstrong," *Sport*, June 1963
507 Carroll, "Triple Champ Armstrong Has 'No Regrets,'" *The Ring*, May 1959
508 Bromberg, "Armstrong Pilot Cracked Ban Here on Mixed Bouts," *The Knockout*, July 24, 1943; Nagler, "Hammerin' Henry Armstrong," *Sport*, June 1963; *California Eagle*, July 3, 1941 and February 6, 1958; *Pittsburgh Courier*, December 26, 1942
509 *Oregon Daily Journal*, June 27, 1918
510 *Oakland Tribune*, June 2, 1942
511 *Oakland Tribune*, June 2, 1942
512 *The Ring*, June 1942
513 *Sacramento Bee*, July 4, 1942; *Oakland Tribune*, September 18, 1942
514 Fleischer, "Nat Fleischer Says," *The Ring*, September 1942
515 *Oakland Tribune*, August 27, 1942
516 *Los Angeles Daily News*, October 14, 1942; *San Francisco Examiner*, October 29, 1942
517 Ackerman, "Armstrong, the Fighter of the Month," *The Ring*, December 1942; *The Ring* November and December, 1942
518 *New York Times*, September 11, 1942; *San Francisco Examiner*, October 2, 1942
519 *The Ring*, February 2022; boxrec.com
520 *San Francisco Examiner*, October 18, 1942
521 *San Francisco Examiner*, October 24 and 25, 1942
522 *San Francisco Examiner*, October 27 and 28, 1942
523 *San Francisco Examiner*, October 27, 1942; *Los Angeles Daily News*, October 27, 1942
524 Heller, 217; Armstrong and Libby, "Now I Fight for God," *Boxing Illustrated*, January 1964
525 *Pittsburgh Courier*, November 7, 1942
526 Fleischer, "Nat Fleischer Says," *The Ring*, January 1943; *The Pittsburgh Courier*, November 7, 1942
527 Fleischer, "Nat Fleischer Says," *The Ring*, January 1943; *The Pittsburgh Courier*, November 7, 1942
528 Roberts, *Boxing Register*, 685; *Pittsburgh Press*, May 17, 1984; boxrec.com
529 Pantalone, 98, 107-112
530 Pantalone, 113
531 Pantalone, 114; Armstrong and Libby, "Now I Fight for God," *Boxing Illustrated*, January 1964; *Oakland Tribune*, December 5, 1942
532 Pantalone, 165

533 Pantalone, 170
534 Pantalone, 175
535 Pantalone, 168, 177
536 *San Luis Obispo Telegram-Tribune*, December 3, 1942; *Los Angeles Daily News*, December 8, 1942
537 Daniel, "Robinson Named Fighter of the Year," *The Ring*, February 1942
538 Haygood, 145
539 *The Ring*, April 1943
540 *San Francisco Examiner*, December 15, 1942; *Los Angeles Evening Citizen News*, January 30, 1960
541 *Los Angeles Daily News*, January 6, 1943
542 Van, "Van-O-Grams," *The Knockout*, March 6, 1943; *Los Angeles Daily News*, February 25 and March 2, 1943; *The Ring*, February 2022; boxrec.com
543 *Los Angeles Daily News*, March 3, 1943; *Los Angeles Times*, March 3 and March 4, 1943
544 *Los Angeles Times*, March 3, 1943
545 *Los Angeles Times*, March 3, 1943
546 *Los Angeles Times*, March 4, 1943
547 *New York Daily News*, June 6, 1945
548 *Los Angeles Times*, March 3, 1943; *Los Angeles Daily News*, March 4, 1943
549 *New York Times*, December 19, 1942; boxrec.com
550 *San Francisco Examiner*, March 7, 8, and 10, 1943
551 *Ridgewood Herald News*, January 30, 1958; *Hazelton Standard Speaker*, February 22, 1958
552 *Tucson Citizen*, March 13, 1943
553 *Philadelphia Inquirer*, March 24, 1943; boxrec.com
554 *San Francisco Examiner*, March 30, 1943; *New York Times*, April 2, 1943
555 *Brooklyn Daily Eagle*, March 31, 1943
556 Fleischer, "Hank's Rally Too Late," *The Ring*, June 1943; Van, "Van-O-Grams," *The Knockout*, March 6, 1943; *Imperial Valley Press*, March 30, 1943; *San Francisco Examiner*, March 31, 1943; *Waterbury Democrat*, March 31, 1943; *New York Times*, April 2, 1943; *New York Daily News*, April 2, 1943; *New York Age*, April 3, 1943; *Beatrice Daily Sun*, April 4, 1943
557 Mullins, 110; *New York Times*, April 3, 1943; *Los Angeles Daily News*, April 3, 1943
558 *New York Times*, April 3, 1943
559 Fleischer, Nat, "Hank's Rally Too Late," *The Ring*, June 1943; *New York Times*, April 3, 1943; *Los Angeles Daily News*, April 3, 1943
560 Fleischer, "Hank's Rally Too Late," *The Ring*, June 1943; *New York Times*, April 3, 1943; *New York Daily News*, April 3, 1943; *Los Angeles Daily News*, April 3, 1943; *Beatrice Daily Sun*, April 4, 1943; *Oakland Tribune*, April 4, 1943; *Hanford Morning Journal*, April 4, 1943
561 Mullins, 112; *Los Angeles Daily News*, April 3, 1943
562 Armstrong, "Now I Fight for God," *Boxing Illustrated*, January 1964
563 Sugar, 179; Roberts, *Boxing Register*, 442-445

**Chapter 19: Sugar Ray**
564 *The Ring*, June 1943; *Springfield News-Sun*, April 4, 1943; *San Francisco Examiner*, April 10, 1943
565 *Evansville Courier and Press*, April 4, 1943
566 *Oakland Tribune*, May 25, 1943
567 McHugh, 140
568 *New York Times*, March 20, 1943
569 *New York Times*, June 11 and 12, 1943; *New York Daily News*, June 12, 1943; Kafka, "Scene in New York," *The Knockout*, June 26, 1943
570 *New York Daily News*, June 12; 1943; *New York Times*, June 12, 1943
571 *New York Daily News*, June 12, 1943
572 *New York Times*, June 12 and 13, 1943; *New York Daily News*, June 12, 1943
573 *Los Angeles Daily News*, October 14, 1943
574 *New York Times*, June 13, 1943
575 McHugh, 142; Roberts and Skutt, 275; *New York Daily News*, June 14, 1943; boxrec.com
576 Haygood, 152
577 Robinson, 114-115
578 *New York Age*, June 26, 1943
579 Haygood, 144
580 *Los Angeles Times*, July 25, 1943
581 Robinson, 7
582 Robinson, 38
583 Robinson, 43
584 Robinson, 53-54
585 boxrec.com
586 *New York Times*, August 2, 1943; britannica.com
587 Robinson and Anderson, 115
588 *New York Daily News*, August 27, 1943; boxrec.com
589 *New York Daily News*, August 28, 1943; boxrec.com
590 Robinson and Anderson, 116; *New York Times*, August 28, 1943
591 Robinson and Anderson, 115
592 *Los Angeles Daily News*, August 28, 1943
593 Heller, 217; *Los Angeles Daily News*, August 28, 1943
594 Heller, 217
595 *New York Times*, August 28, 1943
596 Haygood, 148
597 Christie, "On This Day: Sugar Ray Robinson Beats a Shell of the Legendary Henry Armstrong," boxingnewsonline.net; *Los Angeles Daily News*, August 28, 1943; *New York Times*, August 28, 1943; Fleischer, "Nat Fleischer Says," *The Ring*, November 1943
598 *Los Angeles Daily Times*, August 28, 1943
599 Robinson, 116
600 Heller, 217; Armstrong, "Now I Fight for God," *Boxing Illustrated*, January 1964
601 boxrec.com

**Chapter 20: "Tired of Fighting"**
602 Fleischer, Nat Fleischer Says," *The Ring*, November 1943
603 *New York Daily News*, September 1 and 8, 1943; *Los Angeles Times*, September 2, 1943
604 *California Eagle*, October 28, 1943
605 *St. Louis Post-Dispatch*, September 10, 1944
606 Bromberg, "Armstrong Pilot Cracked Ban Here on Mixed Bouts," July 24, 1943
607 *St. Louis Post-Dispatch*, September 10, 1944

[608] *Ogden Standard-Examiner*, August 3, 1947
[609] Stump, "Hammerin' Henry," *Sport*, January 1955; *California Eagle*, October 28, 1943; *Detroit Tribune*, November 22, 1944; *Hill Top Times*, April 5, 1945; *St. Louis Star and Times*, April 11, 1945; *West Los Angeles Independent*, April 13, 1945; *Los Angeles Evening Citizen News*, April 20, 1945
[610] Robinson, 369
[611] Leonard, xiii and 286
[612] Leonard, 264; Dixon, 228
[613] *The Ring*, October 1944
[614] *New York Times* June 18, 1944
[615] Armstrong, 239; *Chicago Tribune*, June 4, 1944; *New York Daily News* June 15, 1944
[616] Lardner, "Notes on Sports," *The New Yorker*, June 10, 1944
[617] boxrec.com; njboxinghof.org
[618] *Los Angeles Times*, February 15, 1945; *Los Angeles Daily News*, February 15, 1945
[619] Stump, "Hammerin' Henry," *Sport*, January 1955
[620] *Hawaii Tribune-Herald*, January 22, 1945
[621] Armstrong, 242; *Hartford Courant*, January 1, 1946
[622] *Mason City Globe-Gazette*, August 2, 1945; *Pittsburgh Courier*, August 25, 1945
[623] *Pittsburgh Courier*, August 25, 1945
[624] *Coos Bay World*, October 4, 1950; boxrec.com
[625] *Oakland Tribune*, February 14, 1945
[626] *Brooklyn Daily Eagle*, December 11, 1945
[627] *Hazleton Plain Speaker*, March 12, 1945
[628] *Ogden Standard Examiner*, August 3, 1947
[629] *Salt Lake City Deseret News*, January 8, 1948
[630] *Los Angeles Daily News*, April 19, 1949; boxrec.com
[631] boxrec.com; legacy.com
[632] boxrec.com
[633] *New York Age*, December 21, 1946; *New York Age* January 18 and July 5, 1947
[634] *New York Age*, March 1, 1947 and September 24, 1948
[635] *California Eagle*, August 19, 1948

## Chapter 21: God's Ball of Fire
[636] bible.com
[637] Ryan, James, "Boxer Henry Armstrong Dead at 75." upi.com
[638] *Kansas City Star*, December 25, 1946
[639] Armstrong, 244
[640] Armstrong, 245; *Los Angeles Mirror*, January 22, 1949
[641] *Los Angeles Mirror*, January 22, 1949; *Los Angeles Daily News*, January 22, 1949
[642] Armstrong, 246; *Los Angeles Mirror*, January 22, 1949
[643] Armstrong 249; Armstrong, "I Fought for Keeps," *Argosy*, October 1955; Madden, "Henry Armstrong," *Missouri Life*, January-February 1980; *Springfield-News Leader*, January 2, 1950
[644] Stump, "Hammerin' Henry," *Sport*, January 1955
[645] *Los Angeles Times*, September 7, 1949; *Modesto Bee and News-Herald*, September 7, 1949; *The Pittsburgh Courier*, September 17, 1949
[646] *Springfield News-Leader*, January 2, 1950
[647] *Arizona Sun*, October 12, 1951
[648] *Arizona Republic* October 13, 1951
[649] *Arizona Republic* October 13, 1951
[650] *Springfield News Leader*, January 2, 1950; *Ogden Standard-Examiner*, January 14, 1950; *St. Louis Globe-Democrat*, September 1, 1961
[651] *Arizona Republic*, October 13, 1951
[652] Stump, "Hammerin' Henry," *Sport*, January 1955
[653] *Santa Maria Times*, October 3, 1957
[654] Daniel, "Hall of Fame," *The Ring*, October 1954
[655] *New York Times*, June 4, 1956
[656] Armstrong, 10
[657] *Redding Record Searchlight*, January 24, 1959; *Los Angeles Mirror*, January 24, 1959; *New York Times*, January 25, 1959
[658] *Los Angeles Mirror*, January 24, 1959; *California Eagle*, January 29, 1959; *Los Angeles Evening Citizen News*, July 26, 1960
[659] *Los Angeles Times*, August 14, 1988
[660] *Los Angeles Evening Citizen News*, July 27, 1960; *Napa Valley Register*, July 27, 1960
[661] boxrec.com
[662] *Miami News*, October 26, 1960
[663] *Miami Herald*, February 6, 1961
[664] *Miami Herald*, October 27, 1960
[665] *Miami Herald*, October 27, 1960
[666] *Miami Herald*, December 28, 1960
[667] Roberts, *Boxing Register*, 459-460
[668] *Miami News*, February 3, 1961
[669] *Miami Herald*, February 6, 1961
[670] *Miami Herald*, February 3 and 6, 1961; *Pomona Progress-Bulletin*, February 7, 1961
[671] *Tampa Times*, February 8, 1961
[672] *St. Louis Post-Dispatch*, February 10, 1961
[673] *Miami News*, February 8, 1961

## Chapter 22: Tolling Ten
[674] Armstrong, "Now I Fight for God," *Boxing Illustrated*, January 1964
[675] Hauser, 17
[676] *St. Louis Post-Dispatch*, February 20, 1962
[677] *Long Beach Telegram*, February 5, 1963
[678] *The Fresno Bee*, February 11, 1964
[679] Armstrong, "Now I Fight for God," *Boxing Illustrated*, January 1964
[680] Armstrong, "Now I Fight for God," *Boxing Illustrated*, January 1964
[681] Brown, "Henry Armstrong: Fighter for God," *Negro Digest*, January 1962
[682] Nagler, Barney, "Hammerin' Henry Armstrong," *Sport*, June 1963
[683] *London Guardian*, October 25, 1988

684 Friedman, "Fifty Years After the Glory," *People*, November 21, 1988
685 Haygood, 151
686 Letters from Henry Armstrong to George Luckman, January 3 to August 18, 1979. Author's collection.
687 ancestry.com
688 Friedman, "Fifty Years After the Glory," *People*, November 21, 1988
689 *St. Louis Post-Dispatch*, May 3, 1981
690 *St. Louis Post-Dispatch*, October 25, 1988
691 *St. Louis Post-Dispatch*, October 25, 1988
692 *Los Angeles Times*, August 14, 1988
693 *Tampa Bay Times*, November 13, 1982
694 *Los Angeles Times*, August 14, 1988 and July 29, 1989
695 Haygood, 152
696 *Los Angeles Times*, August 14, 1988
697 *Los Angeles Times*, October 29, 1988

**Afterword**
698 *Santa Maria Times*, October 24, 1988
699 Carroll, "Sepia Sockers to the Fore," *The Ring*, Mach 1947

www.ingramcontent.com/pod-product-compliance
Lightning Source LLC
Chambersburg PA
CBHW032031300426
44117CB00009B/1022